OXFORD READINGS

The series provides students selection of the best and most author, work, or subject. No single school or style of approach is privileged: the aim is to offer a broad overview of scholarship, to cover a wide variety of topics, and to illustrate a diversity of critical methods. The collections are particularly valuable for their inclusion of many important essays which are normally difficult to obtain and for the first-ever translations of some of the pieces. Many articles are thoroughly revised and updated by their authors or are provided with addenda taking account of recent work. Each volume includes an authoritative and wide-ranging introduction by the editor surveying the scholarly tradition and considering alternative approaches. This pulls the individual articles together, setting all the pieces included in their historical and cultural contexts and exploring significant connections between them from the perspective of contemporary scholarship. All foreign languages (including Greek and Latin) are translated to make the texts easily accessible to those without detailed linguistic knowledge.

OXFORD READINGS IN CLASSICAL STUDIES

Homer's *Iliad*
Edited by Douglas L. Cairns

Virgil's *Aeneid*
Edited by S. J. Harrison

The Roman Novel
Edited by S. J. Harrison

Euripides
Edited by Judith Mossman

Aristophanes
Edited by Erich Segal

Greek Tragedy
Edited by Erich Segal

Menander, Plautus, and Terence
Edited by Erich Segal

The Greek Novel
Edited by Simon Swain

Ancient Literary Criticism
Edited by Andrew Laird

Aeschylus
Edited by Michael Lloyd

Ovid
Edited by Peter E. Knox

The Attic Orators
Edited by Edwin Carawan

Lucretius
Edited by Monica R. Gale

Catullus
Edited by Julia Haig Gaisser

Vergil's *Georgics*
Edited by Katharina Volk

All available in paperback

Oxford Readings in Classical Studies
Vergil's Eclogues

Edited by
KATHARINA VOLK

OXFORD
UNIVERSITY PRESS

OXFORD
UNIVERSITY PRESS

Great Clarendon Street, Oxford OX2 6DP

Oxford University Press is a department of the University of Oxford.
It furthers the University's objective of excellence in research, scholarship,
and education by publishing worldwide in

Oxford New York

Auckland Cape Town Dar es Salaam Hong Kong Karachi
Kuala Lumpur Madrid Melbourne Mexico City Nairobi
New Delhi Shanghai Taipei Toronto

With offices in

Argentina Austria Brazil Chile Czech Republic France Greece
Guatemala Hungary Italy Japan Poland Portugal Singapore
South Korea Switzerland Thailand Turkey Ukraine Vietnam

Oxford is a registered trade mark of Oxford University Press
in the UK and in certain other countries

Published in the United States
by Oxford University Press Inc., New York

© Oxford University Press 2008

The moral rights of the author have been asserted
Database right Oxford University Press (maker)

First published 2008

All rights reserved. No part of this publication may be reproduced,
stored in a retrieval system, or transmitted, in any form or by any means,
without the prior permission in writing of Oxford University Press,
or as expressly permitted by law, or under terms agreed with the appropriate
reprographics rights organization. Enquiries concerning reproduction
outside the scope of the above should be sent to the Rights Department,
Oxford University Press, at the address above

You must not circulate this book in any other binding or cover
and you must impose the same condition on any acquirer

British Library Cataloguing in Publication Data
Data available

Library of Congress Cataloging-in-Publication Data
Vergil's Eclogues / edited by Katharina Volk.
p. cm.—(Oxford readings in classical studies)
Includes bibliographical references and index.
ISBN 978–0–19–920294–2   ISBN 978–0–19–920293–5
1. virgil.   Bucolica.   2. Pastoral poetry, Latin—History and criticism.   3. Country life in literature.   4. Rome—In Literature.   I. Volk, Katharina, 1969–
PA6804.B7V43 2008
872'.01—dc22   2008009944

Typeset by SPI Publisher Services, Pondicherry, India
Printed in Great Britain
on acid-free paper by
Biddles Ltd., King's Lynn, Norfolk

ISBN 978–0–19–920293–5 (Hbk)   978–0–19–920294–2 (Pbk)

1 3 5 7 9 10 8 6 4 2

Preface

As Vergil observes in *Eclogue* 8.63, *non omnia possumus omnes*, and it is a special pleasure to acknowledge those without whose help I would not have been able to see this volume to completion. My thanks go to Hilary O'Shea for initiating the project (originally conceived as one single collection of *Oxford Readings* on both the *Eclogues* and the *Georgics* but ultimately realized as two separate books) and to Jenny Wagstaffe and the staff at Oxford University Press for their assistance in the volume's production. Niklas Holzberg, Bob Kaster, Jim Zetzel, and the anonymous referees gave me helpful suggestions for the choice of articles; I am also grateful to Niklas for letting me use his invaluable bibliographies (see Introduction, note 3) and to Jim for his comments on the Introduction. Thanks to a generous grant from the Stanwood Cockey Lodge Fund (Columbia University), I was able to employ a research assistant, Kristin Robbins, whom I thank for her wonderful job in compiling and editing the papers and bibliography.

More than to anyone else, I am indebted to the authors. In addition to agreeing to have their articles reprinted, they made themselves available to answer queries, make revisions, and either provide themselves, or discuss and correct, the English translations of Latin and Greek passages—and, in the case of the two German contributions, even of the papers themselves. I am delighted to have been able to gather such a distinguished group of Vergilians between covers; this truly is their volume.

KV

New York
September 2007

Contents

1. Introduction: Scholarly Approaches to the *Eclogues* since the 1970s — 1
   Katharina Volk
2. Arcadia: Modern Occident and Classical Antiquity — 16
   Ernst A. Schmidt
3. The Style of Virgil's *Eclogues* — 48
   R. G. M. Nisbet
4. Bucolic *nomina* in Virgil and Theocritus: On the Poetic Technique of Virgil's *Eclogues* — 64
   Lorenz Rumpf
5. Allusive Artistry and Vergil's Revisionary Program: *Eclogues* 1–3 — 79
   Thomas K. Hubbard
6. On *Eclogue* 1.79–83 — 110
   Christine G. Perkell
7. Virgil's Third *Eclogue*: How Do You Keep an Idiot in Suspense? — 125
   John Henderson
8. Virgil's Fourth *Eclogue*: Easterners and Westerners — 155
   R. G. M. Nisbet
9. The Sixth *Eclogue*: Virgil's Poetic Genealogy — 189
   David O. Ross, Jr.
10. An Interpretation of the Tenth *Eclogue* — 216
    Gian Biagio Conte
11. Eclogues *in extremis*: On the Staying Power of Pastoral — 245
    Seamus Heaney

Bibliography — 261
Acknowledgements — 285
Index of passages cited — 287

1

Introduction: Scholarly Approaches to the *Eclogues* since the 1970s

Katharina Volk

SORTES VERGILIANAE: TRENDS IN VERGILIAN SCHOLARSHIP

To an extent unparalleled by any other text from Graeco-Roman antiquity, the works of Vergil have been considered capable of producing meaning.[1] Their status as an engine of unlimited signification finds its emblem in the *sortes Vergilianae*, the practice (attested from the second century AD onward) of consulting Vergil's poems as an oracle by opening the text at random and interpreting the first verse chanced on as pertaining to the consultant's situation.[2] While modern critics typically approach Vergil in a less haphazard fashion, the variety of divergent interpretations at which they are able to arrive, and the ways in which these interpretations respond to the enquirers' own intellectual and ideological concerns, attest to the poet's

---

[1] This introduction has a counterpart in that of this book's 'sister volume', *Oxford Readings in Classical Studies: Vergil's 'Georgics'*. I originally wrote a single introduction to what was supposed to be a single volume on both works. When the Press decided to publish two separate books instead, I had the task of splitting up the introduction as well, which explains the identical structure of the two chapters, as well as the overlap in the first section. Readers interested in how the trends in Vergilian scholarship described here play out in the *Georgics* are invited to consult the other volume.

[2] On the *sortes Vergilianae*, see briefly Comparetti 1997: 47–8, as well as Martindale 1997b: 6, who likewise considers the practice emblematic of approaches to Vergil in general.

continuing appeal as a provider of meaningful answers to a multitude of different questions.

The resultant lack of consensus in Vergilian scholarship has—especially in recent, poststructuralist times—been viewed as a positive thing, with the inherent openness and polysemy of Vergil's works being regarded as indicative of their quality. To take just a few examples, S. J. Harrison concludes the introduction to his 1990 *Oxford Readings in Vergil's 'Aeneid'* with the observation that 'the volume and variety of recent criticism is a tribute to the continuing literary interest and stature of the *Aeneid*', a work that, in the same sentence, he characterizes as 'great poetry' (20). Also that year, Christine G. Perkell predicted that future scholarship on the *Eclogues* would 'deemphasize the notion of a proper understanding, of a correct reading, in favor of opening up the text, of acknowledging ambiguities and not simplifying complexities' (1990*b*: 47). As for the *Georgics*, Philip Hardie's remark about the story of Aristaeus—that 'to insist on a single interpretation may be to do violence to this polymorphous and Protean text' (1998: 45)—could easily be extended to the poem as a whole, about which Hardie concludes that 'many contemporary readers are left feeling that this is a text with more problems than answers' (52). However, the very elusiveness of the work contributes to its greatness, as maintained, among others, by William W. Batstone, who writes that 'the diversity of compelling interpretations is part of the *Georgics*' larger value and meaning' (1997: 125).

If the ability to produce divergent readings is thus, by general consensus, an intrinsic feature of Vergil's poetry, and if the extant interpretations of his works are as many as the leaves blown about in the Sibyl's cave, giving an overview of Vergilian scholarship is a daunting task, one that might appear doomed from the start. Fortunately, though, my purpose in the following pages is rather more circumscribed. Since the present volume is concerned with the *Eclogues* only, works on the *Aeneid* and *Georgics* appear only in supporting roles. Likewise, since the papers collected here date exclusively from 1975 onward, my discussion of Vergilian criticism is similarly restricted to works since the 1970s. This starting date is somewhat arbitrary and was chosen on the assumption that scholarship from the last third of a century or so may still be considered vaguely contemporary. However, beginning with the 1970s also makes a certain amount of sense since that decade saw a number of important new impulses in the study of the *Eclogues*, ones that have continued to influence scholarship.[3]

In one way or another, Vergil's *Eclogues* (just like the *Georgics*) have often stood in the shadow of the *Aeneid*. As an example of a 'lower' genre and a work of the poet's youth, the book has been regarded as ultimately preparatory for the great epic, the masterpiece in which Vergil's life and work culminated according to the teleological view of the poet's career that is found in the *Vitae* and still colours perceptions of the Vergilian *oeuvre* today.[4] While the bucolic mode has certainly enjoyed periods of great popularity at various points in the history of Western literature, it has long been unfashionable, and if poems about shepherds do not hold much appeal for the general public, professional classicists, too, tend to eye them with a certain suspicion. As a result, the *Eclogues* are studied in colleges and universities less frequently than the *Aeneid*, and scholarly publications on Vergil's epic far outnumber those on his earliest poems. In addition, the very methodologies and approaches critics bring to bear on the *Eclogues* (and the *Georgics* as well) are often ones first developed in the study of the *Aeneid* (this is true especially of the 'Harvard School' pessimistic approach), a fact that neatly illustrates the work's secondary status.

This is not to say, however, that there has not been considerable work done on the *Eclogues*. The last thirty or so years have seen the publication of major commentaries (Coleman 1977, Clausen 1994) and numerous books and articles, which are representative of both Vergilian scholarship (in all its variety and with all its controversies)

---

[3] For scholarship on the *Eclogues*, see Briggs 1981 as well as the more up-to-date and extensive bibliography compiled by Niklas Holzberg (available online at <www.psms.homepage.t-online.de/bucolicabib.html> (2002)). In addition, the journal *Vergilius* publishes an annual Vergilian bibliography. Recent monographs on Vergil, all with discussion of and bibliography on the *Eclogues*, include Hardie 1998 (the best general introduction to the poet), La Penna 2005, Holzberg 2006, and von Albrecht 2006. Two 'companions' to Vergil, Horsfall (ed.) 1995 and Martindale (ed.) 1997, provide articles on individual works and other topics of interest. Finally, the *Enciclopedia Virgiliana* (1985–90) contains a wealth of information on all things Vergilian.

[4] On Vergil's career, see Lipking 1981: 76–93, Theodorakopoulos 1997, and Volk 2002: 152–6.

and the general developments and advances of Latin literary studies in the late twentieth and early twenty-first centuries. While the multiplicity of approaches and results makes it difficult to give even a broad overview or construct a simple narrative, it nevertheless seems to me possible to discern two principal strands in the interpretation of Vergil's work in general and of the *Eclogues* in particular, strands that are not infrequently intertwined but are nevertheless markedly different.

The first trend involves readings that might be called 'ideological'. By this I mean approaches predicated on the idea that Vergil's poems are designed to 'convey a message' (Putnam 1970: 4), which the critic endeavours to uncover. This message may be seen to concern the social and political situation of the work's composition, the poet's own poetry or poetry in general, or (quite frequently) human life and the human condition—or any combination of these and similar issues. As is well known, critical assessments of Vergil's position on such matters have varied considerably over the past decades. While the poet was traditionally credited with a positive or 'optimistic' attitude, not only toward the pastoral life presented in his poems, but also concerning the political ascendancy of Octavian reflected more obliquely in his text, scholars starting in the 1970s began increasingly to detect deep ambivalence and even downright 'pessimism' in the *Eclogues* (and likewise the *Georgics*).[5] This type of approach was clearly influenced by the 'Harvard School' or 'two-voices' pessimistic criticism of the *Aeneid*, which was going strong already in the 1960s[6] but left its mark on the study of Vergil's earlier

[5] The division of ideological readings of Vergil into 'optimistic' and 'pessimistic' is overly simplistic and has been criticized, e.g. by Thomas 1990: 64–5, who prefers 'Augustan' and 'ambivalent' instead (Thomas also points out, in 64 n. 1, that the designation 'Harvard School' is less than appropriate for a critical trend shared by scholars from many universities). For the sake of convenience, however, I shall stick with these terms. As for Thomas's preferred 'ambivalent', it seems to me that there is a wide spectrum of readings that detect some form of ambivalence in Vergil's text. As Hardie 1998: 51 writes (apropos of the *Georgics*), such interpretations are 'more often than not' ultimately pessimistic (since ambivalence is experienced as disruptive); however, a number of scholars maintain that Vergilian poetry is indeed characterized by an (uneasy) balance, in which positive and negative aspects exist side by side, without either one being privileged.

[6] Generally on the 'Harvard School', see Serpa 1987: 76–88; on pessimistic interpretations of the *Aeneid*, see Harrison 1990: 5–6.

poems with characteristic delay.[7] Ideological readings since this paradigm shift have concentrated on determining the nuances of Vergil's optimism or pessimism, often concluding that the poet's texts are characterized by a deep and deliberate ambiguity, which mirrors the complexity of the world and of human life as represented in the poems. It should be pointed out, however, that recent years have seen a reassessment of Vergil's political stance especially and that, in a kind of New Augustanism, scholars these days are again much more inclined to see the poems as reflecting positively on Octavian and his politics.[8]

The second approach might be labelled 'literary' and characterizes a wide variety of studies that examine the *Eclogues* primarily as works of literature. These include discussions of the poems' genre, an issue made especially problematic by the existence of a long subsequent tradition of European pastoral, a genre whose exact relationship to Vergilian bucolic is anything but clear. Another major field of interest—in Latin studies in general and in Vergilian scholarship in particular—has been intertextuality and the ways in which poems allude to and position themselves vis-à-vis their models. In this context, much attention has been paid to the influence on the *Eclogues* of Theocritus and Callimachus. Finally, critics have focused on questions of poetics, that is, on how Vergil in the *Eclogues* presents his own endeavour and ambition and how he undertakes to inscribe his own efforts into a particular literary tradition.

As mentioned above, these two approaches are not mutually exclusive. Ideological readings frequently concern themselves with the role of the poet, while primarily literary studies may have much to say about the poems' political or more generally philososphical

[7] This trajectory can be traced nicely in the monographs of Michael C. J. Putnam, one of the most eminent representatives of the 'Harvard School': only after his first book on the *Aeneid* (1965) did he tackle the *Eclogues* (1970) and only later still the *Georgics* (1979).

[8] See e.g. one of the most recent monographs on Vergil, Holzberg 2006. Already in 1990, Richard F. Thomas (1990: 65; with reference to Don Fowler) detected an Augustan backlash to the 'Harvard School' approach, but it would appear that his New Augustans are simply old Augustans who resist the contemporary shift to pessimism. By contrast, today's New Augustans, such as Holzberg, have gone through the pessimists' school, are attuned to the complexities and ambivalences of Vergil, but still conclude that the poet projects a largely positive image of Octavian (and of whatever else is at stake).

outlook. Still, not only do many works of Vergilian criticism fall fairly clearly into the one category or the other, but there has also been, over the past few decades, a kind of metapoetic turn, a shift away from reading Vergil for his message and toward studying him for his poetics. Practitioners of present-day *sortes Vergilianae* are thus less likely to ask 'What do these poems tell us about life?' than 'What do these poems tell us about poetry?' The following overview of scholarship on the *Eclogues* will further illuminate this tendency.

THE *ECLOGUES*

The 1970s saw a sudden flourishing of studies on Vergil's *Eclogues*, especially in the Anglophone world, where Putnam 1970, the first English-language monograph since Rose 1942, was followed in quick succession by Berg 1974, Leach 1974, van Sickle 1978, and Alpers 1979, as well as the commentary of Coleman 1977. It is possible to identify a number of interrelated impulses that contributed to this renaissance. First, literary studies had seen a general rise of interest in pastoral poetry of all periods (witness, for example, Rosenmeyer 1969 and Poggioli 1975), a phenomenon that led Eleanor W. Leach to proclaim, in the preface to her 1974 book, a new 'golden age of pastoral criticism' (7). Second, inspired by New Criticism, the prevalent strand of literary analysis during the Cold War years, at least in the United States, scholars found in the riddling and complex *Eclogues* fertile ground for close readings and symbolic interpretations.[9] And third, it was only a question of time before the pessimism of the 'Harvard School' readings of the *Aeneid* (which were themselves much influenced by New Criticism) spilled over into scholarship on Vergil's other works. As has often been pointed out, the dark view of Vergilian poetry proposed by many critics of this period may be relatable to the political atmosphere of the 1960s and particularly to the experience of the Vietnam War.[10]

[9] Connolly 2001 examines the influence of New Criticism on Cold War readings of the *Eclogues*.
[10] This point is made e.g. by Segal 1981: 7 and Harrison 1990: 5; see also Serpa 1987: 76–7.

Pessimistic readings of the *Eclogues* can be found in Putnam 1970, Leach 1974, Segal 1981 (a collection of articles on Theocritean and Vergilian bucolic originally published between 1965 and 1977), Boyle 1986: 15–35, and M. O. Lee 1989, among others.[11] These works react to a view of pastoral in general and the *Eclogues* in particular according to which Vergil's poems, like other pastoral texts, present an idealized dreamworld, an escapist rural fantasy far removed from the grim urban reality of the author and his readers. The idea that Vergil in the *Eclogues* created a 'spiritual landscape' ('geistige Landschaft') that he called Arcadia had been put forth by Bruno Snell in 1945 and greatly influenced especially German scholarship.[12] In the pessimistic interpretations, however, the *Eclogues* never present an ideal pastoral world, but always one that is endangered, has been lost, or is being abandoned. Factors such as love, death, political upheavals, and the poet's own ambitions are identified as constant threats to the pastoral ideal.

While Anglophone critics were deconstructing Snell's view by drawing attention to the dark sides of Vergilian pastoral, a German Latinist, Ernst A. Schmidt, attacked 'Arcadia' from a different angle. Schmidt was able to show that Snell and his followers had retrojected Renaissance ideas of an idealized pastoral world onto the *Eclogues* and that the romantic notion of a Vergilian Arcadia was an anachronism.[13] In Schmidt's eyes, any ideological reading of Vergil's poems was based on 'misunderstandings' (1972: 120–85): the *Eclogues* were not about political panegyric, (Epicurean) praise of the countryside, or some ideal state of human life such as the Golden Age or 'Arcadia'. Pointing out that the *Eclogues* (just like Theocritus' bucolic poems)

---

[11] Alpers 1979 belongs to the same general critical climate but takes a more conciliatory view, arguing that in the *Eclogues*, Vergil typically presents oppositions (which in more pessimistic interpretations are seen as essentially disruptive) in a state of 'suspension', showing the opposing terms to exist side by side without privileging one or the other.

[12] E. A. Schmidt 1975 (reprinted in this volume) traces the history of Snell's idea. Among the scholars representative of this kind of utopian view of the *Eclogues*, note especially Friedrich Klingner, who worked on Vergil throughout his career, influenced Snell and was influenced by him in turn, and in 1967 published as a monograph a summary of his lifelong Vergilian studies.

[13] See E. A. Schmidt 1972: 154–85 and especially 1975; a similar argument is found in Jenkyns 1989.

always concern herdsmen *qua* singers, Schmidt concluded that the poems were about poetry itself, 'Dichtung der Dichtung' (1972: 108). While Schmidt's approach is somewhat radical, his work is symptomatic of a larger development within *Eclogues* criticism. A great number of scholarly publications from the last few decades are concerned either with the *Eclogues* as poetry or with what they have to say about poetry. Formalist examinations of Vergil's bucolic style and language include Lipka 2001, as well as the papers of R. G. M. Nisbet 1991 and Rumpf 1999 (both reprinted in this volume); see also O'Hara 1996: 243–52 on etymological wordplay in the *Eclogues*.

Questions of genre have always been central to studies of the *Eclogues*, but while many critics used to view Vergil's poems in the light of the later development of pastoral, scholars now increasingly stress—especially since the important work of Halperin 1983—that ancient 'bucolic' is sufficiently different from the ensuing pastoral tradition and thus better studied in isolation (for an up-to-date introduction to many aspects of Greek and Roman bucolic poetry, see now Fantuzzi and Papanghelis (eds.) 2006).[14] In a departure from previous attempts to define pastoral through its content (for example, an idealized if perhaps threatened pastoral world), Hubbard 1998 proposed that the genre was instead constituted by each poet's self-positioning vis-à-vis his predecessor(s) (compare also Muecke 1975 and Alpers 1990 specifically for Vergil's contributions to this process). His insistence on the 'intertextual construction' (1998: 18) of pastoral is a neat illustration of the metapoetic turn and also of the increasing importance of the concept of intertextuality, which has played a major role in numerous individual studies on the *Eclogues*, including many mentioned in what follows.

Another important focus of scholarship has been the structure of the *Eclogue* book, a topic treated by van Sickle 1978 (2nd edn. 2004) and Seng 1999, among others. Building on important earlier work (especially on the observation of Maury 1944—picked up in particular by Otis 1964: 128–43—of pervasive ring composition around a centre constituted by *Eclogue* 5: *Eclogue* 1 corresponds to *Eclogue* 9, 2

---

[14] A strict distinction between 'bucolic' and 'pastoral' has not caught on in *Eclogues* scholarship, and I shall continue to use the two terms (largely) interchangeably.

to 8, 3 to 7, and 4 to 6), critics have pondered the significance of ('synchronic') architectural schemes versus the experience of a linear ('diachronic') reading through the book as a whole.[15] The tension between the written nature of the *Eclogue* book and the purported culture of orality of its herdsmen protagonists is examined in Breed 2006*a*.

Consideration of the place of individual *Eclogues* within the book as a whole has largely replaced discussion of the chronology of the poems' composition, a central topic of earlier scholarship. However, one major chronological issue was raised by Bowersock 1971, who suggested that the dedicatee of *Eclogue* 8 (addressed in lines 6–13) is not Pollio, as previously assumed, but rather Octavian and that the mention of warfare in Illyria (6–7) is a reference to the latter's campaign in the area in 35 BC. As a result, the completion of the *Eclogues* (traditionally placed in 39) would be dated down to the mid-30s. Bowersock's thesis has engendered a lively controversy, which remains as yet unresolved.[16] The considerably more extreme scenario of Luther 2002, who maintains that the work was published only in 28–27/6 (which would move the *Georgics* to the mid-20s), will presumably not win general acceptance.

The relationship of the *Eclogue* book to its historical background and its overt or hidden references to contemporaries, especially Octavian, remain controversial. Nauta 2006 gives an overview of all panegyric passages (or ones that might be taken as such). Mayer 1983*a* (see also Green 1996) is sceptical especially of Octavian's presence in the *Eclogues*, but see Korenjak 2003 for a discussion of how Vergil's text actively invites a biographical reading and the identification of bucolic characters with historical figures.

As Karl Galinsky has observed, '[t]here is no such thing as a "typical *Eclogue*"' (1965: 162), and there is also no such thing as a typical

---

[15] Breed 2006*b* provides a thoughtful introduction to the issues; Rudd 1976: 119–44 surveys various architectural schemes, from a decidedly sceptical perspective.
[16] In support of Bowersock, see, among others, Clausen 1972 and 1994: 233–7, E. A. Schmidt 1974, van Sickle 1981, Köhnken 1984, Mankin 1988, and Nauta 2006; opponents include Tarrant 1978 (with a response by Bowersock 1978), Mayer 1983*a*, Farrell 1991*a*, Green 1996, Seng 1999, and now Thibodeau 2006 (with attractive new arguments). See also Zetzel 1984, who demonstrates the unreliability of Servius (who identifies the addressee as Octavian) in this and similar matters.

interpretation of any single *Eclogue*. Many of the monographs cited above deal extensively with the individual poems (Putnam 1970 in particular offers close readings of all ten); there are also detailed discussions of *Eclogues* 1, 2, 4, and 5 by Ian M. Du Quesnay (1976, 1976/7, 1979, and 1981) and interpretations by different scholars of all the poems in Gigante (ed.) 1981. In addition, I single out the following, with no aspiration to completeness.

Eclogue 1 has rightly been regarded as programmatic for the collection as a whole; see especially Putnam 1970: 20–81 and Alpers 1979: 65–95, as well as Perkell 1990*a* and Hubbard 1995: 41–6 (both reprinted in this volume). Wright 1983 examines the poem's relation to Theocritus and Callimachus; Cairns 1999 draws attention to ancient etymologies of the name Tityrus (see also the response of van Sickle 2004); E. A. Schmidt 1998 (responding to Du Quesnay 1981) reconsiders the issue of Tityrus' manumission; Winterbottom 1976 and Wimmel 1998 discuss the historical background; and Rundin 2003 uses the *Eclogue* as the starting point for an Epicurean reading of the collection (see also Davis 2004).

Studies of the second *Eclogue* have understandably focused on the relationship to Theocritus 11; see especially Du Quesnay 1979. Mayer 1983*b*, Cancik 1986, and van Sickle 1987 present different views on the social status of Corydon and Alexis.

Schäfer 2001 treats *Eclogue* 3 together with *Eclogue* 7 as examples of ancient 'Streitdichtung' (poetry of verbal contest); Currie 1976 argues for an influence of Roman and Italian comedy; Powell 1976 and Henderson 1998*b* (reprinted in this volume) likewise focus on the poem's dramatic (and aggressive) aspects, which Karanika 2006 contextualizes in Mediterranean cultural practices; and Monteleone 1994, Schultz 2003, and Tracy 2003 all (in very different ways) use the figure of Palaemon as a key to reading the poem as a comment on pastoral poetics and/or the contemporary literary scene.

The prophetic fourth *Eclogue* has always struck readers as the most 'optimistic' of the ten poems and has attracted special attention on account of both its reception (especially the Christian interpretation, on which see Benko 1980) and its possible sources. The latter issue (see the classic treatment of Norden 1924) is tackled by R. G. M. Nisbet 1978 (reprinted in this volume); Beaujeu 1982 revisits the question of the identity of the mysterious *puer*, whom Binder 1983

Introduction 11

identifies as Octavian; and Hubbard 1995/6 and Lefèvre 2000 discuss intertextuality with Catullus 64. For a discussion of the poem as a whole, see the monograph of van Sickle 1992.

In his discussion of *Eclogue* 5, G. Lee 1977, rather than focusing on the songs about Daphnis, finds humour in the exchanges of Mopsus and Menalcas and points out that Mopsus clearly knew Menalcas' song beforehand; Baumbach 2001 posits a homoerotic subtext and suggests that Mopsus is wooing Menalcas with his song.

On the poetics of *Eclogue* 6, see Deremetz 1987 and Rutherford 1989. The highly metapoetic Song of Silenus is treated by Ross 1975: 18–38 (reprinted in this volume) and Courtney 1990. Thomas 1998 suggests that the *Eclogue*'s speaker is a bucolic character 'Tityrus' (see line 4) rather than 'Vergil'.

Readers of the seventh *Eclogue* have always wondered why Corydon wins the singing contest rather than Thyrsis; Fantazzi and Querbach 1985, Egan 1996, Papanghelis 1997, and Sullivan 2002 offer various explanations for Corydon's victory. Frischer 1975 provides a close reading of the poem as a whole.

Eclogue 8 is the subject of the monograph of Richter 1970. Sallmann 1995 (see also 1998) considers the songs of Damon and Alphesiboeus reflective of two different kinds of love (generally on the theme of love in the *Eclogues*, see Stroppini 1993 and Papanghelis 1999); Segal 1987 focuses on intertextuality with Theocritus 2; and Faraone 1989 and Katz and Volk 2006 discuss the love magic in the song of Alphesiboeus. Solodow 1977 offers a pessimistic reading of the sequence *Eclogues* 8–10 as expressive of the failure of poetry.

Henderson 1998*a* views the ninth *Eclogue* as a mime and considers various ways of realizing its 'script'; in the interpretation of Perkell 2001, Moeris and Lycidas figure respectively as pessimistic and optimistic 'readers' of (Menalcas') poetry; and Rupprecht 2004 offers a metapoetic (and pessimistic) reading in which the absent and ever-elusive Menalcas stands for bucolic poetry.

Eclogue 10, Vergil's farewell to pastoral (see Kennedy 1983 on the final three lines), has elicited enormous interest because it features Gallus and is assumed to have programmatic and metageneric connotations (the monograph of Rumpf 1996 helpfully surveys earlier interpretations). Thus, for example, Conte 1986: 100–29 (reprinted in this volume) interprets the placement of Gallus in Arcadia as a juxtaposition of elegy and bucolic, while Kennedy 1987 sees Arcadia as an elegiac, specifically Gallan, motif rather than a pastoral one (compare Whitaker 1988; generally on Gallus in the works of Vergil, see Ross 1975 and Gagliardi 2003). Perkell 1996 views the poem less pessimistically than many, pointing out, that after all, Gallus, unlike his Theocritean model Daphnis, gives in to love and thus chooses life over death.

As already mentioned, the *Eclogues* have frequently been studied as part of the tradition of European pastoral, and every work on the pastoral genre deals to some extent with the reception of Vergil's poems. In addition to the titles quoted earlier, note especially Patterson 1987 and now Skoie and Velázquez (eds.) 2006, as well as Lerner 1984, Jenkyns 1992 (on pastoral with an eye to Vergil), Martindale 1997*a* (on the *Eclogues* with an eye to reception), and von Albrecht 2006: 58–64; for the influence of the *Eclogues* on particular works and authors, see Ziolkowski 1993, Heaney 2003 (reprinted in this volume), and the papers in Paschalis (ed.) 2007.

THE PRESENT VOLUME

The papers in this volume have been chosen with the purpose of creating an anthology that will serve as an introduction to scholarship on the *Eclogues* since 1975. Two main considerations have directed my choices. First, wanting to represent a wide variety of approaches, I have included scholars from different countries, with different styles and different critical convictions, whose views on the texts they treat vary considerably. Second, I have aimed to cover major topics of contemporary research on the *Eclogues* while also highlighting particularly prominent poems. Of course, there is no way to do so comprehensively, and, out of considerations of space, I have not been able to include contributions on each individual *Eclogue*.[17]

---

[17] Just as the views of Vergil's work expressed in the ten papers vary considerably, so too do the authors differ over the correct way to spell the poet's name. Should it be *Vergil* or *Virgil*? To preserve the individuality of the contributions, no attempt has been made to unify the spelling.

Introduction

The volume opens with Ernst A. Schmidt's 'Arcadia: Modern Occident and Classical Antiquity' ('Arkadien: Abendland und Antike', 1975), which treats an important chapter in the history of the reception of Vergil as well as the history of ideas. Schmidt is able to show that the belief of Bruno Snell and others that the *Eclogues* present a utopian dreamland called 'Arcadia' is deeply influenced by concepts found not in Vergil, but in Renaissance pastoral, especially the *Arcadia* of Jacobo Sannazaro (1504); in the few *Eclogues* in which Arcadia actually appears, it stands not for some lost ideal but rather for the very present realm of bucolic poetry itself.

The next two pieces are concerned with Vergil's creation of a specifically bucolic language. In 'The Style of Virgil's *Eclogues*' (1991), R. G. M. Nisbet discusses primarily syntactic and metrical features (often adapted from Theocritus) that are typical of the *Eclogues*. By artfully creating an impression of artlessness, these elements, which include repetition, ellipsis, parenthesis, and a preference for the feminine caesura and the bucolic diaeresis, set the collection apart from Vergil's other works.

Lorenz Rumpf, in 'Bucolic *nomina* in Virgil and Theocritus: On the Poetic Technique of Virgil's *Eclogues*' ('Bukolische Nomina bei Vergil und Theokrit: Zur poetischen Technik des Eklogenbuchs', 1999), concentrates on the poet's use of adjectives, nouns, and proper names. Arguing that certain rules and restrictions govern the employment of such words and their distribution across the *Eclogue* book, Rumpf throws light on how these 'bucolic *nomina*' function as the very building blocks of Vergil's bucolic world.

Thomas K. Hubbard then explores the programmatic significance of the first three *Eclogues* in 'Allusive Artistry and Vergil's Revisionary Program: *Eclogues* 1–3' (1995), demonstrating how, through his allusions to Theocritus in these poems, Vergil stakes out his own position within the genre. By interpreting interactions between herdsmen (such as Meliboeus and Tityrus in *Eclogue* 1 and Damoetas and Menalcas in *Eclogue* 3) as confrontations between representatives of old and new types of bucolic, Hubbard shows how the Roman poet deals with his 'anxiety of influence' and positions himself in relation to his Greek predecessor.

The next five papers present studies of individual *Eclogues*. Christine G. Perkell in 'On *Eclogue* 1.79–83' (1990) argues that the quintessentially pastoral closing lines of *Eclogue* 1 are not, as has been suggested, a mere 'pastoral tag' attributable, as it were, to Vergil himself (rather than to Tityrus). Instead, the melancholy beauty of these lines may be seen to express a moral and aesthetic development in Tityrus, his response to Meliboeus' haunting songs of loss. Although the one poet goes into exile, there remains in the country a newly awakened pastoral voice. The poem thus finely dramatizes the power of pastoral to move and to seduce.

John Henderson's 'Virgil's Third *Eclogue*: How Do You Keep an Idiot in Suspense?' (1998) reads through *Eclogue* 3 as mime to text and discusses, or rather re-enacts, the experience we readers have when attempting to 'direct' Vergil's script. We are continually scrambling to make sense of the aggressive interactions of Menalcas, Damoetas, and Palaemon (presented to us without an authorial frame), trying to understand the 'rules of the game' and define our own position vis-à-vis the bucolic world—but never quite succeeding.

In 'Virgil's Fourth *Eclogue*: Easterners and Westerners' (1978), R. G. M. Nisbet reconsiders the question whether Vergil's *Cumaeum carmen* owes more to Near Eastern, especially Jewish, traditions or to its Graeco-Roman background. Surveying parallels for the manifold concepts expressed in the poem, Nisbet establishes that while the *Eclogue* is an amalgam of Eastern and Western elements, the influence of Jewish Sibylline oracles is profound.

Discussing the sixth *Eclogue*, a poem 'largely concerned with poetry', David O. Ross, Jr. in 'The Sixth *Eclogue*: Virgil's Poetic Genealogy' (1975) focuses in particular on the initiation of Gallus, a scene that he suggests is based on an episode in Gallus' own writing. Ross shows how Vergil, following Gallus, constructs a 'poetic genealogy' that leads to Gallus from Apollo, via Orpheus and Linus, Hesiod, and Callimachus and other Alexandrian authors, and how the poet places himself in that same tradition.

Gian Biagio Conte in 'An Interpretation of the Tenth *Eclogue*' (1986; Italian 1980) provides a metaliterary reading of *Eclogue* 10 as a confrontation of the genres of bucolic and elegy. Placed in the bucolic world by his well-meaning friend Vergil, the character Gallus is tempted to give up his elegiac poetry and lifestyle and become a bucolic poet, but in the end he yields to love after all; despite their short flirtation, the bucolic and elegiac codes thus turn out to be ultimately irreconcilable.

The volume ends with a reflection on the continuing relevance of the pastoral mode, Seamus Heaney's essay 'Eclogues *in extremis*: On the Staying Power of Pastoral' (2003). Discussing poems of Michael Longley, Vergil, Czeslaw Milosz, Louis MacNeice, and Miklos Radnoti, Heaney concludes that pastoral, for all its formalism and traditionalism, remains uniquely able to confront reality, including in the most desolate and threatening circumstances, and to deeply engage its readers.

2

Arcadia: Modern Occident and Classical Antiquity

Ernst A. Schmidt

There is no name in Greece which raises in the mind of the ordinary reader more pleasing and more definite ideas than the name Arcadia. It has become indissolubly connected with the charms of pastoral ease and rural simplicity. The sound of the shepherd's pipe and the maiden's laughter, the rustling of shady trees, the murmuring of gentle fountains... —these are the images of peace and plenty which the poets have gathered

[The original article appeared in 1975 and was reprinted with some revisions in E. A. Schmidt 1987: 239–64. The difficult task of translating the text was undertaken by Dr Ben Schmidt, Swindon, UK. I am most grateful to the translator for his mastery in giving the essay a true English ring without betraying the author's German style of writing and thinking, and to Katharina Volk for additional suggestions.] Prior works by the author concerning the questions and answers of the present essay include Chapter C III 'Goldenes Zeitalter und Arkadien' in E. A. Schmidt 1972: 154–85 and Chapter 11 § 8, 'Pan und Arkadien in den drei späten Eklogen' in E. A. Schmidt 1987: 208–13, first published in E. A. Schmidt 1974: 37–46.

[As a new introduction to this translation I insert a passage from Kerkhecker 2000: 415: 'For a decade now, a consensus has been growing that, about Virgil's Arcadia, Snell was wrong (R. Jenkyns, 'Virgil and Arcadia', *JRS* 79 [1989], 26–39; cf. his book *Virgil's Experience. Nature and History: Times, Names, and Places* [Oxford, 1998], pp. 156–69). The case 'against' Snell was summed up (in a rather different spirit) twenty-five years ago, in an article that goes far beyond mere refutation (E. A. Schmidt, 'Arkadien: Abendland und Antike', *A&A* 21 [1975], 36–57; revised in his book *Bukolische Leidenschaft oder Über antike Hirtenpoesie* [Frankfurt am Main, Berne, and New York 1987], pp. 239–64; quoted by D. F. Kennedy, 'Arcades ambo: Vergil, Gallus and Arcadia', *Hermathena* 143 [1987], 47–60, at 57 n. 13; cf. n. 12). Schmidt

about that ideal retreat. There are none more historically false, more unfounded in the real nature and aspect of the country, and more opposed to the sentiment of the ancients.... How, then, did this false notion of our Arcadia spring up in modern Europe? How is it that even our daily papers assume this sense, and know it to be intelligible to the most vulgar public? The history of the change from the historical to the poetical conception is very curious, and worth the trouble of explaining, especially as we find it assumed in many books, but accounted for in none.... Thus we reach the year 1500 without any trace of a poetical Arcadia. But at that very time it was being created by the single work of a single man....

Appearing in 1502, the 'Arcadia' of Sannazaro went through sixty editions during the century, and so this single book

saw that the Arcadia of the *Eclogues* could not be identified with the Arcadia of pastoral poetry, and recognized the rôle of Sannazaro in the process of transformation. He described the conditions of Snell's misapprehension, and examined the question: if Virgil's Arcadia is not pastoral—what is it?'

This essay is an attempt to lift some of the layers that have come to cover the bucolic poetry of Vergil. Such an attempt must be most careful in the use of its terms and concepts. Therefore the ancient bucolic poetry in hexameter verse (from Theocritus to Nemesianus) is always called 'bucolic poetry', never 'pastoral poetry' (whereas a novel such as *Daphnis and Chloe* would have to be termed a 'pastoral novel'). The characters of bucolic poetry are always called 'herdsmen' (German: 'Hirten') and not 'shepherds'. The use of the term 'shepherd' in this essay is limited (1) to the herdsmen of sheep as opposed to 'goatherd' and 'cowherd' (not in this essay) and (2) to the characters of later pastoral poetry (German: 'Schäfer'). Since the term 'shepherd' evokes Renaissance and post-Renaissance pastoral poems, novels, dramas, operas, figurines of Meissen china, the pedantic use of 'herdsman' for Vergil helps us to be wary of anachronisms. The name of the poet is spelt 'Vergil' both in my own use and where I am translating. The form 'Virgil' (which was still in use with my academic teachers in Germany and at the time also the prevalent spelling in England) occurs only in quotes. Terms that defy translation into English include 'Abendland', 'Historismus', 'antik', 'die Antike'; the English terms used are no more than vaguely similar at best: 'Occident' or 'Western culture'; 'historicism'; 'ancient' or 'classical', 'classical antiquity'.—In general the translation differs slightly from the German original in two respects: (1) There are occasional short additions in order to facilitate understanding for readers without a German cultural or academic background. These additions are not marked. (2) Additions in square brackets, mostly to the notes, reproduce marginal notes by the author in his copy of the original essay, some of which were inserted already in the 1987 reprint. These notes do not postdate the publication of the original article. The omission of reference to later scholarly work is intentional.]

created that imaginary home of innocence and grace which has ever since been attached to the name.

J. P. Mahaffy, *Rambles and Studies in Greece*, 2nd edn.[1]

1. THE PROGRAMME

The poet who in the decade following Caesar's murder was working on the poems that for the first time present Arcadia as a symbol was born in 70 BC. The poet whose major work, written in AD 1480, revolves once again around Arcadia as its central symbol, following a period of oblivion that lasted for one and a half millennia, died in AD 1530. Thus the year 1930 saw both the 2,000th anniversary of Vergil's birthday and the 400th anniversary of Sannazaro's death. How did the cultural and academic world celebrate the heavenly twins of the Arcadia symbol, the discoverers of Arcadia? Not a single contribution to the celebrations of Vergil's birthday, certainly none in Germany, even mentioned Sannazaro[2]—the poet to whose grave Johann Gottfried Herder (1744–1803)[3] still paid a visit and for whom his friend Pietro Bembo composed the following inscription:

Da sacro cineri flores. Hic ille Maroni
Syncerus Musa proximus ut tumulo.

Give flowers to the holy ashes: Here lies Syncerus, as close to Vergil's grave as to his Muse.

---

[1] Mahaffy 1878: 324–9. Quote discovered by my friend John A. Crook, Cambridge. [Chapter 12 on 'Arcadia—Andritzena—Bassae—Megalopolis—Tripolitza', from whose first pages the quotes are taken, was not contained in the 1st edition.]

[2] Contemporary classical scholars in Germany seem ignorant of Sannazaro's *Arcadia*. This is illustrated for example by a remark made in Gercke 1921. Gercke traces the 'atmosphere' of paintings of Schidone (read: Guercino) and Poussin that illustrate the phrase 'Ego et in Arcadia' back to lines 31 ff. in Vergil's *Gallus-Eclogue*, but remarks (317 n. 1): 'Influence through Italian bucolic poetry cannot be ruled out: an expert may be able to trace it'—directly after a mention of the 'Death Rites for a Shepherdess in Arcadia' by Poussin! Cf. Sannazaro, *Arcadia*, *Proses* X and XI: Massilia's Grave.

[3] Cf. letter to his wife dated 19 January 1789 (see Kuhn, Hofmann, and Kunz 1966: 118–19).

Appreciations of Sannazaro remained sparse and did not extend beyond Italy.[4] While Vergil was mostly invoked as the 'Father of the Occident', particularly as the author of the *Aeneid*, the herald and interpreter of the order of the state and the hero's historical mission, his *Bucolics* also attracted praise. But just as Sannazaro was mostly ignored, so the Arcadia of the *Eclogues* was mentioned either not at all or only in passing. And even though appreciations of Sannazaro would occasionally celebrate Vergil as well, the Roman poet's Arcadia was generally omitted.[5]

In Vergil's work, Arcadia may be a limited element, but it is certainly one that cannot easily be ignored. Nonetheless, for almost one and a half millennia the symbol had no effect whatsoever.[6] Neither the poetry of the Augustan age, directly indebted to and heavily influenced by the atmospherical emanations of the *Bucolics*, nor the bucolic poetry of the Imperial age, which takes its point of departure from Vergil and uses his terms and motifs, his forms and symbols as poetic elements, nor indeed the ancient commentaries on Vergil; neither medieval nor early Renaissance pastoral poetry, all of which emerged from a knowledge of Vergil's *Eclogues* and the web of traditions originating from them—none of them display even the most minute trace of Vergil's Arcadia. After a few preliminaries,[7] the stream of living Arcadia symbolism that was to last for the next three hundred years begins with Sannazaro's *Arcadia*. Following that period, it runs almost completely dry for more than a century, only to be rediscovered by twentieth-century academic research, with an impact on the field of classical studies and far beyond, in the seminal 1945 essay by Bruno Snell.[8]

---

[4] A list of such contributions can be found in Corti 1969: 307 n. 1.

[5] Vergil's Arcadia mentioned in studies on Vergil: Wili 1930: 39: in passing and in inverted commas ('in Arkadien') of *Ecl.* 5 as opposed to *Ecl.* 4; Klingner 1931*b*: 134–5: Bucolic poetry with its 'nostalgia for a Golden Age' as a 'paradise imagined along Arcadian lines'.—[Vergil's Arcadia not mentioned in studies on Sannazaro: cf. e.g. Momigliano, 'Jacopo Sannazaro (24 Aprile 1530–1930)' (1930) and 'L' "Arcadia"' (1930), reprinted in Momigliano 1948: 43–9 and 50–6.]

[6] Cf. Panofsky 1936 ~ 1955; there 302: '... Boccaccio's Ameto, where more than thirteen hundred years after Virgil *at least the name* of Arcadia *reappears*' (italics EAS).

[7] Cf. n. 6 and section 3.

[8] Cf. section 2 with n. 22. Mambelli 1940 does not include the entry 'Arcadia' in his 'Indice dei soggetti' on the roughly 4,000 titles of the years 1900–40 while including entries such as 'arcano', 'arboricultura', 'arazzi', 'aratri'!

That third discovery of Arcadia is itself oblivious of the Arcadia oblivion that marks the period between Vergil and Sannazaro; it remains trapped in a peculiar bias, unaware of Sannazaro's unique historical significance and character, unaware of his necessary transformation of Arcadia symbolism, unaware of the latent power and potential influence of this modern version of Arcadia. While it does take note of the cessation of Arcadia towards the end of the eighteenth century, even furnishing the correct interpretation for that event,[9] it still regards Vergil's Arcadia as the first element in a continuous chain of tradition. It sees itself as the interpretation of a discovery made by Vergil, overlooking the fact that the only reason it can even perceive that symbol in the *Eclogues* is owed to the fact that it has already assimilated the modern version of Arcadia. I will show how it fails to capture the essence of Vergil's Arcadia for the simple reason that the notion of Arcadia implied by its interpretation of Vergil is none other than the very notion of the new Arcadia. In other words, a symbol inspired by Vergil, a symbol of the Renaissance reception of classical antiquity, is now read into Vergil.

It seems to me a worthwhile task to analyse the three discoveries of Arcadia—Vergil, Sannazaro, Snell—by going back in time and exploring their interdependence. The enquiry will also have to take into account the aforementioned dual mystery in the history of Arcadia: the big intervals between Vergil and Sannazaro, and between the age of German classicism and the inter-war period; as well as the fact that this rather obvious finding with respect to classical antiquity and the Middle Ages has not been noticed and interpreted before. The historical interpretation of the end of Sannazaro's fame has not yet been brought to bear on our understanding of the self-image of the scholarly generation that rediscovered Vergil's Arcadia.

My intention is not to destroy a vital web of mutual influences and tradition under the guise of a pseudo-scientific objectivity, nor is it my wish to rescue Vergil from his friends by evacuating him to a museum of well-tempered sterility. There is no naive going back from the history of his reception to Vergil's presumed intention. Instead, I offer preparations for a new and historically more aware understanding of Vergil's bucolic poetry. Nor should adversaries of

---

[9] Cf. below, section 3, last paragraph.

Klingner and Snell take any comfort in my argument—it is an in-house disagreement, which may ultimately be about the extent of one's love for Vergil. But why do I single out Snell's essay? Why only this contribution to Vergil's Arcadia? Why do I not engage with Reitzenstein's theory of an Arcadian school of bucolic poetry prior to Theocritus,[10] with Wilamowitz' derivation of Vergil's Arcadia from lost *prolegomena* to the scholia on Theocritus,[11] or with Jachmann's hypothesis of a post-Theocritean Arcadia?[12] Or even with Raper's Arcadian club in Rome under the presidency of Asinius Pollio[13] and Bayet's similarly daring hypothesis constructing a poets' circle of 'Arcadians' around Pollio and Vergil?[14] Let alone Brugioni's argument that the originality of Vergil's bucolic poetry is due to its anti-Arcadian character[15] or Levi's interpretation of Arcadia as echo poetry?[16] [Why not Webster's[17] speculation that the popularity of Arcadia in later pastoral poetry originated in its significance as the Attalids' mythical country of origin (fresco in Herculaneum with Arcadia, Heracles and Telephos; Telephos frieze in Pergamon) and in the *mystai* of Dionysos in Pergamon, whom he seems to interpret as both *boukoloi* (= *mystai* as well as bucolic characters) and tragic poets and/or actors?[18]] Not because Snell (following Ernst Kapp and Erwin Panofsky in their derivation of Vergil's Arcadia)[19] is more convincing or, more importantly, because he makes Vergil the actual discoverer of Arcadia, but rather because his essay is the only really significant contribution. Its significance consists among other factors in the fact that Snell is the

[10] R. Reitzenstein 1893: 121 ff., 131–2 (n.), and 243 ff.
[11] Von Wilamowitz-Moellendorff 1906: 111 n. 1. Cf. C. Wendel 1920: 71–2.
[12] Jachmann 1952*b*, in particular 171 ff.
[13] Raper 1908: dinner hall for Augustus' secret 'Celebration of the 12 Gods' (Suet. *Aug.* 70) decorated as Arcadia; musical contributions from this Arcadian scenery are preserved in *Ecl.* 4, 6, and 10.
[14] Bayet 1930*b*, here 380–4.
[15] Brugioni 1940. Brugioni's interpretation is revived by Fantazzi 1966: 180, who calls Damon's song in *Ecl.* 8 'anti-Arcadian': an amusing paradox indicative of the unthinking assumptions and terminological confusions of research into Arcadia, as it calls Vergil's earliest Arcadian song (cf. section 4) a negation of Arcadia.
[16] Levi 1967/8.
[17] [Webster 1964: 193–200, in particular 201.]
[18] [Cf. Webster 1964: 165–6, 196–7, 198–9, 201–2, 215.]
[19] Cf. E. A. Schmidt 1972: 173 n. 209.

only one to focus on the fascination that Vergil's Arcadia began to exert even on the modern reader, the only one to make this fascination the subject of his analysis, and the only one to reveal that his interpretation builds on the assumption that Vergil's Arcadia and the new Arcadia are identical. In other words, Snell is most emphatic in the mistaken belief that his own rediscovery of the new Arcadia, which made Vergil's Arcadia visible and significant for him, is identical with Vergil's discovery of Arcadia. Snell's essay thus becomes the instrument of its own defeat, opening up a new access to Vergil's Arcadia. By the same token, all other attempts at deducing Arcadia from other origins, including Kapp-Panofsky-Snell's Polybios hypothesis, forego their claim for individual refutation by losing their premise. They are errors of academic research whose sole value is to serve as illustrations of the secret power and potential influence of the new Arcadia.[20]

2. BRUNO SNELL, 'THE DISCOVERY OF A SPIRITUAL LANDSCAPE'

Snell's essay 'Arkadien: Die Entdeckung einer geistigen Landschaft', which was published three decades ago[21] in the first volume of the yearbook *Antike und Abendland* (1945), founded by him, and published again in 1946 in his book *Die Entdeckung des Geistes*,[22] characterizes Vergil's Arcadia as a blissful existence constituted by three new qualities in the life of the soul: the poetic/dreaming, the all-encompassing/loving, and the sensitive/suffering. Snell's key

[20] C. Wendel's (1920) criticisms of Reitzenstein, Legrand, and Wilamowitz and generally of specific attempts to find a source for Vergil's Arcadia have not prevailed; his indication of the familiar mythological connections between Arcadia and Pan / Pan and Syrinx was disregarded. The same happened when the idea was repeated (as a criticism of Snell) by Büchner 1957: 241–3.
[21] [i.e. thirty years before the date (1975) of the original article which is reproduced here in translation.]
[22] Snell 1945 = 1955: 371–400 (all the quotes refer to this edition, the translations are by Dr Ben Schmidt). Reprinted in Oppermann (ed.) 1963: 338–67. [Snell's book appeared also in English (Snell 1953), with the Arcadia essay on pp. 281–309; the English version of the essay was reprinted in Commager (ed.) 1966: 14–27.]

words for this 'land of the soul that longs for its far-away home'[23] are: escape, loss, longing, feeling, and emotion. While Snell focuses on the most 'Arcadian' of the *Eclogues*, i.e. the tenth, which is the Gallus poem, Arcadia is to him a symbol for the whole of Vergil's bucolic poetry. In terms of literary history, Snell's Arcadia is the confluence of the notion of a Golden Age with a prevailing elegiac mood.

Snell's essay throws into stark relief a general condition for the reception of scholarly writing. Anyone who intends to say something new must necessarily make reference to what is already known and established, otherwise they will neither be understood nor believed. Snell, who saw in Vergil the discoverer of that Arcadia 'which is now the notion that comes to the minds of all who hear that name',[24] could not but describe Vergil's bucolic poetry in such a way as to align its novelty in the history of classical literature and its uniqueness in terms of its Arcadian character with the Renaissance notion of Arcadia. But on the other hand the description of Vergil's bucolic poetry as Arcadia had to result in a picture of the *Eclogues* that was aligned with or at least had references to his readers' image of Vergil, although the readers would not have called that image Arcadia, even where they read Arcadia in the *Eclogues*. Snell fulfils both preconditions, which explains the immense influence of his essay. The preconditions are fulfilled because Snell and his readers went through the same kind of schooling with respect to Vergil's bucolic poetry and Arcadia. The main achievement in his conception is the discovery of the convergence between the prevailing interpretation of the *Eclogues*—which remained silent about Arcadia—with the modern Arcadia. Snell aligned Vergil's bucolic poetry as it was conceived by German Latinists (not *hommes de lettres*) with the modern Arcadia as it was perceived by Romanists and art historians. Specifically, without Jachmann's 'Bukolische Technik Vergils' (1922) and Panofsky's 'Et in Arcadia ego' (1936) Snell's article would not have been possible; it would not have been understood nor would it have had any influence.[25]

Panofsky 1936 provided the immediate impulse for Snell's Arcadia essay. In a brief article (Snell 1938) the core of the later study with all its central points

---

[23] Snell [1945] 1955: 392.   [24] Snell [1945] 1955: 371.
[25] [The following passage in small print reproduces an original footnote.]

is already present: the emphasis on 'sentimentality', the 'soulful', the 'emotional' in Vergil's bucolic poetry as opposed to the 'simple' 'factualness' of Theocritus; the longing, the 'dream' of a more meaningful life; even the comparison between Roman wishful poetry with Greek philosophy and the connections between the Golden Age and Arcadia. And the reference to Panofsky 1936 in a note on Vergil's Arcadia, which is mentioned here for the first time, stands within the following context (Snell 1938: 242): '... Vergil's concept (one might even say: *discovery*) of bucolic Arcadia...' (italics EAS). Cf. Panofsky 1936: 227: 'Thus it was Virgil who achieved the paradisiacal conception that the modern mind automatically connects with the term "Arcadia"'.—Friedrich Klingner's first articles on Vergil in 1927 (1927*b* = 1956*a*: 294–308; 1927*c*; cf. also 1927*a*, on Vergil: 22–4) and 1930/31 (1930 = 1956*a*: 256–74; 1931*a*; 1931*b*) had not mentioned Arcadia (with the exception quoted in n. 5 above). It emerges in his research report 'Virgil' (1942 = 1956*a*: 221–55), now with the subtitle 'Wiederentdeckung eines Dichters' ('Rediscovery of a poet'); cf. there 244, 245 and in particular 229: '... transported into the desired blissful realm of Arcadia, where the songs of herdsmen make love and suffering sound purer and more beautiful than in the confused and devastated reality that had surrounded the poet', and 231: 'While already in the early poems of the collection a peculiar seriousness can be heard beneath the playfulness, when the joys and sufferings of life are mirrored and transfigured in the herdsmen's Arcadia, the later poems are replete with the sounds of more mysterious and significant words, singing of fortune and misfortune...., mourning, interpreting, comforting and praising...'. Then in Klingner 1943 (= 1956*a*: 275–93), we read, '... Herdsmen's songs in the dreamlike imaginary country of Arcadia, the Arcadia *discovered* by Vergil for all generations to come' (280; Italics EAS).—The influence of Snell 1938 becomes particularly probable here; the author of the 1942 research report—see above—knew it, of course, even though he does not mention it there. The works of Klingner already mentioned in turn influence Snell's essay on Arcadia—cf. Snell [1945] 1955: 380 n. 1, and in particular the terms 'existence', 'transfigured', and 'imaginary country'—, which in turn had an influence on statements in Klingner 1947 (= 1956*a*: 142–72). Further Klingner [1943] 1956*a*: 280–1: 'In this musical imaginary country of Arcadia joy and suffering in the songs of the herdsmen...sound pure and full and beautiful. Nay, this Arcadia is nothing but a different, secret side of his own existence discovered by the poet. That is why like in a dream he is one with all his herdsmen and with that wonderful, blissful land.... As a backdrop one needs to keep in mind the terribly devastated life that surrounded him as he was writing: civil war, revolutions, death, misery, brutality, and depravity'; the 'imaginary land of Arcadia' as a 'transfigured home' like the Italian land in the *Georgics*; cf. also 282–3. Again [1947] 1956*a*: 162: 'Virgil's Arcadia is no different' (sc. than Catullus' 'artificial world'), an 'imaginary sphere of life': thus shortly before on the same page following Snell [1945] 1955, cf. in particular 397; in later editions Snell in turn makes reference to exactly this passage in Klingner's article: Snell [1945] 1955: 394 n. 1: 'Imaginary country and soulscape, one with the artificial world of bucolic poetry, a desired home, accessible to the homeless poet's song, who finds there what he is searching here in vain in the soulless, terribly brutal reality of common existence.' Klingner again in 1956*b*, here 136: ' "Arcadia", a sphere beyond, the realm of a higher and consecrated existence in the midst of a brutal, murderous, soulless reality, a dreamscape and home for the soul.' And again in Klingner 1967: 109–10: '. . . a great and consuming love and the new art . . . made the escape possible from the soulless and murderous Rome, in godless times to participate in a higher existence where the divine and the human were still united'—' "Arcadia" is a consecration of existence, the imaginary land where song is the highest value, where in the songs of the herdsmen everything that is confused, distraught, and out of tune here will sound pure and full and beautifully harmonious. "Arcadia" is ennobled by a sublime force that transfigures any heavy elements, making them hover in delicate balance, the epitome of the Muses' art.'

Panofsky characterized the Arcadia of Sannazaro and the Renaissance as a Utopia of bliss and beauty, brimming with nostalgia and melancholy, and presented the elegiac mood as the prevailing quality of Renaissance Arcadia.[26] It is not necessary to have read Sannazaro in order to understand Snell; a general idea of Arcadia as exemplified e.g. in Schiller's *Resignation* or, to a lesser degree, in Goethe's *Faust II* will suffice. But only someone who knows Panofsky's article will be able to fully appreciate some of Snell's sentences. In particular the fact that Snell identifies as genuinely Arcadian the elegiac poet Gallus, Vergil's confrontation of Gallus with his own poetry, and the play with elegiac poetry as a theme within bucolic poetry, is only possible and understandable against the backdrop of Sannazaro and Panofsky: '. . . the elegiac feeling . . . impresses us as the essential

---

[26] Cf. Panofsky 1936: 230–1; more detailed and more developed Panofsky 1955: 303–4. Cf. the remarks of Saxl 1927: 22, to which Panofsky refers: 'the sentimental', 'sweet pain', 'idylls full of melancholy'; Saxl points to the first line of Garcilaso de la Vega's first *Eclogue*: 'El dulce lamentar de dos pastores' ('The sweet wailing of two shepherds').

quality of the Arcadian atmosphere', Panofsky states.[27] The notion that Vergil's bucolic poetry views its world 'as something that has been lost'[28] is hard to understand on the basis of Vergil's text but becomes clear upon reading Panofsky: 'According to Sannazaro, Arcadia is mostly a Utopian realm, and that is why it is shrouded in the gentle veils of melancholy'.[29]

Within the field of Latin studies in Germany, the view of the *Eclogues* most influential on Snell was that of Günther Jachmann. The impact of his 1922 article 'Die dichterische Technik in Vergils Bukolika' can hardly be overestimated.[30] Many later statements and articles on Vergil's bucolic poetry are constructed on the foundations laid by him; many use his terminology and phraseology without acknowledging the source, sometimes even unwittingly. The celebrations surrounding Vergil's anniversary had consolidated Jachmann's views, if not within the whole field of Classical Studies, then certainly among German Latinists, and Snell's essay on Arcadia served to further anchor his interpretation of the *Eclogues* among scholars of modern languages and literatures[31] as well as the general public.

Jachmann's essay attempts to go beyond the previous decades' analytical approaches to Vergil without doing away with their

[27] Panofsky 1936: 231; for a more precise appreciation of this as Sannazaro's unique achievement, see Panofsky 1955: 304.
[28] Snell [1945] 1955: 381.
[29] Panofsky 1936: 231. More strongly and, while making a point concerning Vergil, actually criticizing Snell, Panofsky 1955: 304: 'Sannazaro's Arcadia is a utopian realm like Vergil's. But it is also [sc. in Sannazaro as opposed to Vergil] a realm that is irretrievably lost, viewed through a veil of melancholy memory.' Exactly these characteristics had, however, already been assigned to the *Eclogues* at Vergil's 1930 anniversary. 'Melancholy', for example, is a key term in the lecture 'Vergil' of 1930 by Johannes Stroux (Stroux 1932); and Santucci 1930 interprets nature in the *Eclogues* as 'sentimento' and 'malinconia', in remarkable coincidence with A. Sainati's phrase quoted by Saxl 1927: 22 n. 3 (Sainati 1919: 184) and Panofsky 1936: 231 with n. 1: 'La musa vera del Sannazaro è la malinconia.' 'Memory' and 'longing' are key words in Walter Wili's interpretation of the *Eclogues* in his book on Vergil (1930: 22 ff., 45).
[30] Already in 1927 Klingner points out the significance of this essay: Klinger 1927c: 576–7.
[31] Cf. e.g. Corti 1969: 291: 'Scrive lo Snell...' ('Snell writes...') with a quote from Snell [1945] 1955: 381 ('...like something lost...', '...more longing than happiness...'). She therefore speaks of Vergil's bucolic poetry as a 'paesaggio di evasione' ('escapist landscape': Snell's 'escape and 'imaginary country'), thus finding a feature of Sannazaro's Arcadia already in the Roman poet's *Eclogues*.

results.[32] He does not negate the objections made by the analysts; he makes no attempt to eliminate contradictions and ambivalences. On the contrary, he welcomes them and seeks them out since he regards them as intentional devices employed by Vergil to lift the reader away from the factual, real, and specific[33] into a world of feelings and emotion.[34]

The world of bucolic poetry as a whole as well as the individual *Eclogues* with all their contradictions and factual ambivalences are unified in their mood. The inconsistencies are technical devices to produce moods: such is Jachmann's paradoxical, even absurd, yet unchallenged and influential argument. His key word is 'mood' ('Stimmung'): it appears ten times in his 20 page essay![35] In the contributions to Vergil's 1930 anniversary, the term is once again of central importance. Where Jachmann stated that the events in Vergil's bucolic poetry are 'steeped in a sentimental mood' or that their 'unified character' consists in their 'mood', Wili 1930 writes that the *Eclogues* are 'nothing but their mood', and Stroux 1932 that they are 'steeped in a unified sentimental mood'.[36]

Snell tended to avoid the term 'mood', preferring other terms used synonymously by Jachmann, such as emotion, feeling, sentimentality, the sentimental, and longing, particularly because these terms converge more strongly with the elegiac notion of Arcadia as described by Panofsky.

[32] While Jachmann greatly inspired academic research, he also represents a step back and the beginning of a problematic development. By not going beyond analysis, such as that found in Bethe 1892, he remains below the level of interpretation reached by Leo 1903. And by doing without an actual interpretation of the poems, seeing their purpose fulfilled in the creation of a vague mood, he gives carte blanche to the interpreter's arbitrary subjectivity, accepting even celebratory mood, self-enjoyment, and nostalgia as adequate interpretations.

[33] A late descendant of this interpretation of Vergil's technique, transferred to Horace, is Eduard Fraenkel's interpretation of *Epode* 16 (1957: 42 ff.), in particular 46–7: the 'apparent inconsistency' between the phrases used in the senate proceedings and those used in the national assembly 'fulfils an important purpose', namely to create an impression of 'complete unreality'.

[34] In the construction of this peculiar process, Jachmann does not seem to have made a proper distinction between fictionality (as opposed to reality) and non-realistic literature (as opposed to realism).

[35] Klingner 1927c has five occurrences of 'mood' and five occurrences of 'feeling' on seven pages.

[36] Jachmann 1922: 103 and 114; Wili 1930: 23; Stroux 1932: 7; cf. Klingner 1927c: 582.

The elegiac-sentimental bucolic poetry in Jachmann's interpretation was not the only factor to influence classical studies up to and beyond Snell. Another aspect in the mood of Vergil's bucolic poetry as seen by Jachman is at least as important, viz. its presentation by means of a vocabulary normally used as linguistic devices for the description of specific types of landscape painting. From Jachmann 1922 to Snell [1945] 1955 via Stroux 1932 and Wili 1930, Vergil's bucolic poetry is evoked in the language of specific effects of space and light. Atmosphere, twilight, dusk, veil, shimmer, colour, distance are frequently used terms. The favourite term is 'shimmer' ('Schimmer'); Wili uses it five times. The verbs used in conjunction with these nouns are illustrated by the following quotes: 'everything lies in the uncertain shimmer of twilight' (Wili), 'a bucolic mood spreads its shimmering light' (Wili), 'everything steeped in the colours of emotion' (Snell), 'the whole scene bathed in a mild light' (Jachmann). The phrase 'steeped/bathed in…' ('eingetaucht in…') is a particular favourite: Jachmann uses it three times, Stroux and Snell once. Other verbs either emphasize the notion of being embraced by light and atmosphere—'spreads over, lies in, stands in; embraced by, encompassed by, flooded by, hovering'—or they imply an internal abundance, foregrounding emotion over light and atmosphere—'filled with mood, ethos, feeling, emotion' (Jachmann, Stroux, Snell), 'permeated by', 'saturated by'. The compound verbs most commonly used in these characterizations of Vergil's bucolic poetry are of the type using the German prefix 'ver-': 'vergolden' ('to bathe in gold') and 'verklären' ('to transfigure'), 'verwischen' ('to blur', transitive) and 'verschleiern' ('to veil'), 'verschwimmen' ('to blur', intransitive) and 'verschweben' ('to float, hover away'), 'verdämmern' ('to fade away') and 'verschimmern' ('to shimmer away'). It will be immediately evident that an interpretation of bucolic poetry that paraphrases *usque ad aquam* in *Ecl.* 9.9 with the words 'the shimmering meanders of the distant river'[37] presents romantic landscapes to the inner eye; in one instance, they are even explicitly named as such: 'everything is bathed in uncertain shimmering twilight like Romantic landscape paintings'.[38] Since this allows associations with heroic and idyllic, pastoral, 'classical', and 'elegiac'

---

[37] Wili 1930: 31.   [38] Ibid. 30.

landscapes, the circle to 'Poussin and the Elegiac Tradition'—thus the new subtitle given by Panofsky to his reworked essay 'Et in Arcadia ego' in 1955—is closed (with or without the detour via Claude Lorraine). In other words, this aspect, too, of the interpretation of the *Eclogues* as constituted by Jachmann holds the possibility of connecting them with the modern Arcadia and its longing for classical antiquity.

Jachmann's 1922 interpretation of the *Eclogues* is in turn nothing but the transfer of Richard Heinze's characteristics of the *Aeneid* onto the *Bucolics*.[39] The paragraph 'Ethos' of the 1903 book *Virgils epische Technik*[40] contains six times in nine pages the term 'emotion', eight times the term 'feeling', and nine times the term 'mood'. It is not difficult to recognize in Heinze's core statement that Vergil's narrative 'is thoroughly soaked with feeling'[41] the linguistic and conceptual model for the designation of Vergil's bucolic poetry discussed above.

If this relationship to Heinze's book on the *Aeneid* is correctly diagnosed, then in terms of its place in cultural history, the new understanding of the *Eclogues* must be located within the German rediscovery of Vergil (originally as an epic poet) by means of categories that have their origin in Schiller's treatise 'Über naïve und sentimentalische Dichtung' ([1795] 1989).[42] Heinze appreciates the *Aeneid* as the work of a sentimental poet as opposed to Homer's naïve epic poems.[43] What he has to say, following the passage on 'ethos', about 'the emergence of the poet's personality', for example, is a direct extension of Schiller's juxtaposition between the *Iliad* and

---

[39] Or rather, it is the generalization of a view stated by Bethe 1892: 590 (cf. Jachmann 1922: 115 n. 1) about Vergil's intention to create a mood, under the impact of Heinze's interpretation of the *Aeneid*.

[40] The dependence in terms of the general approach is already indicated in the expression 'technique' used by Jachmann in his title. On the interpretation of Jachmann's approach as a transfer of Heinze's, cf. Klingner [1942] 1956a: 229; Holtorf 1953: 51.

[41] Heinze 1903: 362. Besides the passages quoted, cf. also Jachmann 1922: 104: '...saturated with mood and emotion, in a word: sentimental.'

[42] Fuchs 1930/1: 75 hypothetically attempts to locate Schiller's admiration for Vergil within the same context: 'Was it the fundamental difference between the sentimental and the naïve poet, recognized by Schiller and shared by both, that brought them together, or was it...?'

[43] Explicitly Hosius 1930: 44: '...on Homer's naïve and Vergil's sentimental poetry, if I may use these terms'. The vocabulary used in the context of this remark, 44–6, might be transferred from Homer to Theocritus, from the *Aeneid* to the *Eclogues*, in any contemporary appreciation of Vergil's bucolic poetry: 'descriptions

the *Orlando Furioso*.[44] The transfer of the distinction between naïve and sentimental from 'Homer *vs.* Vergil, *Aeneid*' to 'Theocritus, bucolic *Idyll vs.* Vergil, *Eclogues*' has caused the stubborn persistence of the notion of a naïve, simple, objective, factual, realistic Theocritus, which is quite bizarre given the results of individual research on the Alexandrian era and Theocritus.

This description, informed by Schiller, of Vergil's bucolic poetry set the seal on its identification with modern pastoral poetry, which was itself understood in terms of Schiller's categories; the reference to Arcadia as understood by Schiller from within the contemporary modern tradition (he had no knowledge of Vergil's Arcadia) had become almost necessary. Schiller subdivides the elegiac poetic style ('in its wider sense'), which together with the satirical poetic style constitutes sentimental poetry, into elegy ('in its specific sense') and idyll ('in its widest sense'). Integral aspects of the elegiac poetic style, whose character as sentimental poetry is to be in search of Nature Lost, include 'lamentations of lost joys, of the Golden Age that has disappeared from the world'. Schiller's criticism of the pastoral idyll concerns its 'unfortunate' constitutive failure that it 'posits the aim as something that lies behind us'; instead, he calls for an idyll 'that would lead humans, who after all cannot return to Arcadia, all the way into Elysium'.[45]

3. SANNAZARO, *ARCADIA*

Sannazaro's *Arcadia* was written around 1480; after a number of pirate prints, an expanded version was published in 1504 as the

---

of deeds and facts' *vs.* 'impact of facts on feeling', 'the soul's emotional vibrations'; 'deeds are not Vergil's main concern, he is indifferent to time, place and probability'. (On a scene in the *Odyssey*:) 'Everything is vivid and clear, everything is possible' *vs.* (in the *Aeneid*:) 'All events are saturated with psychology.' Similarly also Schott 1930: 843: Vergil the dreamer and spinner of yarns, Homer clear and simple. 'It is here if anywhere that Schiller's distinction between naïve and sentimental poetry applies. Homer's is a naïve view on a great and rich nature; Vergil's mind drapes his invented fables with the sentimental excitements of his ingenious mind.'

[44] Heinze 1903: 370–3; Schiller [1795] 1989: 713–15.
[45] Cf. Schiller [1795] 1989: 721, 728–30, 747, 750. Cf. on this topic Rüdiger 1959, in particular 237 ff.

Arcadia 31

first edition that was authorized by the poet. It enjoyed wide dissemination in numerous editions and commentaries throughout the sixteenth century.[46] There was no work of comparable fame and influence: I only mention Tasso's *Aminta*,[47] Guarini's *Pastor fido*, the Marcela episode in *Don Quijote*[48] as well as contemporary painting.[49] Drawing on a summary of modern research, I will now present not so much the content but rather the character and historical significance of this work—the origin of modern pastoral poetry and the constitution of the new Arcadia.

The elements of the elegiac and the melancholy in Sannazaro's *Arcadia* have already been mentioned; let me add here three further characteristics of fundamental importance, taken from a number of articles by Petriconi,[50] from the Sannazaro essays in the book *Metodi et Fantasmi* by the Italian scholar Maria Corti, and from Ulrich Töns' unpublished habilitation thesis 'Vergil und die Ekloge in den romanischen Ländern'.[51] These three characteristics are: the Italian lyricism as established by Petrarch, the Golden Age, and the freedom of love. In light of these points, the epochal difference between Sannazaro's and Vergil's Arcadia becomes particularly evident.

In Maria Corti's work, the novelty of Sannazaro's *Arcadia* is presented as a further development of the Tuscan pastoral of the

---

[46] Different authors cite different numbers: Mahaffy 1878; Weisbach 1930; Corti 1969: 305–23; [Schunck 1970: 93; Töns 1977: 143 n. 1]. [For the year 1504 as publication date of the authorized edition in Naples cf. Töns 1977: 143; the year 1502 which is universally given is not correct: in that year an unauthorized and incomplete edition came out in Venice; cf. ibid. My quotations come from the 1961 edition by Alfredo Mauro.]
[47] Cf. Petriconi 1930.
[48] Cf. Köhler 1966.
[49] Cf. besides Panofsky's essay in particular Weisbach 1930, esp. 130–5. This outstanding essay (the Giorgione circle—Guercino—as the mediator between Sannazaro and Poussin; an excellent artistic interpretation and historical juxtaposition of the 'Et in Arcadia ego'-paintings by Guercino and Poussin) is not superseded by Panofsky. Superseded are Hubaux 1929 and Gercke 1921. Weisbach and Panofsky have recently been complemented by Himmelmann-Wildschütz 1973. (The humanist *memento mori* 'I too in Arcadia' goes back to the visual motif 'Two shepherds contemplating a skull' on Italic gems of the late Hellenistic period, interpreting it in an allegorical-elegiac mode; connection between the gems and bucolic poetry considered; Arcadia not mentioned.) I am grateful to Fritz Schalk for directing my attention to this title as well as to Maria Corti's book (1969).
[50] Petriconi 1930, 1948, and 1959.   [51] Töns 1973; cf. Töns 1977.

Quattrocento through direct and conscious reference to Vergil in the spirit of Petrarch's *Canzoniere*. Töns arrives at the same result. Both researchers reckon that Sannazaro wrote *Arcadia* after the *Bucoliche elegantissime* (published in 1482 but partly circulating already prior to that date), which would mean that he was familiar with the pastoral code of Quattrocento pastoral poetry in Siena and Florence, while also writing in a context of Vergilian reception shaped by the influence of Petrarchism as represented by the first vernacular translation of Vergil's *Eclogues* by Bernardo Pulci in the aforementioned edition of *Bucoliche elegantissime*.[52]

Töns shows vividly how Pulci emphasizes idyllic sentimentality and emotionality in Vergil's *Eclogues* through the use of lyricisms and a language of emotions in the Petrarchist style. From Pulci onward, Vergil's *Eclogues* are read through the eyes of Petrarch and reproduced accordingly, particularly and with complete mastery in Sannazaro's *Arcadia*.

This work is characterized by extremes of mellowness and sweetness, by sentimentality and powerful moods. Tears, sighs, and mourning are the prevalent motifs, touching lamentations about love the main theme. Töns argues[53] that since Petrarch the lover's situation had become incomparably more mellow and sentimental than it had been in Vergil. Pain and suffering are enjoyed as a mellow mood in which the hardness and acuteness of suffering disappear under the veil of a deep melancholy. Sentimentality loses itself in its own contemplation; lamentation is a painful, passive meditation.

The main moments of this lyricism—sentimentality, melancholy, the intoxication of lamentation, the enjoyment of the self in suffering ('si mi è dolce il tormento', *Ecl.* 2.90: 'so sweet is torment to me'), self-pity ('una compassione grandissima di me stesso', *Pros.* 7 § 26: 'overwhelming compassion for myself')—can be found in Snell's analysis of Gallus' verses in Vergil's tenth *Eclogue*. Gallus 'contemplates... his own death with sentimental delight', he 'views himself as if in a mirror and enjoys the notion that others think of him with great emotion'.[54] The fact that he chooses Gallus' verses in *Ecl.* 10

[52] Cf. Töns 1973: 184.   [53] Cf. Töns 1973: 137.
[54] Snell [1945] 1955: 386–7. The text says (v. 34): *vestra meos olim si fistula dicat amores*! To read into this passage Gallus' expectation to be celebrated by the Arcadians in soulful-sentimental songs means simply to add the desired interpretation to

reveals the strength of Snell's guiding (pre-)conception of Arcadia. For among Vergil's *Eclogues*, it is exactly this constellation—the lover in Arcadia—and its character that had the strongest effect on Sannazaro. In *Ecl.* 10 one can grasp one of the roots of Renaissance Arcadia: a text that contains Arcadia and fits well with Sannazaro's notion of poetry as evolved from Petrarch. The only questionable aspect is the fact that Snell makes Gallus' words the constituent of Vergil's Arcadia just because Vergil has him speak about Arcadia in Arcadia. But is this not rather a matter of the bucolic poet letting the (non-Arcadian) elegiac poet speak within his own world—one will find parallels to Gallus' notions in the Roman elegiac poets[55] much rather than in the other *Eclogues*—and characterizing him through his lamentations? This is not Vergil's world itself, just as the characterization of Tibullus in Horace's *Ode* 1.33 cannot be directly equated with the lyrical poet's notion of love. Gallus' words to the Arcadian herdsmen are purely elegiac in tone and attitude; they represent an elegiac version of Vergil's poetical world, an alternative to his bucolic poetry. In a nutshell, they are the elegiac misconception of Vergil's Arcadia. The agreement of Snell's interpretation of Arcadia with Sannazaro's novel, whose elegiac character is obviously different from Vergil's bucolic world, relies on the equation between the text's effect with one of the textual elements that exert this effect, on the identification of two different textual elements due to their fusion in the history of the text's reception. Reference to the fact that Gallus' words in *Ecl.* 10 were written by Vergil and spoken in his Arcadia and thus formed part of his bucolic poetry does not constitute a valid counter-argument. For this fact I wish to neither deny nor play down; on the contrary, it is the very origin of the new Arcadia. If the whole of Vergil's bucolic poetry is Arcadia, why then focus on the elegiac poet

---

the text—after all the whole direction of the argument is to demonstrate the sentimental-emotional quality of Vergil's Arcadia in the first place. A comparison between Gallus' words with Tibullus 1.1.61 ff. leads to the almost necessary conclusion that Vergil takes up an elegiac motif (by Gallus), probably even weakening the elegiac bliss of self-pity in the imagination of one's own death ('only Styx can wash away the pains of love'). Cf. Stroh 1971: 229 with n. 7.

[55] Cf. above n. 54 and Berg 1974: 187. Hubaux 1929 points to Prop. 1.17.21–4 and Ov. *Trist.* 3.3.76 with respect to *mihi molliter ossa quiescant* (*Ecl.* 10.33) as the elegiac equivalent to *sit terra tibi levis*. (He sees the origin of the motif 'music at the grave' in Leonidas of Tarentum, *Epigr.* 19 Gow-Page = *Anth. Pal.* 7.657.)

Gallus in *Ecl.* 10? Why not, for example, take the lamentation of the herdsman Meliboeus in *Ecl.* 1.4 and 71: *nos patriam fugimus, en quo discordia civis*... as the core of Vergil's discovery of Arcadia?[56]

The elegiac character of Sannazaro's *Arcadia* is in a certain respect a repetition of the situation in the tenth *Eclogue*—the love-sick love poet in Arcadia. In another respect it is the integration of the elegiac, namely the attitude of the elegiac poet Gallus towards Vergil's Arcadia, into the symbol of Arcadia: Arcadia itself becomes elegiac. This shift takes place within the sphere of influence, and with the help of the stylistic devices, of Petrarch's vernacular poetry.

Hellmuth Petriconi's essay 'Über die Idee des goldenen Zeitalters als Ursprung der Schäferdichtungen Sannazaros und Tassos' ('On the Idea of the Golden Age as the Origin of the pastoral poems of Sannazaro and Tasso') was published in the year of the Vergil and Sannazaro anniversaries of 1930. It is the most important and influential contribution on the subject of Renaissance pastoral in this century. Vergil's bucolic poetry, Vergil's Arcadia are not mentioned. Petriconi later repeated his insights in two further essays whose titles precisely mirror the author's arguments: 'Das neue Arkadien' ('The New Arcadia') and 'Die verlorenen Paradiese' ('Paradises Lost').[57] The first of these two articles, published in the third volume of the yearbook *Antike und Abendland* in 1948, three years after Snell's essay on Arcadia, is a striking demonstration of the influence of the rediscovery of Arcadia. For in a sense it is the repetition of the 1930 article under a new title—since Arcadia now existed again—and while it does not explicitly refute Snell, such refutation had already been latently present in Petriconi's premises in 1930. The title itself—'The *new* Arcadia'[58]—does, however, implicitly lay claim to a falsification of Snell's thesis.

Petriconi's thesis, which has been widely accepted, argues that the idea and origin of the Arcadia symbol in Renaissance pastoral poetry is the Golden Age, in the sense that the Golden Age is lost and that only Arcadia preserves a trace of its glory. Arcadia is a mental space constituted by the longing for a Golden Age. In spite of

---

[56] Cf. also section 4.   [57] Petriconi 1948 and 1959.
[58] Italics EAS. [Cf. also Schunck 1970: 106 n. 63: 'Sannazaro achieved roughly what Bruno Snell had seen in Vergil as the discovery of a "landscape of the mind".']

widespread acceptance of this interpretation, the latent influence of the new Arcadia is responsible for the continuing obliviousness vis-à-vis the fact that Vergil's Arcadia is in no way connected with the Golden Age, that it has nothing to do with it, that the only way Petriconi's argument can be true is if we accept that such a connection did not exist in Vergil.[59] I am not making any new claims here, only reminding us of a fact to which attention has been called occasionally ever since von Finckenstein 1806,[60] and lately increasingly more often, and which should therefore be considered well known. Individual more recent statements connecting Vergil's Arcadia with the Golden Age do no harm to the validity of claims to the contrary; they deserve our interest as evidence that documents how modern pastoral poetry has influenced academic research on Vergil via Snell and Klingner. The connection between Arcadia and the Golden Age as the origin and central idea of Renaissance pastoral is a Renaissance achievement; it is the uniquely Renaissance element in

---

[59] The first connection between the Golden Age and pastoral song (not 'Arcadia'!) is made by Neronian bucolic poetry (Calpurnius Siculus and the *Carmina Einsidlensia*), which is ignorant of Arcadia. The first and probably for many centuries the only theoretical statement about these connections is the following passage by Donatus: ... *bucolicum carmen originem ducere a priscis temporibus, quibus* vita pastoralis *exercita est et ideo velut* aurei saeculi *speciem in huiusmodi personarum simplicitate cognosci* ... (Hagen 1867: 742 = Diehl 1911: 23, 29 ff. = Brummer 1912: 13, 240 ff.). After Donatus the first to connect 'in a systematic fashion bucolic poetry with the notion of a Golden Age' seems to have been Rapin 1659. Cf. Krauss 1938: 180–1, 190. Even Iulius Caesar Scaliger in his 1561 poetics did not mention the Golden Age in the passage on 'Pastoralia' ([1561] 1994: Book I, Chapter 4) (although he, too, already connected the *vetustissimum ... poematis genus* with the *antiquissimus vivendi mos*). Sixteenth-century literary theory did not keep up with the contemporary development of pastoral poetry. Just like Scaliger, late Renaissance poetics continue to draw on the classical prolegomena to the scholia on bucolic poetry. The triumphant progress of the Golden Age throughout the theory on bucolic poetry seems to have begun with Rapin, for the unknown editor (and translator) (= Friedrich L. K. von Finckenstein) of the collection *Arethusa oder die bukolischen Dichter des Alterthums*, Part I makes the following knowledgeable and witty remark at the beginning of his 'Versuch über das bukolische Gedicht' (von Finckenstein 1806: 3): 'Most of the more recent poetics posit the essence of the pastoral as the representation of a supremely blissful country life or a so-called Golden Age. Their theories are founded on such a notion, which seems to have been derived from a number of more recent works of that kind, and quite a few of the bucolic works of classical antiquity had to put up with being philosophized out of their proper sphere.'

[60] Cf. the previous n.

Renaissance pastoral; it is not part of classical antiquity nor of Vergil.[61]

It is not even likely that Vergil's fourth *Eclogue* acted as catalyst in the fusion process.[62] But even if that was the case: the lack of connection between Arcadia as arbiter in a poetical contest (towards the end of the poem) and the prophecy of the Golden Age is evident and has been emphasized on various occasions. The influence of the fourth *Eclogue* cannot be ruled out *a priori*, although it is unlikely; in any case, the tenor of the poem must not be confused with the character of Vergil's bucolic poetry in general—unless one is prepared to declare the messianic poem Vergil's bucolic poem par excellence and to make it the measure of bucolicity for all the other *Eclogues*. However, scholars more often tend to come up with analyses that place the fourth *Eclogue* outside the sphere of bucolic poetry altogether.

It is more likely that the integration of notions of a Golden Age in Sannazaro originates in motifs of Roman elegiac poetry, particularly in Tibullus, in whose retrospective idylls the rural sphere of herdsmen and farmers appears as an ideal world (cf. in particular 1.1; 1.10; 2.5) and the long gone reign of Saturn is favourably compared to the present (1.1.35–48).[63]

The feeling of loss and longing is characteristic only of the new Arcadia. Besides the Petrarchist notion of love and immersion in

---

[61] In his dissertation, which gives ample consideration to *Ecl.* 4.87–103, Gatz 1967 is right not even to mention Arcadia, neither in connection with the Golden Age nor as one of the other imaginary ideas of classical antiquity (cf. index). Similar endeavours with respect to the modern age, however, cannot do without Arcadia. Following Petriconi 1948, Gatz 1967: 211 points out that it was only during the Renaissance period that the Golden Age entered the pastoral idyll (which is a certain exaggeration: cf. above n. 59). Similarly already H. Wendel 1933: 9; Veit 1961: 146; [Stephan 1971: 11; Werner-Fädler 1972: 19–20; only Sannazaro connected Arcadia and Golden Age: 21 ff.]. Under the influence of Snell and Klingner, however, Mähl 1965: 59 and 111 returns to the superseded and historically unaware interpretation.

[62] In spite of its echoes in *Ecloga* VI of *Arcadia*: but this poem about the Golden Age draws on classical literature on the subject.

[63] Since motifs in Tibullus can be traced not only to the *Georgics* but also to *Ecl.* 4 (cf. Wimmel 1968: 171–4 and 234–40; for criticism of Wimmel's continuation of the 'bucolic' Tibullus cf. E. A. Schmidt 1972: 142–3), one could posit an indirect impact of Vergil's poem on Renaissance Arcadia; the fact, however, that the term Arcadia is used in *Ecl.* 4 is not significant in this context.

emotion, the elegiac character of the new Arcadia poetry is based on the Golden Age as the lost origin and idea of Arcadia.

It is finally Petriconi's achievement to have pointed out the element of the freedom of love in Renaissance Arcadia and to have demonstrated the likelihood of its origin as a motif in Tibullus 1.3.63–4 (the same poem that contains the praise of the reign of Saturn). Further explanations on this important aspect are not necessary here. Suffice it to point towards Tasso's 'Erlaubt ist, was gefällt' ('If you like it, then it is allowed')[64] and Faust's 'Arkadisch frei sei unser Glück' ('May our happiness be free like Arcadia's').[65] For Erich Köhler, too, in his essay 'Wandlungen Arkadiens' in the essay collection *Esprit und arkadische Freiheit*, Arcadian freedom is the main topic of pastoral poetry since the Renaissance.[66]

So the main characteristics of Sannazaro's *Arcadia* have their origin in Roman elegy: freedom of love and the Golden Age in Tibullus,[67] enjoyment of suffering etc. in an elegiac motif (probably from Gallus) that Vergil incorporated into *Ecl.* 10. Petrarchist Renaissance pastoral is thus a repetition of classical antiquity, fusing its bucolic and elegiac poetry to create Arcadia.

It is evident that the element of the freedom of love is absent, and necessarily so, from classical bucolic poetry. This is where the fact becomes particularly poignant that Renaissance Arcadia, the Arcadia that comes to our minds when we hear Arcadia, cannot be Vergil's Arcadia, because what we find evoked under the title of Vergil's Arcadia is the classical-pagan world itself in all its naturalness and freedom, in its beauty and perfection, in its mythology and poetry—as a lost world viewed with longing desire from the perspective of a present that is markedly different. The elegiac character of Sannazaro's Arcadia is the fusion of a Petrarchist attitude towards

---

[64] Goethe, *Tasso*, v. 994 following Tasso, *Aminta*, v. 681: 'S'ei piace, ei lice'.
[65] Goethe, *Faust II*, v. 9573. Cf. the last but one paragraph of section 3.
[66] Cf. Köhler 1966.
[67] In Tasso the chorus 'O bella età de l'oro' (*Aminta*, Act 1, Scene 2) ends with 'Amiam, che 'l Sol si muore e poi rinasce: | a noi sua breve luce | s'asconde, e 'l sonno eterna notte adduce' ('Let us love, for Sun dies and then is born again: | For us his short light | hides itself, and the sleep brings eternal night'). Here it is the first Basia poem (5.4–6) by Catullus—the 'great holy kisser' according to Goethe's remark about Johannes Secundus, who wrote his *Basia* forty years prior to *Aminta*—that provides the motif of free erotic desire in connection with an elegiac mood.

love as sentimentality, melancholy, and narcissistic enjoyment of suffering, with the sentimental longing for classical antiquity as the Golden Age of an innocent and free nature.

Even though Vergil's Arcadia may have lent its name and individual features to that modern symbol, living on as its transformed cause and origin, it is not identical with it; identity is a historical impossibility. The symbol of lost antiquity does not belong to antiquity.

Sannazaro has an acute sense of epochs, that is, a feeling of difference from the Middle Ages and of distance from classical antiquity, and yet, in a truly humanistic vein, he endeavours to win antiquity back over the abyss of time and to renew it in his poetry. Thus, in *Prose X* of *Arcadia* he tells the story of a splendid syrinx that hangs in a pine tree in the holy forest of Pan on Mount Maenalus. It is Pan's syrinx, which later fell into the hands of a Syracusan herdsman, who bequeathed it to the Mantuan Tityrus after his death. The latter, in turn, taught the woods to echo the name of Amaryllis and sang the ardour of Corydon's passion (and similarly to these references to *Ecl.* 1 and 2, Sannazaro goes on to allude to *Eclogues* 3, 8, 5, 6, 10, 7, 9, and 4). Vergil did not pass on the syrinx. It hangs on the holy tree where Tityrus placed it: 'appresso al quale non venne mai alcuno in queste selve, che quella sonare potuto avesse compitamente' ('and never did anyone come to it in these woods who would have been able to play it in an accomplished way'). But now Sannazaro (Sincero) takes up again 'Corydon's humble pipe' ('l'umile fistula di Coridone': *Prologo* 6); for the first time after a long time there will again be a poet who composes bucolic song in the ancient way. That the syrinx of the Arcadian god Pan had been mute all the time till Sannazaro and that Arcadia was now created: these are complementary aspects of the same event in literary history.[68]

While Sannazaro's relationship to Vergil is quite different from Vergil's relationship to Theocritus, it is in principle similar to the relationship that Calpurnius sees himself as having towards Vergil. Vergil almost strove to replace or at least surpass Theocritus, his

---

[68] This paragraph is a corrected version of the original section of E. A. Schmidt 1975: 51, following Töns 1977: 159–60 with n. 76 (where the author also refers to *A la Sampogna*, v. 16).

gratitude and admiration directed at the founder of the genre, who provided him with preformed patterns of expression for use in his own poetry. He saw his own poetic project as already underway in Theocritus, whose earlier forms of expression he was now absorbing and subsuming. For Calpurnius and Sannazaro, however, Vergil remains intact as a poet of unattainable greatness, as a sublime exemplar, as a reality towards which the constitutive relationship is one of yearning. It is true that the reader of Vergil is also meant to notice and appreciate how elements of Theocritus are present and transformed. But he is meant to understand what is typically Vergilian in those elements, whereas in Sannazaro—and to a certain extent already in Calpurnius—the reader is meant to recognize and admire the Vergilian quality as Vergilian, as a devotional image of longing and a manifestation of the gold standard. The presence of Theocritus in Vergil is the instrument of Vergil's overcoming of Theocritus and an emphasis of his own achievement, while the presence of Vergil in Sannazaro is the instrument of admiration for the unattainable Vergil, the admiration for something lost. From Sannazaro's point of view, Vergil is the past, a reality long gone. Vergil's relationship to Theocritus does not evoke the same notion of temporal distance. But we have seen how crucial this temporal aspect is in Sannazaro: Pan, Theocritus, Vergil form a chain that after them broke, never to be renewed.

With respect to the development of the notion of Arcadia, the only discernible preliminary stage to Sannazaro, besides the isolated instance in Boccaccio's *Ameto*,[69] is the Pan symbolism in the circle around Lorenzo il Magnifico.[70] While Pan and his realm Arcadia may in part have been influenced by Vergil's *Eclogues*—although I fail to see anything that would suggest this—the image and significance of the god seem to originate first and foremost in mythographical tradition and theological-philosophical speculation.

---

[69] Cf. Panofsky 1955: 302.
[70] Cf. Saxl 1927: 21–5: Luca Signorelli's painting of Pan; Poliziano, *Sylva* 2. [Cf. also Vossler 1950: 86, who connects the Platonic academy in Florence (Ficino and Pico della Mirandola) with Sannazaro's Arcadia and mentions their discovery of 'a separate mythical world for beautiful souls and tender feelings, a kind of metaphysical landscape, an Arcadia, a land of shepherds and nymphs, a realm of cultivated and materialized longings.']

Which would mean—although this is no more than a speculation at this point—that the first reception of Vergil's Arcadia, the foundation of the new Arcadia by Sannazaro, was not inspired by the text of the *Eclogues* itself, but that Vergil's Arcadia captured the eye and mind of the reader because the Arcadian god had only just been revived from a different classical tradition, for example when Lorenzo evoked Pan in a poem as the great god of coming and going, birth and death.[71]

The apogee and at the same time the symbolical end of Arcadia—of the new, the Renaissance Arcadia—is the third act of *Faust II*. Arcadia appears under the dual aspect of divine nature and—'thoroughly transformed'—as the symbol of modern poetry from the Renaissance period up to Goethe's own century.[72] At first, Arcadia is a vision arising from the loving encounter between Faust and Helena, between the medieval-occidental mind and classical beauty—a vision of Greek antiquity as ahistorical nature, as the primal phenomenon, as beauty combining ideal perfection with conformity to natural laws. And while at first the creative, visionary character of Arcadia will not tolerate anything that is temporal, yearning, past—which is why the Arcadia poem must not be confused with the Golden Age—it later comes to represent an inner space, in which the spirit of modern poetry, as symbolized by Euphorion and the opera, emerges from the loving union between Faust and Helena: 'Arkadisch frei sei unser Glück' ('May our happiness be free like Arcadia's'). For Goethe this Arcadia of Arcadian freedom is the historical symbol of what took place during the Renaissance period in terms of the emergence of modern poetry.

It is no accident that this historical interpretation of Arcadia at the threshold to Historicism simultaneously also marks the end of Arcadia.[73] Following Snell[74] and Krauss,[75] we may also link the phenomenon to the rediscovery of the Greeks. But this is ultimately no different. Already Goethe had lost the Arcadian view of Vergil's

---

[71] Cf. Saxl 1927: 24–5.
[72] On this passage cf. Lohmeyer 1975: 334 ff.
[73] Cf. Vossler 1906 = 1965: 181–93, here 182 and 186. [The opinion that Arcadia ceased to exist around the beginning of the nineteenth century must be modified in the light of Stephan 1971; cf. in particular his conclusion, 159–62.]
[74] Snell [1945] 1955: 400.   [75] Krauss 1938: 198.

bucolic poetry.[76] And when Hegel speaks sarcastically of the idyll and devalues Vergil as opposed to Theocritus with the famous sentence in his *Aesthetics* that 'Vergil in his *Eclogues* is already more barren', one may be forgiven for thinking that this was any of the nineteenth-century classical scholars of the period from Niebuhr to Wilamowitz speaking.

4. VERGIL'S LATE *ECLOGUES*: *INCIPE MAENALIOS MECUM, MEA TIBIA, VERSUS*

Apart from differentiations in terms of literary history, apart from questions of reception, the discussion of Arcadia in the context of an interpretation of Vergil's *Eclogues* would be much helped if certain questions were considered or even deemed possible and meaningful—questions such as: What are the contexts in which the terms 'Arcadia' and 'Arcades' occur? What specifically is the evidence that would necessarily lead to questions about the origin of Arcadia in Vergil? Should we call Arcadian all of Vergil's *Eclogues* or only those in which those words occur? Or should we call Arcadian only the phenomena that Vergil calls by this name? Is Arcadia a symbolic term for the whole of Vergil's bucolic poetry or just for one aspect of the whole? For example, is the whole of *Ecl.* 9 Arcadian, which would make Moeris' expulsion from his farm an Arcadian event?

The issue of Vergil's Arcadia first raises questions about its scope and extent. 'Arcadia' and 'Arcades' play a role only in the four *Eclogues* 4, 7, 8, and 10. While Snell did note that *Ecl.* 2 takes place not in Arcadia but in Sicily, he explicitly called *Ecl.* 2 Arcadian, although he stated that from one *Eclogue* to the next the herdsmen turn more and more into 'Arcadian shepherds'.[77] The use of 'shepherd' ('Schäfer') instead of 'herdsman' ('Hirte')—analogous to the shift from the German neuter 'das Idyll' ($\tau\grave{o}$ $\epsilon i\delta\acute{v}\lambda\lambda\iota ov$) to the feminine form 'die Idylle'[78]—is an almost unmistakable symptom of the

---

[76] Cf. Grumach 1949: 1.318 and 360: 'the good Vergil' takes second place to *Daphnis and Chloe* (Eckermann, *Gespräche mit Goethe*, 9 March 1831).
[77] Snell [1945] 1955: 372 and 377.
[78] Cf. in this context Böschenstein-Schäfer 1967: 2.

hidden influence of modern pastoral poetry on the reception of classical bucolic poetry. This is further proof that Snell takes his point of departure from the modern Arcadia rather than from Vergil's Arcadia or the text. One should also keep in mind that none of Vergil's *Eclogues* takes place in Arcadia. Even in the poem for which such a statement would almost be true, in *Ecl.* 10, it is only within the goatherd Vergil's song that Arcadia is the scene of events; the song of the bucolic poet, however, the herdsman's song itself is not located in Arcadia (cf. *Ecl.* 10.1–8, 70–7).

Is *Ecl.* 1, for example, Arcadian in Vergil's sense of the term? Or are there any scholars fully aware of what they are saying who would want to call the entire first *Eclogue* Arcadian, in whatever sense? Both characters in the poem, Schadewaldt says, are 'Italian herdsmen, not the citizens of some blissful nowhere'.[79] But even Italians can be Arcadians like Corydon and Thyrsis at the banks of the Mincius in *Ecl.* 7. But again: is the exiled Meliboeus' mode of existence Arcadian? And if not, if we admit only Tityrus as an Arcadian, how then would the whole of *Ecl.* 1 be Arcadian? But if we accept notions such as the ones indicated by the article title 'Exile and Arcadia in Eclogues 9 and 1'[80] or the notion that Vergil's *Eclogues* are a mixture of Rome and Arcadia,[81] we forego from the start any opportunity to understand Arcadia as a symbol of Vergil's bucolic poetry as a whole; at best we subsume its idyllic[82] aspects into the notion of Arcadia.

But if the notion of the idyllic does not fully cover the significance of Vergil's bucolic poetry, if the idyllic aspect is not congruent with the content indicated by the references to Arcadia in Vergil, how will one be able to control the terminological confusion?

The significance of the symbol of Arcadia in Vergil should be construed from textual evidence, from the interpretation of the poems that make reference to Arcadia, from the connections between those references, and from the relations between the references and the poems in terms of chronology and content. The four *Eclogues* that contain

---

[79] Schadewaldt 1931 = 1970: 1.701–22, here 708 (repr. also in Oppermann (ed.) 1963: 43–68).
[80] Segal 1965.
[81] R. D. Williams 1972/3: 29.
[82] In Snell and others often synonymous with 'Arcadian'; cf. Snell [1945] 1955: 384–5: 'idyllic peace'—'Arcadian dreams'; 'Arcadian-idyllic'.

references to 'Arcadia', 'Arcades' or to Arcadian localities, i.e. *Ecl.* 4, 7, 8, and 10, have one thing in common besides the fact of these common references: they are the four latest poems in the book of *Eclogues*. However controversial the position of *Ecl.* 7 may have been for a long time—Snell[83] explicitly assumes an early date, as does Becker[84] and even Jachmann's essay on Arcadia, with the consequence of a misrepresentation of Vergil's Arcadia[85]—today the tendency is increasingly towards a later date, and there is indeed no way around that fact.[86]

In spite of their temporal proximity, these four latest poems still do not form a coherent group. Rather, 7, 8, and 10 make up a block of three later poems, with a similar unity in terms of content and character as the earlier group formed by the three *Eclogues* 2, 3, and 5, and with an analogous positioning of both triads in the two halves of the book, whereas *Ecl.* 4 is the final poem in the group of four *Eclogues* 9, 1, 6, 4, which are chronologically in the middle. While the early group was written by 42 BC at the latest, the middle group as a whole dates from 40 BC: because of its address to Varus in his capacity as legate in the Transpadana, which he became only in 40 BC, the earliest poem in this group, *Ecl.* 9, belongs to the same year as the latest one, which is the Pollio *Eclogue*. Because of its fairly strong coherence, the late triad of poems can also be assumed to have been written in quick succession. Depending on the dating of *Ecl.* 8 that would mean 39 or 35 BC.[87]

The earliest reference to Arcadia, which occurs towards the end of *Ecl.* 4 (58–9), invokes Arcadia as the home of Pan and as arbiter in a musical contest between that god and the poet Vergil. Vergil hopes to defeat the god Pan, even in Arcadia and with Arcadia as arbiter, with an epic poem expected for the future. It is important to note that this is the first reference; it is the cause of, and point of reference for, the notion of Arcadia in the three later *Eclogues*. For what those three poems represent is a return to bucolic poetry in the true sense of the term, following the *paulo maiora canamus* of the prophetic poem as if

---

[83] Snell 1938: 241.   [84] Becker 1955: 320 n. 4.
[85] Jachmann 1952*b*: 167 and 169–70.
[86] Cf. [Rohde 1963: 117–39, here 138]; Büchner 1957: 233–4; E. A. Schmidt [1974] 1987: 201–4.
[87] Cf. E. A. Schmidt [1974] 1987, Chapter 11: A plea for 35 BC.

they were its palinode. Just as the proem of *Ecl.* 4 rose above the previous *Bucolics*, in *Ecl.* 8, 7, and 10 Vergil returns to his bucolic world, which he now explicitly calls Arcadia, because of the programmatic position Arcadia occupied in *Ecl.* 4. No, Vergil says, Arcadia will not get to hear any epic poem of mine; it will continue as the land of Pan, the inventor of the syrinx, it will continue as the poetic world of his followers, of herdsmen playing the syrinx, it will continue as the land of pastoral poetry. 'The woods of Maenalus are ever musical, | His pines talk; he is ever hearing pastoral loves | And Pan, who first found work for ineffective reeds' (*Ecl.* 8.22–4, trans. G. Lee),[88] as Vergil's herdsman sings in the first poem after *Ecl.* 4—a clear contrast to the epic poem announced earlier about the deeds of the *puer* grown up to be a young man.

In so far as Arcadia is a symbol of Vergil's return to bucolic poetry such as that of *Ecl.* 2, 3, 5, 9, 1, and 6, it requires only a slight widening of focus to extend the notion also to these earlier *Eclogues*. Already *Ecl.* 2 had emphasized Pan and the herdsman-poet's discipleship to Pan (2.31–3). It should, however, be noted that calling these poems Arcadian because of Pan and song does not imply inclusion of the Golden Age and elements of *Eclogue* 4; on the contrary, they then remain definitely excluded.

No further demonstration will be necessary for the fact that this use and notion of Arcadia does not require any literary or historical derivation. Arcadia is the land of Pan, who is the inventor of the syrinx and the god of herdsmen: bucolic poetry is poetry by herdsmen playing the syrinx. It is as such a land that Arcadia appears in *Ecl.* 4, and that is what it remains in the later *Eclogues*. The search by classical scholars for precursors must be seen as driven by an unconscious identification of Vergil's Arcadia with the new Arcadia. The insistent urge to identify specific traditions that pre-date Vergil can be explained not with the textual evidence but with the projection of modern Arcadia symbolism onto Vergil's bucolic poetry. This fact alone renders refutations of individual such interpretations not only ineffectual but superfluous. Since they remain trapped in the same fundamental mistake, they are methodologically wrong and ought to be rejected.

[88] G. Lee 1984.

This leaves us with the task to characterize Vergil's Arcadia as Vergil's bucolic poetry. To my mind, Vergil's Arcadia is poetry—not an imaginary, a desired, or a lost world, not a Utopia or an ideal, not nowhere or elsewhere, but poetry here and now: the poet and poetry in the historical moment of preparation for the challenges ahead: for the transformation of neoteric into classical poetry. This is poetry declaring itself autonomous and absolute, expressing and experimenting with its new-found self-confidence and self-awareness, unfolding its potential, its commitments, its insights and principles in terms of *ludus* and *labor*.

Crucial insights from Snell's essay—such as the autonomy of poetry, the new self-awareness of the poet, art as a symbol—can be integrated into this picture. It does not deny the central, even constitutive role of love nor the power of emotion; it does not exclude the lyrical qualities of Vergil's bucolic poetry as emphasized by Schadewaldt.[89] It does, however, posit beauty as a complement to love, and adds to the notions of soulfulness and lyrical quality those of clarity and architecture, of masculine power and greatness, and the classical quality of Vergil's bucolic poetry so glowingly invoked by Walter F. Otto.[90] It rejects any notion of soft passivity, any suggestion that this poetry was dreamlike, associative, sliding, wavering, wallowing in emotion, oblique, characterized by dusk and twilight, uncertain, fluctuating, or vague.

If, however, one prefers to restrict the scope of Vergil's Arcadia symbolism to the three later *Eclogues*, one would have to concede one point to Snell and Klingner, although they would not accept such a restriction: one would then have to concede that escapism seems to be a driving force. For in those poems, Vergil does not construct a poetic world in which to assert himself and his poetry. He retreats from a task he has already envisioned and deemed possible; he retreats from the challenge of historical poetry into the world of existing bucolic poetry. As the symbol for this retreat into absolute poetry, for the renewed play of poetry with itself, Arcadia has a clearly delineated function that can almost be stated in terms of literary history: it is the symbol of poetry on stand-by, of poetry remaining at

---

[89] Cf. Schadewaldt [1930] 1970: 709.
[90] Otto 1931 (repr. in Oppermann (ed.) 1963: 69–92).

home after the premature writing of the fourth *Eclogue*, waiting until the Roman world would evolve to a point where poetry of that world[91] would become possible.

The fact that here, too, the world of poetry is present marks a fundamental difference to Sannazaro. The worlds of Vergil and Sannazaro are opposites in terms of present *vs.* past, presence *vs.* loss, actuality *vs.* longing, clear outline and firmness *vs.* melancholy. The difference is striking in a comparison between Vergil's *Ecl.* 8.22–3: 'The woods of Maenalus are ever musical, | His pines talk; he is ever hearing pastoral loves' (trans. G. Lee) and Sannazaro's Arcadia, *Prose* X § 2: 'There was a time, when the world was not so full of corruption: then all pine trees would talk... here [sc. on Mount Maenalus] and respond to the love songs of the herdsmen.' These two texts should not be juxtaposed as Arcadia present and past. In the second text, too, Arcadia is present, with the sense of past being an integral part of the present Arcadia. In other words, the 'new Arcadia' is the way nostalgia is directed towards classical antiquity as the Golden Age—*Ecl.* 6 of the *Arcadia* praises the Golden Age as 'tempi antichi'—to which Vergil's Arcadia contributes some essential features.

Bruno Snell's Arcadia is a symbol for the rediscovery of Vergil's bucolic poetry after Historicism and Positivism. It may be a symbol for the renewed closeness to Roman poetry in Germany after the one-sidedness of German philhellenism; it may even be seen as forming part of tendencies to overcome Historicism among scholars of classical antiquity in Germany after World War I.

This supposed closeness to Vergil is not without its dangers. Where the King of Dunois says in Schiller's *Jungfrau von Orleans*: 'to found a realm of innocence and purity | within the rough, barbaric nature of the real world',[92] Klingner, following Snell, says: 'Arcadia [sc. Vergil's Arcadia], the far-away world of a higher and consecrated existence

---

[91] [The German word used in the original, 'Weltdichtung' ('world poetry'), cannot be translated into English. It is not identical with 'Weltliteratur', it refers to the term 'Weltgedicht', now and then applied in German literary criticism to works such as the *Divine Comedy* since the nineteenth century and used in a famous essay by Zinn (1956). 'Weltdichtung' or 'Weltgedicht' (tentatively rendered in English with 'cosmic' or 'cosmical poetry' by Zinn) is poetry that represents not just one aspect of the world or one theme but a whole world, it is a poetry of universal character. The above translation narrows the meaning to 'poetry of the Roman world'.]
[92] Vv. 504–5. Cf. Rüdiger 1959: 245.

within a brutal, murderous, soulless reality, a dreamscape, a home for the soul.'[93] This retrospective idyll[94] has become the expression of an internalized Utopia of the past. Walter Wili's criticism of the nineteenth century applies equally to the reading of Vergil that he, too, advocates:[95] 'It is the nature of our minds', he says, 'to make the transition from history to the myth of our own nostalgia far too quickly, and to grasp onto it as if it were history.'

Sannazaro's Arcadia, the new Arcadia, Arcadia—for it is only this Arcadia that can lay claim to the title!—is a symbol of the reception of classical antiquity in the Renaissance period. From Sannazaro to Schiller it has a dual aspect, that of longing for mankind's lost state of innocence—'I, too, was born in Arcadia' in the fantasy *Resignation*— and that of longing for the lost world of classical antiquity—'Sweeter in its melting tones the flute did sound, played by the herdsmen's god' in the first version of Schiller's *Die Götter Griechenlandes*. It is a backward-looking Utopia characteristic of its time, it is a melancholy-elegiac vision of the ideal as past, as a lost paradise of identity between nature and culture, nourished by an acute feeling of inadequacy. Arcadia unites classical antiquity with the modern world, but not in the sense that the same symbol could serve for the self-interpretation or the historical reading of two different eras, which would make them symbolically identical, overcoming the epochal difference through the power of a symbol. Instead, Arcadia unites the epochs by symbolizing modern Western culture in its relation to classical antiquity.

In the narrower sense, Vergil's Arcadia is a poetical symbol for the poet's interim return to the bucolic world of poetic self-reflection; in its wider sense, it is a symbol for the threshold from neoteric to classical poetry, from Alexandrian play, from passion and subjectivity to the notion of art as the interpretation of and responsibility for the historically necessary step of declaring itself an independent realm governed by rules of its own making. A historical understanding in the context of European pastoral poetry will not be possible without understanding the paradox that, as such a symbol, Vergil's Arcadia is not Arcadia.

---

[93] Klingner 1956*b*: 136.
[94] Cf. in this context Schiller [1795] 1989 and Rüdiger 1959: 237–9 and 245.
[95] Wili 1930: 6.

3

The Style of Virgil's *Eclogues*

R. G. M. Nisbet

The style of a poet is the most important thing about him, the element that cannot be translated, without which nobody but a scholar could endure to read him. But it is also the hardest part to characterize, which is why we all prefer to talk about other matters. Lists of vocabulary and metrical statistics provide useful raw material, but they may communicate very little; a count of dactyls does not tell us what the *Eclogues* are actually like. I believe that here as elsewhere the best approach is to concentrate on particular passages where the idiosyncrasy of the poet appears in its most undiluted form. Such passages give a flavour to the whole, but this quality is easily dissipated in a statistical treatment; after all, in most works of literature, including even the *Eclogues*, there are many lines that could have belonged somewhere else.

Virgil in the *Eclogues* set out to do a Theocritus in Latin, that is to say to transfer the charm and precision of a very individual poet to his own slow-footed language. Partly of course he does the trick by specific imitations, and commentators have collected a store of more or less parallel passages, which for the most part will be omitted here. Such parallels are most evocative when they preserve the movement of the original; thus at 8.41 *ut vidi, ut perii* ('when I saw, then I was

This paper appears here as it was published in 1991 and reprinted in R. G. M. Nisbet 1995: 325–37, with the addition of translations of the quotes from Greek and Latin by the author.

lost') the use of the second *ut* as a correlative[1] strains the possibilities of Latin, but it recalls the Theocritean prototype χὼς ἴδον ὣς ἐμάνην (2.82). Then there is the notorious case of 8.58 *omnia vel medium fiat mare* ('let everything become mid-ocean'); Theocritus had said πάντα δ' ἔναλλα γένοιτο ('let everything become contrary', 1.134), and by a process of free association more characteristic of modern than classical poetry Virgil represents ἔναλλα ('contrary') as if it were ἐνάλια ('in the sea'). But quite apart from parallel passages there is a more indirect imitation of style that cannot be associated with any single model. This type of imitation is really the more subtle, though it is harder to pin down; in the same way the best parodies are not the sort most common in antiquity, where a well-known line is modified by some ridiculous adaptation. The really clever parodies suggest the idiom of the original in an absurd way without referring to any particular passage; such is Calverley's skit on Browning, 'The Cock and the Bull', or the hexameter of Persius that catches the quintessence of the old Roman tragedians, *Antiopa aerumnis cor luctificabile fulta* ('Antiopa whose heart is supported by tribulation', 1.78).

The *Eclogues* deal with what Milton called 'the homely slighted shepherd's trade', and so they affect a simplicity that is an accomplishment of art. That is why Tityrus at the beginning of the book plays on a thin oat, *tenui avena*, with reference to the style of the poems as well as the shape of the instrument; in the same way Virgil at the end of the last *Eclogue* says that he has been weaving a basket from slender hibiscus, *dum sedet et gracili fiscellam texit hibisco*. Words for rustic objects like *avena*, 'oat', and *fiscella*, 'basket', give a suggestion of simplicity; however natural oats and baskets may have been in the context, the ancient sensitivity to levels of diction was such that they must have seemed to lower the style. Just as Theocritus talks of onions and snails, and the more realistic Greek epigrammatists describe cottage utensils and artisans' implements, so Virgil flavours his bucolics with thyme and garlic, chestnuts and cheese. Theocritus had one great advantage: by writing in a kind of Doric, however bogus it often was, he produced a whiff of the countryside,

---

[1] Timpanaro 1978: 219 ff., citing (p. 274) Catull. 62.45 *sic virgo, dum intacta manet, dum cara suis est* ('so a maiden, as long as she stays untouched, so long she is dear to her family'), 62.56.

and because of the dialect's poetic status he could do this without seeming prosaic or banal. In view of the very different literary traditions of Latin, Virgil could not go to the backwoods for poetic expressions. His efforts in this direction were very limited: we may note the archaic *nec vertat bene* for *ne vertat bene* (9.6), perhaps *his* for *hi* in a passage whose interpretation is disputed (3.102 *his certe— neque amor causa est—vix ossibus haerent* ('These lambs certainly— and love is not the reason—hardly hang on to their bones.'), most notoriously *cuium pecus* for 'whose flock?' (3.1). That provoked the well-known retort *dic mihi, Damoeta: cuium pecus anne Latinum* ('Tell me, Damoetas, is *cuium pecus?* Latin?', Donat. *Vit. Verg.* 43), and Virgil did not venture again on what Catullus would have called the language of goat-milkers (*caprimulgi*).

Apart from words for rustic objects, the most striking thing about the vocabulary of the *Eclogues* is the number of diminutives. There are only three proper diminutives in the whole of the *Aeneid*, *palmula* (5.163), *sagulum* (8.660), and most memorably *parvulus Aeneas* (4.328). In the *Eclogues*, on the other hand, there are a dozen diminutives, words like *agellus, gemellus, luteolus, munusculum, novellus*, with no fewer than thirteen instances of *capella*, 'a nanny-goat'; this is out of line with other serious poetry apart from Catullus and elegy. Other instances of unpoetical words are not very common; *suavis*[2] occurs 4 times and *formosus* 16 times, though they were avoided in the *Aeneid* and most other epic. In spite of the sprinkling of rusticity, there is plenty of stylistic heightening; the Latin poetic vocabulary is freely used, words like *amnis* (5.25), *pontus* (6.35), *ratis* (6.76), poetic plurals like *otia* (1.6, 5.61) or the notorious *hordea* for barley (5.36), forms like *arbos* (3.56) or *risere* (4.62), infinitives like *suadebit inire* (1.55), retained accusatives like *suras evincta* (7.32), Grecisms like *suave rubenti* (4.43). It is true that Tityrus mentions *caseus* or cheese (1.34), not a word that could be found in epic, but when he invites Meliboeus to supper he turns to a more dignified periphrasis, *pressi copia lactis* (1.81). It is this blend of the commonplace and the exquisite that gives the *Eclogues* some of their characteristic quality.

---

[2] Axelson 1945: 35 ff.

The Style of Virgil's Eclogues

'The most prominent single characteristic of Theocritus' style is his repetition or partial repetition of words': I quote Dover's commentary (1971: xlv), and I base my analysis partly on his. The repetition of a single word is too common to need much illustration, but one may note in particular the *geminatio* of a proper name (2.69 *a Corydon, Corydon*, Theoc. 11.72 ὦ Κύκλωψ Κύκλωψ). More typical[3] are lines like 1.74 *ite meae, felix quondam pecus, ite capellae* ('Forward, my own, once a happy flock, forward, nanny-goats!'), where a word in the first foot is repeated in the fifth; by a rather mannered distribution *meae* is attached to the first *ite* and *capellae* to the second. The same pattern can be seen in Theocritus: cf. 1.64 ἄρχετε βουκολικᾶς, Μοῖσαι φίλαι, ἄρχετ' ἀοιδᾶς ('Begin, as sung by herdsmen, dear Muses, begin a song.'). Another type can be seen at 6.20–1 *addit se sociam timidisque supervenit Aegle, | Aegle Naiadum pulcherrima* ('Aegle adds herself as an accomplice and reinforces them as they hesitate, Aegle the fairest of the Naiads'); here the subject is repeated with some expansion, though the figure does not permit a second verb. Such epanalepsis is in no way particularly bucolic, but significantly is found at Theocritus 1.29–30 μαρύεται ὑψόθι κισσός, | κισσὸς ἑλιχρύσῳ κεκονιμένος ('Ivy winds above, ivy spotted with ivy-flowers'). A more characteristically bucolic idiom occurs when a whole clause is repeated with slight modifications: *Daphninque tuum tollemus ad astra. | Daphnin ad astra feremus; amavit nos quoque Daphnis* ('Your Daphnis we shall exalt to the stars, Daphnis to the stars we shall carry; I too was loved by Daphnis', 5.51–2). So in Theocritus Βουκολιάζεο, Δάφνι· τὺ δ' ᾠδᾶς ἄρχεο πρᾶτος, | ᾠδᾶς ἄρχεο, Δάφνι, ἐφεψάσθω δὲ Μενάλκας ('Make herdsmen's music, Daphnis, and do you begin the song first; begin the song, Daphnis, and let Menalcas follow', 9.1–2).

That leads us to more complex repetitions where we shall take as prototype Theocritus 1.4–6, which must have derived particular prominence from its place in the early editions:

αἴ κα τῆνος ἕλῃ κεραὸν τράγον, αἶγα τὺ λαψῇ·
αἴ κα δ' αἶγα λάβῃ τῆνος γέρας, ἐς τὲ καταρρεῖ
ἁ χίμαρος· χιμάρῳ δὲ καλὸν κρέας, ἔστε κ' ἀμέλξῃς.

---

[3] Gimm 1910: 80 ff.

If he chooses the horned goat you will take the she-goat, and if he takes the she-goat for his prize, the kid falls to you; a kid's flesh is fine until you milk her.

Here words for 'take', 'she-goat', and 'kid' reappear at different places in the line, sometimes in a different tense or case; the lines derive their charm from the ringing of the changes. The pattern is not confined to bucolic poetry, and is found also in Callimachus's *Hymn to Apollo* (2.9–11):

ὠπόλλων οὐ παντὶ φαείνεται, ἀλλ' ὅτις ἐσθλός·
ὅς μιν ἴδῃ, μέγας οὗτος, ὃς οὐκ ἴδε, λιτὸς ἐκεῖνος.
ὀψόμεθ', ὦ Ἑκάεργε, καὶ ἐσσόμεθ' οὔποτε λιτοί.

Apollo does not appear to everybody but to him that is good. Who sees him, he is great; who has not seen him, he is lowly. We shall see you, Apollo, and we shall never be lowly.

Virgil must have felt the movement as typically bucolic, and so we find similar juggling with words in the eighth *Eclogue* when he assesses the relative guilt of Medea and Cupid (8.48–50):

crudelis tu quoque, mater.
crudelis mater magis, an puer improbus[4] ille?
improbus ille puer; crudelis tu quoque, mater.

You too were cruel, mother [i.e. Medea]. Was the mother more cruel or that boy [Cupid] more wicked? That boy was wicked, but you too were cruel, mother.

Commentators are offended by the pointlessness of it all: Heyne wished to delete the last two lines, and Coleman finds the triple repetition of *crudelis* and *mater* very jejune. In fact Virgil is using a pattern that he regarded as particularly Theocritean; no doubt this pattern has its origin in the jingles of shepherds, but in the hands of a poet the artlessness is contrived.

The same movement is found in the bucolics of Calpurnius, and it has been observed also by modern imitators. Tennyson's 'Come down o maid from yonder mountain height' is a beautiful pastoral poem, and everybody knows 'the moan of doves in immemorial elms', reflecting Virgil's onomatopoeic *nec gemere aeria cessabit turtur*

---

[4] In view of the following line I take *improbus* to be predicative, not attributive.

The Style of Virgil's Eclogues

ab ulmo ('nor will the turtle-dove cease to moan from the lofty elm', 1. 58). Less attention is paid to what goes before: 'and sweet is every sound, Sweeter thy voice, but every sound is sweet'; here in a line and a half Tennyson shows that he has caught one of the most characteristic features of the bucolic idiom. The point has not been lost on so gifted a verse-composer as J. B. Poynton; see his rendering of Shakespeare's 'In such a night as this':[5]

> advenit, ecce, leo, Thisbe nec viderat ipsum.
> umbra est, quam vidit; visa tamen aufugit umbra.

Another form of balance is found in the poetic competitions where one shepherd caps the song of another, naturally in the same number of lines; the movement is familiar not only from Theocritus but from the rival choruses of Catullus's epithalamium. The pattern must have its antecedents in popular poetry: Dover quotes the Greek children's song where one speaker says: 'Where are my roses, where are my violets, where is my beautiful parsley?' and the other replies: 'Here are the roses, here are the violets, here is the beautiful parsley.'[6] The possible complexities of the pattern may be seen from the end of Virgil's seventh *Eclogue* (61–8):

> *Corydon*: populus Alcidae gratissima, vitis Iaccho,
> formosae myrtus Veneri, sua laurea Phoebo;
> Phyllis amat corylos: illas dum Phyllis amabit,
> nec myrtus vincet corylos nec laurea Phoebi.
> *Thyrsis*: fraxinus in silvis pulcherrima, pinus in hortis,
> populus in fluviis, abies in montibus altis:
> saepius at si me, Lycida formose, revisas,
> fraxinus in silvis cedat tibi, pinus in hortis.

Corydon: The poplar is dearest to Hercules, the vine to Bacchus, the myrtle to fair Venus, his own bay-tree to Apollo. Phyllis loves hazels; as long as Phyllis loves those, neither will the myrtle surpass hazels nor the bay-tree of Phoebus. Thyrsis: The ash is loveliest in the woods, the pine-tree in parkland, the poplar in streams, the fir in the high hills. But if you should revisit me often, fair Lycidas, the ash would give place to you in the woods, the pine-tree in parkland.

---

[5] Poynton 1936: 100, translating Shakespeare, *Merchant of Venice*.
[6] PMG 852 ποῦ μοι τὰ ῥόδα, ποῦ μοι τὰ ἴα, ποῦ μοι τὰ καλὰ σέλινα; | ταδὶ τὰ ῥόδα, ταδὶ τὰ ἴα, ταδὶ τὰ καλὰ σέλινα.

Here we should observe the degrees of correspondence not only between one speaker and another but within each separate quatrain and often within single lines. We may notice in particular the paratactic comparison, most simply illustrated from the opening of Theocritus 1; instead of saying 'your piping is as sweet as the whisper of the pine' we find instead 'sweet is the whisper of the pine-tree and sweet too is your piping'. Another bucolic pattern may be seen very clearly in the second of these two stanzas: the statement of the first two lines 65–6 is followed by the hypothesis, *saepius at si me, Lycida formose, revisas*, which leads to the conclusion in the last line. For the same movement we may compare Theocritus(?) 8.41–4:

> παντᾷ ἔαρ, παντᾷ δὲ νομοί, παντᾷ δὲ γάλακτος
> οὔθατα πιδῶσιν, καὶ τὰ νέα τράφεται,
> ἔνθα καλὰ Ναῒς ἐπινίσσεται· αἰ δ' ἂν ἀφέρπῃ,
> χὡ τὰς βῶς βόσκων χαἰ βόες αὐότεραι.

Everywhere is spring, and everywhere pastures, and everywhere udders gush with milk and younglings are fattened where fair Nais comes; but if she goes away, the cowherd and the cows dry up.

The shepherds' monologues, as well as their dialogues, seem to be influenced by popular poetry. This is seen most clearly with the repeated refrains, which tend to break speeches into snatches; but even when there is no refrain, there may be a lack of orderly progression. Stories are not told in any systematic way; the narrative about the capture of Silenus (6.14 ff.) is quite exceptional. In Damon's love-song (8.17 ff.) the reader has to piece together what is going on,[7] a natural consequence of the broken-up character of the bucolic style; the same is true to some extent with Corydon in 2 and Gallus in 10, though in the latter case the fluctuating movement of Gallus's own elegies seems to play a part. Tityrus in the first *Eclogue* cannot give a coherent account of himself; though this is meant to suggest the rustic wiseacre's garrulity and love of mystification, Virgil may have been influenced in his strategy by the inherent bittiness of shepherds' songs. As T. E. Page pronounces on *modulans alterna notavi* ('setting to music I marked the alternations', 5.14), 'You cannot sing and play a pipe at the same time.'

Another kind of disjointedness in bucolic arises from the frequency of parenthesis. Sometimes this involves quite a long hyperbaton; for a

---

[7] Otis 1964: 105 ff.

The Style of Virgil's Eclogues

possible instance see 9.37–8 *id quidem ago et tacitus, Lycida, mecum ipse voluto | si valeam meminisse neque est ignobile carmen* ('This is the very thing I am doing and silently, Lycidas, go over in my mind—if I could only remember, nor is it contemptible—the song'). Here editors usually regard *id* as the object of *voluto*, but this does not combine satisfactorily with the idiomatic *id ago*, 'I am busy with that'; it might be more elegant to take *voluto* with *carmen* and to mark off the intervening phrases with dashes. Sometimes a parenthesis gives an impression of spontaneity, which is of course achieved by art; cf. 3.93 *frigidus, o pueri— | fugite hinc—latet anguis in herba* ('cold-blooded, my lads—run away—there is lurking a snake in the grass'), where the disruptive *fugite hinc* indicates the speaker's sudden alarm. See also 8.109 *parcite—ab urbe venit—iam parcite, carmina—Daphnis* ('Stop, there is coming from town, now stop, my chants—Daphnis!'); here the separation of *venit* from *Daphnis* is highly mannered, but at the same time it indicates the excitement of the speaker and produces a climax with the lover's name. For an even longer hyperbaton see 9.2–4:

> o Lycida, vivi pervenimus, advena nostri
> (quod numquam veriti sumus) ut possessor agelli
> diceret 'haec mea sunt; veteres migrate coloni.'

Oh Lycidas, we've lived to come to this, that a newcomer, something we never were afraid of, should take possession of *my* small-holding and say 'This is my property; former cultivators, move off!'

Here the long separation of *nostri* from *agelli* puts great emphasis on the possessive, and the parenthesis helps to suggest the breathless indignation of Moeris.

Ellipse is another feature that is colloquial at least in origin. It is found in the clipped civilities of Theocritus (14.1–2):

> χαίρειν πολλὰ τὸν ἄνδρα Θυώνιχον–ἄλλα τοιαῦτα
> Αἰσχίνᾳ. ὡς χρόνιος–χρόνιος–τί δέ τοι τὸ μέλημα;

A very good day to friend Thyonichus.—The same to Aeschinas. It's a long time.—A long time.—What's the trouble?

So too the beginning of the third *Eclogue* (a passage directly imitated from Theocritus (4.1 ff.)):

dic mihi, Damoeta, cuium pecus? an Meliboei?
non, verum Aegonis.

'Tell me Damoetas, whose flock? Is it Meliboeus's?' 'No, Aegon's rather.' Sometimes the ellipse is more mannered than genuinely colloquial, *quo te, Moeri, pedes?* ('Whither, Moeris, do your feet...?', 9.1) may look idiomatic, but it is not what anybody would actually say; it is as artificial as 'whither away?' So too when Menalcas forgets an astronomer's name, the interrupted construction gives an illusion of spontaneity: *in medio duo signa Conon—et quis fuit alter | descripsit radio totum qui gentibus orbem...?* ('In the middle two figures—Conon, and who was the other one who mapped out with his pointer the whole sky for mankind?', 3.40). Ellipse may also be used for euphemistic reasons; Virgil would not dream of imitating the rustic obscenities of Theocritus, still less the unimaginable bad language of real *pastores*, a rough body of men, so he contents himself with the discreet impropriety of *novimus et qui te* ('I know who did what to you', 3.8).

A marked feature of the Theocritean style is the number of appositions, which suggest the disjointed afterthoughts of colloquial discourse; cf. 15.19–20 ἑπταδράχμως κυνάδας, γραιᾶν ἀποτίλματα πηρᾶν | πέντε πόκως ἔλαβ' ἐχθές, ἅπαν ῥύπον, ἔργον ἐπ' ἔργῳ ('yesterday he bought five fleeces, seven-drachma dog-skins, pluckings of antiquated haversacks, nothing but filth, one job after another'). Appositions in the *Eclogues* are much less conspicuous, but there is one notable type that is mannered rather than colloquial; this is the appositional sandwich as in 1.57 *raucae, tua cura, palumbes* ('full-throated, your charges, the wood-pigeons'). This pattern is not paralleled in Theocritus, but is attested in Archilochus and Greek epigram.[8] Otto Skutsch has commented on the resemblance between *raucae, tua cura, palumbes* and a line in Propertius *et Veneris dominae volucres, mea turba, columbae* ('and lady Venus's birds, my flock, the pigeons', 3.3.31); he plausibly suggests a common source in Gallus,[9] and has named the construction the 'schema Cornelianum'. The word-order appears intermittently in later Latin poetry, and Juvenal still uses it for sardonic effect (7.120 *veteres, Maurorum epimenia,*

[8] An authoritative treatment of the figure is provided by Solodow 1986: 129 ff.
[9] O. Skutsch 1956: 198–9; he also cites *Ecl.* 10.22 *tua cura Lycoris.*

bulbi, 'old onions, the rations of Moors'); no extant work favours it so much as the *Eclogues*, but it must be regarded as a neoteric rather than a bucolic feature.

Some of the elements that I have been mentioning are brought together in a concentrated form in a passage in the ninth *Eclogue* (23–5):

> Tityre, dum redeo—brevis est via—pasce capellas,
> et potum pastas age, Tityre, et inter agendum
> occursare capro—cornu ferit ille—caveto.

Tityrus, till I get back—it's a short journey—feed the nanny-goats, and when fed drive them to water, Tityrus, and as you drive them a clash with the billy-goat—he butts with his horns—you must avoid.

This is an isolated snatch of song, typical of the bittiness to which I have referred. The passage is broken up by two parentheses (*brevis est via* and *cornu ferit ille*) that hint at the disorganized character of colloquial speech, though once again Virgil's disorganization is deliberately organized. We may also note the repeated reiteration of key words to produce the traditional bucolic jingle: *Tityre Tityre, pasce pastas, age agendum*. And there is a distinctive metrical point that I have not yet dealt with, the so-called bucolic diaeresis.

A diaeresis occurs when a word ends at the end of a foot, and the bucolic diaeresis is sometimes defined as any word-break at the end of the fourth foot; thus on this definition there would be a bucolic diaeresis after *cornu ferit*. Such word-breaks are notably common in Theocritus, and more common in the *Eclogues* than in Virgil's other hexameters; but a more restrictive definition brings out more clearly a distinguishing characteristic of bucolic poetry. According to this a bucolic diaeresis occurs when there is not only a word-break but a pause in sense at the end of the fourth foot, as after *brevis est via* in the passage under discussion; by the normal rules of the Latin hexameter this pause is preceded by a dactyl, often produced by a pyrrhic word of two short syllables (as here *via*). The bucolic diaeresis in this strict sense is much more common in the *Eclogues* than in Virgil's other works: I have counted 62 cases in the *Eclogues* compared with 4 in *Aeneid* 2 (including one incomplete line). If we look at the distribution of these 62 cases the effect is even more striking: the early third *Eclogue* has ten, the early seventh *Eclogue* has twelve, and though the first *Eclogue* has only four, three of these occur in the first eleven lines, where the characteristic tone is being established. It is also worth noting that the grander manner of the fourth *Eclogue* allows no place for a bucolic diaeresis in the strict sense (i.e. followed by a pause).

Other metrical points may be mentioned more summarily. One feature with a higher incidence than in the *Aeneid* is a line like *Daphnin ad astra feremus: amavit nos quoque Daphnis* (5.52); here after *feremus*, that is to say after the trochee in the third foot, there is not only a word-break but a pause. This so-called feminine caesura is often found with Greek words, as at 2.6 *o crudelis Alexi*; significantly there are three of these caesuras in the first seven lines of the early second *Eclogue*. Then again the runs without strong punctuation at the end of the line are shorter than in the *Aeneid*, even if the statistics are exaggerated by the short snatches of dialogue between the shepherds. The relatively frequent elision of long vowels that is so characteristic of the *Aeneid* is much less common in the *Eclogues*; but such a feature is too negative to give us much sense of the tone of the poems.

I shall mention briefly a few metrical abnormalities. Quadrisyllabic endings may be noted at 2.24 *Actaeo Aracyntho*, 6.53 *fultus hyacintho*, 10.12 *Aonie Aganippe*; in all these cases the last word is Greek, and the Greek effect is underlined by a preceding hiatus or in one instance by an irrational lengthening; metrical licences often come two by two. Sometimes there is a shortening of a long final vowel before another vowel, again in the Greek manner; the abnormality is encouraged by the Greek name at 2.65 *o Alexi*, though not at 8.108 *an qui amant, ipsi sibi somnia fingunt?* ('Or do people in love make up their own dreams?').The effect is more typically bucolic when the licence is combined with a bucolic diaeresis, as at 6.44 *ut litus 'Hyla Hyla' omne sonaret* ('so that all the shore sounded "Hylas, Hylas"'). Here the first final *a* is long by Greek accidence, and the second is shortened by Greek correption before the vowel; the scansion of the same word in two different ways, a favourite Hellenistic trick,[10] here gives hints of an echo. So again at 3.78–9:

> Phyllida amo ante alias: nam me discedere flevit
> et longum 'formose, vale vale' inquit 'Iolla'.

---

[10] Nisbet and Hubbard 1970 on Hor. *Carm.* 1.32.11; Hopkinson 1982: 162 ff.

I love Phyllis more than other girls, for she wept that I was going away and said with lingering voice 'Farewell, my beautiful, farewell—Iollas!'

The final *e* of the second *vale* is shortened before *inquit*, suggesting that the speaker is moving into the distance. Perhaps in passing I may give my version of the situation, which is different from the usual account. Phyllis wept that Menalcas was going, and said 'goodbye, goodbye my beautiful'. One naturally assumes that she is going to say 'my beautiful Menalcas', but then by a surprise she adds 'Iolla'; it transpires that she is going off with Menalcas, and that the farewells are being addressed to the other man.

Some of the features that I have been discussing are not specifically bucolic, and we must look for further antecedents. Horace described the style of the poems as *molle*, soft;[11] of course that is one side of Theocritus, but as a Hellenistic poet he could also be crisper and spikier than the *Eclogues* ever are. Virgil must have owed much to Catullus and no doubt Gallus for his emotional sentimentality, harmonious resonances, bright colouring, and elaborate word-patterns. If this paper deals only incidentally with these aspects it is because I wish to isolate the more purely bucolic elements, but a full analysis of the style would recognize an element of neoteric *mollitia* that is not really Theocritean. When Horace characterized the *Eclogues* he combined *molle* with *facetum*; as Quintilian saw (6.3.20), *facetum* refers not to humour, though there is humour in the *Eclogues*, but to a neatness and elegance that may be distinguished from the lush sensuousness of the neoterics proper.

Here it must be emphasized that in spite of a dominant tone, ancient poetry-books are not necessarily written in a uniform style. Theocritus himself shows a considerable variation between the purely bucolic idylls and the mime-like *Adoniazusae* (15), and Virgil introduces elements that properly belong to different types of poem; in such cases Kroll talked of the crossing of the genres,[12] but where the abnormality is incidental Francis Cairns's term 'inclusion'[13] seems more appropriate. For a simple instance see the beginning of the song of Silenus (6.31–2):

---

[11] Hor. *Sat.* 1.10.44–15 *molle atque facetum | Vergilio annuerunt gaudentes rure Camenae* ('A sentimental and humorous [or: elegant] style the Muses who love the countryside have granted to Virgil.').
[12] Kroll 1924: 202 ff.   [13] Cairns 1972: 158 ff.

> namque canebat uti magnum per inane coacta
> semina terrarumque animaeque marisque fuissent.

He sang how through the immense void the atoms of earth and air and sea had been brought together.

Here *uti* is clearly Lucretian, particularly at that place in the line, and so is some of the vocabulary, though not the use of *que*. I have already referred to the subsequent lines on Hylas (6.43–4):

> his adiungit Hylan nautae quo fonte relictum
> clamassent, ut litus 'Hyla Hyla' omne sonaret.

He adds also at what well Hylas had been left when his ship-mates had shouted his name, so that all the shore sounded 'Hylas, Hylas'.

Here a neoteric effect is produced not only by the scansion of *Hyla Hyla* but by the learned allusiveness of *quo fonte*. Another style is found in a snatch of song by Corydon at 7.29–30:

> saetosi caput hoc apri tibi, Delia, parvus
> et ramosa Micon vivacis cornua cervi.

This head of a bristling boar little Micon (dedicates) to you, Diana, and the branching antlers of a long-lived stag.

That is the manner of dedicatory epigram, even if it is written in two hexameters rather than an elegiac couplet. Then again, at 8.80 *limus ut hic durescit et haec ut cera liquescit* the rhyming jingle suggests a magic spell. For a more thoroughgoing conflation of styles one may turn to the tenth *Eclogue*, where the bucolic themes give way to a pastiche in hexameters of the love-elegies of Gallus:

> a! te ne frigora laedant!
> a! tibi ne teneras glacies secet aspera plantas!
> ibo et Chalcidico quae sunt mihi condita versu
> carmina pastoris Siculi modulabor avena. (10.48–51)

Ah, may the frosts not hurt you! Ah, may the rough ice not cut your tender soles! I'll go and the songs that I have composed in Chalcidic verse [i.e. in the manner of Euphorion] I'll play with the oaten pipe of a Sicilian goatherd.

Here one may note the sentimental *a*, the sentimental theme of the ice taken from Gallus by Propertius,[14] followed by the resolute *ibo*,

---

[14] Prop. 1.8.7–8 *tu pedibus teneris positas fulcire pruinas, | tu potes insolitas, Cynthia, ferre nives* ('Can you tread with your tender feet the lying frost? Can you endure, Cynthia, the unfamiliar snows?').

suggesting (as Gallus himself must have done) the fluctuating moods of the lover.

The most persistent change of style is in the fourth *Eclogue*, where Virgil himself describes his matter as *paulo maiora*, 'somewhat grander':

> ultima Cumaei venit iam carminis aetas;
> magnus ab integro saeclorum nascitur ordo;
> iam redit et Virgo, redeunt Saturnia regna,
> iam nova progenies caelo demittitur alto.
> tu modo nascenti puero, quo ferrea primum
> desinet ac toto surget gens aurea mundo,
> casta fave Lucina,[15] tuus iam regnat Apollo. (4–10)

The last age of the Sibylline song has now come; the great sequence of the centuries is born afresh. Now both the Virgin returns and returns the reign of Saturn; now a new stock descends from high heaven. If you but favour the baby being born, with whom the iron generation will first come to an end and through the whole world a golden generation will arise, chaste Lucina, your Apollo is already reigning.

This resonant passage is intended to suggest a sacred chant, though it is more resonant than the Jewish Sibylline oracles to which Virgil owes so much of his content. We may note the almost entirely end-stopped lines and the formal patterning in groups of 2 + 2 + 3; groups of 7 are in fact attested in the Jewish prototypes. But the most striking feature is the incantatory rhyming of *o: integro, ordo, virgo, caelo, alto, puero, quo, toto, mundo, Apollo*.[16]

The fourth *Eclogue* has a manner of its own in other respects. One may note *saeclorum*, a molossus without elision in the centre of the line; there are 10 instances of this neoteric pattern in 63 lines, a greater incidence than in the other *Eclogues* and considerably greater than in the *Aeneid*. The artistic distribution of adjective and noun, again in imitation of Catullus 64, is also more marked than usual, even if there is only one 'golden' line in the strict sense: 28 *incultisque rubens pendebit sentibus uva* ('and a reddening cluster will hang from

---

[15] Against the general opinion I put a comma after Lucina and interpret 'provided that Lucina favours the birth, Apollo is already as good as reigning' (R. G. M. Nisbet 1978: 62, reprinted in this volume).

[16] This was pointed out in an early article by R. G. Austin (1927: 100 ff.).

untended thickets'). Then there is the grandiloquent address to the baby himself (48–9):

> adgredere o magnos (aderit iam tempus) honores,
> cara deum suboles, magnum Iovis incrementum.

Assume, I pray, great dignities (the time will soon be here), dear offspring of the gods, great increase of Jupiter.

Here *incrementum* at the end of the line produces a spondeiazon almost unique in the *Eclogues*, though found occasionally in Theocritus; the rustic word is given dignity by its position, producing an ambiguity characteristic of this oracular poem. In the following lines we meet some more resonant rhymes (50–2), again quite unlike the normal style of the *Eclogues*:

> aspice convexo nutantem pondere mundum,
> terrasque tractusque maris caelumque profundum;
> aspice, venturo laetentur ut omnia saeclo.

Look at the cosmos, swaying with its vaulted weight, the lands and the stretches of the sea and the deep sky—look how everything rejoices in the coming age.

As the poem nears its end the tone suddenly changes (55–9):

> non me carminibus vincet nec Thracius Orpheus
> nec Linus, huic mater quamvis atque huic pater adsit,
> Orphei Calliopea, Lino formosus Apollo.
> Pan etiam, Arcadia mecum si iudice certet,
> Pan etiam Arcadia dicat se iudice victum.

In song neither Thracian Orpheus will surpass me nor Linus, though his mother is of help to one and his father to the other, Calliopea to Orpheus, fair Apollo to Linus. Even Pan if he were to compete with me with Arcadia as judge, even Pan with Arcadia as judge would say that he was defeated.

Coleman calls attention to the apparently pointless repetitions, which he regards as a possible indication of textual corruption. I believe that his observation could be explained in a different way: Virgil is changing gear and reverting in a rather exaggerated way to his normal bucolic idiom. In much the same way Catullus in his eleventh poem, after using the Sapphic metre inappropriately for cynical gibes at his friends and tasteless invective against his lady,

The Style of Virgil's Eclogues

reverts in his last stanza to a genuinely Sapphic image, the flower broken by the ploughshare.

I conclude with the last lines of the tenth *Eclogue*: evening appropriately closes the poem and the book:

> surgamus: solet esse gravis cantantibus umbra,
> iuniperi gravis umbra; nocent et frugibus umbrae.
> ite domum saturae—venit Hesperus—ite capellae.

Let's arise; the shade is wont to be oppressive for singers; oppressive the juniper's shade, shade harms also the crops. Go home sated, the evening star is coming, go home, nanny-goats.

Here we have the same jingling repetition that we found at the beginning of Theocritus 1: *gravis, gravis, umbra, umbra, umbrae*. At *iuniperi gravis umbra* there is the enanalepsis that has already been mentioned, for it is surely wrong to understand *est*; that would disrupt the correspondence with the next clause, where *et frugibus* balances *cantantibus*. It may also be suggested that *gravis umbra* is a delicate oxymoron of the sort familiar in sophisticated Roman poetry: a shade in all its senses is naturally *levis*. In the penultimate line we have the soft feminine caesura after the trochee in the third foot, and in the last line the even more typical bucolic diaeresis, the break after *Hesperus*. Also characteristic are the parenthesis *venit Hesperus*, the repetition of *ite* in the first and fifth feet, the artificial distribution by which *saturae* is combined with the first *ite* and *capellae* with the second; there seems also to be a whimsical implication that the audience like the animals now have had their fill. The poem closes with a Grecism for the Evening Star (*Hesperus*), and a diminutive for the humble nanny-goats (*capellae*), the word that is found in the *Eclogues* thirteen times; the blend of the poetic and the familiar that is so typical of these poems is here given special emphasis. Virgil has ended the book with his bucolic signature-tune, and if I am asked to define the bucolic style I can only point to these lines and say 'That is what it is like.'

4

Bucolic *nomina* in Virgil and Theocritus: On the Poetic Technique of Virgil's *Eclogues*

Lorenz Rumpf

A collection of ten poems closely related to one another by content as well as language, Virgil's book of *Eclogues* forms a poetic whole. Its unity is created, among other things, by a specific 'nominal' vocabulary[1] that pervades the collection.[2] In this paper, I will consider the typically bucolic adjectives, nouns, and proper names used regularly throughout the *Eclogues* (e.g. *formosus, tener, viridis; silva, arbustum, pratum; Tityrus, Daphnis, Menalcas*), not just on a semantic level (as

I wish to thank Willibald Heilmann (to whose memory the English version is dedicated), Lutz Lenz, Bernd Manuwald, and Oliver Primavesi for their suggestions; Benno Rumpf for his help with the statistics in section 2; and Katharina Volk, Joshua T. Katz, and Axel Jansen for correcting my English. Thanks also to the audiences at the annual meeting of the American Philological Association in San Diego in December 1995 and the Mittelrheinisches Symposion at Marburg University in January 1997. In this version of the original 1999 paper, some references have been added and a few alterations made.

[1] *Nomina* and 'nominal' are used here in their broader German sense (i.e. including nouns, proper names, and adjectives).

[2] There is no such system of typical verbs. Among the words that occur at least 10 times in the *Eclogues*, there are 13 verbs and 35 nouns, adjectives, and proper names, and only three of the verbs *(cano, canto, pasco/-or)* are in some way typically 'bucolic' (four if we include *incipio*, which typically introduces bucolic song); others include *video, venio, duco, facio, fero, possum*. On the other hand, we find a large number of characteristically bucolic words among the nouns and adjectives (*silva, pecus, herba, mons, ovis, umbra, capella, pastor, lac, tibia; formosus, mollis, tener, viridis*), as well as the proper names *Daphnis, Corydon, Tityrus, Amyntas, Menalcas, Amaryllis, Nympha, Phyllis*. As the nouns are thus far more distinctive for the vocabulary of the *Eclogues*, this paper confines itself to an examination of these.

symbols and conveyors of motifs), but as material, as the very 'building blocks' of the bucolic sphere. My aim is to show how they are systematically used as objects of a poetic game.[3]

The use of bucolic *nomina* and the way in which they recur are subject to certain restrictions and peculiarities that I attempt in this paper to demonstrate and interpret from a poetological point of view. In sections 1 and 2, I will show how typically bucolic adjectives and nouns are continually repeated throughout the collection, while at the same time there is a tendency towards variation and a remarkable economy in their use. In a different yet comparable manner, the use of proper names, too, is characterized by an interplay of continuity and change. They recur regularly, but as will be shown in section 3, the identity of the individuals to whom they refer is systematically blurred.

Some methodological problems arise. First, I need to demonstrate my hypotheses with reference to specific examples, whose selection may well seem arbitrary. The only way to substantiate my claims is thus through cumulative argument. While my use of charts and numbers may raise the suspicion of pseudo-exactness, such a comprehensive survey is necessary in order to prove that the overall result corresponds to the individual observations with which I am starting out. The value of my numbers is thus qualitative rather than quantitative. In a number of cases it may be disputed whether a word is specifically bucolic or not, but in spite of an inevitable fuzziness, there can be no doubt but that there is such a thing as a typical bucolic *nomen*. The number of borderline cases is low and without any decisive influence on the results. At the beginning of each section, I will briefly explain the criteria by which the individual words have been selected.

Some of the phenomena described here may certainly be observed in other literary works as well, but in the *Eclogues* they can be shown to be more pronounced and dominant. To make this point, I provide

---

[3] Pietzcker 1965 examines bucolic nouns (141–4) and adjectives (145–53) semantically. The aims of Kollmann 1973*a*, 1974, and 1975 are likewise different from those of this study: he analyzes the absolute frequency of specific words, the specific vocabulary of the *Eclogues* in comparison to the *Georgics* and *Aeneid*, and Virgil's independence from his predecessors, especially Theocritus. Vaccaro 1966 exclusively deals with questions of word order.

a comparison with Virgil's later works in section 1 and return in sections 2 and 3—the difference in language notwithstanding—to Theocritus as the literary model of the *Eclogues*.

1. ADJECTIVES

The *Eclogues* feature a repertoire of adjectives that denote natural qualities (usually ones subject to sense perception), which characterize objects, animals, or persons belonging to the bucolic world and which are often typical of the bucolic sphere and its specific ambience. The frequent use of a number of these adjectives is one of the devices that create a certain homogeneity throughout the collection.

When these adjectives are used attributively, the following restriction can be observed: there is a tendency not to make them fixed epitheta of *one* substantive, but to vary the combinations. This is most obvious with *viridis*, *pinguis*, *amarus*, and *candidus*. Each of these adjectives occurs regularly throughout the *Eclogues*, but each of its combinations with nouns and proper names comes up only once: viridis occurs eleven times in the ten poems and is combined with *antrum* (1.75), *frons* (1.80), *lacertus* (2.9), *hibiscum* (2.30), *cortex* (5.13), *herba* (6.59), *ripa* (7.12), *arbutus* (7.46), *ulva* (8.87), *umbra* (9.20), *alnus* (10.74); pinguis is used eight times, in combination with the following words: *caseus* (1.34), *ervum* (3.100), *arvum* (5.33), *olivum* (5.68), *ovis* (6.4), *taeda* (7.49), *electrum* (8.54), *verbena* (8.65); candidus seven times, in combination with *barba* (1.28), *Nais* (2.46), *Daphnis* (5.56–7), *inguen* (6.75), *Galatea / cycnus* (7.37–8: comparative[4]), *populus* (9.41); amarus six times, combined with *salix* (1.78), *amor* (3.109–10), *cortex* (6.62–3), *apium* (6.68), *herba* (7.41: indirectly, in a comparison), *Doris* (10.5). Formosus is used 16 times in 17 combinations (on the method of counting, see n. 4), 12 of which occur only once: it is combined with *Amaryllis* (1.5), *Alexis*

---

[4] In the case of adjectives in the comparative form, in most instances the object or person *compared* and the object *to which* the comparison is made have been taken into account. This is why in my list the number of combinations sometimes exceeds the number of instances of the respective adjective.

(2.1; 5.86; 7.55), *puer* (2.17, 45), *annus* (3.57), *Iollas* (3.79), *Apollo* (4.57), *Daphnis* (5.43–4), *pecus* (5.44), *pedum* (5.88–90), *Galatea / hedera* (7.37–8; comparative), *Venus* (7.62), *Lycidas* (7.67), *Adonis* (10.18). Only the combinations with *Alexis* and *puer* (the latter likewise referring to Alexis in *Ecl.* 2) are used more than once—an obvious exception to the rule.

A survey of further adjectives shows the same pattern in the *Eclogues* as a whole.[5] The tendency to construct a system of typical adjectives is obvious but, on the whole, Virgil seems to avoid fixed epithet combinations. Not only are attributive adjectives *able* to be interchanged, but there seems to be a veritable *pressure* for interchange, with the result that typically bucolic qualities are ascribed to a broad variety of objects and persons throughout the collection. Of course, variation is a ubiquitous poetic phenomenon, but the characteristic vocabulary of the *Eclogues* is unusually dense, that is, restricted to comparatively few words, which renders more conspicuous the principle of variation described here.[6]

---

[5] <u>Mollis</u> is used attributively 14 times, with the following nouns (12 of these combinations occur only once): *castanea* (1.81), *vaccinium* (2.50), *iuncus* (2.72), *acanthus* (3.45), *herba* (3.55; 7.45: comparative), *arista* (4.28), *folium* (5.31), *viola* (5.38), *hyacinthus* (6.53), *somnus* (7.45: comparative), *vitta* (8.64), *clivus* (9.8), *pratum* (10.42); <u>tener</u> 11 times (9 combinations occurring only once): with *agnus* (1.8; 3.103), *fetus* (1.21), *lanugo* (2.51), *mundi orbis* (6.34), *myrtus* (7.6), *harundo* (7.12), *herba* (8.15), *virgultum* (10.7), *planta* (10.49), *arbor* (10.53–4); <u>niger</u> 5 times (3 combinations occurring only once): with *vaccinium* (2.18; 10.39), *ilex* (6.54), *postis* (7.50), *violae* (10.39). <u>Lentus</u> is something of an anomaly: it occurs eight times, combined with *viburnum* (1.25), *vitis* (3.38; 9.42; 10.40), *salix* (3.83; 5.16), *hasta* (5.31), *palmes* (7.48). Exceptionally, a sort of fixed formula (*lenta vitis*) is used three times, but still three combinations are found only once. In addition, I give an abbreviated overview of the bucolic attributes used less often (two to four times): e.g., 4/2 means that a specific word is used 4 times in combination with nouns or proper names and that 2 of these combinations occur only once: *aërius* (3/3), *albus* (2/2), *argutus* (4/4), *asper* (2/2), *aureus* (3/1), *densus* (3/3), *dulcis* (4/4), *florens* (4/2), *fragilis* (3/3), *frigidus* (4/2), *gelidus* (2/2), *hirsutus* (2/2), *liquidus* (2/2), *maturus* (2/2), *niveus* (3/3), *pallens* (4/4), *pulcher* (2/2), *puniceus* (2/2), *purpureus* (2/2), *roscidus* (2/2), *rubens* (3/3), *sanguineus* (signifying a colour) (2/2), *silvestris* (3/3), *suavis* (2/2), *tenuis* (2/2). The count shows that 132 out of the 154 combinations in the *Eclogues* taken into account (85.7 %) are 'singlets'. (Quotations from the *Eclogues* come from Mynors 1969, translations from Fairclough 1999. I have made use of the concordance of Lecrompe 1970; see also Najock 2004).

[6] An especially striking example of this tendency is *formosus*, which reappears only once in Virgil's later works (*G.* 3.219); see Heuzé 1970; Marchetta (1994). If we check the use of the adjectives examined above in the *Georgics* (which after all treats a

In the interplay of continuity and variation, the quality of each single adjective as a freely usable poetic building block becomes obvious. These observations concerning the employment of adjectives hint at broader patterns of a specific use of language in the *Bucolics*. Further clues concerning this will emerge from a consideration of nouns and proper names.

2. NOUNS

In the case of the bucolic nouns (i.e. words denoting natural objects or qualities, manmade objects, and types of animals and humans found in the bucolic sphere),[7] there is again a tendency for each

similar sphere), we find that *pinguis* (28 instances), *tenuis*, and *dulcis* (22 instances each) stand out, while the frequency of most other adjectives is under-proportional: in the *Georgics*, *viridis* occurs 9 times as an attribute (11 times in the *Eclogues*), *tener* 10 times (11 times in the *Eclogues*), *lentus* 12 times (8 times in the *Eclogues*), *candidus* 4 times (6 times in the *Eclogues*), *amarus* 3 times (6 times in the *Eclogues*), *mollis* 20 times (quite frequently, but still under-proportionally compared to 13 instances in the *Eclogues*). A quantitative comparison of all instances of these words (which cannot be fully documented here) shows that the single adjectival attribute in the *Georgics* is used with significantly lower frequency than in the *Eclogues* (4.46 times in the *Eclogues*; 7.85 times in the *Georgics*, which is more than 2.5 times as long): thus, the adjectival vocabulary of the *Eclogues* is more repertoire-like (and there are no tendencies to create a new, structurally comparable adjectival repertoire in the *Georgics*). The use of attributive adjectives in the *Aeneid* is governed by different rules: the *variatio* of epithet there—see e.g. Worstbrock 1963: 177–90—is always in creative contrast to a fundamental tendency to imitate a 'Homeric' formulaic style with stock epithets. A relatively small number of adjectives used very frequently (size characterizations such as *altus*, *magnus*, *ingens*) show a tendency to become fixed epithets: e.g. *altus* is found 8 times in the *Aeneid* with *caelum*, 3 times with *mare*, 5 times with *moenia*, and 11 times with *mons* (which also means that formulae like *pius Aeneas*, *infelix Dido*, *audax Turnus*, *fidus Achates* are not the only fixed epithet combinations in the *Aeneid*). Adjectives that show variations similar to those described in the *Eclogues* occur far less often in the *Aeneid*, considering the length of the work (whose number of verses is twelve times as high). Those listed above as 'bucolic' may serve as an example: e.g. *mollis* occurs 20 times, *viridis* 15 times, *tener* 6 times. In the *Idylls* of Theocritus there is no elaborate system of adjectives: only a few of them (e.g., ἁδύς, καλός, and μαλακός) occur frequently or regularly; a comparison with Virgil thus makes no sense in this case.

[7] A few remarks on my criteria of selection: *leo* (*Ecl.* 4.22; 5.27) and *tigris* (*Ecl.* 5.29), e.g., have not been included because these exotic animals—differently from *lupus*—without doubt do not belong to the core of the bucolic sphere. *Cautes* ('cliff') has not been taken into account because the speaker in *Ecl.* 8.43 evokes a

single word to recur throughout the collection (on account of their symbolic meaning, *silva* and *myrica* are especially well known). Again, though, their use is governed by a restriction: in many cases they occur exactly once per poem. *Fagus* may serve as an example. This tree name ('beech'), which symbolically opens the book in *Ecl.* 1.1, occurs five times in five different *Eclogues*.[8] Repetition makes it a characteristic word, while its uniqueness per poem has the consequence that in no individual *Eclogue* does the *fagus* become a stable object and a firm point of reference. In *Eclogue* 1, for example, it does not turn into a leitmotif symbolizing Tityrus' *otia* (1.6), which one might have thought a possible way to use such a word.

Other examples of nouns used with some frequency throughout the *Eclogues* and only once per poem (or at least in extreme moderation) include *aper* (*Ecl.* 2.59; 3.75; 5.76; 7.29; 10.56), *arbustum* (1.39; 2.13; 3.10; 4.2; 5.64), *canis* (1.22; 3.67; 6.77; 8.28; 10.57), *cornu* (3.87; 6.51; 7.30; 9.25; 10.59), *cytisus* (1.78; 2.64; 9.31; 10.30), *fons* (1.39, 52; 2.59; 3.97; 5.40; 6.43; 7.45; 9.20; 10.42), *ignis* (3.66; 5.10; 6.33; 7.49; 8.81), *iugum* (2.66; 4.41; 5.76; 9.8; 10.11), *litus* (1.60; 2.25; 5.83; 6.44; 9.43), *myrica* (4.2; 6.10; 8.54; 10.13), *pratum* (3.111; 4.43; 7.11; 8.71; 10.42), *quercus* (1.17; 4.30; 6.28; 7.13; 8.53), *ulmus* (1.58; 2.70; 5.3; 10.67), *uva* (4.29; 5.32; 9.49; 10.36). A comprehensive survey shows that in the *Eclogues* the normal situation is an even distribution of individual nouns over the poems, not a concentration in a single poem.[9] The words *capella, flumen, herba, mons, ovis, pecus* (*-oris*),

---

clearly anti-bucolic scenery, whereas *rupes* is counted, which in *Ecl.* 1.56 and 76 is emphatically included in the bucolic sphere. The words denoting the seasons of the year have been included because these are, in a way, part of the bucolic world. Below the same criteria will be applied to Theocritus.

[8] *Ecl.* 1.1 (*Tityre, tu patulae recubans sub tegmine fagi*); 2.3–4 (*tantum inter densas, umbrosa cacumina, fagos | adsidue veniebat*); 3.12–13 (*aut hic ad veteres fagos cum Daphnidis arcum | fregisti et calamos*); 5.13–14 (*... in viridi nuper quae cortice fagi | carmina descripsi...*); 9.9 (*usque ad aquam et veteres, iam fracta cacumina, fagos*).

[9] The following 152 bucolic substantives occur at least twice in the *Eclogues*. In parentheses, first the absolute number of instances is given, then the number of poems in which the word occurs. If necessary, the number of poems in which the word occurs exactly once is added in the third position: *acanthus* (2/2), *aequor* (2/2), *aestas* (2/2), *aestus* (3/3), *ager* (7/5/3), *agnus* (5/4), *agricola* (2/2), *alnus* (3/3), *amomum* (2/2), *anguis* (2/2), *ansa* (2/2), *antrum* (6/4/3), *aper* (5/5), *apis* (3/3), *aqua* (4/3), *arator* (2/2), *aratrum* (2/2), *arbor* (7/5/4), *arbustum* (5/5), *arbutus* (2/2), *aries* (2/2), *arista*

silva, umbra, which are very frequent, sometimes occur several times in the same *Eclogue*, but their appearance per poem is still sparing and their distribution relatively even.[10] A comparison with Theocritus' *Idylls* shows that this way of employing nouns is in fact specific to

(2/2), *armentum* (4/3), *arvum* (2/2), *avena* (3/3), *aura* (2/2), *Auster* (2/2), *baccar* (2/2), *bos* (4/3), *cacumen* (3/3), *calamus* (8/6/4), *calathus* (2/2), *canis* (5/5), *capella* (13/8/5; see n. 10), *caper* (6/3/1), *castanea* (2/2), *cera* (3/3), *cervus* (4/4), *cicada* (2/2), *cicuta* (2/2), *collis* (3/2), *cornu* (5/5), *cortex* (3/3), *corylus* (5/3/1), *culmen* (2/1), *cycnus* (3/3), *cytisus* (4/4), *examen* (2/2), *fagus* (5/5), *falx* (2/2), *fera* (2/2), *fistula* (6/5), *flos* (8/6/4), *fluctus* (3/3), *flumen* (11/8/6; see n. 10), *fluvius* (2/2), *focus* (2/2), *folium* (2/1), *fons* (9/8), *fraxinus* (2/1), *frigus* (10/5/2), *frons* (3/3), *frux* (4/3), *gramen* (3/2), *grex* (9/7/6), *haedus* (8/6/4), *harundo* (2/2), *hedera* (5/4), *herba* (15/8/3; see n. 10), *hibiscum* (2/2), *hircus* (2/1), *hortus* (3/3), *humus* (5/4), *hyacinthus* (2/2), *ignis* (5/5), *ilex* (3/3), *imber* (3/3), *iugum* (5/5), *iuncus* (2/2), *iuniperus* (2/2), *iuvencus* (5/4), *lac* (10/6/3), *lapis* (2/2), *laurea* (2/1), *laurus* (7/5/4), *lilium* (2/2), *litus* (5/5), *lucus* (3/3), *lupus* (8/6/4), *malum* (6/4/2), *mare* (5/4), *mel* (2/2), *messis* (2/2), *messor* (2/2), *mons* (15/7/3; see n. 10), *myrica* (4/4), *myrtus* (4/2/1), *narcissus* (3/3), *nemus* (8/4/1), *nubes* (2/2), *nux* (2/2), *Nymphae* (10/7/5), *oliva* (2/2), *ovis* (15/6/3; see n. 10), *palumbis* (2/2), *pastor* (11/8/5; see n. 10), *pecus, -oris* (17/7/4; see n. 10), *pecus, -udis* (2/2), *pinus* (6/4/3), *pirus* (2/2), *piscis* (2/2), *poculum* (5/3/2), *pomum* (5/4), *populus* (3/2), *pratum* (5/5), *quercus* (5/5), *rete* (2/2), *ripa* (3/2), *rivus* (5/4), *ros* (2/2), *rupes* (6/4/2), *rus* (3/3), *saepes* (2/2), *salix* (5/4), *saltus* (3/2), *saxum* (2/2), *seges* (3/3), *sertum* (3/2), *silva* (22/9/1), *sol* (4/3), *solum* (2/1), *stabulum* (3/2), *sulcus* (2/2), *taurus* (6/5/4), *tellus* (3/1), *terra* (9/5/0), *thymum* (2/2), *tibia* (10/1; a clear exception: the word occurs only in the *versus intercalaris* of Damon's song), *uber* (5/4), *ulmus* (4/4), *umbra* (15/7/2; see n. 10), *unda* (3/3), *uva* (4/4), *vacca* (2/2), *vaccinium* (3/2), *vallis* (3/3), *vellus* (2/2), *ventus* (3/2), *ver* (2/2), *viola* (3/3), *vitis* (9/7/5), *vitula* (5/1; see n. 10).

[10] In the case of *silva*, the most frequent of these nouns (22 instances), a special form of 'uniqueness per poem' can be observed: the use of different *case forms* is restricted. Both nominative (*Ecl.* 2.62; 3.57; 4.3; 5.28; 6.39; 10.8) and accusative (*Ecl.* 1.5; 2.60; 3.46; 4.3; 5.58; 6.2), each appearing in six *Eclogues*, are used exactly once per poem. The ablative plural forms show a relatively even distribution as well (*Ecl.* 2.31; 5.43; 7.65, 68; 8.56, 97; 10.52); the vocative plural is used twice (*Ecl.* 8.58; 10.63), the dative singular once (2.5). The instances of the remaining bucolic nouns used more than 10 times in the *Eclogues* are: <u>*pecus (-oris)*</u> (17 instances): 1.50, 74; 2.20; 3.1, 3, 6, 20, 34, 83,101 (twice); 5.44, 60, 87; 7.47; 8.15; 10.17; <u>*herba*</u> (15 instances): 2.11, 49; 3.55, 93; 4.24; 5.26; 6.54, 59; 7.41, 45, 57; 8.2, 15, 95; 9.19; <u>*mons*</u> (15 instances): 1.83; 2.5, 21; 5.8, 28, 63, 76; 6.40, 52, 65, 71; 7.56, 66; 8.59; 10.32; <u>*ovis*</u> (15 instances): 1.21; 2.33 (twice), 42; 3.3, 5, 94, 98; 6.5, 85; 7.3; 8.52; 10.16, 18, 68; <u>*umbra*</u> (15 instances): 1.4, 83; 2.8, 67; 5.5, 40, 70; 7.10, 46, 58; 8.14; 9.20; 10.75, 76 (twice); <u>*capella*</u> (13 instances): 1.12, 74, 77; 2.63, 64; 3.96; 4.21; 7.3; 8.33; 9.23; 10.7, 30, 77; <u>*flumen*</u> (11 instances): 1.51; 3.96; 5.21, 25, 84; 6.64; 7.52, 56; 8.4; 9.40; 10.18; <u>*pastor*</u> (11 instances): 1.21; 2.1; 5.41, 59; 6.4, 67; 7.25; 8.1, 23; 9.34; 10.51. With decreasing number of instances, distribution approaches single use per poem. The frequency of *pecus, ovis*, and *vitula* (see n. 9) in *Ecl.* 3 is the exception that proves the rule. Here for once the animals are of importance for the 'action' of the poem (e.g. the *vitula* as the wager in Damoetas' and Menalcas' singing contest becomes an object of contention between them).

Bucolic nomina *in* Virgil and Theocritus 71

the *Eclogues*.[11] In the case of both works, I have taken into account not only those bucolic nouns with two or more occurrences,[12] but those that appear only once as well,[13] for they constitute a significant portion of the total. The following chart (p. 72) can be assembled.

The count shows that in Virgil bucolic nouns occur significantly more often in relation to the number of verses, while the number of different bucolic nouns used by both poets is practically equal. This

[11] The lists are based on Theocritus' *Idylls* 1–7 and 10–12 in Gow's edition (1952a), which are (a) universally accepted as authentic and (b) bucolic or important for Virgil's bucolic poetry (e.g. *Id.* 2 as a model for Alphesiboeus' song in *Ecl.* 8). *Id.* 10, the 'Reapers', is at any rate close to the bucolic sphere; *Id.* 12 in lines 3–6 features a bucolic priamel. In nn. 12 and 13, the occurrences in Theocritus have for reasons of space not been documented in detail; cf. Rumpel 1961; Lembach 1970.

[12] In the *Idylls* singled out in n. 11, these are the following 129 words: ἀγέλα (3/3), ἀέλιος / ἠέλιος (3/3), ἀηδών (3/3), αἴγειρος (2/1), αἱμασιά (3/3), αἴξ (23/6/1), αἰπόλος (12/4/1), ἄκανθα (4/4), ἀκρίς (3/2), ἀλκυών (2/1), ἄλσος (5/4), ἀλωά (2/2), ἀλώπηξ (2/2), ἀμνίς (2/1), ἀμνός (3/1), ἄμπελος (2/2), ἄνθος (3/2), ἄντρον (6/4/2), *ἀρήν (6/4/2), ἄρκευθος (2/2), ἄρκτος (3/3), αὔλιον (2/2), αὐλός (3/3), βαίτα (2/2), βάτος (2/2), βάτραχος (2/2), βοῦς (4/2/0), βούτας (5/3), βράβιλον (2/2), γάλα (6/3/1), γαυλός (2/1), γεώλοφον (2/2), δαμάλα (2/2), δάφνα (3/2), δέπας (2/1), δέρμα: hide of an animal (2/2), δράγμα (2/2), δρυμός (3/2), δρῦς (9/4/1), ἔαρ/εἶαρ (3/2), εἴριον/ἔριον (2/1), ἔλαιον (2/2), ἐλίχρυσος (2/2), ἔριφος (5/3/2), θάλασσα: sea as part of the Sicilian bucolic scenery (4/3), θαλλός (2/2), θέρος (6/3/0), θηρίον (3/3), θώς (2/1), ἴον (2/2), ἵππος (2/1), καλάμα (2/2), καρπός (2/2), κηρίον (3/2), κηρός (3/2), κισσός (4/3), κνύζα (2/2), κορύνα (2/1), κότινος (2/1), κράνα (7/5/3), κρέας (3/3), κῦμα (5/4), κύπειρος (2/2), κύτισος (2/2), κύων (8/5/3), λαγωβόλον (2/2), λᾷον (2/1), λάρναξ (2/1), λίθος (3/3 without *Id.* 6.18), λύκος (7/6), μάκων (2/2), μᾶλον/μῆλον (apple) (10/8/6), μᾶλον/μῆλον (sheep) (3/3), μέλι (4/3), μέλισσα (6/4/3), μελίτεια (2/2), μηκάς (2/2), μοσχίον (2/1), μόσχος (2/2), μυρίκα (2/2), νάκος (2/2), νεβρός (2/2), νέκταρ (2/1), Νότος (2/1), Νύμφαι (14/4/1), οἶνος (2/2), ὄϊς (9/7/5), ὀπώρα (2/2), ὄρνις (3/2), ὄρος (19/6/2), ὄχνη (2/2), πέτρα (7/6), πήρα (2/1), πίθος (2/2), πίτυς (4/3), ποία (2/2), ποιμήν (9/3/0), ποίμνα (3/3), ποίμνιον (3/2), πόντος (3/3), πόρτις (5/3/1), ποταμός (4/2/0), πτελέα (3/2), πτέρις (2/2), πῦρ (7/4/2), πῶλος (2/1), ῥόδον (4/3), ῥόος (2/1), σέλινον (2/2), σκίλλα (2/2), σμᾶνος (2/2), σποδός (2/2), στέφανος (5/5), στιβάς (2/2), σῦριγξ (8/4/3), σχοῖνος (2/2), τάλαρος (2/2), τάμισος (2/2), ταῦρος (4/2/0), τέττιξ (5/4), τράγος (6/3/1), τυρός (3/2), ὕδωρ (9/4/2), φάσσα (2/1), φυτόν (2/1), χειμών (3/2), χίμαιρα (3/2), χίμαρος (2/2), χιών (3/3).

[13] In Virgil, these are the following 132 words: *abies* (7.66), *agellus* (9.3), *agna* (2.21), *alga* (7.42), *alium* (2.11), *anethum* (2.48), *animal* (6.40), *anser* (9.36), *apium* (6.68), *aquila* (9.13), *arcus* (3.12), *arena* (3.87), *baca* (10.27), *bitumen* (8.82), *Boreas* (7.51), *caespes* (1.68), *calta* (2.50), *cantharus* (6.17), *capreolus* (2.41), *carduus* (5.39), *carectum* (3.20), *casia* (2.49), *catulus* (1.22), *clivus* (9.8), *colocasium* (4.20), *columba* (9.13), *cornix* (9.15), *corymbus* (3.39), *cratera* (5.68), *creta* (1.65), *cupressus* (1.25), *damma* (8.28), *ebulum* (10.27), *electrum* (8.54), *equus* (8.27), *ervum* (3.100), *fascis* (9.65), *fax* (8.29), *ferula* (10.25), *fetura* (7.36), *fiscella* (10.71), *flamma* (8.105), *fragum* (3.92), *frondator* (1.56), *fuligo* (7.50), *gemma* (7.48), *glans* (10.20), *hasta* (5.31), *hiems*

72 Lorenz Rumpf

	Virgil, Ecl. 1–10	Theocritus, Id. 1–7, 10–12
Total number of verses	830 (Ecl. 8.28a included)	964
Bucolic nouns with 2 or more occurrences	152	129
Number of occurrences	671	477
Bucolic nouns with one occurrence	132	157
Total number of bucolic nouns	284	286
Total number of their occurrences	803	634
Ratio of verses to occurrences of bucolic nouns	1.03	1.52
Average number of occurrences per bucolic noun	2.83	2.22

(10.66), *hordeum* (5.36), *iuvenca* (8.2), *labrusca* (5.7), *lana* (4.42), *lanugo* (2.51), *liber* (10.67), *libum* (7.33), *licium* (8.74), *ligustrum* (2.18), *limes* (1.53), *limus* (8.80), *lolium* (5.37), *lutum* (4.44), *lynx* (8.3), *minium* (10.27), *mola* (8.82), *morum* (6.22), *mulctra* (3.30), *murex* (4.44), *muscus* (6.62), *nectar* (5.71), *novale* (1.70), *olivum* (5.68), *olor* (9.36), *ornus* (6.71), *ovile* (1.8), *pabulum* (1.49), *paliurus* (5.39), *palmes* (7.48), *palus* (1.48), *papaver* (2.47), *pascuum* (1.48), *pedum* (5.88), *pellis* (2.41), *pluvia* (9.63), *praesepe* (7.39), *prunum* (2.53), *quadrupes* (5.26), *racemus* (5.7), *ramus* (8.40), *rastrum* (pl. *rastri*) (4.40), *rosetum* (5.17), *rubus* (3.89), *ruscum* (7.42), *saeptum* (1.33), *salictum* (1.54), *saliunca* (5.17), *sandyx* (4.45), *sata* (3.82), *semen* (6.32), *sentis* (4.29), *serpens* (4.24), *serpyllum* (2.11), *silex* (1.15), *solstitium* (7.47), *specula* (8.59), *spelaeum* (10.52), *spina* (5.39), *spinetum* (2.9), *stipula* (3.27), *subulcus* (10.19), *sucus* (3.6), *taeda* (7.49), *taxus* (9.30), *tegmen* (1.1), *tugurium* (1.68), *turtur* (1.58), *tus* (8.65), *ulula* (8.55), *ulva* (8.87), *umbraculum* (9.42), *umor* (3.82), *upilio* (10.19), *verbena* (8.65), *viburnum* (1.25), *villa* (1.82), *vimen* (2.72), *vinea* (4.40), *vinum* (5.71), *virgultum* (10.7), *vitta* (8.64), *vulpes* (391), *Zephyrus* (5,5). In Theocritus the following 157 words with a single instance are taken into account: ἀγριέλαιος, αἰγιαλός, αἴγιλος, αἰγίπυρον, ἀιών, ἀκανθίς, ἄκανθος, ἄκρατος (wine)\comma ἀκριδοθήρα, ἄκυλος, ἄλειφαρ, ἀλέκτωρ, ἄλφιτον, ἀμαλλοδέτας, ἀμητήρ, ἀμνάς, ἄνδηρον, ἄνεμος, ἀνεμώνα, ἀνθέρικος, ἄπιον / ἄπιος, ἀρνακίς, ἄροτρον, ἀσπάλαθος, ἀσφόδελος, ἀτρακτυλλίς, αὖλαξ, ἄχυρον, ἄωτος, βδέλλα, Βορέας, βοτάνα, βοτόν, γαλάνα, γέρανος, γλάχων, γλυκύμαλον, δένδρον, δρυτόμος, ἐέρση, ἐλαία, ἔλαφος, ἐνόρχας, ἔποψ, ἐργάτας, ἐργατίνας, ἐρείκα, Εὖρος, Θαλύσια, θάψος, θύννος, ἱππομανές, ἰσχάς, κάκτος, κάλπις, κάλυξ, κάνθαρος, κέδρος, κισθός, κίσσα, κισσύβιον, κνάκων, κνίδα, κόμαρος, κόρθυς, κορυδαλλίς, κορυδαλλός, κόρυδος, κρίνον, κριός, κύαμος, κυκλάμινος, κύκνος, κύλιξ, κύμινον, κυνόσβατος, κυπάρισσος, κώμυς, κῶνος, λανός, λεπύριον, λεύκα, λευκόιον, λίμνα, λόφος, λυκιδεύς, μᾶζα, νᾶμα, νάρκισσος, νομεύς, ξύλον, ὄγμος, οἴς, οἰνάρεος, ὀλολυγών, ὀμφαξ, ὄξος, ὀπλά, ὀροδαμνίς, ὀρομαλίς, ὄρπαξ, ὄρχος, ὄχθη, παγά, πακτά, πέλλα, πεύκη, πῖδαξ, πίτυρον, πλαταγώνιον, πόκος, πρῖνος, πρώξ, πτύον, πτώξ, πῶμα, ῥάμνος, ῥίον, σακίτας, σαύρα, σαῦρος, σίον (or οἴσυον), σῖτος, σκαφίς, σκιά, σκοπιά, σκύλαξ, σκύμνος, σκῦφος, σκώψ, σπόρος, σταφυλά, στάχυς, σῦκον, συριγκτάς, σφάξ, σχαδών, σχῖνος, σωρός, ταρσός, τέμπεα, τηλέφιλον, τόξον, τραγεία, τρυγών, τρύξ, τρύχνος, ὑάκινθος, ὕλα, ὗς, φακός, φηγός, φλόξ, φραγμός, φυκίον, φύλλον, χεῖμα.

means that in the *Eclogues* the 'network' of bucolic words is (a) more tightly knit and (b) more like a repertoire, as the tendency to repeat each single word is higher. But most importantly, in a considerable number of cases, a noun carries specific weight as part of the action or functions as a leitmotif in an individual Theocritean poem, which results in a high unevenness of distribution across the poems.[14] Apart from such striking cases—which already make a fundamental difference—it can be shown by way of a comprehensive survey that in the *Eclogues*, the overall distribution of occurrences is in fact more even, that is, the single bucolic noun is used more 'sparingly' per poem.[15] The importance of this fact is reinforced by the observation that Virgil, as shown above, uses such words more frequently than Theocritus. These two tendencies add up to the effect that in Virgil, the single bucolic noun becomes a poetic element with a value of its own and with a constitutive function for the *Eclogues* as a whole, namely to create relations *between* single poems. This means, on the other hand, that the bucolic noun in Virgil is less integrated in the action of individual poems than it is in Theocritus.

3. PROPER NAMES

Since the material basis is evident, it is relatively unproblematic to examine the bucolic proper names: the Greek pastoral names—about half of them taken over from Theocritus[16]—form a clearly delineated

---

[14] Especially remarkable are αἴξ (*Id.* 1.4, 5, 14, 25, 57, 143; *Id.* 3.1, 3, 34; *Id.* 4.39; *Id.* 5.1, 12, 27, 73, 84, 89, 128, 145, 148; *Id.* 7.87, 97; *Id.* 10.30 (2x)); δρῦς (*Id.* 1.23, 106; 5.45, 61, 102, 117; 7.74, 88; 11.51); Νύμφαι (*Id.* 1.12, 66, 141; *Id.* 4.29; *Id.* 5.12, 17, 53, 70, 140, 149; *Id.* 7.92, 137, 148, 154); ὄρος (*Id.* 1.77, 115, 123, 136, 152; *Id.* 2.49; *Id.* 3.2, 46; *Id.* 4.35, 56, 57; *Id.* 7.46, 51, 74, 87, 92, 111, 152; *Id.* 11.27).

[15] The evenness of distribution can be described by the following quotient, which for any specific word gives a measure of the *average deviation* of its number of instances per poem from the *average number* of its instances per poem: $\Sigma(x_{ik} - \bar{x}_i)^2 / \Sigma(x_{ik})^2$ (*x* signifying a specific number of instances, the index *i* a specific word, and the index *k* a specific poem). The result will be between 0 and 1, with a smaller quotient meaning greater evenness of distribution. If this is applied to all instances of bucolic substantives listed above, the result is 0.63 for the *Eclogues* and 0.73 for Theocritus, *Idylls* 1–7 and 10–12.

[16] Lipka 2001: 176–91.

group of words. However, already Servius saw that they are employed in a most striking manner: proper names recur regularly in the *Eclogues*,[17] but it is impossible consistently throughout the book to identify the individuals named by them. This way of using proper names can clearly be related to the peculiarities of the nouns described above.

The name *Tityrus*, so prominent in *Ecl.* 1, has always been regarded as a Virgilian mask (e.g. in Calp. *Ecl.* 4.64 this identification is taken for granted). But Servius comments on *Ecl.* 1.1: *et hoc loco Tityri sub persona Vergilium debemus accipere; non tamen ubique, sed tantum ubi exigit ratio* ('Here, too, it is Virgil we have to understand behind the mask of Tityrus; however, this is the case not everywhere, but only where common sense tells us so').[18]

At some moments, a 'tangible' *Tityrus* identity seems to appear, which then again is called into question. In *Ecl.* 1, the name refers to the shepherd who has been granted the *otia* that allow him to dedicate himself to a quiet bucolic existence and to sing. In this poem, the name, like a leitmotif, returns in the vocative (1. 4, 13, 18, 38) and once (38 again) in the nominative. In the given sequence of the poems, the name occurs next in *Ecl.* 3 (20: ... *Tityre, coge pecus*..., 'Tityrus, round up the flock!', and 96: *Tityre, pascentis a flumine reice capellas*..., 'Tityrus, turn back from the stream the grazing goats...'). Here *Tityrus* is someone who receives orders; so the same name can be used for persons of low as well as high status. The next time the name appears (*Ecl.* 5.12 [Menalcas]: *incipe: pascentis servabit Tityrus haedos*, 'Begin. Tityrus will tend the grazing kids'), it again points to a person of low rank who takes care of the herd while the others are singing. The poet of the highest dignity in *Ecl.* 5 is called *Menalcas*, who in 86–7 expressly pronounces himself the author of *Ecl.* 2 and 3. But then in the prologue of *Ecl.* 6, Apollo

---

[17] On bucolic proper names as genre constituents, see Korfmacher 1960.
[18] Cf. C. Wendel 1900: 50: '... satis ut puto probatum est Vergilium nomina bucolica non eidem semper personae dedisse, sed—praeter paucissima exempla...—ad unum quodque carmen pangendum de integro permiscuisse atque elegisse'; see also Coleman 1977: 25; Jachmann 1922. An extreme counterexample is the allegorizing reading of Herrmann 1930 e.g. 7: '*à chaque pseudonyme correspond un nom réel et un seul*' (H.'s italics); for a non-allegorizing but similar position see Flintoff 1975/6.

programmatically addresses the speaking persona, who appears to be the *Eclogues* poet, as *Tityrus* (4–5): *pastorem, Tityre, pinguis | pascere oportet ovis, deductum dicere carmen* ('A shepherd, Tityrus, should feed sheep that are fat, but sing a lay fine-spun'). Here at the beginning of the second half of the book, we thus find an echo of the Tityrus of *Ecl.* 1. But this identity remains fleeting; even in *Eclogue* 6 itself it is not reaffirmed. In *Ecl.* 8.55 the name *Tityrus* appears once more, again denoting a singer:... *certent et cycnis ululae, sit Tityrus Orpheus* ('... let owls, too, vie with swans, let Tityrus be an Orpheus'). In an *adynaton* figure and in contrast with Orpheus, the name is here used as a symbol for 'humble' singing. It has thus become a sort of emblem for *the* bucolic singer as such, recalling several other expressions of 'bucolic modesty'.[19] Finally, in *Ecl.* 9.23–4 (in a quotation from a song of Menalcas given by Lycidas that echoes *Ecl.* 3.96), *Tityrus* is once more used as the name of a person receiving commands (*Tityre, dum redeo* (*brevis est via), pasce capellas, | et potum pastas age, Tityre...*, 'Tityrus, till I return—the way is short—feed my goats; and when fed, drive them, Tityrus, to water...').

The situation is similar with *Menalcas*, another 'great name' of the *Eclogues*. In *Ecl.* 2.15 *Menalcas* is the name of a lover mentioned by Corydon as a possible alternative to Alexis; in *Ecl.* 3 the younger[20] of the two competing singers is named Menalcas; and in *Ecl.* 5 Menalcas is the older and more dignified singer[21] whom Mopsus extols to the highest degree. In the sphragis at the end of this last poem (*Ecl.* 5.85–7) Menalcas momentarily 'is' the *Eclogues* poet, who immediately afterwards, in the prologue of *Ecl.* 6, is addressed by Apollo with *Tityre* (4). In *Ecl.* 9 Menalcas is an absent and almost mythical bucolic singer, which recalls his being extolled in *Ecl.* 5. However, in *Ecl.* 10 a downfall follows: in line 20 of this poem (*uvidus hiberna venit de glande Menalcas*, 'Menalcas came, dripping, from the winter's mast [i.e. acorns, presumably wet from being steeped in water; L.R.]')

[19] Cf. *Ecl.* 4.1–3 and the prologue of *Ecl.* 6.
[20] e.g. *Ecl.* 3.32–4 (Menalcas): *de grege non ausim quicquam deponere tecum: | est mihi namque domi pater, est iniusta noverca, | bisque die numerant ambo pecus, alter et haedos* ('From the herd I'd dare not stake anything with you. I have at home a harsh father and stepmother; and twice a day both count the flock, and one of them the kids as well').
[21] *Ecl.* 5.4 (Mopsus): *tu maior; tibi me est aequum parere, Menalca...* ('You are the elder, Menalcas: it is fitting that I obey you...').

a mute bucolic figure appearing together with shepherds and swineherds bears this name. The question whether this is 'the same' *Menalcas* as before remains systematically open. A survey of the proper names of figures who play a role in at least one *Eclogue* largely shows the same phenomenon of fluctuating identity (11 cases out of 14).[22] There are no doubt some traces of continuing identity. In the case of *Tityrus*, for example, we can speculate whether the hints of a servant Tityrus simply refer to the time before his manumission (*Ecl.* 1.27).[23] This is possible but remains elusive. In the end, the reader of the *Eclogues* is left with unanswered questions. Each time a bucolic name is used, we ask ourselves whether it refers to the same person as before, but while there are some indications that would support such an interpretation, others militate against it. Ultimately, it is impossible simply to assume identical characters.

In Theocritus, by contrast, there is no such wavering of identities. The opposite case is the rule: ten names of main figures occur in exactly one poem (taking into account *Id.* 1–7 and 10–12 again),[24] while only four names that are used for a main figure in one poem reappear

[22] *Alphesiboeus*: minor character (dancing shepherd) in 5.73; main character (singer) in *Ecl.* 8; *Corydon*: main character unhappily in love in *Ecl.* 2; quotation from 2.1 in 5.86; singer (main character) in *Ecl.* 7; *Damoetas*: former owner of Corydon's *fistula* in 2.37, 39; singer (main character) in *Ecl.* 3; marginal figure (singing shepherd) in 5.72; *Damon*: marginal figure in *Ecl.* 3 (17: owner of a goat, 21–4: Damoetas tells he defeated Damon in a singing contest); singer (main character) in *Ecl.* 8; *Daphnis*: in beauty comparison in 2.26; owner of *arcus* and *calami* in 3.12–13; shepherd-hero whose death and apotheosis are extolled in *Ecl.* 5; introduces the singing contest in *Ecl.* 7; *coniunx* of the persona of Alphesiboeus' song in *Ecl.* 8; addressed in the prophecy about the *Caesaris astrum* (in a song of Moeris overheard by Lycidas) in 9.46, 50; *Lycidas*: lover praised in 7.67; main character in *Ecl.* 9; *Meliboeus*: main character in *Ecl.* 1; marginal figure (owner of cattle) in 3.1, a line quoted in part again in 5.87; framing narrator in *Ecl.* 7; *Menalcas*: see above in the text; *Moeris*: sorcerer in 8.96, 98; main character in *Ecl.* 9; *Mopsus*: main character in *Ecl.* 5; Nysa's bridegroom in Damon's song of *Ecl.* 8 (26, 29); *Tityrus*: see above in the text. In the case of *Alexis*, there is an exceptional continuity: in *Ecl.* 2 it is the name of the boy with whom Corydon is hopelessly in love (2.1, quoted in 5.86), and in 7.55 the singer who praises *formosus Alexis* is again called Corydon. We learn nothing about 'identities'; still, the same pair of names reappears. Two names of main characters occur in one poem only: *Palaemon* (referee in the singing contest of *Ecl.* 3) and *Thyrsis* (one of the contestants of *Ecl.* 7).
[23] Flintoff 1975/6, esp. 19.
[24] Θύρσις (*Id.* 1); Δέλφις, Σιμαίθα (*Id.* 2); Βάττος (*Id.* 4); Λάκων, Μόρσων (*Id.* 5); Δαμοίτας (*Id.* 6); Λυκίδας, Σιμιχίδας (*Id.* 7); Βουκαῖος (*Id.* 10).

elsewhere.[25] For example, *Idyll* 1 is, as it were, the poem of Thyrsis, and the avoidance of the name in the other poems only highlights this fact. In Theocritus, then, the individuality of the single poem is created by, among other things, the individuality of its respective protagonist(s): Thyrsis' reappearance would have a disturbing effect. There is thus nothing like the up-and-down movement so typical of the *Eclogues*, the constant oscillation of a name between 'margin' and 'centre'. If a name reappears within the *Idylls*, the identity of the person with a character already established is sometimes affirmed through explicit allusion (see n. 25). Marginal names remain almost exclusively marginal.[26] This comparison with his literary model shows even more clearly how Virgil turns names into pieces of a systematic 'puzzle'. Again and again, he seems to put up signposts and suggest more or less clearly defined identities, but these soon dissolve.

4. CONCLUSION

The following devices turn Virgil's bucolic nouns, adjectives, and proper names into poetic elements used with a relatively high degree of freedom: (a) combinations of bucolic adjectives with nouns or

[25] Thyrsis in *Id.* 1 sings the dirge for *Daphnis*, whose sufferings are alluded to again in *Id.* 5.20 and 7.73 (and in 5.81, *Daphnis* is mentioned as a singer), while in *Id.* 6 one of the main singers, who seems to have no connection with this *Daphnis*, is given the same name (this way of reusing a name is reminiscent, for once, of the *Eclogues*). The goatherd *Komatas* is a singer (main character) in *Id.* 5, and Lykidas in his song in 7.78–89 mentions the miraculous saving of *Komatas*, who again is a goatherd (78) and a singer (88–9). The name of *Korydon*, a main character in *Id.* 4, reappears in 5.6; *Milon* in *Id.* 4 is the shepherd who takes part in the Olympic games and in *Id.* 10.7, 12 one of the two singers (and a beautiful boy in [Theocr.] *Id.* 8.47). The name *Menalkas*, which becomes so important in Virgil, occurs in the pseudo-Theocritean *Idylls* 8 and 9 only.

[26] Typical names of marginal figures are for example Τίτυρος (*Id.* 3.2; 7.72) and Ἀμαρυλλίς (*Id.* 3.1, 6, 22; 4. 36, 38: a kind of generic name for a beloved woman who is praised). Of course, some names are always names of marginal figures in the *Eclogues* as well (e.g., *Amaryllis*, *Amyntas*, *Galatea*, *Phyllis*), but even with them we find some fluctuations: *Galatea* in 9.39 and 7.37 is clearly the sea nymph, but in *Ecl.* 1.30, 31 and 3.64, 72 the name signifies a 'bucolic' mistress without any hint of the nymph. *Amaryllis* in most cases is the name of a beloved woman, as in Theocritus: *Ecl.* 1.30, 36 (Tityrus'); 2.14, 52 (Corydon's); 3.81 (in a stanza of Damoetas); 9.22 (Lycidas addressing Moeris), but in Alphesiboeus' song in *Ecl.* 8 *Amaryllis* is the name of the servant assisting in the love spell. Names occurring in just one single poem are exceptions on this level as well (e.g., *Thestylis*, the name of a servant in *Ecl.* 2.10).

proper names are continually varied; (b) bucolic nouns are used sparingly in one and the same poem; (c) proper names are employed in a way that blurs individuality.[27] Each of these phenomena reduces the degree of integration of the pieces of bucolic vocabulary into their respective contexts. The bonds are loosened (a) between adjectival attributes and the nouns they qualify, (b) between nouns and the contexts of the poems in which they find themselves, and (c) between proper names and individuals. Virgil's bucolic words can thus not be reduced to their function as conveyors of specific semantic content each and every time they are used, but the way in which they are systematically made to 'float' makes them assume an emblematic value of their own. Through this playful use of language, the *nomina* become parts in a mosaic of language, with the result that the notion that words are, as it were, 'objects in the hand of the poet' is turned into poetic reality.[28] Virgil's bucolic sphere is a world created by the poet, a phenomenon explicitly described in lines 19–20 of *Eclogue* 9, where Lycidas evokes the disastrous consequences that would have obtained if the great bucolic singer Menalcas had been killed in the turmoil of civil war: *quis caneret Nymphas? quis humum florentibus herbis | spargeret aut viridi fontis induceret umbra?* ('Who would sing the nymphs? Who would strew the turf with flowery herbage, or curtain the springs with green shade?').[29] Not only does Menalcas praise the bucolic world in his song, but he alone is able to assemble the bucolic elements: the bucolic world exists only through his singing. The words of the poet and the objects of his poetry have become indistinguishable.

[27] These observations may also shed some new light on what since Jachmann has been described as the curious 'unreality' of the bucolic sphere. Jachmann correctly describes the fluctuation of identities in the *Eclogues* (1922: e.g. 107, 114), but sometimes goes even further, e.g. when he observes that Virgil does not 'stick to the objects themselves' ('haftet nicht so stark an den Dingen als solchen', 1922: 104). This claim can now be supported by section 2 of this paper. As E. A. Schmidt 1972: 177–8 has shown, Jachmann's mistake was to interpret this peculiarity as an expression of an emotional state of the author and of the 'sentimental' character of the *Eclogues* as compared to Theocritus' 'naïve' *Idylls*. Cf. Rumpf 1996: 27–8.

[28] Wellek and Warren 1949: 190: '...poetry organizes a unique, unrepeatable pattern of words, each an object as well as a sign and used in a fashion unpredictable by any system outside of the poem'; see also Jakobson 1981.

[29] For the motif see Lieberg 1982: 5–13 and 1985.

5

Allusive Artistry and Vergil's Revisionary Program: *Eclogues* 1–3

Thomas K. Hubbard

Vergilean criticism over the decades has tended to dismiss *Ecl.* 2 and 3 as early and derivative. The abundance of Theocritean material in these texts has been assumed *ipso facto* to be a sign of imaginative poverty and immature technique.[1] However, beginning with the influential work of Pasquali in the 1940s, a number of critics have suggested that allusion to Greek (and particularly Alexandrian) models in neoteric and Augustan poetry is often not so innocent as to be mere imitation for imitation's sake, but can be a conscious technique for bringing into the text a supplemental level of literary significance beyond the content of the allusion itself.[2] A learned literary audience might be expected to see in an allusion not only testimony to the author's erudition, but a vector of meaning which extends beyond the specific locus of reference to incorporate or challenge the broader context and program of the work or author

---

This paper was first published in 1995 and reprinted in a revised version in Hubbard 1998: 45–75. The version published here is that of 1995, with translations from the 1998 reprint added.

[1] La Penna 1963: 490–2 is virtually alone in not placing these eclogues as the earliest. For the more conventional chronology, see Cartault 1897: 51–77; Kumaniecki 1926; Hahn 1944: 199–205; Barra 1952; Büchner 1955–8: 1251–4; De St. Denis 1942: 3–18; Terzaghi 1963: 829–39; E. A. Schmidt 1974; Coleiro 1979: 93–4.

[2] Pasquali 1951: 11–20 = 1968: 273–82. For a succinct appraisal of Pasquali's successors in this field, see Farrell 1991*b*: 13–25.

alluded to.[3] Conte and others have insisted that the phenomenon of 'poetic memory', on the part of both author and reader, even goes beyond such cases of conscious and specific *aemulatio* to include broader generic allusions, which may function as an implicit grammar of poetic discourse.

Working within a different literary tradition, the critic Harold Bloom has evolved the concept of 'anxiety of influence' and articulated a set of 'revisionary ratios' whereby a belated poet can both acknowledge and repress the influence of a dominant literary precursor.[4] While the revisionary ratios of Latin poetry are very different from those of the nineteenth-century English poets with whom Bloom was concerned, the general concept nevertheless has obvious relevance to interpreting the intersubjective relationship between some Latin poets and their Greek models. Seen in this light, the dense Theocritean allusiveness of *Ecl.* 2 and 3, far from indicating undeveloped poetic skills, may well reflect Vergil at his most sophisticated and self-conscious.

I have argued elsewhere that the Alexandrian bucolic tradition evolved as a genre always already conscious of its literary past, ever concerned with framing the poet's relationship to his precursors.[5] It is thus only natural that this is the genre to which the young Vergil would turn in introducing his literary persona to Roman letters, even as it became the starting point for many other literary careers. Coming from a background of neoteric interest in Alexandrian allusiveness, as evidenced in the works of Catullus, Calvus, Cinna, and perhaps even in early minor works of his own,[6] Vergil found the programmatic self-consciousness of the bucolic mode congenial

---

[3] This theory thus depends on the concept of a 'Model Reader', whose competence is established by a text; on which, see Conte 1986: 30.

[4] Bloom 1973, 1975, 1976, and 1982.

[5] Hubbard 1993.

[6] For the influence of Parthenius and the neoterics on the early Vergil, see Clausen 1987: 4–12. Some poems of the *Catalepton* (especially 5 and 8), a polymetric collection in the style of Catullus, are esteemed as Vergilean, and some critics even regard the whole collection as authentic: see, for example, Westendorp Boerma 1949: xxxi–xlix, and Marmorale 1960: 85–193. For strong metrical arguments in favor of the young Vergil's authorship of the neoteric epyllion *Culex*, see Duckworth 1969: 81–3; for other arguments in favor of its authenticity, see, among others, Arnaldi 1943: 197–214; Barrett 1970: 348–62; Berg 1974: 95–6.

to his intentions in making his first major poetic statement. At the same time, he saw in the limited self-containment of the Theocritean 'green cabinet' a paradigm inviting its own polemical deconstruction, a ripe target for a concerted progression of antithetical poetic responses.

Vergil's Arcadia is a 'poetic memory' of Alexandrian bucolic, albeit a highly selective one, projecting into an assumed background landscape the occasional moments of leisure and fulfillment which we find in Theocritus, whether with the relaxing shepherds at the beginning of *Id.* 1 or the townsmen at the Harvest Festival ending *Id.* 7. However, even within Vergil's own work, this idealized Arcadian life of pastoral innocence seems evident more in its violation or transcendence than in its presence. Arcadia is simultaneously Vergil's own construction and object of deconstructive counterpoint. This dynamic opposition forms the core of Vergil's poetic practice both within individual eclogues and in the Eclogue Book as a whole, which as many scholars have emphasized, must in a sense be read as one continuous poem manifesting itself in different phases.[7] The first half of the book has often been seen as a positive construction of a pastoral vision, while the second half dramatizes progressive alienation from that vision, as each poem of the first half is taken up and responded to in reverse order.[8] There is thus a systematic revisionary tension between the poems of the Eclogue Book itself, complementing the intertextual dynamics which position each poem in its relation to the work of Theocritus and Vergil's other precursors. Overlapping the book's division into mutually reflecting halves is a division into triads,[9] with *Eclogues* 1–3 articulating Vergil's revisionary challenge to his precursor Theocritus most directly and personally in terms of self-conscious *aemulatio*, *Eclogues* 4–6 challenging and transcending the norms of bucolic as a generic category, *Eclogues* 7–9 presenting Vergil's own poetic voice as an already established model for subsequent dialogic revisionism, with *Eclogue* 10 embodying and recapitulating all three movements. Joseph Farrell has recently argued for an 'allusive program' in the *Georgics*, with

---

[7] See the studies of Maury 1944; Otis 1964: 128–43; Rudd 1976: 119–44; van Sickle 1978; Coleiro 1979: 94–101. On the concept of the 'Augustan poetry book' generally, see Van Sickle 1980: 5–42.

[8] See especially Becker 1955: 317–28 and Otis 1964: 130–1.

[9] For this structure, see Hahn 1944: 239–41 and Galinsky 1965: 171–91.

Vergil progressing from one set of didactic models (Hesiod and Aratus) in *Geo.* 1 to another (Lucretius) in *Geo.* 2 and 3, finally abandoning the didactic mode with the Homeric texture of references in *Geo.* 4. The program of the *Eclogues* is not so much one of selecting different allusive foci as a reflection of Vergil's progressive self-realization as a poet, expressed through his evolving allusive relationship with his literary predecessors, who are most dominant as a personal presence in the first poems of the Book, and progressively less so as the Book unfolds, transforming them into a recessive background of 'poetic memory'. This notional self-development says nothing about the actual biographical date of each eclogue's composition, if there even was such a thing as a single *imprimatur* date for each.[10] Vergil surely intended us to read the *Eclogues* as a developing sequence in exactly the order in which they have been transmitted, whatever the date of each one's conception. Accordingly as a prelude to a larger study of the development of Vergil's allusive program in the whole Book, I shall examine in this paper the first group of *Eclogues*, 1–3, from the standpoint of Vergil's conscious use of *aemulatio* as a technique of poetic self-definition.

Eclogue 1 is both exemplary and programmatic for Vergil's technique of utilizing allusion to the Theocritean subtext in a way that is constitutive of literary significance, and not merely ornamental or material. The famous opening of the poem (and thus of the Eclogue Book) clearly evokes the opening lines of *Idyll* 1,[11] which almost certainly stood at the beginning of Vergil's edition of Theocritus as in ours:[12]

---

[10] The various numerological symmetries which scholars have noted in the collection suggest at least some revision of poems at the time they were assembled into book form. While I do not accept most attempts to create numerological symmetries through textual surgery and am sceptical of many supposed symmetries internal to the poems, I do believe that some correspondences are undeniable (e.g. that *Ecl.* $2 + 8 = Ecl.$ $3 + 7 = 181$ lines, and *Ecl.* $1 + 9 = 150$ lines, corresponding to *Ecl.* $4 + 6 = 149$ lines). In addition to the studies cited in n. 8 above, see E. L. Brown 1963 and Lallemant-Maron 1972 for the intellectual background to Vergil's use of numerology.

[11] See Pöschl 1964: 10–11; Wright 1983: 108; Van Sickle 1986: 39–40. There may also be some contamination with *Id.* 7.88–9, as argued by Cartault 1897: 346.

[12] Although the order of Theocritus' *Idylls* varies in different manuscripts, all of those that contain *Idyll* 1 place it at the beginning, suggesting that it was so placed in the archetype. For a thorough review of the manuscripts and papyri, see Gow 1952b: 1.xxx–lxix.

Tityre, tu patulae recubans sub tegmine fagi
silvestrem tenui Musam meditaris avena... (*Ecl.* 1.1–2)
Tityrus, resting beneath the cover of the spreading beech
You ponder the woodland Muse with your thin reed of oat.

ἁδύ τι τὸ ψιθύρισμα καὶ ἁ πίτυς, αἰπόλε, τήνα
ἁ ποτὶ ταῖς παγαῖσι μελίσδεται, ἁδὺ δὲ καὶ τύ
συρίσδες· μετὰ Πᾶνα τὸ δεύτερον ἆθλον ἀποισῇ. (*Id.* 1.1–3)
Goatherd, there is some sweet whisper as that pine tree
Near the spring sings out, and you also sweetly
Play the pipe; after Pan you will take the second prize.

In each case, a shepherd encounters another piping under the shade of a tree and compliments his song. However, the echo is undercut by a significant deviation from the model, as the Theocritean pine is transformed into a Vergilean beech. This change seems intended as a conscious correction of the original:[13] pines are tall, narrow, low-branching, and drop needles and cones, making them far from satisfactory as a locus for pastoral music, whereas Vergil's beech is a large tree with spreading branches (emphasized by the epithet *patulae*), ideal for noontime shade and relaxation.[14] Vergil's more careful consideration of the physical milieu is coupled with a more intensive focus on the person of the singer, named as the first word of the poem (*Tityre*), in contrast to the nameless Theocritean goatherd who is introduced almost as an afterthought to the description of the pine tree and spring, which seem to make a melody on their own. In Theocritus the shepherd appears merely as an element in the landscape, whereas Vergil subordinates the landscape to its proper role as a background to the activity of the shepherd.

The prominence accorded the name 'Tityrus' thus signals a conscious effort on Vergil's part to foreground what is secondary in his

---

[13] On the use of allusion as a form of programmatic correction, see Thomas 1982*b*: 148 and 1986: 185–9. This is related to the concept of *oppositio in imitando* elaborated by Giangrande 1967: 85.

[14] On the size and spreading habit of Mediterranean beech trees, see the discussions of Sargeaunt 1920: 43–5 and Abbe 1965: 80–1. The beech tree comes to have a programmatic significance in Vergil's *Eclogues*: the site of Corydon's lament (*Ecl.* 2.3), the wood for Alcimedon's cup (*Ecl.* 3.37), the bark on which Mopsus' song is written (*Ecl.* 5.13), the broken deadwood symbolizing the death of the pastoral world (*Ecl.* 9.9). For a different explanation of Vergil's choice of the beech as his programmatic tree, see Kenney 1983: 49–50. On the other hand the pine is characteristically Theocritean, the locus for song not only in *Idyll* 1 but also in *Id.* 3.38.

source. This is particularly clear when we consider the provenance of the name within the Theocritean corpus. Tityrus appears in *Id.* 7.72, where Lycidas describes him as singing of Daphnis and Comatas; he is little more than a name here, parallel to the two unnamed flute-players providing entertainment and subordinate in interest to the banqueting Lycidas as well as to the legendary Daphnis and Comatas of whom he sings. Equally illuminating is *Id.* 3.1–5, where Tityrus is asked to tend the goats while the singer of the idyll serenades Amaryllis. The framing vocatives *Tityre, tu* and *tu, Tityre* of *Ecl.* 1.1 and 4 seem to be modelled on the framing Τίτυρ'... Τίτυρε of *Id.* 3.3–4. Even more significant is Vergil's adaptation of the beloved Amaryllis, first mentioned in *Ecl.* 1.5 and revealed as Tityrus' contubernalis in *Ecl.* 1.30–7. The subordinate Tityrus of Theocritus in effect supplants the goatherd to become the lover of Amaryllis himself. Moreover, whereas the goatherd of *Id.* 3 was an unsuccessful and rejected suitor, Vergil's Tityrus wins Amaryllis' loyalty and devotion: their relationship embodies pastoral love in something close to an ideal form, in contrast with Tityrus' former and more oppressive relationship to Galatea (another unsuccessfully wooed figure in Theocritus). The secondary figure in Theocritus thus becomes primary for Vergil, taking over where Theocritus' goatherd left off and succeeding where he failed. This dynamic of erotic succession can only be meant as a trope for the relationship of literary succession between Theocritean bucolic and Vergilean pastoral, with Vergil making central the marginal in Theocritus and 'succeeding' (in both senses of the word) where his predecessor failed. In teaching the woods to 'echo' (*Ecl.* 1.5 *resonare*) the name Amaryllis, Tityrus expresses Vergil's allusive echoing of Theocritus through appropriation of Amaryllis.

However, in addition to being emblematic for Vergilean pastoral and its place within literary tradition (an identification reconfirmed by the invocation of Tityrus in *Ecl.* 6.4–5),[15] Tityrus appears as a

[15] While I do not accept the Servian identification of Tityrus and his farm with Vergil and his, so long a commonplace of criticism (but most recently and devastatingly refuted by du Quesnay 1981: 32–8), it is legitimate to see 'Tityrus' as one of several voices who may stand as a programmatic synecdoche for the world of Vergilean pastoral: see the intelligent discussion of this question by Kollmann 1973*b* and Wright 1983: 112.

dramatic character within the dialogic situation of *Eclogue* 1. His emergence from secondary to primary character within the pastoral tradition parallels his dramatic story within *Eclogue* 1, as he moves from slavery to freedom. Sitting in leisure under the shady beech tree, he encounters the goatherd Meliboeus, a character whose story of alienation from the pastoral world stands in stark contrast to Tityrus' happy fulfillment. Meliboeus' progression from good fortune as owner of his own farm to calamity in loss of his land is a clear foil to Tityrus' opposite turn of fortune. To the extent that Tityrus is a programmatic figure for the emergence of Vergil's pastoral vision, Meliboeus becomes a contrapuntal figure of doubt and denial, a living testimony that not all men share in the benevolence of Tityrus' *deus* and the political order which he represents.

Meliboeus' status as the antithesis and negation of the pastoral vision is carefully reinforced by the allusive structure of his utterances within the dialogue. It must first be noted that Meliboeus is not even a character from the world of Theocritean bucolic, nor is his story of dispossession one with any parallels in the *Idylls*. Rather Meliboeus' story represents the intrusion of Roman political reality into the bucolic genre's characteristic state of Epicurean detachment. After learning of Tityrus' good fortune, Meliboeus gives a concrete illustration of his own misery and that of his herd by pointing to a sick she-goat, who had just abandoned her twin offspring after giving birth to them on a rock (*Ecl.* 1.13–15). Twin births are normally signs of fertility and good fortune, and indeed the she-goat who has just given birth to twins is a detail taken from *Id.* 1.25–6, the very same idyll alluded to and corrected in the opening line of *Eclogue* 1. However, in Theocritus the she-goat is mentioned in a very positive context as part of the prize offered Thyrsis for his song of Daphnis: even after nursing her twin offspring, the she-goat still has enough milk left over to fill two pails a day. The symbol of bounty and profusion in Theocritus is transformed into a symbol of sterility and failure for Meliboeus.[16] The stark contrast between the two she-goats would accentuate the pathos of Meliboeus' situation for those readers who recognize the allusion. Moreover, Meliboeus' struggling she-goat, like the more vigorous one offered Thyrsis, is

[16] See Gigante 1981: 39–40.

mentioned as a preliminary to the request for a song—Thyrsis' song of Daphnis in *Idyll* 1, Tityrus' story of the young deus in *Eclogue* 1. In Meliboeus' case, however, the she-goat is not a prize, but an indication of his destitution and inability to offer a prize in return for what he wants to hear. Meliboeus also echoes Theocritus at the end of Tityrus' story, again in a manner suggesting his utter alienation from the world of bucolic bounty and plenitude. Complimenting the old man on his good fortune, Meliboeus pours out an almost lyrical description of the life of pastoral leisure which Tityrus leads:

> fortunate senex, hic inter flumina nota
> et fontes sacros frigus captabis opacum;
> hinc tibi, quae semper, vicino ab limite saepes
> Hyblaeis apibus florem depasta salicti
> saepe levi somnum suadebit inire susurro;
> hinc alta sub rupe canet frondator ad auras,
> nec tamen interea raucae, tua cura, palumbes
> nec gemere aeria cessabit turtur ab ulmo. (*Ecl.* 1.46–58)

> Fortunate oldster, here among familiar streams
> And sacred springs you will enjoy the shady coolness;
> As always before, from the neighbor's boundary lines here
> The willow hedge with its flowers feeding Hyblaean bees
> Will often lull you to sleep with its soft whisper;
> Here beneath the high cliff the vine pruner will sing to the breeze
> And neither the noisy pigeons, your favorites,
> Nor the turtledove will cease to moan from the lofty elm.

It has generally been recognized that this passage is based on Simichidas' relaxed celebration of the harvest festival at the end of *Idyll* 7:[17]

> πολλαὶ δ' ἄμμιν ὕπερθε κατὰ κρατὸς δονέοντο
> αἴγειραι πτελέαι τε. τὸ δ' ἐγγύθεν ἱερὸν ὕδωρ
> Νυμφᾶν ἐξ ἄντροιο κατειβόμενον κελάρυζε.
> τοὶ δὲ ποτὶ σκιαραῖς ὀροδαμνίσιν αἰθαλίωνες
> τέττιγες λαλαγεῦντες ἔχον πόνον· ἁ δ' ὀλολυγών
> τηλόθεν ἐν πυκιναῖσι βάτων τρύζεσκεν ἀκάνθαις·
> ἄειδον κόρυδοι καὶ ἀκανθίδες, ἔστενε τρυγών,
> πωτῶντο ξουθαὶ περὶ πίδακας ἀμφὶ μέλισσαι. (*Id.* 7.135–42)

---

[17] However, Cartault 1897: 348–9, anxious to valorize the element of personal experience in *Eclogue* 1, denies any Theocritean influence here.

> Many poplars and elms rustled above our heads,
> And nearby the sacred spring trickling down
> From the cave of the Nymphs made its plashing noise;
> On the shady branches the unseen cicadas
> Did their work, chattering away; the tree frog
> Far off cried in the dense thornbushes;
> Larks and finches sang, the dove moaned,
> And nimble honeybees flitted about the springs.

Trees, shade, a sacred fountain, a gentle breeze, singing birds and humming bees are all appropriated by Vergil from this subtext.[18] The source is subtly acknowledged by the designation of the bees as 'Hyblaean', referring to Theocritus' native Sicily. But Vergil imports into this bucolic picture two non-Theocritean details, the singing pruner (*Ecl.* 1.56 *frondator*) and the boundary hedge (*Ecl.* 1.53 *vicino ab limite saepes*). We have introduced into the pretty picture of bucolic leisure two antithetical elements embodying the demands of the real world—labor and property. The issue of property is of course the crux of Meliboeus' problems, as he is expelled from his farm and wanders with his dwindling herd to some unknown destination.[19] The image of violated boundaries is brought to the fore with the adynata of *Ecl.* 1.59–62 (deer in the sky, fish on land, the Parthian in Gaul, the German in the East) and Meliboeus' imagined wanderings to the four corners of the Earth (*Ecl.* 1.64–6). The evocative rustic tableau thus reminds us of the real world's intrusion and Meliboeus' own alienation from such happiness; the perfect pastoral moment contains within itself the seeds of its potential loss and negation. Where the Theocritean subtext was a first-person description of pleasure as it was experienced, the Vergilian rewriting of that subtext becomes the description of a style of life from which the first-person has been disenfranchised and which he will never know again. Even as Tityrus is by deployment of allusions set up to be

---

[18] The Theocritean subtext itself may bear an allusive relation to Callimachus' use of the pure sacred fountain and honeybees as programmatic symbols for the high standards of his poetic doctrine (*Hymn* 2.110–12), and Vergil may well be alluding to this secondary subtext as well, counterposed to the 'muddy stream' (Callim. *Hymn* 2.108–9) of the 'chalk-bearing' Oaxes, Meliboeus' allotted venue (*Ecl.* 1.65). See Wright 1983: 137–8.

[19] On the concept of 'property' here as an antithetical negation of the ideal pastoral community of possessions, see Putnam 1970: 46–54.

the rightful successor of Theocritean bucolic, Meliboeus is by an equally resonant network of allusions set up as its antithesis and denial. There is little reason to believe the Servian identification of Tityrus with Vergil himself and to regard the eclogue as an allegory for Vergil regaining lost property through Octavian's intervention. We should rather see in the two shepherds illustration of the inevitable result of Octavian's land policy: there are both winners and losers from such wholesale changes. From the standpoint of Tityrus and the mainstream pastoral program, Octavian may well be a god, but there is within *Eclogue* 1 that dialogic 'other' voice of Meliboeus, divorced from the pastoral locale and the advantages of Octavian's New World Order.

Through the mechanism of a single speaker, *Eclogue* 2 dramatizes the same ambivalence of pastoral self-presentation: Corydon's invitation to Alexis is phrased as an extended encomium of rustic life, but the recognition of his love as a form of *dementia* also calls into question the value and appeal of the proffered life-style. On a second plane of signification, the text makes careful use of Theocritean subtexts both to assert and deny its own efficacy as a poetic expression. Its chief model, *Idyll* 11, explicitly presents Polyphemus' song to Galatea as an example of poetry's curative powers; *Eclogue* 2 not only lacks the extended didactic prologue of *Idyll* 11 emphasizing this idea, but ends on a note of studied ambiguity. Moreover, in the tradition of *Idyll* 5, this eclogue exploits the theme of pederasty as a metaphor for poetic influence: Corydon's rejected love for the city boy Alexis is in a sense a reflection of Vergil's anxiety about the failure of his own pastoral poetry in the eyes of his sophisticated literary audience. Corydon's yearning for a boy-lover to whom he can teach the country arts is clearly associated with a desire for poetic influence among a generation of successors. Corydon's failure in his quest stands as a gesture of poetic self-doubt at this point in the program of Vergil's Eclogue Book.

Although *Idyll* 11 is the dominant model for *Eclogue* 2, it is not in fact alluded to until v. 19. The opening lines incorporate seriatim a parade of references to other Theocritean texts which in one way or another also reflect the principal themes of poetry, love, and their interaction. The very name Corydon alludes to the aspiring young shepherd/poet of *Idyll* 4, coming into his own under the wry scrutiny of the urban sophisticate Battus (= Callimachus).[20] But where Theocritus' Corydon ultimately proved himself in the eyes of his hitherto condescending interlocutor, Vergil's Corydon fails to move Alexis with his poetic appeal.[21] This poetic failure is foregrounded with the first words of his address to Alexis, imitating the first words of the goatherd's unsuccessful serenade to Amaryllis in *Id.* 3.6–9:

> o crudelis Alexi, nihil mea carmina curas?
> nil nostri miserere? mori me denique cogis?   (*Ecl.* 2.6–7)
>
> O cruel Alexis, do you care nothing for my songs?
> Do you pity us not at all? Will you force me finally to die?

> ὦ χαρίεσσ' Ἀμαρυλλί, τί μ' οὐκέτι τοῦτο κατ' ἄντρον
> παρκύπτοισα καλεῖς, τὸν ἐρωτύλον; ἦ ῥά με μισεῖς;
> ἦ ῥά γέ τοι σιμὸς καταφαίνομαι ἐγγύθεν ἦμεν,
> νύμφα, καὶ προγένειος; ἀπάγξασθαί με ποησεῖς.   (*Id.* 3.6–9)
>
> O charming Amaryllis, why do you no longer call on me,
> Your love-toy, peeping out of this cave? Do you hate me?
> Is it, my nymph, because I look snub-nosed and pointy-jawed
> When I am close? You will make me hang myself.

The parallels of word-order are obvious (*o* + epithet + vocative name at the beginning, infinitive + *me* + second-person verb at the end), but it is significant that Vergil varies the Theocritean focus on physical appearance by instead emphasizing Corydon's songs as the thing rejected in the very first line.

Corydon's next two lines allude to the opening of Lycidas' greeting to Simichidas in *Id.* 7.21–3:[22]

> nunc etiam pecudes umbras et frigora captant,
> nunc viridis etiam occultant spineta lacertos...   (*Ecl.* 2.8–9)

---

[20] The view that Battus is the Battid Callimachus originates with R. Reitzenstein 1893: 229–34.

[21] The name Alexis is foreign to Theocritus and is fundamentally a figure of Hellenistic erotic epigram (see *Anth. Pal.* 7.100 (Plato), 12.127, 12.164 (Meleager); Robinson and Fluck 1937: 50 and du Quesnay 1979: 47), and may even be meant to evoke the idea of 'Alexandria' itself, the center of learning and sophistication. Hubaux 1927: 46–64 sees this as one in a series of borrowings from Hellenistic erotic epigram in *Eclogue* 2. For the urban provenance of Corydon's Theocritean interlocutor Battus, see Lattimore 1973: 322–3.

[22] On the parallel, see Posch 1969: 35.

Now even the flocks seek shade and cool;
Now the thorn-brakes hide even the greeen lizards.

Σιμιχίδα, πᾷ δὴ τὺ μεσαμέριον πόδας ἕλκεις,
ἁνίκα δὴ καὶ σαῦρος ἐν αἱμασιαῖσι καθεύδει,
οὐδ᾽ ἐπιτυμβίδιοι κορυδαλλίδες ἠλαίνοντι; (*Id.* 7.21–3)

Simichidas, whither do you drag your feet at noon,
When even the lizard sleeps in the stone wall
And not even the tomb-crested larks wander about?

The intensity of the noontide heat is exemplified in both passages by the retreat of even the sun-loving lizard; in Vergil's text the lizards are paired off with the herds of livestock who seek shade, in Theocritus with birds. For both authors, however, the animals' retreat from the sun is contrasted with the extraordinary presence of a man exposed to its full ardor. The noontide encounter of *Idyll* 7 appears to be a numinous moment,[23] the backdrop for Simichidas' investiture as a poet by the mysterious Lycidas. *Idyll* 7 celebrates poetry as a tool of emotional detachment and self-distancing from pederastic love, as reflected both in Lycidas' nonchalant farewell to the boy Ageanax and in Simichidas' song advising Aratus to free himself from the clutches of the boy Philinus. The tendency of the subtext behind this allusion is thus in many ways antithetical to that of the first allusion, asserting poetic efficacy as against the poetic futility of *Idyll* 3, Epicurean detachment from love as opposed to *Idyll* 3's uncritical self-immersion in love.

The next two lines parade before us yet another conspicuous allusion to the opening lines of a Theocritean lover. The Thestylis who is involved in mixing herbs for the harvesters' lunch (*Ecl.* 2.10–11) cannot help but evoke the Thestylis of *Id.* 2.1–2, the maid directed by Simaetha to bring herbs and ingredients for her magical brew.[24] Here too we see the theme of a seemingly hopeless love for a beautiful youth, whom the speaker of the idyll attempts to recapture by a binding song. While the effectiveness of that song in winning back her lover is dubious, Simaetha does through her narrative retelling of events achieve a certain emotional distance and ability to endure her abandonment.[25] In a sense the three

[23] See F. J. Williams 1971; Segal 1981: 121–2; E. L. Brown 1981: 93.
[24] In addition to these opening lines, we also see Thestylis mixing ingredients in *Id.* 2.18–19 and 59–62.
[25] See Griffiths 1979: 87–8; Segal 1981: 83–4 and 1985: 114–18, with the qualifications of Parry 1988: 48.

Theocritean idylls evoked in *Ecl.* 2.6–11 form a priamel of different possibilities for the interaction of love and song: song attempting to persuade the beloved but failing (*Idyll* 3), song releasing the lover from love (*Idyll* 7), and song attempting to persuade the beloved and failing, but succeeding in releasing the lover from love (*Idyll* 2). We thus see a gradual intertextual progression toward the dynamics of *Idyll* 11, the primary model for the eclogue, first called to mind explicitly in *Ecl.* 2.19–22.

Lines 12–13 return to *Idyll* 7 for their source, but trope the original in a significant way:

> at mecum raucis, tua dum vestigia lustro,
> sole sub ardenti resonant arbusta cicadis.   (*Ecl.* 2.12–13)

But along with me only the vineyards echo with their croaking cicadas
Beneath the burning sun, while I track down your footsteps.

> τοὶ δὲ ποτὶ σκιαραῖς ὀροδαμνίσιν αἰθαλίωνες
> τέττιγες λαλαγεῦντες ἔχον πόνον.   (*Id.* 7.138–9)

On the shady branches the unseen cicadas
Did their work, chattering away.

Vergil places the cicadas, like the speaker himself, beneath the 'burning sun' (*Ecl.* 2.13 *sole sub ardenti*), appropriately externalizing the 'burning' passion of Corydon (*Ecl.* 2.1 *ardebat*). But for Theocritus, the cicadas were associated specifically with shade, again like the speaker himself, who is here relaxing at the harvest festival after a long journey from town.[26] The frenetic pacing of Corydon is implicitly contrasted with the idle lounging of Simichidas and his friends on beds of leaves and grass (*Id.* 7.131–4); the heat of *Ecl.* 2 is contrasted with the deep shade and cool spring emerging from the Nymphs' cave in Theocritus' *locus amoenus* (*Id.* 7.135–7).[27] Simichidas' community of friends at the harvest festival contrasts with Corydon's lonely alienation (*Ecl.* 2.4 *solus*), even as his Epicurean

---

[26] Of course, Theocritus' cicadas are themselves an allusion to Callimachean poetics, for which the shrill cicada represents the slight and delicate character of Alexandrian lyric (*Aetia* 1, fr. 1.29–30; see also *Id.* 1.52 and Hubbard 1993: 29 n. 9). By here calling the cicadas *raucis*, Vergil consciously associates them with harshness (like that of Callimachus' braying asses) rather than sweetness, and in so doing challenges Alexandrian convention.

[27] Vergil has *arbusta* making noise, even as Theocritus has trees humming (*Id.* 7.135–6); but for Theocritus, the trees' sound is the rustling of a gentle breeze (an image of coolness and comfort), whereas the cicadas' noise in Vergil reflects heat and discomfort.

detachment from passion, announced in his song (*Id.* 7.96–127), forms a counterpoint to Corydon's complete absorption in passion. Indeed, the harvest celebration so vividly and sensuously described at the end of *Idyll* 7 is a poetic paradigm of the Epicurean ideal. This is of course the same passage which formed the basis for Meliboeus' wistful description of the life now available to Tityrus, but no longer available to himself (*Ecl.* 1.51–8). By evoking it here and metonymically negating it (transforming the cicadas from an image with connotations of leisure and detachment to one with connotations of intense physical and emotional discomfort), Corydon expresses the impossibility of the Epicurean bucolicism of *Idyll* 7 for himself, even as it was impossible for Meliboeus. By allusively discounting the solution of *Idyll* 7, this passage suggests the unlikelihood of any cure for Corydon's love through poetry.

In lines 14–15 we have an allusion to *Idyll* 3, another one of the three Theocritean texts programmatically evoked in the opening sequence of *Ecl.* 2.6–11:

> nonne fuit satius tristis Amaryllidis iras
> atque superba pati fastidia?   (*Ecl.* 2.14–15)
> Wasn't it better to put up with the unhappy tantrums
> And lofty disdain of Amaryllis?

Amaryllis, of course, is the indifferent beloved addressed by the miserable goatherd of *Idyll* 3, whose opening lines are imitated by *Ecl.* 2.6–7. By suggesting that her temper and quarrelsomeness would be more bearable than the cold disdain of Alexis, Corydon characterizes his own situation as even worse than that of the Theocritean goatherd. Amaryllis, however, also reminds us of *Eclogue* 1, where the unsuccessful goatherd of *Idyll* 3 has been supplanted by Vergil's Tityrus as Amaryllis' lover; only for Tityrus, she was no longer a temperamental and difficult *prima donna*, but had become a caring and supportive wife (*Ecl.* 1.30–2).

Lines 12–13 and 14–15 thus both serve to expand the Theocritean frame of reference set up in the three allusions of *Ecl.* 2.6–11, by alluding to two of the same idylls again, but with specific reference to points which had already been used in a creatively revisionary way in the preceding eclogue: in alluding to Theocritus here, Vergil also alludes to his own programmatic use of Theocritus. In the present context, both allusions are polemical, the first denying the possibility of Theocritean bucolic leisure (such as that of *Id.* 7.131–9) for Corydon, the second implying that Corydon's love is even more hopeless than the passion of Theocritus' most lovelorn pastoral singer (the goatherd of *Idyll* 3). That both Theocritean passages had already been used by Vergil in a polemical fashion in the first poem of the Eclogue Book only reinforces their polemical character here.[28] After an initial parade of straightforward Theocritean allusions, we are here given two double-allusions which tropologically announce Vergil's capacity for changing and even negating his Theocritean models.[29]

Much the same function is served by the following allusion to Menalcas, another Theocritean foil to Corydon's Alexis:

> nonne Menalcan,
> quamvis ille niger, quamvis tu candidus esses?
> o formose puer, nimium ne crede colori:
> alba ligustra cadunt, vaccinia nigra leguntur.   (*Ecl.* 2.15–18)
>
> Wasn't it better to have Menalcas,
> Although he is dark and you are white?
> Fair boy, don't rely on your complexion too much;
> Pale privets fall to the ground, but dark hyacinths are plucked.

Vergil introduces Menalcas as a swarthy, rustic contrast to the pale city-boy Alexis. Menalcas is indeed a figure from the countryside of Theocritean bucolic, but he is presented there as a fair, red-haired youth (*Id.* 8.3), equal in age and appearance to Daphnis, the paradigm of male beauty. Vergil thus appropriates Menalcas, like Amaryllis, by a form of reversal. Indeed, we shall see *Eclogue* 3 make Menalcas its principal programmatic character, a symbol of Vergil's challenge to established bucolic tradition as represented by the older Damoetas. In the foils of Amaryllis and Menalcas, we thus see two Theocritean figures who are taken over by Vergil and consciously transformed in persona, putting the transformation of Polyphemus/Corydon and Galatea/Alexis in this eclogue into the

---

[28] This also calls into question the general assumption that *Eclogue* 2 is one of the two earliest poems in the collection, for which see Otis 1964: 120, Galinsky 1965: 162, and the sources listed in n. 1 above.

[29] For the sophistication with which Vergil practices such 'self-reference', sometimes in conjunction with allusions to other authors, see Thomas 1986: 182–5.

context of the revisionary program evident in the poems which precede (*Eclogue* 1—Amaryllis) and follow it (*Eclogue* 3—Menalcas). The parallels between Corydon's praise of his own wealth and talents (*Ecl.* 2.19–24) and Polyphemus' (*Id.* 11.34–40) are obvious and have been amply discussed.[30] But as so often, what is really most interesting is the way Vergil chooses to vary and enrich his model. Where Polyphemus boasted of owning 1,000 animals (*Id.* 11.34 βοτὰ χίλια),[31] Corydon specifies 1,000 female lambs (*Ecl.* 2.21 *mille agnae*), appealing to Alexis' sense of refinement and delicacy, and at the same time also implying that he has many other sheep as well.[32] That the lambs are characterized as wandering in Sicilian mountains (*Ecl.* 2.21 *Siculis in montibus*) seems a self-conscious allusion to the Theocritean context and provenance of the line. The second point at which Corydon departs from the Cyclops' model is in his description of his own song: whereas Polyphemus boasted merely that he was the best piper among the Cyclopses (not terribly strong competition, one supposes), Corydon presumes to sing such things as 'Dircaean Amphion in Actaean Aracynthus' (*Ecl.* 2.23–4). Amphion, of course, was legendary for musical powers which could move even stones to form the walls of Thebes. But Amphion was not a particularly pastoral figure (as is almost acknowledged with the qualification *si quando armenta vocabat*); the recherché, geographical learning of the laborious Alexandrian line with four names seems awkward and out of place in a context where the speaker has just been talking about his fresh milk and lambs. The learning appears particularly pretentious and overblown if, as some commentators believe, this allusion is meant by Vergil to be understood as a solecism.[33] Far from moving stones, Corydon is in the end revealed as unable to move even a boy.

[30] Cf. Cartault 1897: 93–5; Posch 1969: 38; du Quesnay 1979: 64–5.
[31] βοτά can refer to sheep and cattle mixed together, or grazing animals in general. See the review of the word's usage by Gerber 1969: 178–9.
[32] See du Quesnay 1979: 64. Mayer 1983*b* fails to understand the hyperbole inherent in this boast and thus misinterprets these lines as proof that Corydon was not a slave. Van Sickle 1987: 127–9 speaks of a slave's *peculium*, but even here, we should emphasize the excess inherent in Corydon's boast; whatever his civil status, Corydon clearly exaggerates in a naive attempt to impress Alexis.
[33] See Rose 1942: 34; Putnam 1970: 97–8; and Moore-Blunt 1977: 28–9. However Coleman 1977: 96–7 denies any solecism here. For what may be a similar usage of intentional solecism, see the allusion to Oaxes in *Ecl.* 1.65 and Hatzikosta 1987.

Whereas the Cyclops' self-praise is prefaced by a certain diffidence about his grotesque physical appearance (*Id.* 11.30–3), Corydon extends his self-praise to this category as well (*Ecl.* 2.25–7), moving away from *Idyll* 11 as a model to the shepherd Damoetas' ironic song delivered in the persona of the Cyclops (*Id.* 6.34–8). Corydon clearly misses the irony of these lines, in which the Cyclops is imagined as seeing himself in reflective water and finding his ugly image beautiful.[34] But we can be sure that Vergil did not miss it and at the authorial level transfers the irony of the Theocritean subtext into an ironic reflection on Corydon, who exaggerates the dissonance of the subtext even further by going so far as to compare himself to the legendary Daphnis. The comparison to Daphnis is more than just Corydon's self-flattery concerning outward appearance, but constitutes a literary self-comparison as well, when we remember that Daphnis was the co-singer and equal of Damoetas in *Idyll* 6 (see especially 6.42–6): for Corydon to be the equal of Daphnis is thus to be the equal of his teacher Damoetas (*Ecl.* 2.37–9) and the Theocritean subtext for which both Damoetas and Daphnis are metonyms. Corydon's capacity for self-deception is implicitly acknowledged, however, with the qualifying *si numquam fallit imago* (*Ecl.* 2.27 'if a reflection never deceives') attached to his self-comparison; we are only too aware, with Polyphemus' case in mind, that reflections do indeed deceive, whether in regard to one's appearance or one's song.

The imitation of Polyphemus is continued with Corydon's appeals to Alexis to inhabit a humble pastoral hut with him, hunt deer, and drive herds (*Ecl.* 2.28–30); we are reminded of the Cyclops' appeal to Galatea to sleep in his cave (*Id.* 11.44–9) and ply the shepherd's trade along with him (*Id.* 11.65–6). Hunting is an act which Corydon adds to his Theocritean model, particularly relevant in this context as a form of male adolescent initiation and bonding, often with homoerotic overtones.[35] In *Ecl.* 2.31–9, a passage long seen as almost entirely

---

[34] Moore-Blunt 1977: 31 notes the harsh metrical texture (3 elisions) and comic diction (*adeo* in the sense of 'excessively') undercutting the assertion of beauty in *Ecl.* 2.25. On the ironizing force of the Theocritean allusion here, see Putnam 1970: 117–18.

[35] Moreover, in Cretan ritual, the initiatory hunt was especially framed as a period of homosexual association with an older man: see Brelich 1969: 198–200; Calame 1977: 1.421–3; Vidal-Naquet 1986: 117–22; Sergent 1986: 7–48.

without Theocritean precedent,[36] Corydon's invitation is expanded to include instruction in the art of the pan-pipe:

> mecum una in silvis imitabere Pana canendo
> (Pan primum calamos cera coniungere pluris
> instituit, Pan curat ovis oviumque magistros),
> nec te paeniteat calamo trivisse labellum:
> haec eadem ut sciret, quid non faciebat Amyntas?
> est mihi disparibus septem compacta cicutis
> fistula, Damoetas dono mihi quam dedit olim,
> et dixit moriens: 'te nunc habet ista secundum';
> dixit Damoetas, invidit stultus Amyntas.

> Together with me you will imitate Pan in the woods by singing
> (Pan first taught us to join several reeds with wax;
> Pan cares for sheep and the masters of sheep),
> Nor should you be ashamed to have rubbed your lips with the reed:
> What would Amyntas not do to learn these same arts?
> I have a pan-pipe fixed together out of seven unequal reeds,
> Which Damoetas once gave me as a gift,
> And he said as he died: 'Let it now have you as its second owner.'
> Damoetas so spoke, and the fool Amyntas was envious.

Again, the associations of such tutelage are both initiatory and homoerotic. Pan's discovery of the pan-pipe is explicitly motivated here by a desire for teaching, connected with his care for 'sheep and the masters of sheep'.[37] Pan's reputation as a lover of fair country youths is familiar especially in the artistic tradition.[38] Most likely to be known by Vergil and his audience was a famous Hellenistic sculpture group by Heliodorus (c.100 BC) and existing in numerous Roman copies, at least one of which Pliny (*HN* 36.35) tells us was in the Porticus of Octavia in Rome.[39] In it we see the smiling goat-god

---

[36] See Cartault 1897: 97–8; Galinsky 1965: 164–5; Posch 1969: 41–2, although the last sees some precedent for the gift of the syrinx in Aegon's gift to Corydon in *Id.* 4.28–30 and Lycon's gift to Lacon in *Id.* 5.8; these parallels seem to be generally intertextual rather than specific allusions.

[37] Of course, the syrinx was also from the first connected with Pan's unrestrained sexuality. See Borgeaud 1988: 79–87.

[38] The tradition is at least as old as the name vase of the so-called 'Pan Painter' (*ARV* 550.1), depicting an ithyphallic herm watching an ithyphallic Pan chasing a Phrygian youth. In literature, see Callim. fr. 689 Pf., Theoc. *Epigr.* 3, and Borgeaud 1988: 74–5.

[39] About twenty replicas are extant. See Bieber 1961: 147 and pl. 628 and R. R. R. Smith 1991: 131 and pl. 160.

putting his arm around a slender youth as he instructs the boy in the syrinx; in a beauty-and-the-beast pose, the boy looks at the pipe with a mix of tentative fascination and shy uncertainty. In proposing to be Alexis' music teacher, Corydon wishes to replicate the relationship of Pan to his shepherd darlings, and of his own teacher Damoetas to himself. By being encouraged to 'imitate' Pan, Alexis is imagined as engaging in a tradition which reaches back from student to teacher through the generations all the way to the original divine teacher himself.

In the relationship of Damoetas and Corydon we see the pederastic teacher-student interaction, familiar from Theocritus' *Idyll* 5, become highlighted as a metaphor for poetic influence and succession. The dying Damoetas bequeaths his syrinx to Corydon, who alone is worthy to be its second owner. That Damoetas is chosen as the name for Corydon's musical precursor and mentor is significant. Damoetas is the Theocritean shepherd of *Idyll* 6 who composes a song in the persona of the Cyclops Polyphemus: he is thus Corydon's model in 'imitating' Polyphemus, and is indeed the direct source for *Ecl.* 2.25–7, as we have observed. The relation of Damoetas and Corydon can thus in a certain sense be seen as expressing the relationship of literary succession between Theocritus and Vergil.[40] But Corydon's lack of success in fostering such a relationship of succession between himself and Alexis must then be seen as an expression of Vergilean self-doubt, a sense that he has not yet attained the status and pre-eminence requisite to the role of being a 'literary father'.

The pan-pipe is one of many gifts which Corydon offers Alexis, all allusively evoking the world of Theocritean bucolic and more particularly the gifts which Polyphemus offers Galatea. Vergil, if anything, emphasizes the inappropriateness of the gifts relative to their recipient. Whereas a she-goat with two kids might be an appropriate gift for the shepherdess Amaryllis (*Id.* 3.34–6) or the eleven collared fawns and four bearcubs offered Galatea would be a true marvel (*Id.* 11.40–1),[41] the two foundling goats which Corydon offers Alexis (*Ecl.* 2.40–4) are neither a rarity nor even likely to interest a boy who lives in the city. While it is plausible that Galatea was interested

---

[40] See Van Sickle 1986: 41–2.
[41] On the conflation here, see Cartault 1897: 98–9; Posch 1969: 42–3; du Quesnay 1979: 67.

in flowers such as those the Cyclops offers (*Id.* 11.56–9), since she once came to pluck hyacinths (*Id.* 11.25–7), we have no reason to think that a boy like Alexis would care for the many flowers which Corydon gathers for him (*Ecl.* 2.45–50). Indeed, the flowers play a significant role in Polyphemus' self-recognition: he explicitly notes that snowdrops and poppies grow in different seasons, and thus admits the absurdity of his offer to bring her both flowers. Corydon's catalogue is equally absurd in its collocation of flowers that bloom at different times of the year.[42] But where this was a moment of self-recognition for the Cyclops, adumbrating his final recognition of the futility of his love for Galatea, Corydon seems not to recognize the impossibility of the flowers he names being woven into a crown. The flowers represent merely one more instance of Corydon's overworked fantasy and self-delusion, emphasized by contrast with the self-consciousness of the Theocritean subtext.

Corydon does, however, come to a partial self-recognition in *Ecl.* 2.56–9: 'You are a rustic, Corydon; neither does Alexis care for your gifts | nor would Iollas take second place, if you should try to compete with gifts . . .'. Corydon now recognizes that his syrinx and pastoral music are as irrelevant to Alexis as his offer of goats and flowers. Corydon makes one last appeal to Alexis, based on reference to mythological exempla. 'Even the gods and Dardanian Paris have lived in the woods' (*Ecl.* 2.60–1). Paris is a curious and singularly ill-omened example. He is indeed a refined and handsome young townsman who comes out to the country to herd sheep, but the result of this interlude is the Judgment of Paris and the disaster which ensues therefrom. The ultimate implication of the example is clear enough: town and country are better left unmixed, particularly when matters of love are concerned. Alexis proves every bit as destructive for Corydon as Paris did for Troy. As with Corydon's solecistic reference to Amphion earlier in his song, the allusion is inappropriate for the purpose which he has in mind; but in this case at least, it also proves true in a sense which he does not suspect. Every allusive reference within the text of Corydon's song bears a secondary

---

[42] On the mix of spring (e.g. narcissus, casia) and summer flowers (e.g. anethum, caltha), see Coleman 1977: 101–2.

meaning, revealed only through consideration of the allusion's background.

The final and climactic allusion in the song recalls the close of Polyphemus' monologue in *Idyll* 11:

> a, Corydon, Corydon, quae te dementia cepit!
> semiputata tibi frondosa vitis in ulmo est:
> quin tu aliquid saltem potius, quorum indiget usus,
> viminibus mollique paras detexere iunco?
> invenies alium, si te hic fastidit, Alexin.   (*Ecl.* 2.69–73)

> Ah Corydon, Corydon, what madness has seized you!
> The leafy vine on the elm tree has been only half pruned by you:
> Why don't you rather undertake to weave something useful
> Of withes and soft rush?
> You will find another Alexis, if this one disdains you.

> ὦ Κύκλωψ Κύκλωψ, πᾷ τὰς φρένας ἐκπεπότασαι;
> αἴ κ' ἐνθὼν ταλάρως τε πλέκοις καὶ θαλλὸν ἀμάσας
> ταῖς ἄρνεσσι φέροις, τάχα κα πολὺ μᾶλλον ἔχοις νῶν.
> τὰν παρεοῖσαν ἄμελγε· τί τὸν φεύγοντα διώκεις;
> εὑρησεῖς Γαλάτειαν ἴσως καὶ καλλίον' ἄλλαν.
> πολλαὶ συμπαίσδεν με κόραι τὰν νύκτα κέλονται,
> κιχλίζοντι δὲ πᾶσαι, ἐπεί κ' αὐταῖς ὑπακούσω.
> δῆλον ὅτ' ἐν τᾷ γᾷ κἠγών τις φαίνομαι ἦμεν.
> οὕτω τοι Πολύφαμος ἐποίμαινεν τὸν ἔρωτα
> μουσίσδων, ῥᾷον δὲ διᾶγ' ἢ εἰ χρυσὸν ἔδωκεν.   (*Id.* 11.72–81)

> 'O Cyclops, Cyclops, whither have you flown with your wits?
> If you would go and weave cheese crates or cut greenery
> And bring it to your lambs, you would be much more sensible.
> Milk the one who is here. Why pursue the one who flees?
> You will perhaps find another, even fairer Galatea.
> Many girls ask me to come play with them at night,
> And they all giggle when I listen to them.
> It is clear that on land even I appear to be somebody.'
> So Polyphemus shepherded his love as he played,
> And he passed his time more easily than if he had spent gold.

For Theocritus' clarity and dramatic resolution Vergil substitutes ambiguity. For Theocritus' humor and ironic detachment we see Vergilean pathos. One never could take the love of a one-eyed troglodyte giant for a beautiful sea nymph very seriously, whereas the love of Corydon for Alexis is at least plausible in human terms, even though the two are separated by barriers of place and culture not dissimilar to the geographical divide between the land-based Cyclops and sea-based Nereid. Indeed the very nature of pederastic love involves such barriers, being by definition a relationship between unequals, with scripted roles of pursuer and pursued, in which an attractive youth is courted by an unattractive older man with a combination of gifts, pedagogical guidance, and verbal persuasion; even when consummated, such man–boy relationships are seldom mutual and reciprocal. Pederastic love replicates the artist's pursuit of beauty by positing a quintessential ideal of male beauty which is never fully tenable, both emotionally distant and evanescing into temporal change with the passing of that brief moment of adolescent bloom. Such love is necessarily an eternal quest for perfection, never to be satisfied or fulfilled. In this sense, Corydon's human limitations and lack of success in pursuing Alexis are very real, not unlike the experience of all true pederasts. By seeing in the Cyclops' hopeless love the dramatic outline for a description of Greek man–boy love in a less hospitable Roman context, Vergil transforms buffoonery and bathos into something far more subtle and naturalistic.

It is thus no surprise that we find more complexity in Vergil's resolution of the matter. Since Polyphemus' love was never realistic in the first place, it is not difficult to imagine it being cured through song and through the Cyclops' fantasy that he is desired by other girls. But neither of these alternatives are explicitly presented in Vergil's text. Indeed what is most striking is the abruptness with which Corydon's monologue ends.[43] Whereas *Idyll* 11 framed Polyphemus' song with a lengthy narrative introduction and a two-line conclusion, both emphasizing the theme of song as a cure for love, *Eclogue* 2 has no conclusion and only a much shorter introduction with no such *fabula docet*. The poem ends merely with Corydon telling himself that he will find 'another Alexis'. But what does this mean? That he will find a boy who reciprocates his love, even as

---

[43] On the more negative conclusion of *Eclogue* 2, see Posch 1969: 53 and Galinsky 1965: 165–72, who sees Epicurean influence in Vergil's questioning of the efficacy of music. See also du Quesnay 1979: 58–9, who, however, misinterprets the condition of the final line as the logical equivalent of a relative clause. I cannot agree with Otis 1964: 124 that Corydon's 'self-awareness emerges and cures an irrational passion'.

Polyphemus expects to find maidens who love him? Or that he will find another boy who rejects him like Alexis? And even in the former case, is not the hope of finding reciprocated love illusory, as it surely was for Polyphemus? We are merely left hanging with these questions unresolved. The wording 'another *fairer* Galatea' makes it clear that Polyphemus' hope is a positive one, as is further demonstrated by his lines on the maidens who have pursued him; the carefully constructed frame of the song leaves the matter in no doubt. But Vergil's deliberate omission of any follow-up exposition of Corydon's line seems intended as a device of conscious ambiguation. The informed reader is at once invited to assimilate Corydon's lines to the Theocritean subtext and to note their divergence from the subtext. As in *Eclogue* 1, we see the Theocritean world evoked as a positive model, but Vergil adds to it notes of doubt and uncertainty. Here the uncertainty encompasses not only the viability of the pastoral ideal in the modern Roman world, as in *Eclogue* 1, but extends to the efficacy of song itself.

Eclogue 3 is the first overtly agonistic piece in the Eclogue Book, and may be seen as a dramatic embodiment of Vergil's challenge to literary tradition. The two shepherds who encounter each other, Menalcas and Damoetas, are both familiar to us as minor characters in Corydon's autobiography in *Eclogue* 2. Damoetas was the older poetic father-figure from whom Corydon inherited his syrinx (*Ecl.* 2.36–9), inspired by the Theocritean Damoetas who was Corydon's precursor in imitating the persona of the Cyclops (*Id.* 6.21–41). Menalcas, on the other hand, was the dark-skinned boy whom Corydon loved prior to his obsession with the fair Alexis (*Ecl.* 2.15–16). As we have observed, his Vergilean persona seems a deliberate counterpoint to the Theocritean Menalcas, who like Daphnis was notable for his fair skin and red hair (*Id.* 8.3).[44] We thus have a contrast in identities already set up for us in the two characters of *Eclogue* 3: Damoetas an older friend of Corydon's, Menalcas younger, Damoetas a character who represents the Theocritean past, Menalcas representing a change and deviation from Theocritus. Menalcas

---

[44] However, like Theocritus' Menalcas, he is young and still under his parents' control: see *Id.* 8.15–16 and *Ecl.* 3.33–4.

twice appears later in the Eclogue Book: in *Eclogue* 5, he sings of Daphnis' apotheosis and gives as a gift to Mopsus the pipe which taught him *Eclogue* 2 and 3 (*Ecl.* 5.85–7), and in *Eclogue* 9 he is retrospectively cited by Lycidas and Moeris as the master poet of Vergilean pastoral. As the voice of youth challenging tradition, this identification of Menalcas as a genuine voice of Vergil's own art is implicit already in *Eclogue* 3.

This contrast between Menalcas and Damoetas is set up from their opening exchange of lines, modelled on the opening of Theocritus' *Idyll* 4:

Men. dic mihi, Damoeta, cuium pecus? an Meliboei?
Dam. non, verum Aegonis; nuper mihi tradidit Aegon. (*Ecl.* 3.1–2)

Men.: Tell me, Damoetas, whose flock is this? Is it Meliboeus'?
Dam.: No, it's Aegon's. Aegon recently handed it over to me.

Ba. εἰπέ μοι, ὦ Κορύδων, τίνος αἱ βόες; ἦ ῥα Φιλώνδα;
Co. οὔκ, ἀλλ' Αἴγωνος· βόσκειν δέ μοι αὐτὰς ἔδωκεν. (*Id.* 4.1–2)

Ba.: Tell me, Corydon, whose cattle are these? Are they Philondas'?
Co.: No, they are Aegon's. He gave them to me to pasture.

Theocritus' phraseology is followed down to the very details of word-order. However, where Damoetas reproduces the name Aegon from the original, Menalcas changes the names, asking if the herd which Damoetas tends is that of Meliboeus. This name is significant not only as a deviation from Theocritus (as we have observed, the name is not present in the Theocritean corpus), but resonates with haunting echoes of the situation in *Eclogue* 1, where Meliboeus is the shepherd who unjustly loses his farm; here we have the acid implication that Damoetas has taken over the forlorn shepherd's flock as well.

Menalcas' reply to Damoetas continues his technique of imitating, but altering the Theocritean model. Like Battus in *Idyll* 4, he calls the herd wretched (*Ecl.* 3.3 *infelix o semper, oves, pecus!*, 'always unhappy flock, you sheep'; cf. *Id.* 4.13 δειλαιαί γ' αὗται, τὸν βουκόλον ὡς κακὸν εὗρον, 'they are miserable since they have met with a bad cowherd') and avers that their new master must be milking them twice a day (*Ecl.* 3.5–6; cf. *Id.* 4.3).[45] But unlike *Idyll* 4, which reveals Aegon to be

---

[45] On the parallels and changes here, see Cartault 1897: 127–9; Jachmann 1922: 102; E. A. Schmidt 1972: 62–5.

off competing at Olympia, Menalcas insinuates that Aegon is busy pursuing interests of a more romantic nature, and uses this as an opportunity to vaunt his own youth and sexual attractiveness (*Ecl.* 3.3–4 *ipse Neaeram | dum fovet ac ne me sibi praeferat illa veretur*..., 'while he is hot for Neaera and is afraid that she might prefer me to him'). This introduction of the sexual dimension gives the older Damoetas an opportunity to assert his advantage of masculine maturity (*Ecl.* 3.7 *parcius ista viris tamen obicienda memento*, 'be careful not to make so many remarks like that to real men'), bolstered by an implication that Menalcas allowed himself to be buggered (*Ecl.* 3.8 *novimus et qui te transversa tuentibus hircis*, 'we know who did what to you when even the goats looked on in disgust'; note the masculine relative *qui* and Menalcas' grammatical status as a direct object, passively acted upon). Menalcas' youth makes him still a pederastic mignon in Damoetas' eyes, passive, effeminate, and excessive in his sexual urges (as implied by the act's commission in a sacred precinct—*Ecl.* 3.9).[46] That Menalcas was a passive love object of older men has already been indicated by Corydon's reference to him in *Ecl.* 2.15–16. However, Damoetas' accusation also appeals to a clear Theocritean parallel in *Id.* 5.41–2, where Comatas replies to the younger Lacon's impertinence by reminding him of his onetime pederastic subordination, again with goats looking on. Reminding Lacon of his sexual submission is a way of reminding him of his pedagogical dependence on the older shepherd's musical teaching; as we have observed, this conflict probably had a programmatic significance (innovation vs. tradition) even in Theocritus.[47] By insulting Menalcas with this Theocritean allusion, Damoetas, the representative of poetic tradition, reminds the younger poet of his indebtedness and dependency on tradition.

However, Menalcas is revealed as a figure resistant to the hierarchies and appointed order of poetic succession: at the site of the 'old' (*Ecl.* 3.12 *veteres*) beech trees, he breaks the bow and reeds of the

---

[46] The myth of Atalanta and Hippomenes' transformation into lions for sexual pollution of a sanctuary of the Great Mother (or in some sources, Zeus) evidences the equation of sanctuary violation with bestial lack of self-restraint. See Ov. *Met.* 10.686–704, doubtless based on Alexandrian sources. Cf. Apollod. *Bibl.* 3.9.2; Hyg. *Fab.* 185; Serv. ad *Aen.* 3.113.
[47] See Hubbard 1993: 34–6.

master poet Daphnis out of envy, after seeing Daphnis give them to another boy (*Ecl.* 3.12–15). Not only does Menalcas' active hostility pick up on his embittered defeat by Daphnis in *Id.* 8.90–1,[48] but it also foreshadows the envy Amyntas will later feel when the dying Damoetas bequeaths his pan-pipe to Corydon (*Ecl.* 2.35–9). The reference is thus Vergilean auto-allusion as well as a response and continuation of Theocritus. Menalcas' style is an aggressive, even violent competitiveness in emulation.

Menalcas' counter-charge against Damoetas is one of theft (*Ecl.* 3.16–20), appropriately expressed with an opening line closely imitating (if not exactly stolen from) Catullus' translation of Callimachus' *Coma Berenices* (*Ecl.* 3.16 *quid domini faciant, audent cum talia fures?*, 'what are masters to do when thieves dare such things?'; cf. Catull. 66.47 *quid facient crines, cum ferro talia cedant?*, 'what is hair to do, when such things give way to the cutting blade?'). Damoetas is accused of grabbing one of Damon's goats, and Menalcas exhorts Tityrus, the paradigmatic Vergilean herdsman, to watch their flock lest he steal one of theirs. Damoetas' response is that the goat was properly his, owed him by Damon for a victory in a musical contest (*Ecl.* 3.21–4). Surely the charges and counter-charges here are meant to express extreme conceptions of the poetic positions occupied by the two shepherds: Damoetas' traditionalism, viewed unsympathetically, might be construed as 'theft' of other poets'/ shepherds' material, and Menalcas' brash anti-traditionalism might be seen as destructive and invidious iconoclasm.

Damoetas proposes a musical contest to resolve their respective claims and stakes as his wager a heifer who has given birth to twin offspring and still comes to the milk-pail twice a day (*Ecl.* 3.28–31). Menalcas offers nothing from the herd, since it is not his and is counted twice a day by his father and stepmother (*Ecl.* 3.32–4; cf. *Id.* 8.11–20), but he does offer splendid beech-wood cups inscribed with the figures of two astronomers (*Ecl.* 3.35–43). Both pledges are derived from Theocritus, *Id.* 1.25–60, where the goatherd offers Thyrsis both a she-goat who milks twice a day and a splendid ivy-cup, described with considerable ecphrastic detail. Where Theocritus had

---

[48] There may also be some allusion to a soured love-relationship between Daphnis and Menalcas, a story attributed to Hermesianax by Σ *Id.* 8.53–6d (Wendel). See R. Reitzenstein 1893: 257–9.

connected the two as one offer, Vergil separates them into competing wagers of two shepherds, thus creating a division between the conventionally pastoral pledge of the traditionalist Damoetas and the more modern, technologically wrought offering of the young anti-traditionalist Menalcas.[49] The opposed value systems represented by the two pledges are reinforced by Damoetas' possession of two such cups of Alcimedon and explicit devaluation of them in comparison with the heifer (*Ecl.* 3.44–8). Even as the Theocritean ivy-cup was an import from abroad, brought to Cos by the Calydnean ferryman and containing scenes of an epic world quite separate from the bucolic,[50] so also Menalcas' cups invoke a world of Alexandrian learning and didactic. The astronomers not only remind us in a general way of Aratus' *Phaenomena*, but the specific mention of Conon, the discoverer of the Coma Berenices, recalls Callimachus' elegiac poem on the constellation, which describes Conon as πάντα τὸν ἐν γραμμαῖσιν ἰδὼν ὅρον ᾗ τε φέρονται ('he who sees the entire heaven on the charts and the way in which the stars revolve', fr. 110.1 Pf. = Catull. 66.1 *omnia qui magni dispexit lumina mundi...*, 'he who discerned all the stars of the great universe...'), here appearing as Vergil's *descripsit radio totum qui gentibus orbem* (' he who with his pointer mapped out the whole world for the races of men', *Ecl.* 3.41, of the other unnamed astronomer).[51] This line, as well as Menalcas' earlier echo of Catullus' translation of the Coma Berenices (*Ecl.* 3.16 ∼ Catull. 66.47), exhibits a desire to transcend mere Theocritean imitation and the world of bucolic enclosure into a broader horizon of generic reference, a desire actualized in *Eclogues* 4–6 and most particularly in Menalcas' song of Daphnis' catasterism in *Eclogue* 5. The astronomical interests of *Eclogue* 3 may be read as an allusive build-up to this climax.

The actual amoebaean contest of the two shepherds appropriately positions Damoetas, the older representative of literary tradition, as

---

[49] The separation of the two gifts is also inspired in part by the conflation of *Idyll* 1 with *Id.* 8.11–20, where Menalcas offers a syrinx (instrument of art) as his wager rather than a lamb, since his parents count the herd every night. See Jachmann 1922: 104–5. Cartault 1897: 131–4 also sees influence of *Id.* 5.104–7 here. On Vergil's transformation of Theocritus and the significance of the two gifts as representing a cleavage between the realms of the 'rustic' and 'poetic', see Segal 1981: 238–42.

[50] See Hubbard 1993: 29–30. On the influence of *Idyll* 1 here, see in addition to Segal: Gallavotti 1966: 433–6 and La Penna 1981: 140.

[51] See Cassio 1973: 329–31 and La Penna 1981: 142.

the first to sing a couplet, and Menalcas, the young challenger, as his respondent. The initial exchange opens with praise of the gods:

> Dam. ab Iove principium Musae: Iovis omnia plena;
> ille colit terras, illi mea carmina curae.
> Men. et me Phoebus amat; Phoebo sua semper apud me
> munera sunt, lauri et suave rubens hyacinthus. (*Ecl.* 3.60–3)
>
> Dam.: The Muse's beginning is from Jove; all things are full of Jove.
> He cares for the earth, and my songs are dear to him.
> Men.: Phoebus loves me too. His own gifts are always
> Available to Phoebus at my house, laurels and the sweet-blushing hyacinth.

Damoetas' opening closely imitates Cicero's translation of the first line of Aratus' *Phaenomena* (fr. 1 Ewbank = *Leg.* 2.3.7 *ab Iove Musarum primordia*, 'the Muses' beginnings are with Jove'), whereas Menalcas' closely follows Lacon's response to Comatas at the opening of the amoebaean contest of *Idyll* 5 (*Id.* 5.82 καὶ γὰρ ἔμ' Ὠπόλλων φιλέει μέγα, 'and Apollo loves me greatly'; note the close parallels of word order to *et me Phoebus amat*). Although Damoetas may start out with the more powerful god (Jupiter), Menalcas responds by declaring a closer and more intense relationship with his god (Apollo): not only are his songs a care to Apollo, but Apollo *loves* him. The laurel (symbol of Apollo's passion for Daphne) and hyacinth (symbol of his passion for Hyacinthus)[52] are both Menalcas' tokens, claiming for him a special access to Apollo's erotic interest and artistic inspiration. As in *Idyll* 5 (and *Eclogue* 2, where we first meet Menalcas), the themes of pederasty and musical instruction are closely intertwined.

The next exchange of couplets focuses on these erotic themes quite explicitly:

> Dam. malo me Galatea petit, lasciva puella,
> et fugit ad salices et se cupit ante videri.
> Men. at mihi sese offert ultro, meus ignis, Amyntas,
> notior ut iam sit canibus non Delia nostris. (*Ecl.* 3.64–7)
>
> Dam.: Galatea, the wanton girl, aims at me with an apple
> And flees to the willows, hoping that she will be seen before she gets there.

---

[52] They are so interpreted by Serv. *ad Buc.* 3.63.

Men.: But Amyntas, my flame, offers himself to me of his own will,
Such that now not even the Moon is more familar to our dogs.

The image of a playful Galatea teasing a shepherd by pelting his flock with apples is derived from Daphnis' and Damoetas' songs of the Cyclops in *Id.* 6.6–22:[53] by naming his mistress Galatea, Vergil's Damoetas remains firmly within his Theocritean persona as imitator of the Cyclops. Menalcas, on the other hand, returns to the young upstart Lacon of *Idyll* 5 for his inspiration, progressing beyond the claim of Apollo's love and tutelage to an active pederastic pursuit of his own, even as Lacon does (*Id.* 5.90–1). Moreover, Menalcas claims as his lover none other than Amyntas, whom we know from *Ecl.* 2.35–9 to have revered Damoetas and envied Corydon for inheriting his pan-pipe; given Damoetas' own relation with Amyntas, Menalcas' claim seems designed to stir his anger. Where Damoetas' Galatea merely teased and provoked, Menalcas' Amyntas freely offers himself (*Ecl.* 3.66). As in the other exchanges, Menalcas carries Damoetas' statement to a higher level of intensity and outdoes him.[54] And as suggested in the controlling model of *Idyll* 5, Menalcas' movement from erotic passivity to dominance becomes metaphorical for his emergence as an independent and influential poetic voice.[55]

The centrality of poetic concerns is apparent throughout the amoebaean exchange, whether in the praise of Pollio's *nova carmina* and censure of Bavius and Mevius (*Ecl.* 3.84–91)[56] or in the riddles at the end, both of which seem to be learned allusions to works of Alexandrian poetry (*Ecl.* 3.104–7): the place where the sky is no more than three ulnae in extent may be the papyrus roll of Aratus' *Phaenomena*,[57] and the place where the names of kings are inscribed in the hyacinth flower may be Euphorion's *Hyacinthus*.[58] Both represent themes of grandeur reduced to the compressed form of Alexandrian

---

[53] This passage is also influenced by *Id.* 5.88–9, which Cartault 1897: 141–2 sees as primary.

[54] On the dynamics of the competition between the two throughout the contest, see the useful observations of Powell 1976: 116–17.

[55] See Hubbard 1993: 34–6.

[56] Leach 1974: 180–1 contends that the river imagery of *Ecl.* 3.94–7 and 111 references the 'river of poetry' topos, originating of course with Callimachus.

[57] This is the solution of Campbell 1982/3: 123–4, based on Servius' definition (*ad Ecl.* 3.105) of an *ulna* as a measure of about six feet.

[58] See Wormell 1960: 29–30; E. L. Brown 1978: 27–8; La Penna 1981: 153–4.

poetry.[59] Of course, many other solutions to these riddles have also been proposed, and Vergil may well have intended for us to guess at a plurality of meanings behind them. The indeterminacy of their resolution helps adumbrate the indeterminacy of the contest's resolution: the shepherd Palaemon cannot decide between the two singers and judges them equal. The challenge of Menalcas' newer mode of Vergilean pastoral proves itself the peer of traditional Theocritean pastoral, as represented by Damoetas. We thus see the emergence of Vergil's poetic voice as one worthy of its predecessor and yet independent. At this stage, the dominant Theocritean bucolic model can be transcended and other, grander generic forms brought into play, as we see with the various allusions to Aratus, Callimachus, and Catullus,[60] all building up to Vergil's most ambitious transcendence of the bucolic genre in *Eclogues* 4 and 5.[61]

To summarize our argument, Vergil made aggressive and pointed use of *arte allusiva* at critical junctures in his texts as a conscious technique of characterization. Vergil's method of deploying allusions in *Eclogues* 1–3 is to be seen as a modality of self-assertion vis-a-vis poetic tradition by an emerging young poet. *Eclogue* 1 programmatically inverts Theocritean themes and valuations in demarginalizing the Theocritean character of Tityrus and presenting the non-Theocritean Meliboeus as a figure alienated from the world of bucolic tradition. Against this programmatic challenge is set the critical self-doubt of *Eclogue* 2, in which Theocritean subtexts are deployed such as to make Corydon's erotic misfortunes paradigmatic for the young poet's hopes and doubts. *Eclogue* 3, however, returns to *Eclogue* 1's stance of challenge to tradition by presenting a contest between the

---

[59] Both riddles point to the idea of great things (the sky, kings) reduced to small compass (six *ulnae*, hyacinth flowers). See Clay 1974: 62–4.
[60] In addition to the allusions we have discussed already, the final line (*Ecl.* 3.111 *claudite iam rivos, pueri; sat prata biberunt*) seems modelled on the close of Catullus' wedding hymn for Manlius Torquatus and Junia (Catull. 61.224–5 *claudite ostia, virgines: lusimus satis*). See Berg 1974: 193–4; La Penna 1981: 156. Could this perhaps be an adumbration of the epithalamic context to follow in *Eclogue* 4? Or of the dominant Catullan influence in that poem?
[61] For a detailed study of passages near the end of *Eclogue* 3 which seem to look forward to the imagery and vocabulary of *Eclogue* 4, see Segal 1981: 265–70. Interestingly, these anticipatory allusions begin with the mention of Pollio in *Ecl.* 3.84.

ambitious young shepherd Menalcas and the older, more established Damoetas; the draw which results establishes Vergil as at least on a par with his precursor Theocritus. *Eclogues* 1–3 can thus be viewed as the first act in an intertextual drama of Vergil's poetic self-emergence, in which a tentative, intersubjective beginning is made in what will become with *Eclogues* 4–6 a more broadly intergeneric/intertextual confrontation, culminating in the juxtaposition of Vergil (= Menalcas) and Gallus in *Eclogues* 9 and 10 as the respective masters, however problematized, of their separate, but interrelated generic spheres.

6

On *Eclogue* 1.79–83

Christine G. Perkell

In his interesting study of the *Eclogues*, Paul Alpers points to a crucial problem in *Eclogue* 1.[1] He observes that while many current critics view Tityrus as being of pedestrian imagination, callous, evasive, and morally insensitive,[2] it is he, nevertheless, who speaks the splendid final verses of the poem, verses which, in their haunting and melancholy beauty, essentially characterize Virgil's poetry:

> et iam summa procul villarum culmina fumant
> maioresque cadunt altis de montibus umbrae.

> Already smoke rises from the distant farm-house roofs
> And deeper shadows fall from the towering hills.

With their 'vespertinal mixture of sadness and tranquility',[3] these verses are model expressions of Virgil's dissonant sensibility and exemplify the emotive power of his pastoral voice.

Yet, to return to Alpers' point, these verses are out of character, if the generally accepted negative evaluations of Tityrus' previous utterances are valid. Alpers tries to solve this problem in a lengthy,

---

This paper first appeared in 1990 and is here reprinted with minor modifications and added translations of the Latin texts. In the translations I have wanted, above all, to capture the melancholy, haunting tone of the poem that is the essential subject of this essay. Translations of the *Eclogues* are from Boyle 1976, with slight modifications. I translated the *Georgics* passage myself.

[1] Alpers 1979, e.g. 65–71. For Latin citations I have used the text of Coleman 1977.
[2] e.g. Coleman 1977 *ad* 11, 19, 59, 79 and 90; Boyle 1986: 16, 17 n. 5, 18–19; Segal 1965: 275–6; Leach 1974: 118; Putnam 1970: 39.
[3] Alpers 1979: 67 n. 3, citing Panofsky 1955: 300.

difficult, and often shifting discussion,[4] by denying that dramatic consistency is an essential feature of the pastoral mode in general or of this poem in particular. As a consequence he can also, therefore, deny that the identity of the speaker of any given verse need have significance. Rather he argues that pastoral is lyric to a great degree ('the peculiar poetics of the *Eclogue*, somewhere between drama and lyric', 1979: 84), that it seeks to create a certain mood—with no necessary correlation between parts (e.g. 1979: 18), and that it is the character of the utterances that signifies, not the speaker. Extrapolating from some views of Klingner, he argues that readers who are troubled by Tityrus' speaking the conclusion fundamentally mistake the mode of the poem, misread its tensions, and hence fall into interpretive errors, among which he would include negative moral judgments about Tityrus. When Alpers says that 'the static, undramatic view of the poem, though not wholly adequate, at least enables us to avoid some misleading commonplaces about it' (1979: 81), he refers to negative judgments about Tityrus by such critics as Putnam (or Boyle or Coleman). If one relaxes one's requirements for dramatic consistency and logical, linear coherence,[5] one can see, he argues, that the poem's conclusion is appropriate to pastoral, regardless of who speaks it. (An extreme statement of this view is Wright's, who asserts that the poem proper really ends at 77–8 and that the conclusion is merely a pastoral tag, 'poetic sleight-of-hand', to obtain a serene and peaceful conclusion.[6]) I quote Alpers now at some length in order to avoid suspicion of misrepresenting him: 'In the most subtle and convincing of such ["essentially nondramatic"] readings, Tityrus' *adynata* (59–62) are interpreted as a breakthrough to the sublime *for the whole poem* (Alpers' italics)[7] [i.e. despite the apparent deficiencies of Tityrus as a character]; the ironies are to be referred not to the speakers and their relations, but to the situation as a whole and the tensions inherent in it. *By the same token, the final*

---

[4] Alpers 1979: 65–95.
[5] Such a relaxed reading fits well with Pöschl's concept of the 'lässige Spannung' of the Roman classic (1964: 82). It is to this loose structure that Pöschl attributes e.g. Tityrus' forgetting to answer the question of the god's identity. Cf. Pöschl 1964: 35.
[6] Wright 1983: 112.
[7] He takes this thought from Klingner 1967: 25–6, who argues that l.62, by evoking the fate of Rome, completes the poem's 'Durchbruch zum Erhabenen'.

lines are taken as a powerful conclusion to the poem as a whole; they are attributed, so to speak, to Virgil, rather than to Tityrus' (1979: 71). (Italics here and material in brackets supplied by present author.)

Alpers' argument for the essentially non-dramatic nature of the *Eclogue* and the consequent irrelevance of the individual speaker, although provocative, seems not, finally, convincing. Most basically, it *feels* wrong; it is counter-instinctive and requires us to deny that we feel what we feel in reading, namely that the characters do have identity and that the ending is, therefore, inappropriately dismissed as merely impersonal or pastoral. Less subjectively, one might also argue that no speech in *Eclogue* 1 should, as Alpers suggests, be 'attributed above all to Virgil himself'; for while the *Eclogue* poet (perhaps to be identified with Virgil)[8] does speak in other poems, here he does not. Rather he allows all issues to emerge from the interaction between the two speakers. The reader must respond to the poem's pressures without authorial authentication of either speaker in the drama.

I use the term 'drama' deliberately, for I wish to argue, against Alpers, that the poem is, in fact, precisely a miniature drama. It is conceived with careful attention to consistency of speaker and suggestive of character in so much detail as to belie the irrelevance of the individuality of the speakers. Tityrus' speaking of the final verses is an organically motivated climax to the miniature drama enacted in the poem. Tityrus is drawn out of his self-absorption and made responsive, I suggest, by the power of Meliboeus' pastoral voice; and the demonstration of this power is a climax and major purpose of the *Eclogue*. This proposed reading of the poem's conclusion and of Tityrus' appropriateness for speaking it will be seen to make possible some new perspectives on the poem's tensions and achievements.

---

[8] Leach is most interesting on the subject of the *Eclogue* poet, whom she considers the unifying figure of the *Eclogues*. His own ideal 'is the search for a viable form of poetic expression, a self-critical search that gives ultimate unity to the collection by its relinquishment of pastoral poetry' (1974: 50). He speaks directly in *Eclogues* 2, 4, 6, 8, and 10. Leach cautions that 'neither the *Eclogue* poet nor any other character in the *Eclogues* is to be taken as a definitive spokesman for Vergil, or as a representative of his personality or ideas' (1974: 262). Patterson conceives of authorship as a 'strategy' and adds, 'And by throwing into structural and linguistic question the location of his own voice throughout the ten poems, Virgil effectively demonstrated how a writer can protect himself by dismemberment, how he can best assert his ownership of a text by a wickedly shifting authorial presence' (1987: 4).

To begin, we can establish consistency of dramatic characterization by considering several different features of the speakers' utterances. For example, a great difference in values between the two speakers emerges from a comparison of their attitudes towards the country. For Tityrus the country signifies the realities of physical labor and financial worry (31–2, 34, 40). 'For him it is a place of work and hard-earned savings (*peculi*, 32) and frustrations (*pinguis et ingratae premeretur caseus urbi*, 34).'[9] Tityrus is represented, in his responses to country life, as concerned with practical and material realities. In Meliboeus, on the other hand, although he sees its difficult reality:

> et tibi magna satis, quamvis lapis omnia nudus
> limosoque palus obducat pascua iunco. (47–8)
>
> And large enough for you, though naked rock
> And marsh cover over all the pasture with muddy reed.

the country sparks a creative imagination, which, quite indifferent to material reality, transforms and transfigures brackish marsh into a pastoral ideal, into the very quintessence of the pastoral vision:

> fortunate senex, hic inter flumina nota
> et fontis sacros frigus captabis opacum;
> hinc tibi quae semper, vicino ab limite saepes
> Hyblaeis apibus florem depasta salicti
> saepe levi somnum suadebit inire susurro;
> hinc alta sub rupe canet frondator ad auras,
> nec tamen interea raucae, tua cura, palumbes
> nec gemere aeria cessabit turtur ab ulmo. (51–8)
>
> Fortunate old man, here among familiar streams
> And sacred springs you will hunt the shaded cool.
> Here, as always, the hedge by your neighbor's boundary,
> Where Hyblaean bees feed on the willow-blossom,
> Will often coax you into sleep with soothing murmur.
> Here by that high crag the pruner will sing to the breeze,
> While hoarse wood-pigeons, your heart's care, and turtle-doves
> Will moan unceasingly from the soaring elms.

This transforming imagination emerges, then, as the defining characteristic of Meliboeus as pastoral poet and seems, thus, to set him

[9] Segal 1965: 275. Cf. Coleman 1977 *ad* 3–4 and 34.

apart from Tityrus. In this 'most famous piece of pastoralism in the poem',[10] Virgil gives us to see that it is Meliboeus' imagination that creates the pastoral vision—an idyllic vision which never existed historically anywhere or had any substance except in the poet's imagination, as is clearly implied by the juxtaposed descriptions of unlovely reality (46–7) and imagined ideal (51–8).[11] The pastoral vision is revealed as an individual act of imagination and spirit (not of nostalgia or memory).

Related aspects of Meliboeus' pastoral imagination are reflected in his repeated empathetic identification with others—people as well as figures of nature. For example, he apostrophizes the absent Amaryllis, addressing her directly, as if he imagined her present:

> mirabar quid maesta deos, Amarylli, vocares,
> quoi pendere sua patereris in arbore poma. (36–7)
>
> I wondered why, Amaryllis, you called so sadly
> On the gods, and let the apples hang in their trees.

So immediately does he recreate, interpret, and identify with her response to Tityrus' absence. Or again, Meliboeus endows nature with sentience, imagining that the pines, springs, and hedges called and longed for the absent Tityrus:

> Tityrus hinc aberat. ipsae te, Tityre, pinus,
> ipsi te fontes, ipsa haec arbusta vocabant. (38–9)
>
> Tityrus had gone. Even the pines, Tityrus,
> Even the springs, even these orchards called to you.

Although Alpers and Putnam think that Meliboeus imagines Tityrus as some sort of Daphnis figure, a rural divinity upon whose well-being nature depends,[12] I think it easier to propose that his imagining of rural responsiveness to Tityrus' absence is a characteristic of his empathetic sensibility and imagination. Verses 4–5 show this same vision of nature as responsive to man:

---

[10] Alpers 1979: 84.

[11] Putnam 1970 attempts to resolve the inconsistency between the real character of the land and the ideal by translating: 'Fortunate old man, and so your lands will remain. And for you they are large enough, even were naked rock and swamp with marshy reed to cover all the pasture.' This translation, I believe, obscures the creative climax of the poem, Meliboeus' transfiguration of barren reality into pastoral idyll.

[12] Putnam 1970: 41 and Alpers 1979: 89–90 and n. 33.

> tu, Tityre, lentus in umbra
> formonsam resonare doces Amaryllida silvas.
>
> You, Tityrus, lazing in the shade,
> Teach the woods to echo 'lovely Amaryllis'.

(Cf. also 55.) Similarly, Meliboeus' attribution of capacity for happiness to his flock suggests his particular quality of imagination:

> ite meae, felix quondam pecus, ite capellae. (74)
> Onward, my little goats, once happy flock, onward.

All these verses contribute to a sustained representation of a particular, fluid, poetic sensibility that focuses on nature, endows it with sentience and responsiveness, and that allows multiple empathetic experiences. In comparison, as we have seen, Tityrus' attitudes appear material and practical. He shows consistently greater attention to external realities.

As Tityrus and Meliboeus differ in their attitudes to the country, so they differ also in their attitudes to the larger outside reality. Although he describes himself as *iners* (27), Tityrus was nevertheless realistic, energetic, and resourceful enough to venture into the larger world in an attempt to resolve his problems and to secure the material bases of his way of life. In Meliboeus, by contrast, one senses an inattentiveness to material reality (16–17) and perhaps a disinclination to struggle, an easy resignation to defeat and loss—which conditions have, in fact, been the very inspiration in this poem of his most haunting, powerful poetry. His loss of and anticipated longing for home, transfigured into song, have a painful beauty, in which he luxuriates (67–8) with pathetic and melancholy drama.[13] (This dimension of Meliboeus will be pursued further, below.)

---

[13] Cf. Alpers 1979: 83 and Leach 1974: 123 on the exaggerations and melodramatic inclinations of Meliboeus. Cf. Segal 1965: 275 and note 24 below. Pöschl 1964: 57: 'Aus seinen Worten spricht "le sombre plaisir de la mélancolie" (Lafontaine)'. One should also note Meliboeus' many self-conscious and/or neoteric rhetorical tropes, which suggest a more deliberate and refined poetic technique than that of Tityrus. Examples are: postponed *namque* (4), neoteric *a* (15), *tricolon abundans* (38–9), accusative with passive past participle (54), onomatopoeia (55), pathetic/disjointed utterance (67–9), pathetic repetition of *post* (67 and 69), triple rhyme of *-os* (72). Cf. e.g. Page 1965 and R. D. Williams 1979 *ad loc.*

Another deft stroke of dramatic characterization is the consistency of Meliboeus' and Tityrus' attitudes towards religion. While Meliboeus is identified with traditional rural piety:

> saepe malum hoc nobis, si mens non laeva fuisset,
> de caelo tactas memini praedicere quercus.   (16–17)
>
> Often I remember—if our minds had not been blind—
> We were foretold this evil by oaks struck from heaven.

and grieved at the advent of a *miles* whom he thinks to term *impius* (70), Tityrus is ready to worship a new, private, urban god, for reasons of expediency:

> o Meliboee, deus nobis haec otia fecit.
> namque erit ille mihi semper deus, illius aram
> saepe tener nostris ab ovilibus imbuet agnus.
> ille meas errare boves, ut cernis, et ipsum
> ludere quae vellem calamo permisit agresti.   (6–10)
>
> O Meliboeus, a god has made this peace for us.
> For a god he will always be to me, his altar
> Often stained with a gentle lamb from our folds.
> He allowed my cattle to wander, as you see,
> And myself to play what I wished on my rustic reed.

> quid facerem? neque servitio me exire licebat
> nec tam praesentis alibi cognoscere divos.
> hic illum vidi iuvenem, Meliboee, quotannis
> bis senos quoi nostra dies altaria fumant,
> hic mihi responsum primus dedit ille petenti:
> 'pascite ut ante boves, pueri, submittite tauros.'   (40–5)
>
> What was I to do? For nowhere else could I escape
> From slavery, nor know such present gods.
> Here I saw him, Meliboeus, that youth for whom
> Every year our altars smoke for twice six days.
> Here he first gave answer to my prayer:
> 'Pasture your cattle as before, boys; breed your bulls.'

The dispensations of this god, materially significant as they are, seem to be independent of moral merit, as least as far as the reader can see.[14]

---

[14] Contrast Pöschl, who thinks the climax of the poem is the merciful act of the divine youth, who secures peace and freedom for poetry to the shepherd (1964: 85). I argue that this putative act of 'grace' is represented as without moral content.

One misses in Tityrus' narrative a dimension of genuine awe for the numinous and mysterious. Tityrus seems neither superstitious nor reverent, but, above all, pragmatic.

Even subtle details in this brief poem suggest two consistently conceived characters. Virginio Cremona points to the characters' different concerns with space, time, and focus of identity. While Tityrus speaks of distant space, uses verbs primarily in the past tense, and founds his present identity on the relationship between *ille* and *mihi*, Meliboeus speaks of present space (*hic*), uses verbs mostly in the present or future, and sees essential contrasts between *tu* and *nos*.[15]

From such differences as these, which range from obvious to subtle, one may infer that the dramatic characters of Tityrus and Meliboeus are consistently conceived and that, therefore, Alpers is probably wrong to suggest that the identity of the speaker of any given sequence of verses is immaterial or without significance. Given the demonstrated consistency and coherence of characterization in the poem, I suggest that it is insufficient to qualify a speech which is apparently out of character as, essentially, 'lyric' or merely appropriately 'pastoral' in mode and attribute it to a speaker external to the poem, even if that speaker is Virgil himself.

How, then, to read the conclusion? I propose that verses 79–83 can make *dramatic* sense (and not only pastoral—if beautiful—nonsense) if Tityrus is seen as responsive, ultimately, to Meliboeus' vision and as sympathetic, consequently, to his plight. Drawn out of his complacency and self-absorption by the beautiful power of Meliboeus' song, Tityrus comes finally to answer Meliboeus' loss with new-found pastoral generosity, thus moving to his own vision of nature and community.[16] This outcome is the climax of the miniature drama enacted in *Eclogue* 1, a moment of communication and communion. Tityrus' responsiveness beautifully and ironically proves the power of the pastoral vision—even as its principal speaker is exiled—to move the listener and to forge shared and humane values. As Alpers himself well observes, Tityrus' final verses have a tonality different from those which he apparently initially sang

---

[15] Cremona 1977: 287–308.
[16] Community is an important theme of Alpers' study throughout. See e.g. pp. 118, 125–7, 162, 221, 225–6.

(1–5).[17] To be more precise, we may observe that he has internalized Meliboeus' bittersweet esthetic, his haunting union of pathos and beauty, and comes finally to sing a song much like his. Therefore I would see Tityrus' invitation both as more sincere and also as more significant than Coleman's perhaps trivializing 'belated offer of hospitality'.[18] Neither, I think, is it quite so grand as Pöschl proposes when he finds it, along with the young god's grace to Tityrus, the exalting proof that the poem's theme is humanity.[19] Rather it has an ambiguity in its diffidence that is harmonious with Meliboeus' mood.[20]

If it is the case that Tityrus has been moved, convinced, converted, that he speaks from internal, organic cause and not merely as the vehicle of a necessary pastoral tag, what is it in Meliboeus' song that brings about this result? I suggest that he is moved, just as certain (not all) readers are, by the peculiar beauty and pathos of Meliboeus' voice. When we consider the totality of Meliboeus' utterances in the poem, we see that they suggest a striking and somewhat problematic portrait of a very particular poetic and creative inclination. We have noted already Meliboeus' empathy, how he humanizes and/or apostrophizes people, pines, goats. We have noted also that the pastoral vision derives from his imagination, not from his memory. And we have proposed that there is a deep, if subtle, relationship between loss and beauty in his song. We can further corroborate these observations.

Let us consider first the poem's opening:

> Tityre, tu patulae recubans sub tegmine fagi
> silvestrem tenui Musam meditaris avena;
> nos patriae finis et dulcia linquimus arva.
> nos patriam fugimus; tu, Tityre, lentus in umbra
> formonsam resonare doces Amaryllida silvas. (1–5)
>
> Tityrus, you, lying under cover of a spreading beech,
> Practice the woodland Muse on a slender oat pipe.
> We leave our homeland's borders and sweet fields;
> We flee our homeland; you, Tityrus, lazing in the shade,
> Teach the woods to echo 'lovely Amaryllis'.

---

[17] e.g. Alpers 1979: 95.   [18] Coleman 1977 *ad* 79.   [19] Pöschl 1964: 86.
[20] Cf. Leach 1974: 137–8, who calls the invitation 'curiously tentative'.

Although most readers assume these verses to be an objective description of Tityrus' posture and thought, the fact is that they are Meliboeus' expression, vision, and interpretation of what he sees.[21] When he speaks the poem's opening verses he defines pastoral values for (as it came to be) the whole Western tradition. *Lentus, tenuis, umbra,* and the quintessential pastoral tree sign or define the enchanting quality of bucolic life. As Patterson puts it, the selfhood of Tityrus (and, therefore, one may add, the pastoral vision itself) is associated with reflection, with echoes, with song, with literary allusion, with leisure, and with protection.[22] She neglects, however, to observe that it is *Meliboeus* who makes this association. As commentators have noted, Meliboeus speaks here in the tradition of Theocritus (cf. *Id.* 1.1 ff. and 7.88–9). He projects his own pastoral vision onto the largely mundane circumstances of Tityrus, a vision which Tityrus corroborates only in limited ways (as in 6, 9–10). It is Meliboeus who personifies the woods and imagines them as responsive to Tityrus' song (5). It is Meliboeus whose emotional depth and fine sensitivity are reflected in his love for home (the *arva* are *dulcia* to him) and attachment to his *patria*. He feels widely and diffusely bonded with his environment, while Tityrus expresses no such flights on his own behalf. Most problematically, I would observe, Meliboeus finds a certain unhappy pleasure in pathetic song. He experiences with intensity, drama, and depth the pain of exile because he so intensely, so responsively finds his fields sweet. It is he who thinks to voice the exquisite pathos of parting.[23] Even in his most idyllic vision (53–8) a touch of sadness enters with the moaning of doves (58), whose cooing sounds mournful to human ears. Not without reason, but yet with intense drama, does Meliboeus translate his exile into an aria of high emotion. Verses 67–9 with their pathetic *en umquam* and fractured syntax artfully express distraction and despair, with Meliboeus himself as the central figure of a tragic scene. Is there not perhaps some gratuitous, luxuriant self-torture in his imaginations

---

[21] Alpers 1979: 81 and 81 n. 4 notes that it is wrong 'to think that Tityrus views his life the way Meliboeus does'. (The reader might note that in this comment Alpers assumes coherent dramatic characters.)

[22] Patterson 1987: 2.

[23] Apparently he is not attached to any female figure, as Tityrus is. His love is, diffusely, the land and its creatures (cf. *hic amor, haec patria est*).

of an *impius/barbarus* defiling his land, in the bitter irony of his having labored for alien intruders (72–3)? In this, significantly the *longest* speech of the poem, Meliboeus envisions what he will never see and never do again.[24]

In his fine sensibility and intense capacity for sorrowful song Meliboeus is parallel to the Orpheus of Virgil's fourth *Georgic.* Orpheus, the archetypal poet, has power to move not only animate and inanimate nature, but also even the dead. Yet Orpheus has as well a predilection for the tragic.[25] Though, for example, Hades contains all the dead, Orpheus' vision fixes on youths and girls unwedded and children dead before their parents (475–7). Eurydice, once lost, becomes the obsessive subject of his song. As Meliboeus failed to heed a warning (16–17) and failed to take such action as Tityrus did in going to Rome, so Orpheus cannot make accommodation to imperfect reality, but wanders lonely woods in hopeless song, even his severed head continuing the lament. Ovid makes a mockery of Orpheus' extravagant mourning;[26] but Virgil sees in it something authentic and true, as he compares Orpheus to the nightingale, nature's paradigmatic singer, whose beautiful song is interpreted, at least by human auditors, as sorrowful, as a lament on the irremediable loss of her offspring:

> qualis populea maerens philomela sub umbra
> amissos queritur fetus, quos durus arator
> observans nido implumis detraxit; at illa
> flet noctem, ramoque sedens miserabile carmen
> integrat, et maestis late loca questibus implet.   (*G.* 4.511–15)

> As a nightingale mourning under a poplar's shade
> Bewails her lost young, hunted by the hard plowman
> And dragged from the nest, unfledged; she weeps
> Through the night, from her perch repeating her piteous plaint,
> Filling woods far and wide with sorrowful song.

The hypothetical explanation of the melancholy of the nightingale's song illuminates the intimate and necessary relationship between

---
[24] Such verses as these Alpers 1979: 92 terms 'frank self-dramatization', citing Waltz 1927: 36.
[25] I treat this topic in Perkell 1989: 82–5. Cf. also Perkell 1978: 220–1 and 1981: 175–7.
[26] Cf. Anderson 1982: 36–50.

tragedy, beauty, and powerlessness. These are inextricably connected in the esthetic to which both Meliboeus and Orpheus adhere. This correlation does not detract from the beauty and value of their song. Rather the irony—if it is that—is that tragic circumstances give song its subject and focus. Aristaeus in the *Georgics* and Tityrus in *Eclogue* 1 are both more successful in the world and more practical in resolution of their problems than are Orpheus and Meliboeus. Their sensibilities are less fine and their griefs, accordingly, less intense. Therefore, while Boyle, for example, wholly idealizes Meliboeus,[27] I suggest that the portrait of him is complex and problematic. The *Eclogue* poet is perhaps implying that the sensibility and imagination that create beautiful song are not fundamentally compatible with success in the world. Perhaps such a sensibility would, in the deepest way, not even wish for success, for success would eliminate the subject of its song, which is loss.

Eclogue 1 deals most fundamentally with different qualities of imagination and value, and with the power of pastoral (both Meliboeus' and Virgil's) to move, to bring together, and continually to transcend in spirit the unpalatable reality of crushing external circumstances. Pastoral poetry in this *Eclogue*, as spoken by Meliboeus, has emotive power and effects a community of longing for shared ideals. The poetry of Meliboeus, with its particular vision and values, converts Tityrus, just as it moves any reader who responds to its idealizing, to its mysterious nostalgia, and to its sadness.[28] Meliboeus' poetry ultimately brings him together with Tityrus and brings responsive readers together with both of them, for it creates a shared longing, a shared esthetic, and consequently shared values. Tityrus' last action, therefore, is the appropriately humane one of reaching out to aid and solace another, even if inadequately. For Meliboeus, exile is postponed and mitigated by the offer of lodging, apples, chestnuts, and cheese. And in the largest sense, to have one's suffering postponed or mitigated is all that any of us can hope for. Tityrus' sympathy for Meliboeus is marked by his taking Meliboeus' esthetic and tone. He comes to close with the same haunting music of loss

---

[27] Boyle 1986: 17.
[28] Cf. Leach for another perspective: '... the garden is not an end in itself but an opportunity. Its function is not to satisfy but to breed a restlessness that impels man toward some higher end' (1974: 36).

and serenity that earlier had characterized Meliboeus, as night is both a natural—and hence reassuring—close, and yet somehow ominous as well.[29]

If this reading of the last verses of the *Eclogue* is legitimate, if affects the meaning of the poem as a whole. Putnam and Boyle, for example, have read the poem as depicting the tragic collision of individual and empire, with the ascendancy of Rome signaling the loss of creative freedom. Meliboeus, the true poet, is lost to the country and will, as he says, no longer sing (77). Remaining are Tityrus, pedestrian and without moral sensibility, and the *impius miles*—a dark picture. If, however, Tityrus' final speech does reflect moral development and esthetic responsiveness, then the tragedy of Meliboeus' exile and of the loss to the country of his voice is somewhat mitigated by Tityrus' awakened sensibility. Pastoral would have a new voice.[30]

This reading allows us to see a fine balance between the opening and closing of the poem. Initially Tityrus, apparently indifferent to others' suffering and loss, plays his own song; but the conclusion finds him reaching out, in a gesture of pastoral community, to share with another. Thus the power of pastoral to effect response and to change values is subtly suggested, even as Meliboeus' own pastoral voice is stilled. This interpretation allows a fine balance also between the tragedy of Meliboeus' exile and the birth of Tityrus' beautiful new tone, and would thus corroborate, if for different reasons, Segal's insight that the poem concludes with an 'atmosphere of suspension amid contraries... [which] sets the tone for the *Eclogues*'.[31]

---

[29] Similarly Pöschl sees the end as both peaceful and dark: 'Man kann also vielleicht von einem offenen Schluß reden. Die Mischung von Melancholie und Serenität, die das ganze Gedicht bestimmt, wäre dann auch hier noch fühlbar' (1964: 63). Cf. Putnam 1970: 65 ff.

[30] See Perkell 2001: 64–88 and Perkell 1996: 128–40 for similarly tensioned readings of *Eclogues* 9 and 10.

[31] Segal 1965: 243–4. *Eclogue* 10 concludes with a comparably paradoxical tension between hope and despair. Gallus, as the *Eclogue* poet 'quotes' him, has failed to find solace or sustaining value in pastoral. His *amor* and the effect of the larger world on him are destabilizing and destructive. Yet even as this is so, the poet's/Virgil's natural and positive love for Gallus is expressed in this poem for him and continues to grow. At the same time as he bids farewell to pastoral and clearly reveals its deficiencies, Virgil makes—in the pastoral mode—the finest statement of its positive values and a moving demonstration of its power. (Interestingly Putnam 1970: 373 finds the idea of growth in *Eclogue* 10 menacing since, he observes, pastoral confines and orders all things and requires limits for its survival.)

Finally I would like to consider the relationship between Meliboeus' pastoral vision and that of the *Eclogue* poet, the composer of the whole poem, Virgil. That is to say, does the substance, vision, or esthetic of Meliboeus' song differ from that of the poem as a whole? I would argue that it does. Meliboeus' pastoral vision, as expressed in 1–2, 4–5, and 53–8 does have a genuinely escapist and idyllic focus, as Meliboeus imagines an ideal, an alternative to reality, although he does not openly acknowledge it to be such. It is Meliboeus' vision that, I believe, led Bruno Snell to see Virgil's pastoral as purely escapist.[32] Meliboeus' capacity for melancholy and his intense observations of unhappy realities seem at variance with his fantasies and longings. Possibly there is no mere, material reality with which he would be content. Virgil's pastoral, on the other hand, as reflected in the substance of the poem as a whole, has a fuller and more complex vision. Although he, too, sees a beauty in pathos and loss (as reflected in Meliboeus' songs), he also suggests something positive as well in Tityrus' invitation and in the birth of his beautiful new tone. Tityrus' (putative) experience of the pastoral idyll (1–5) and his lovely last words literally surround Meliboeus' sorrow. This movement parallels that of Theocritus' first *Idyll*, wherein Daphnis' death is bracketed by the mutual esteem of the shepherd-singers, which opens the poem, and the vigorous vitality of frisking goats, which concludes it.[33]

From its opening to its close Virgil's poem is dialectical, containing tense oppositions that compel the reader to questions of justice, politics, humane value, and the arbitrary nature of experience.[34] These oppositions are susceptible of no easy resolution. Virgil's poetry tends to illuminate and multiply ambiguities rather than to simplify complexities. *Eclogue* 1 expresses a tension in experience and also apprehends a certain, perhaps even promising, balance within it. Thus Virgil is grander in vision than either Meliboeus or Tityrus, each of whom is more limited by his individual perspective and less subtle, less nuanced. Simultaneously present in *Eclogue* 1 are ideal

---

[32] Snell 1953: 281–309. For further references to Snell and Klingner envisioning Arcadia as 'a refuge from the violence of history' see Leach 1974: 21 and 21 n. 6.

[33] Cf. note 31 above for comparable mixing of tone in *Eclogue* 10.

[34] Patterson 1987: 6: 'Virgil bequeathed to us... a dialectical structure, an ancient poetics no less elliptical than those of Plato and Aristotle, and one that has been, I would argue, at least as influential.'

and real in many forms and in unresolved tension.[35] Therefore the reading sketched here, plausible or even compelling as it may seem to some, cannot resolve definitively the questions that absorb readers of this poem. Much discussed questions, for example, about the timeliness, sincerity, and efficacy of Tityrus' invitation, all of which reflect importantly on the moral direction of the poem as a whole, elude resolution because Virgil has left the conclusion open, the future actions of both characters unrevealed.[36] This lack of clarity, this real impossibility of uncomplicated and definitive moral judgment, is Virgil's hallmark and informs, I would argue, the movement of the *Georgics* and *Aeneid* as well.

[35] L. Marx 1964: 25 calls this intrusion of the real the 'counterforce' in the pastoral design. Marx's entire study is of great interest for those working on pastoral of any period.

[36] Indeed, Patterson argues that 'what people think of Virgil's *Eclogues* is a key to their own cultural assumptions, because the text was so structured as to provoke, consciously or unconsciously, an ideological response' (1987: 7).

This essay is a revised version of a paper initially presented at the 1988–89 APA Annual Meeting. I would like to thank Professors Wendell Clausen, Edward Courtney, and the Editor and anonymous readers of *TAPA* for their helpful comments.

7

Virgil's Third *Eclogue*: How Do You Keep an Idiot in Suspense?

John Henderson

1. BEGINNING

I must have your credentials, sing me who you are.[1]

Two herdsmen meet and bicker; bargain over a stake; duel in balladeering; and ballot their umpire for a final decision. The first half of their poem dramatises the process of challenge and defiance from which the bout materialises; the result is a draw.

After the absence of song from *Eclogue* 1 (our first Latin bucolic), where Meliboeus quit the valley for ever, 'taking his songs with him' on the road to nowhere (v. 77, *carmina nulla canam*), and after the solitary solo of *Eclogue* 2's serenade *pathétique*, 'unrefined as it was overwrought' (vv. 4–5, *haec incondite... studio iactabat inani*), Virgil introduces the 'amoebaean' cutting-contest between pastoral singers, the duet as duel. In the movement between *Eclogue* 2 and 3, Virgil brings us straight to the heart of his art—from a solitude into a sociality.

Commentators confine themselves almost entirely to comparing the poem with Theocritean song-contests, and to declaring it among

---

This paper, first published in 1998, was reprinted, in slightly modified form, in Henderson 1999: 146–69 (notes on 304–10). The version appearing here is largely identical with that of 1999.

[1] MacNeice 1966: 37 'Eclogue by a five-barred gate (Death and two shepherds)'.

the poet's first compositions. Coleman 1977: 128–9, for example, spells out the thinking here:

||One of the earliest *Eclogues*... this poem is heavily indebted to Theocritus.... All the innovations have something of the experimental and tentative about them, and the *Eclogue* as a whole is probably the least successful of the ten.||

Such author-centred response represents at bottom a resistance to reading the script as a dramatic mime, preferring to judge the product of Virgil's novitiate (and judge that this is such a product) rather than enter into the rudenesses of his combative herdsmen. Many readers who *have* been prepared to engage with the exchange between the characters have found in their banter a less than pleasant crudity,[2] and ascribed it to the immaturity of a great writer-to-be.

Cups of ink spilled on the poem have attempted what none of its three herdsmen try out loud, namely to solve the pair of riddles with which the song-contest ends, before the judge pronounces the result.[3] The multitude of more or less persuasive solutions spans all the way from putative attribution to the bucolic minds of the riddlers, to ascription to their creator, the intellectual, urban, bookish, Hellenizing poetaster, who here, in any event, dares a touch of rustic needling that he precisely did *not* find in his studies in Theocritus. The *Idylls* (and other Theocritea) include *no* riddle-me-ree stage-business. *Solution* of the riddles has generally seemed the self-evident challenge to scholar-readers.

If we stress the frame-less nature of the *Eclogue*, a narrator-less mime left to situate itself without editorial comment, like the first, and then each successive odd *Eclogue*, we will begin, instead, from the dramatic scenario of the clash between Damoetas and Menalcas. We will get into the 'ring' alongside these competitors, and follow the agonistic rhetoric of their sallies, until the point where riddle and counter-riddle bring the bout to an end. This is the distinctive

---

[2] Esp. Leach 1974: 172, 'The rivalry of Damoetas and Menalcas is one of jealousy and insidious meanness. Their world does not seem to be a free and generous countryside, but sordid and oppressive.'

[3] Cf. Briggs 1981: 1310 for proposed answers to the riddles; esp. Campbell 1982/3, Springer 1983/4, Dix 1995.

approach of B. B. Powell, in his lively ring-side commentary on the trading of verbal punches between the herdsmen in their songs.[4]

On the other hand, if we look over the whole composition, our reading is likely to attend to the internal division where conversational bickering gives way to singing before the appointed judge.[5] The riddles are positioned as the close to singing that began from appropriative rival invocations of the greatest gods of the cosmos and of poetry, Jupiter and Apollo. Thus, C. P. Segal's reading follows a sublative movement through the poem, finding that song raises the singers' horizons up to the aether, as high as the budding poet's imagination can lift them.[6] The business of the wager is now a textual 'operator' which signals the reader to search, in what follows, for the right wavelength for reception of the poem. And the riddles must find uplift to match. The terms of the wager dictate the valorization of the singing, 'proceeding from petty wrangling to an harmonious conclusion'.[7]

No doubt the songs encourage such transcoded reading, not least by their puncturing the world of Galatea, Amyntas and their like, half way through the contest, with flattering praises for Pollio, and scorn for triumviral poetry's Beavis and Butthead—Bavius and Mevius (vv. 84–91).[8] Once the singers play for the approval of Virgil's powerful friend, whose consulate will occasion the straining devotions of the very next poem, the independence of characters from creator is virtually erased. The songs are re-positioned in a scene of rivalry between Virgil's production of his dialogue and *his* rivals' own counter-bids to attract praise and authority. To speak plainly, Virgil has dressed up in rusticity just such a competitive *soirée chez* Pollio as often graced his salon, and for a moment lets the veil slip so we can't miss it.

---

[4] Powell 1976.

[5] Cf. Rosenmeyer 1969: 156, 'The fiction within the poem distinguishes between speaking and singing. But in a sense pastoral singing contests are merely extensions of the potential that resides in the pastoral conversations.' ('Merely'?).

[6] Segal 1967 (= 1981: 235–64).

[7] Otis 1964: 143.

[8] Quite apart from the shock of its appearance in the amoebaean, 'The twice repeated name of Asinius Pollio, soldier, statesman, historian and poet, has the calculated force which only the first direct reference in the Eclogues to a known historical character could possess.' (Putnam 1970: 129).

Yet the poem does more than install the reader, through the figure of Pollio, as judge of Virgil's adolescent promise, ready to patronize or scorn his efforts, just like modern critics. The dramatic scenario is not simply abolished by its inclusion of an orientation beyond the frame of its bucolic horizons: before either singer offers a couplet, their poem has already negotiated the question of what they are singing *for*. That is to say, the 'preliminaries' of *Eclogue* 3 do not simply set up its song-contest, but create an opportunity for the participants to discuss the stake of their bout. To be sure, they *argue* rather than discuss; but the product for the reader is a dramatization within the text of the fundamental question of what is at stake in (the) representation. This text parades explicit terms and a direct answer.

Even the surreal rupture of the characterology through the inclusion of Pollio's name is framed within a performance which has already been evaluated in advance: the stake of the singing was settled before ever the song took wing, so we already know what all the contest contains is worth before it arrives—while our retrospect will re-value the wager, and we shall need to reckon again. Prize and reprise problematize each other. The rustic bet tells what the song's flight of fancy *must* be worth; the urbane conceit says this *can't* be right, so think again.

Or rather, given that the poem stages the scene of self-valuation as *itself* a contest, as well as the exchanges that constitute the song-contest 'proper', what was offered in the first place was no more than a running shuffle of proposals and counter-proposals *toward* fixing a 'pot'. It is not at all clear whether any particular decision was agreed, and what that might be, let alone what it might mean to Virgil, and to us.[9] We were not handed an undisputed and definitive idea of what

---

[9] Almost uniquely, Leach 1974: 174–5 claims that Damoetas' 'boasting gives Menalcas a chance to close the bargain and *dismiss the heifer*.... When the singing is over, Palaemon, the judge, seems unaware that the cups had been offered and assumes the prize was a heifer.' But cf. Rose 1942: 41, 'The heifer has not been wagered.... (Palaemon) does not know what they are singing for but merely assumes that so earnest a contest must be for a considerable prize.' Powell 1976: 115 n. claims that 'Segal, I take it, has not understood that a heifer is the prize': but this, I take it, is not quite to understand Segal's position: while it is true that he slights 'the lowly cow' against 'the elaborate cups' (1967: 307), and forgets what he is about by remarking (302) that 'The cups and the long debate on the relative value of cups and cow

the stake was meant to be, whether or not we come to feel that we have to re-consider what we made of it. Nor, on the other hand, are the contributions to the song made by either singer self-evidently apposite and in keeping with the level of dignity represented by the putative prize.

Our combatants are in no position to *comment* on this themselves, since the singers can call no time-out for critical remarks; but every snippet of song fires a salvo in a running battle of mutual disparagement. If we defer to the poet's surrogate authority-figure, and look to Palaemon for a final arbitration, or at least for a summation of what the singers have achieved, still readers are themselves in the interim on trial.

When judgement *is* duly pronounced on the singing, in a formal declaration of the result and award of the prize the moment has come for stake and songs to bind together the authorized interpretation. We shall be *told* what we have heard, when it is over. But, we should have noticed, the judge Palaemon was not present, as we were, to witness or approve agreement on the stake; he was ushered onto the scene fortuitously, walking into Menalcas' sentence on the very instant he determined to look for someone to play judge (v. 50). Besides, his verdict is a draw, so he doesn't settle the matter by *implementing* his decision. In fact, quite apart from the question of the stake, his pronouncement has itself generated widely different notions of what he (must have) meant. In any case, it is not, ultimately, at all obvious that the judge does speak either representatively, on behalf of some implied rustic community; or authoritatively, in terms of preferring some rustic values to others; let alone

---

(29–43) are now forgotten', and (286) 'Both *the cups* and the contest of which they *are the prize* become meaningful at a level other than that of rustic realism: both are transformed into something symbolic'. Segal wanted his Vergil to find a way to let the Theocritean scenario shine through his own—unresolved—by-play (284): 'Theocritus has the single shepherd offer both cup and goat. The two gifts are of coordinate value.... For Vergil... there is a cleavage between the two realms.... (H)is scene of bargaining... begins to open the dichotomy between practical and aesthetic, "rustic" and "poetic". (286) ... The issue between them, cups or cow, is still unresolved at the moment when Palaemon, the umpire-to-be, appears and brings an end to this first half of the poem.... (302) [With 'Palaemon's closing speech'] the poet returns to and re-affirms the simplicity of his original pastoral setting after he has intimated the larger possibilities that lie within it.' *My* Segal treads a fine line between having his cups and milking them.

authorially, as the surrogate of the poet's viewpoint. The delivery of his verdict actually puts *his* judgement into question. We judge the judge from the dock.

All the same, the question of the stake of this song, of these songs, is, ineluctably, entangled with Palaemon's final judgement. But is this, when it comes, 'a neutral decision'? Thus W. V. Clausen (1994: 91–2) rightly adds to the commentators' highlighted topics, consideration of the question, 'Why does the singing-match of Damoetas and Menalcas end in a draw?' This promising approach, however, will end in (perhaps not unintended) embarrassment. Clausen declares the singers 'virtually indistinguishable—except for sexual orientation'—and he terms the umpire's verdict 'a neutral decision'. The reason why Menalcas spoke first, but Damoetas sang first, thus breaking Theocritus' routine, is 'Because Palaemon intervenes and determines otherwise.... Menalcas and Damoetas, Damoetas and Menalcas—an effect of parity is achieved, and their singing-match appropriately ends in a draw. "Non nostrum inter uos...", says Palaemon (108), without embarrassment.' The circularity, at any rate, of the reasoning here is perfect. Alternatively, we could wonder, is the draw disparagement of both the contenders, indifference, or nonchalance, or dereliction of duty? Does(n't) Palaemon plump for a quiet life, and elude the recriminations of a loser? May this be no honestly adjudicated and honourable draw, but rather a craven ducking of responsibility, if not an (insulting) insouciance, or outright failure of will...? It may.[10] Simple 'parity' is no answer.

So it is, that the three components of the mime—its ceremonies of: dispute and wager; songs and riddles; final judgement—are interimplicated in a contest for mastery of the poem's interpretation. But readers must judge between the contestants, including the judge. Since this is a dramatic script, the reader is also the director: we load our version of the squabbling and its climax in the foolery over agreeing the wager; we take our own measure of the entries for the song contest, somewhere from predictable or state of the art, to astounding, to baffling; and we produce a judge we can, or cannot,

---

[10] Rose 1942: 41–2 ventures: 'His judgement is no more than a modest refusal to judge, and makes it clear that his mind has been busy at least as much with his own thoughts and dreams as with what they have been singing.... He hastily declares a draw.' Alpers 1979: 105 speaks of Palaemon's 'suspension of judgement'.

even must not, trust. This is our beef—it's up to us to load the performance our way.

This is to insist that the poem is dead meat if it is not read in full recognition of this dramatic condition for its realization. Even to pronounce it unsuccessful is, once this is understood, to enter into the scenario. To have judge Palaemon bless, or write off, the singers is also to join in. To answer the riddles is to run the show. To object to Pollio & the gang is to play judge. To fix a price on the contest is to outfox the herdsmen. To enjoy, or deplore, their banter is to understand the rustic other, it may be, all *too* well. But Damoetas and Menalcas here are going to sing whereof they know not, as only the urbane can know, as we read our poet's verses. Poetry in which the bumpkins are caught, beyond their ken.

This mime, in short, is all about representation. Song, poetry; impersonation, empathy; worth, valuation; implication, and self-assessment. This is a contest, but also a hoot; and rumination on the spark of collaborative energy, and the pettiness even of humanity's best moments. We shall ponder each of the main sectors of the poem in turn, and stress the 'ethnographic' problem that arises from our insertion into a milieu which we know to be an imagined construct, one specially contrived to exclude the like of us, and one which performs, but does not explicate, the values its inhabitants hold dear.

2. BICKERING (VV. 1–27)

> I have here an apt occasion, to say, that Virgil, could have written sharper satires than either Horace or Juvenal, if he would have employed his talent that way. I will produce a verse and a half of his, in one of his *Eclogues*, to justify my opinion; and with commas after every word, to show that he has given almost as many lashes, as he has written syllables. 'Tis against a bad poet; whose ill verses he describes. *Non tu, in triuiis, indocte, solebas, stridenti, miserum, stipula, disperdere carmen?* (vv. 26–7)[11]

---

[11] Dryden 1970 (= 1693): 258, 'A discourse concerning the original and progress of Satire, prefixed to the Satires of Decimus Junius Juvenalis...together with the Satires of Aulus Persius Flaccus'.

The exchanges between the herdsmen begin with questions of ownership of animals, and end in insults about talent in song. This could be the most important objective, and we could endure the conversation as a warm-up that evolves the song-contest. Anything unobjectionably plausible by way of striking up dialogue would *do*. In a performance, whether imaginary or staged, Role 1 will approach Role 2, to be joined later, 'settled on a patch of grass', by their arbiter (v. 55). In view, 'this heifer' in Role 2's care (v. 29). The talk starts up from nothing, and only gets to the point once the scene has come together. The singing's the thing.

But a reading on these lines would scarcely amount to more than a formalist's imperious wave of the hand, bidding the script to mean when it is told to start meaning, and not before. If we go back to the *entrée*, *without* knowing quite so much, we'll find that the banter, starting from Role 1's opening question, has much more to mean than it says.

In the abstract, doubtless, it is best to allow the start to an exchange to open the lines of communication, and let what follows orient and define the discourse more narrowly as it proceeds. But Role 1 does more than let us know that he knows Role 2 well enough to call his name, 'Damoetas', and he offers an invitation more precise than 'Will you respond, if I speak?' An opening question presses for an answer, so its function is to engage Damoetas' attention, and participation; but what, the question asks *us*, is Role 1 *saying* with his enquiry? *cuium pecus...?* (v. 1).[12]

At one extreme, 'Tell me: whom's beast/s?' could be ostensively fraternal. Here, then, is rapport. The herder's prime concern is to watch 'his' animals; that is what he is for, why he is here. It must be. This is how one drover sees another. They are fellows. They are defined by the beasts they themselves define. What other question could come first, between such as them?

But this can (also, or instead) be accusation or importunate aggression, whether masquerading as innocent interest in a fellow

---

[12] Critics stick to formal analysis: e.g. Coleman 1977: 109, *ad loc.*, 'the adjective occurs often in comedy... and once in a legal formula... but its subliterary character [is] here deliberately employed for rustic colour', Clausen 1994: 93, *ad loc.*, 'Nor is "*cuium pecus*" rustic speech.... The obvious model for such a scene was Plautus.'

or not. Fixing by name, ordering a reply, demanding to know—this may be intentionally brusque. Is the insinuation that Damoetas is known well enough to the speaker for him to be sure that the/se animal/s *can't* be 'his'? Or, if that goes without saying, because the likes of Roles 1 *or* 2 don't *own* their animals, is the provocation that Damoetas works for one owner after another—who is it this time?— because...he is shiftless,...unreliable,...fast and loose? (The ancient commentator Servius reads the beginning this way: 'He starts from bitterness. For by saying *cuium pecus*, he shows he is a hireling.') Then the insult will be that Damoetas is known through and through; the interrogative was only a modal ruse to frame this calumny. The only thing Role 1 will be *asking* Damoetas is whether he knows a put-down when he hears one; whether he knows he's put down when he's asked if he knows. *Dic mihi*... ('Tell me', v. 1).

In our poem, the reply is to match, for length (v. 2). There is no phatic engagement with Role 1; no naming of him, no pronoun. And no hint to help us with our readerly dilemma with 'Not Meliboeus'?' (v. 1, *an Meliboei?*), that we do not (yet) know how to deal with the inmates of the bucolic valley of the *Eclogue* Book, whether or not to treat the bearer of a name across separate compositions as significantly the 'same' character. Hence we do not know how much sting there is in this suggestion: is collaboration in the dispossession of Meliboeus the point of this abusive insinuation?[13] Damoetas' *mihi* echoes the questioner's *mihi*, but otherwise, the response makes no overture in reciprocation. If the question wanted to learn who owns the beast/s, and made a suggestion; well, the guess was wrong, and the answer is simple. Over, and out: 'No one stole the tarts.' Or else, taking a less aggressive tone, this speaker, Damoetas, accepts that the question is fair enough, because the animal has (or the animals have) only just come into his care: the new arrangement counts as news, in this company.

---

[13] See Flintoff 1975/6: 21–3, on Menalcas, 'We find a series of attempts to give substance and unity to the name.' *Contra*, Patterson 1987: 4–5, on pastoral characters as vacant signs. The commentators are not in the least interested in the reappearance of Meliboeus here. Such hardness of heart; such short memories: *carmina nulla canam*.

Perhaps, though, the repetition of the true owner's name—'neither Damoetas', nor Meliboeus', but Aegon's', yes, Aegon's'—protests over-defensively (v. 2)? And crows aggressively, proud of being trusted, where the questioner (patently) is not? *That* is why *Damoetas* is not free to wander off to prey on other, responsible hands kept busy watching their flocks, unlike *some* people...

So far as the construction of the whole poem is concerned, we'll find that this initial exchange, however low-key, or abrupt, we decide to make it, whether functional in striking up the mime or ethopoeic in giving the first impressions of the interaction between the roles, proves to pinpoint at once the topic which will connect first to last: 'Who do/es the beast/s belong to? Whom's are they now?' (or: 'Who will own it next?').

The first response to Damoetas is to turn away from the human dolt, to pretend solidarity with the sheep: Damoetas is now a non-person: *hic* ('This one', v. 5). He does not relate to the animals, but squeezes them dry, systematically robs the flock of its future; the true owner is the one worthy of rivalry with Role 1, even if he is a loser; what Damoetas is condemned for doing is brought under the heading of the sheep's welfare, from a herdsman's moral high ground (*subducitur*, 'stolen', v. 6). The hierarchy runs down from Aegon, to the flock, and at the bottom comes this displaced nonentity, who does not merit the expenditure of breath or the dignity of address.

The rejoinder to this signals that a 'macho trading of insults' has begun (*uiris... obicienda*, v. 7), and bats back more 'askance' rustic 'derision', this time a cocktail of unspeakable sex, with 'profanation' for mixer (vv. 7–9, the ellipse of the verb hinting at unutterable filth: *transuersa tuentibus... risere... sacello*). Holy cow! Send not to know what peals of nymphette merriment might greet—they palm off a put-on that tolls, sex in the head, for *thee*. The bickering that ensues will hammer on about ownership as a measure of status and worth. Claims to own; the right to appropriate or dominate; stealth as the discourse of propriety, and the property of discourse.

Aegon is supposed to worry whether Neaera rates him as much as Role 1: whom's is *she*? Meanwhile, hireling Damoetas '*steals*' their 'mothers' milk' from the lambs (*subducitur*, v. 6). Someone, and it wasn't Role 1, trust him, vandalized '*Micon's* trees and vine-shoots' (vv. 10–11). Role 1 is, it transpires, 'perverse Menalcas' by name, the one who smashed '*Daphnis'* bow and arrows' in pique (vv. 12–13). Damoetas was spotted bushwhacking '*Dam—on's* billygoat' (vv. 17–20).

The squabbling leads inexorably to the subject of song because that is how 'ownership of a beast' can be won and lost, challenged and vindicated: the voice, or 'the musical instrument you own', can convert into aggrandisement of self (*mea...fistula* ~ *meus...caper*, vv. 22–3). And this equation of selfhood with property leads, even, or even specially, in the idyllic countryside, to dispute and special pleading. Somebody may have a moral right to a possession, but the real world may prohibit its realization: a prize may be 'acknowledged as due, but have to remain owing', however much occasion such a claim gives for scepticism (vv. 23–6).

At the same time, the bickering negotiates towards a further episode in a contentious narrative, of claim and counter-claim to prestige, in terms of ownership arising from musical superiority. On the one hand, this is but the chosen terrain on which to trade insults, boasting laced with spite; but on the other, it obliges Damoetas to prove his claims by risking his winnings, while challenging Menalcas, Role 1, to match him, all the way.

If the trading of insults in this 'flyting' is good-natured, just what you might expect in the country, contemptible gaucherie, or whatever, nevertheless it has performed already a 'tango' of cut-and-thrust abuse and innuendo, and has thus provoked outsiders like ourselves to explore how acute or otherwise the trading of responses has contrived to be, so far. Are these simple folk—or cunning coves? Much the same as us sophisticates, *mutatis mutandis*, or unutterably neanderthal? There is no call to take sides yet. We don't even have to decide, or feel we could decide, whether we have only luckily meandered toward a challenge to a singing match, or were shepherded along the way by two old stagers who know the sequence of moves that result in a wager, and enjoy the release from inhibition that goes together with getting to that point. Is this the best 'that countryside song can do—its worst'? (= *stridenti miserum stipula disperdere carmen?*, v. 27).

3. BARGAINING (VV. 28–54)

'I thought you were satisfied where you were.'
'Every man has his price,' said Morris Zapp. 'Mine is one hundred grand a year and no duties. Have you heard of something new called the UNESCO Chair of Literary Criticism?'[14]

The singers have talked; they have shown us what they are, put before us the pride and shame of their kind—'bent...worst...unschooled' (vv. 13, 17, 26, *peruerse...pessime...indocte*). But they have also triggered the sort of show-down 'the pair' have it 'in common' to relish (v. 28, *inter nos...uterque*). Desire for winning is on a continuum with lust (vv. 3–4, 8–9), it stirs strong, potentially destructive, passions (vv. 14–15), and invests these selves in their successes, their ability to verbalize them, and to command their recognition (vv. 21–4). All the bragging and stabbing have geed up a collision which both men need, as they need each other, and need each other's banter to score from.

The first series of exchanges emphasized that the negotiation is, in a word, a power-play. Its significance may, or may not, be calibrated with the value of the objects put up front, whether in our, or in the actors', reckoning. Like any other possessions, they may only be a convenient currency in personal politics. The dispute gives the chance to meddle, to toy with another's *amour propre*, sting him with loose talk. On the other hand, as the conversation moves toward the formal challenge to sing or be a mockery, the participants jockey for advantage in such a way that they threaten to throw the confrontation into disarray. In retrospect, they have already undermined the security of 'transfer by gift', which may always be 'wrecked' (vv. 12–15), and warped payment of debt by an accusation of 'theft' met with a defence of 'justified assertion of rights' (vv. 16–24). When Damoetas comes to bid first for the stake of the song-contest to come, and challenges Menalcas to name his matching pledge, we are uncomfortably aware that it may be posssible to bet 'when you can't deliver', a trick Damoetas just claimed Damon did with him, for

---

[14] Lodge 1984: 195.

whatever reason, even none (vv. 23–4). The very phrasing of Damoetas' current wager already invites, or betrays, suspicion as the name of the game of bargaining: even before he can spit out his 'pledge of a heifer', he has interrupted himself with a 'precautionary defence' of its worth: *ego hanc uitulam...depono* interrupted by *ne forte recuses...*, vv. 29–31). It is not difficult to play the rhetoric here as an attempt to preempt a counter-bid by seizing the initiative given the utterant by his performance of the contractual speech-act of a wager: he plants the suggestion that 'backing-down' would be a sensible reaction to this impossibly high opening gambit: *forte recuses* (v. 29) construes first with 'heifer' for object, as Damoetas already defends his animal from anticipated scorn; then turns defensiveness into a tack which insinuates that Menalcas may, or would do well to, decline *to make a counter-stipulation*, whether because he is a no-hoper, a mummy's boy wet behind the ears, or because there's nothing on their earth can touch this choice dam and twin calves.

On the other hand, the beauty of the wager is that it always lays a trap for the wary. Why has wily Damoetas (you know he's wily, as wily as you are, Menalcas) bragged out loud the value of his heifer as if it might face his opponent down? Obviously he is guying Menalcas, making sure he can't decide, however he might choose to conceive, phrase, or dress it up, to back down, since that would be to prove Damoetas to have called him right. Obviously his technique is the same one he must have used on Damon, luring him in out of his depth by telling him that was what he was up to, then later robbing him of the bet he was never in a position to make, since he couldn't pay up. After all, he just *told* us that was his strategy. Why else did he lay this bluff on Menalcas?

However we choose to direct the scene, we are here training our sights on 'an animal presently being watched over by Damoetas': *ego hanc uitulam* (v. 29) returns us to where we came in, and Menalcas' question *cuium pecus?* (v. 1). This heifer (or cow), for sure, definitely exists, large as life: but the eyes can't see ownership—is it, too, Aegon's property?[15] Menalcas thinks this way, at once 'refusing to (pretend he can) bet an animal from his herd' (vv. 32–3). For him

---

[15] e.g. Coleman 1977: 113, *ad loc.*, believes the herdsman: 'like the bull in 100 the heifer belongs to himself and not like the sheep to Aegon.'

to do any such thing would be 'reckless daring' (*ausim*, v. 32). Has he seen straight through Damoetas, then? Does he hint as much by spelling out that when an animal comes to be milked and feeds its young 'twice' (a day) (v. 30), these are routinely scheduled opportunities for their actual owners to check up on them, 'twice a day' (v. 34)?

Or is he trumping Damoetas' move? It's not his fault he has 'a fanatical father and wicked stepmother' (v. 33), but rather it's his opportunity to talk down (cow) his opponent. He challenges him not to be impressed by his words, if he can, and presents a description of some beechwood cups he has, stored away untouched (vv. 35–43). It might be telling that he supplies *verbal* cups (bull), but does not produce them. If wagering required actual physical deposition to be in force, this offer would not count as a bet. It is, besides, couched in the future tense: *ponam* (v. 36) does not mean 'I will stake' = 'I am (now) willing to stake', 'I hereby (agree to) pledge', but 'I shall stake' at some later moment, presumably when the cups are directly to hand? At any rate, it does not do to presume that the speech-act can altogether cordon off slippage between the performatively present, and the performatively promissory, guarantee; yet, by the same token, a wary customer should best wait to clap eyes on pledged goods before accepting them as collateral.

So, the suspicion could grow, Menalcas is showing off to his rival his powerful way with language, and telling him so as he does it: the 'crazy' talk (v. 37) of betting with animals they neither of them have, whether to win or lose, gives way to the hyperbolic praise of the artistic object that sets its word-merchant a cut above his fellow (*fatebere maius*, 'you will admit it's colossal by comparison', v. 35), who could only manage his naive one-liner of encomium for the plain and simple 'heifer, and her twins' (v. 30). This ribbing is, so you could run the scene, exactly calculated to drive Damoetas wild: predicting that he will be the one to yield, because he will have to accept that Menalcas will be doing a good job of capturing the worth of his cups in his sales-pitch, his powers of description already acknowledged (vv. 35–6). The exchanges are still in speech, not song, but they already body forth a series of exchanges, they already contest for rhetorical superiority, they already debate the worth of their eloquence, more or less eloquently or indeed blatantly.

Is this all the song-contest we need? If Menalcas has seized his chance to put down his marker, has this actually put him into an unassailable lead? Or does this bartering ruin in advance the singing when it does finally come?

Indeed, let's go one better. Or, at any rate, further. Are these herdsmen spoiling for a fight, or do they mean to spoil their fight? The heifer is 'here', but very likely off-limits as a stake. The cups are only here on the wing of a promise, and there is no attempt to pledge them this instant. They operate, however, as a raising of the stakes to an altogether higher order of magnitude: not the heifer and its routine visits to be milked, her udders to be drunk by her twin calves (v. 30), but (an unspecified number of) 'cups' which 'lips have never touched, pristine and held back from mundane use' (vv. 36; 43).[16] The cups come loaded with cultural baggage, specially designed to psych out Damoetas who has to listen to it. They are a work of art, not just utensils; they carry the trademark of a genius, 'divine Alcimedon', a name you must know, or else forfeit all claim to *chic* status (v. 37). A connoisseur's description works with the material empathetically,[17] as if repeating over again in the materiality of well-turned discourse the craftsman's magical creativity: the cups are 'engraved', but we shall 'add on' detail represented in relief, just as the cup offers to the impressionistic the illusion of 'adding' on the outer layers of carved wood to the wood which has actually been left for the core of the vessels (*superaddita*, v. 38).[18] The simulation of plastic representation by glyptic processes is a marvel not just because 'the chisel' cannot 'add', but only take away, wood, and cannot 'clothe' one layer of relief detail within another (*uestit*, v. 39), however miraculously 'easy' all this may be in the hands of a master (*facili*, v. 39); the 'scattered clusters of berries left to protrude through the tangle of

---

[16] Many readers spy '*two* beech cups' here, presumably reading back from 'For me too did the same A. make two cups' (v. 44, *et nobis idem Alcimedon duo pocula fecit*), as if Damoetas were guessing Menalcas had a pair of cups, and perhaps blurring the detail of the 'two signs' (v. 40, *duo signa*) into the bargain, perhaps, even, not managing or deigning to concentrate (e.g. Putnam 1970: 124. Coleman 1977: 114, *ad* 3.40, *duo signa*, notes, 'either one on each cup or one on either side of each cup').

[17] Cf. Segal 1967: 289–90 for brief appreciation of the artistry paraded here.

[18] On the poetic imagery of working 'in relief', cf. Crinagoras, *Anth. Pal.* 9.545.1 (on Callimachus' *Hekale*), τὸ τορευτὸν ἔπος, with G. D. Williams 1994: 80–1, esp. 81 n. 70; Coleman 1977: 113–14, *ad* 3.38, *superaddita*.

vine-tendrils', implying that many more lie hidden beneath, somehow achieve the relative 'pallor' of ivy (v. 39), whether by some change of hue in the grain of the beech, or as a shading effect from the 'carapace' of vine. The utterance here, whether in Menalcas' rhetoric or in Virgil's hexameters, is *not* 'describing' anything. Rather, it enacts its apprehension of the cups, with the simultaneity intrinsic to apposition (v. 37), followed by a 'pliant' line of 'easy supplementation' (v. 39) that 'clothes' the 'dispersed' units, or 'clusters' of its verbal material in the interlaced *chiaroscuro* of a final 'Golden Line' (v. 39). If the addressee takes all this in his stride, without qualms, worse follows. In the middle of these cups (you would find) 'two figures' (v. 40),[19] 'one of them Conon, whom, again, you *must* know, unless you're a hick from nowhere, and he's such a big name you're getting no clues, and the other—' (v. 40).

At this point, anacoluthon breaks the mood, and the modality. Menalcas has been performing for Damoetas' 'benefit', but his investment in description of the cups has kept him 'before', not 'with', his addressee: now the trap snaps shut, as the name without clues is followed by a clue, with the name to be provided—and provided by Damoetas. Well, 'who was it', represented on those cups, that have never come your way, that have in fact never seen the light of day (v. 43)? If your Menalcas really forgets the name, he comes a cropper, tripping over his own vanity and in his fall suturing and re-establishing the uncrossable divide between herdsmen and urban(e) culture. Perhaps Virgil, and Virgil's educated readers, will find it no trouble to supply the name that Menalcas doesn't recall; if not, this could be because his clues are inconclusive, as gauche as he is, too clumsy by half. Or *that* could be a problem for those among us who don't already know who it is that belongs in a pair with Conon; an artist, an Alcimedon, who knew Hellenistic iconography could perhaps fill in the name without hesitation, and judge accordingly how poor Menalcas' clues are, while deciding what sort of slip it is to forget so famous a name, of a figure on his own, supposedly most

---

[19] Clausen 1994: 100, *ad* 3.36–42 insists that '*in medio*... must mean "in the centre", in the interior of the cup, and not "in the fields, the spaces enclosed by the vine and ivy"... V. had in mind silver cups with a figured medallion occupying the centre of the bowl.'

precious, possessions.[20] Or is this too uncharitable for words—to write someone off for a casual temporary blockage, a name stuck on the tip of the tongue? Would a *friend* help out, take the question at face-value? Should it occur to Damoetas that this surprise question has been planted as a peremptory put-down? '*I've* forgotten—but you don't even *know.*'

The script has Damoetas react by ignoring the bait. He works back from Menalcas' throw-away last line (v. 43), commandeering that for his own parodic punchline (v. 47), before rubbishing it, and the whole routine that it capped, with an emphatic 'total rejection' (v. 48). Damoetas proves he can ham the connoisseur as well as anyone, parroting the designer-label of 'Alcimedon', before verbally replicating the 'embrace' of his cups by the verse-encircling 'soft... acanthus' (v. 45), and making the trees 'follow' Orpheus in the magical illusion of movement across the carving (v. 46). That he has 'two cups', with one figure 'in the middle' (vv. 44, 46 *vs.* 40, 'two figures in the middle', in the middle of the description), shows that he has registered the by-play of 'two-in-one' motifs that featured in Menalcas' rejoinder. Essentially, though, Damoetas squashes Menalcas' elaborate brow-beating and its flourish, the importunate question that put him on the spot. His response to what is (premonitorily) a virtual riddle, is to echo the terms used by the riddler. He dispels the glamour of Menalcas' vivid evocation of his proffered stake-to-be, by turning the gaze back to the physical presence of the heifer—all the more real by contrast with these underwhelming disappointments, the common-or-garden cups. A distinct possibility of 'stalemate' in the preliminaries for the contest stands, in the point-scoring of the disputation, for a victory in Damoetas' favour: the opponent can't produce a worthy stake, so it's a walk-over by default. Cups—who needs 'em?[21]

---

[20] Cf. Rosenmeyer 1969: 59, 'Virgil has his character strain against the rule (*sc.* that 'a herdsman should not be able to talk about matters which are beyond his ken'), but at the last minute pulls back, and by this jolt reminds the reader of the existence of the rule more effectively than if he had never broached the possibility of the herdsman facing up to his test.' I would endorse this classic deconstruction *avant la letter*—but my Virgil pulls back *just too late*.

[21] Cf. Boyle 1975: 194, 'The works of art (the cups) fail to affect the discord manifest in the herdsmen's world. From the artist's values and perceptions, embodied in his creative work, the herdsmen learn nothing'; M. O. Lee 1989: 55, '...there is no indication that either of the boys knows what the figures on the cups might mean.

In reckoning this far, we must have decided whether to take all this at face-value, complete with the coincidence of both herdsmen happening to own cups by the same genius. To put the point strongly, we must determine whether either of the characters in *our* versions of the mime own, or suppose that the other owns, any such objects. Were they Menalcas' fantasy? Might they just as well be, if you are Damoetas—or if you are a reader anxious that there be a song-contest as the dénouement of this bickering? Cups—what cups? Here is the heifer (see?)—where are any cups? These cups are a blind: the cups are, Damoetas knows, just a ruse, a blind, cheap talk: these so-called cups are '*nowhere*' (= *nihil*, v. 48). Damoetas' sarcasm may puncture the grandiose fantasizing of the hopeless name-dropper Menalcas, who conjured up a figure who encompassed the universe, in a worldwide achievement that captured the axes of time and space for all peoples, putting the seasonal round of all civilization on a rational basis by calculating a calendar. For farmers, and for everyone. In caricature, this imaginary figure is mirrored by the figure of Orpheus, drawing the trees to the music of the cups, a counter-myth whose hero outranks any astronomer royale, in or out of a pair, especially when a contest between musician singers is in the offing, and, so far as Menalcas' reverie is concerned, 'following' up that nonsense with his own preferred scene of one single genius leading his audience by the ears. That is his image, the image that will do for him. Not cosmic power of 'description' (v. 41), but affective power of rhetoric, performative clout. Menalcas can chew on *that.*

Menalcas' retort makes it quite clear that he has no intention of doing any such thing. On the other hand, it manages not to commit itself, in so many words, to—just about anything. He insinuates that Damoetas meant his sneer as an exit-line: if Damoetas has played an ace in pointing to the heifer, when Menalcas cannot retaliate directly since (for a start) his arrival on Damoetas' patch denies him on-the-spot access to his prize possessions, then Menalcas can happily sign him a blank verbal cheque. This stunt he pulls off in a breezy gesture that mock-pretends mock-submission: 'Just call and

---

Neither of them, in fact, has ever drunk from the cups'; Leach 1974: 175, 'The cups symbolize all that is lacking in these rustics whose conversation makes disorder its theme and takes no account of the beauty of the natural world.'

I'll meet you there, anywhere' (*ueniam quocumque uocaris*, v. 49). If, that is, it does not rather aim to fudge a way past commitment to any citable terms for the bet. *Has* Menalcas promised to match Damoetas' heifer with one of his own, even if he doesn't have one? Another 'Damon' story coming up?[22]

However we want the bargaining scene played, we find that it has run through a great batch of material as if it mattered in its own right, of vital interest to the herdsmen and essential information for their readers in deciding who they are and what they mean, in much the same way that the bickering already did. The heifer, and then, even more so, the cups seemed so very important to them at the moment they were crying them up. But they are forgotten with such alacrity that we may well wonder if they ever mattered at all. Menalcas' last word declares as much, in decocting terms for the wager into a purely formal matter, which is best pushed aside before it protects either combatant from entering the fray. 'Up the *ante* as high as you please, I'll see you', provokes speedy assent from Damoetas, who again mimics the other, renouncing further 'delaying tactics' (*in me mora non erit ulla*, v. 52 ~ *ueniam quocumque uocaris*, v. 49), agreeing that there is to be 'no running away' from the issue (*nec quemquam fugio*, v. 49 ~ *numquam hodie effugies*, v. 53), and swiftly changing the subject to *Palaemon* (vv. 50, 53, same final *sedes*, position in the line), who steps into the syntax and the type-scene, right on cue to play judge. We could well conclude that the business of settling the wagers has been a prevaricating diversion that both voices finally acknowledge to have been intimidatory scare-tactics, as likely as not meant to save on the nuisance of a show-down. Maybe the moves were more stylized than we (can) know, and the banter has been the shadow-boxing of rough-diamond camaraderie. The swagger on display in Menalcas' threats, in exactly the style of *nemo me impune*

---

[22] So M. O. Lee 1989: 54, 'Through the contest we are never quite sure what the prize will be'; E. A. Schmidt 1972: 178, 'Vergil lasse uns in *Ecl.* 3 im unklaren darüber, welche Preise eigentlich gesetzt werden.' Too sure: Conington and Nettleship 1881: 1.50, *ad* 3.109, 'Both ultimately wagered a heifer', Clausen 1994: 104, *ad* 3.49, *ueniam quocumque uocaris*, 'So confident is Menalcas of winning that he now agrees to meet Damoetas on his own ground, i.e. to stake a cow'. More circumspect, e.g. Coleman 1977: 116, *ad* 3.49, *ueniam quocumque uocaris*, 'The phrase suggests that Menalcas has conceded Damoetas' point and will wager a heifer after all'.

lacessit, is quite explicit: he has come upon the scene precisely to sink his teeth into Damoetas and not let go until he stops the verbal sniping and gets down to serious business (vv. 49, 51): what has happened in the meantime should be forgotten, since the only point that matters is to find a judge and get on with it. And the script, comically or limply (in any event, woodenly), gets *that* hole fixed before the arguments have any opportunity to get going...

However exactly we colour and tone our performance of these negotiations, we may still reserve the right to react to the 'foil' material in the dilatory skirmishing without falling into line with the characters' expressed views of the matter. We may regard the contrapositioning of (unique) heifer and (both players' putative sets of) cups as the poem's way to get us to ponder their relative charisma, and to compare and contrast the valuations we set on them with those of these denizens of the pastoral régime.[23] In effect, the by-play stages a species of rhetorical *praeteritio* (tangential treatment), which brackets the elaboration of the topic of the wager, as a background to the contest to come, a background of uncertain status. Background the heifer and cups may be, but they also foreground the need to call the contest, to gauge its pledge of significance, and find appropriate terms for what is at stake. While the characters' dispute is marked as, for them, inconclusive, we have at least bracketed two dialectically opposed terms and registers within which we can situate our own responses. No way round it, evaluation of the song is, and is not, fore-ordained.

4. BALLADEERING (VV. 60–107)

> The woods of Arcady are dead,
> And over is their antique joy;
> Of old the world on dreaming fed;
> Grey Truth is now her painted toy.[24]

---

[23] For one version, cf. Leach 1974: 175, 'The personalities of both herdsmen are a debasement of the symbolic value of the cups, whose ideal implications are left to the reader.'

[24] Yeats 1965: 1 (= 1889), from *Crossways*, 'The song of the happy shepherd'.

When 'the real song' starts, to put the matter in these terms,[25] both Segal and Powell have found their styles of interpretation already operative in the preliminaries. For Segal, the cups are (in his, and his Vergil's, eyes, far more than the heifer) the appropriate register in which to locate the singing. Not the grubby rivalry of two more or less bovine peasants, but A Song of Nature miraculously conjured by a budding master of cultivated poetry; a cosmology as universally harmonic as any astrologer's calendar; a composition as potently attractive as the music of Orpheus. The cups turn out, as it happens, not to be the agreed stake. But Virgil uses them to implant in us a symbolist impulsion toward the grand vistas that inhere in the confines of art-work.[26] This is the *caelum* in 'the larger vision of the *caelatum opus*' ('heaven' in 'the engraved work', v. 37) which provides the poetic emblem for Segal's title.[27] On the other hand, Powell's *Poeta ludens* enjoys fun at the expense of any who demand high ideals from verse even when the lines themselves mock, for their part, just such inflation of the currency. It's not that the cups programme for our civilized selves what the heifer may stand for in pastoral eyes, but that the herdsmen discard the cups in favour of the heifer. The attraction of entry to the *Eclogues* is precisely that, in this space, values are rated by scales that bear scant, or no, relation to ours. The song-contest will not be a tapestry of antiphonal exultation in universal sympathy, but a grudge match between two lowly primitives whose sole ambition is to do the other down—by hook or by crook. Don't patronize rusticity, try to join in, and play along. Do it 'their' way.[28]

Damoetas already presses upon our judgement the issue of whose perspective is to prevail: when he notifies Palaemon that 'the affair is not trivial' (*res est non parua*, v. 54), does litotes mark a critical

---

[25] Coleiro 1979: 123, 'The real song was from v. 60 to v. 107'.
[26] Cf. Halperin 1983: 185–9, 'Three scenes on an ivy-cup', for the arguments in favour of viewing the goatherd's cup in *Idyll* I as a figure for themes of bucolic poetry. Coleiro 1979: 124–6, for 'allegorical interpretations' of *Ecl.* 3.
[27] Segal 1967: 301; cf. Putnam 1970: 125–6, 'These are strange objects for a humble shepherd to be carrying around—esoteric and highly cultivated....'. Faber 1995 sees in *caelatum* pastoral figured as parody of epic.
[28] Contrast Putnam 1970: 128, 'All in all, this is no competition in the negative sense but an attempt to join in depicting the perfect shepherd's life, with divine assurance and happy love', with M. O. Lee 1989: 55, 'The two shepherds...never really pass beyond Sicilian banter in the contest itself.'

moment for the reader to intervene, and commit the performance to the target of a superlative, or a modest, amplitude? Is this a stage-direction from Virgil, bidding readers to amplify the song-contest as grand as can be;[29] or is it Menalcas sneakily sticking in his oar to influence the judge even as he gets the job, Damoetas seizing the initiative and telling the judge what's what before the action can start?[30]

The point is not simply to scotch either continuities, or *brisures*, between the bickering and the balladeering, nor to invite readers to explore the full range of possibilities opened by the script. Rather, the bucolic cutting-contest unsettles the urbanity of the readers it is written for. Virgil's poem has gone out of its way to create an improvisational feel for his mime, perhaps to place the institution of the amoebaean contest into a social ethos, the herdsman's way of life, so that readers whose first acquaintance with the pastoral world is this very poem can, and afficionados of Theocritean bucolic must, sense their intrusion into a fictional 'parallel universe'. The exchanges in this poem have not been marked as out of the ordinary (as they were in *Eclogue* 1's tangential moment where Meliboeus' catastrophe crosses Tityrus' miracle). Rather, the Roles have interacted with all the emulous intimacy of people in home territory, and on their own turf. Where does this leave us?

'We take our seats' (v. 55), and come under starter's orders: 'Damoetas to start; Menalcas to respond; amoebaean alternation is the rule' (vv. 58–9). The rest, we must 'know', that is: we must realize we do *not* know, but must glean, intuit, guess, or else go with the flow... Palaemon, Damoetas, and Menalcas don't call for a time-out for clarification of procedure; if the singers have any comments, they are obliged to smuggle them into their lyrics; the judge is not going to intervene, interject asides, or interpret, for them or for us, until the songs are done. All this could be otherwise, and is as good as arbitrary for any of us; whereas *they* know the ropes and leave

---

[29] Cf. Segal 1967: 280, 'Vergil explicitly announces, in mock-epic language, that his subject is of no small significance.'

[30] Calpurnius' *Eclogue* 6 springs the surprise of allowing the bickering to overflow past the selection of the judge; no songs are heard; rather, the judge finally loses patience and, for his last word, threatens to get some help in putting an end to the back-biting. *Virgil's* closest influence, in this regard, was Theocritus 5 (but see below).

them unremarked. To realize this is to begin to play the game of apprehending *from play* what the rules of a game are. Games intrinsically consist, on the one hand, of patterned segments which are perceptible through repetition, and, on the other, of a narratival series of junctures and *termini*. The former can be deduced from a single performance; the latter, of course, cannot.

What rules govern the two voices in an amoebaean? Should Role 1 respect, find inspiration from, respond to, Role 2's strictly parallel 'echo' of Role 1's last offering? More generally, presumably Role 2 is already doing well, if they just keep their end up?—but how can Role 1 score points?[31] Is there some notional set of 'licks', a register of topics, even a traditional sequence? Or is this a matter of the *forte* of an individual repertoire, the *ad hominem* agonistics of a game-plan? Are originality, surprise, eccentricity wanted? What does the decision on how long the bursts of song are to last indicate? Would it be more/less aggressive, confident, cavalier, or what, to choose quatrains (as in *Eclogue* 7) rather than the distichs set by Damoetas?

If we are bothered by any of these questions, yet still we can't be bothered by them in the way the characters are. Their quarrel is not ours. Instead, we are regaled with a *duet*. A specially constrained pooling of resources, for sure, but nevertheless, for us outsiders an event in tandem. We want a good show; each of them wants a win.

Let's now try to look to the end. However acutely we have made out a running tally of tactical hits and feints between the players, we don't stand an earthly when the end comes. Remarkably enough, commentators have not yet (I would wager) claimed they would have been able to tell that the end is at hand after v. 106. The fact that a matched pair of riddles are the two singers' final renditions before the

---

[31] To play by the sane regulations of Rosenmeyer 1969: 159, 'If the palm is to go to the singer with the creative imagination, then it should go to the starter, since it is he who sets the pace initially. If, on the other hand, the victory should accrue to the more accomplished artist, then in many cases the second singer, who has his opponent's model to draw on, ought to get the prize.' Leach 1974: 176 follows Jachmann in averring 'that the topical linking of the strophes does not appear natural and effortless,... but artificial and strained. In fact, the singers do not attempt to complement one another or to embroider each other's themes'. Cf. Clausen 1994: 114, *ad* 3.96–7, 'Only here does Damoetas take his cue from Menalcas.' I follow the lines of Powell's analysis in finding oblique but engaged and continuous dialectic running clear through the contest.

148   *John Henderson*

judge makes himself audible (at v. 108) makes the hypothesis tempting, that the three participants all know the riddle as a method of shutting up shop. As we noticed already, this receives no confirmation from the practice in Theocritean, or other, amoebaea. But let's suppose that in 'our' Arcadia it was tried and trusted. In that case, is it a sure sign of exhaustion, panic, satiety in Damoetas that he resorts to riddling? Or does it behove or become the Role who has the lead to contrive some form of 'artistic conclusion' for the duel, so that the sense of an ending can mime a conventional teleology of harmonization,[32] whatever the feelings of the opponents? Since this is a one-off, for us, there is nothing to discount the notion that Damoetas actually had hopes that Menalcas had never come across that old favourite, the ploy of the baited riddle. It might be a poser for any second fiddle to decide if the response should be to attempt an answer. Presumably that is a mistake no one would ever make twice, for riddles are archetypal hermeneutic traps, which illustrate, *in nuce*, just the kind of aporetic play within language in use that the preliminary dialogue exposed to view: a riddle has an answer. A riddle does not have an answer—it has more than one answer. The answer is the answer I choose to tell you after you have taken your pick. Even if I don't cheat on you, and you'll never know the answer to that question, still the answer to my riddle is, in any case, *my* answer to it, the one I choose to make mine. Like an oracle, the power-play of a riddle is therefore a mug's game.[33] Except that it is possible to duplicate it, instead, as Menalcas does.

To judge the performance, or the performances, is to pretend to be *au fait* with the technicalities, but also to impute a set of intentions to the players. Thus we may gather that, between them, the refrains combine to perform a single interactive 'story'. A complex chain of boasts of success and rosy prospects in 'love' grows from Menalcas' first response, where he stresses direct intensity against Damoetas' universality, *Phoebus amat*, v. 62, for (*Ioui*) . . . *curae*, v. 61.[34]

---

[32] 'The matching of perceptive beings in a nexus of friendship and equality', as Rosenmeyer defines the song-contest (1969: 157), without a trace of cynicism.
[33] *Pace* Powell 1976: 120, '. . . the riddles themselves have no answers.'
[34] The fusion of love-poetry-song-contest is cued already at the outset in v. 59, *amant alterna Camenae* ('the Muses—the only Italian Muses in all Virgil—love alternation').

As Damoetas counts up four 'lovers' (Galatea, Phyllis, Iollas, Amaryllis), and Menalcas rivals, disputes, and disdains his claims, they progress, as well as leap, to Pollio's 'love' for poetry (*amat*, vv. 84, 88, cf. 90). Partisan devotion to Pollio gets matched by imprecations on his opponents, and the scene of pastoral poetry then provides images for cutting attacks between Damoetas and Menalcas—'a snake in the grass' *vs.* 'a silly ram got a ducking' (vv. 93; 95).[35] This passes into the call for less recklessness, backed with notification of a take-over bid, and the worry that the preceding outburst of hot temper will make the flow of creativity dry up, with frustration for everyone (vv. 96–9).

Both these catcalls look forward beyond the press of the instant, making pre-emptive strikes to fashion an account of their standing in the realm of song: *ubi tempus erit, omnis in fonte lauabo* ('when the time comes, I shall wash them all in the spring', v. 97) promises safe prospects for pastoral in the care of Damoetas; *si lac praeceperit aestus, | ut nuper, frustra pressabimus ubera palmis* (vv. 98–9, 'if sun cuts off the milk, | as just then, we'll squeeze the dugs with our palms and get nowt') portends a barren time for poetry unless it takes a different path. The next insults turn the mood further to the future, imag(in)ing the death of bucolic. Damoetas poisons the air by caricaturing the 'love' sung by Menalcas as a 'bull-in-a-china-shop'[36] 'destruction' for him and his (*amor exitium*, v. 101). Menalcas agrees on the prognosis, but retorts that the cause is, not 'love', but Damoetas' poisonous 'evil eye' (*neque amor... nescio quis... oculus*, v. 103). The song has represented, manipulated, and wielded, but scotched, smeared, and denied, the 'love' it sings; finally, the disputants have managed to agree, in their disagreement, on one thing: the ultimate insult that they can produce, is that they are *killing* song, none too softly. Does the topic of *exitium* point to 'the way out' from the contest? Is this a recognized final move that the herdsmen know and love? Do those who know their amoebaeans know well that riddling is the only way to say more—i.e. by refusing to 'say' more? Or have

---

[35] 'Another marked change of tone suddenly comes over the poem at line 92', Putnam 1970: 130; Leach 1974: 177, 179 '...here the singers' rivalry takes an explicitly unpleasant turn...From this point on the descriptions of the pastoral world become harsh and unpleasant.'

[36] I borrow this from Powell 1976: 120, though it obscures the force of the bull's rutting lust as a caricature for the herdsman.

these two characters sparked each other into a suicide pact, in which the adrenalin which began the bout coarsened into animus that jettisoned all the courtesies and spoiled the whole game?

It should, then, weigh with judges how they think the performers came to bale out.[37] But this is only the last hurdle in the challenge to comprehend an event we realize is all too easy to assimilate to the games we are familiar with in our own sociality. Indeed, as we saw, both singers have joined in, half-way through as it turns out, by allowing themselves to name Pollio, Bavius and Mevius. *Mutatis mutandis*, wasn't Pollio's recitation-hall the venue for 'amoebaean contests' from poets every bit as cantankerous, prickly, and bitchy as the herdsmen? In this perspective, Virgil uses his rustics to show our values up to us: their value to us is that they oblige us to face, and critique, the nature of our values.

5. BALLOTING (VV. 55–9; 108–11)

'Look, *amigo*,' said Oliver, who had little time for this sort of thing, 'these poems of yours are good, but you smell like a goat. I'll make a bargain with you. I'll publish these poems if you'll have a bath.'

'Do you want to kill me?' cried Louis.

'It's for the sake of art,' said Oliver implacably.[38]

As we remarked, the judgement of Palaemon has been played every which way by readers. He is Virgil's accredited expert witness,[39] to be taken at his word: this *magnum... certamen* is not a 'great quarrel' (i.e. a 'grudge-match'), but a 'great issue'. He heralds to us that the songs have 'intimated the larger possibilities which lie within

---

[37] Thus, '... as if to give final stress to this complete alteration of mood, the shepherds conclude their debate with two riddles...', Putnam 1970: 133.

[38] Bradbury 1978: 164.

[39] Cf. Berg 1974: 192–4, 'Appendix II: The third *Eclogue*: Palaemon', (192) 'the representative of the bucolic genre itself'; Segal 1967: 299, 'The wisdom of a serene and ideal figure like Palaemon... stands beyond the two shepherds' intense involvement in love, just as he stands outside the contest itself. Yet he knows more both of love and of pastoral beauty than they do.'

it... Both shepherds, then, are equally capable of singing of love and of dealing with larger themes. Hence both have cups carved by the "divine Alcimedon".'[40] Palaemon bids us love the song of 'love' from these 'bitter-sweet lover-singers' (*amores | aut... dulcis aut... amaros*, vv. 109–10);[41] they both 'deserve the heifer', or at any rate, they 'deserve a heifer', supposing they could either of them produce one, because their contributions have been so splendid (v. 109, *et uitula tu dignus et hic*. Recall that Palaemon either did, or did not, hear the bargaining over the pot):[42]

> So nice a difference in your singing lies,
> That both have won, or both deserved, the prize.
> Rest equal happy both; and all who prove
> The bitter sweets, and pleasing pains, of love.   (vv. 108–10)[43]

Or, to go to the other extreme, Virgil-Palaemon does not lapse into cheap self-congratulation, but enters into the rancorous spirit of this genuinely hostile collision of wills: 'Neither of you are fit to continue', out on your feet; you have conspired to land yourselves in an impasse, the pair of you, and 'that's *quite* enough' (v. 110, *sat prata biberunt*. ||). And, for Pollio's circle, 'this poem's already plenty big enough' (This *is*, by a short head, the longest poem in the book of *Eclogues*—unless it counts as 'two-in-one', like the other extravaganza, *Ecl*. 8).

[40] Segal 1967: 300, 302, 301.
[41] Segal 1967: 296–7 attempts to cordon 'love' from 'poetry' as a thematic 'alternation' through the song-contest, but the love of poetry modulates into and out of the poetry of love (cf. Schoepsdau 1974). On the incorporation here of address to lovers of reading (of readings in love), cf. Stégen 1957: 7–25, 'Le jugement de Palémon (Virg., *Buc*. III, 108–10)'.
[42] So Putnam 1970: 134, 'The shepherds have not really been challenging each other, as at the poem's outset, but have presented a unity of subject and mood at each stage of the debate. Each is therefore worthy of the prize...'; Powell 1976: 121, 'Palaemon rightly calls it a draw. Each man deserves the sacrificial animal'; Berg 1974: 192, 'Palaemon blesses both: each is worthy of the heifer, for each has shown that he understands what it is to be a poet.' Contrast Boyle 1975: 194, 'Palaemon pronounces both singers worthy of the heifer, not of the cups'; Leach 1974: 175, 181, 'Or perhaps he considers both contenders unworthy of the cups.... It is only fitting that no prizes should be awarded to singers who have distorted their subject to serve their own hostile ends'; M. O. Lee 1989: 55, '... each deserves to win a heifer. Neither, presumably, is worthy of the cups. Works of art have never communicated any message to them.'
[43] Dryden 1961 (= 1697): 15.

In the final instance, how critical *is* judgement in the business of poetry? What credentials are needed to judge, not the judges, but the judging? Is this the quandary set before Pollio's coterie, now ours?

6. BROWSING

CVDDIE.
Fayth of my soule, I deeme ech haue gayned.
For thy let the Lambe be *Willye* his owne:
And for *Perigot* so well hath hym payned,
To him be the wroughten mazer alone.
PERIGOT.
Perigot is well pleased with the doome:
Ne can *Willye* wite the witelesse herdgroome.[44]

As commentators always particularly note, the 'rustic' phrase *cuium pecus* is displayed in the centre of the first verse, after the peremptory insistence of *dic mihi*. The marked lexis prompts a run of questions. Thus: is *pecus* a singularity or collective? How representative is this animal of any in the herd? May the members of this herd stand for any, anywhere? If we are not herdsmen, what are our 'animals'?[45] Does our poet Virgil have an equivalent? Is bucolic poetry not always and ever an invitation to join the favourite dance of Hellenistic poetics, a myth of origins for our poetry, sought in utopic songs of innocence where θύος and Μοῦσα, *oues* and *carmen* recover a fusion in culture at one with nature ('sacrifice, Muse; sheep, song'[46])? As readers versed in, or (much more likely) turned by Virgil to, Theocritean poetry, *cuium pecus* at once prods us toward intertextuality.

When commentaries refer us straight to *Idyll* 4.1 τίνος αἱ βόες; ('Whom's cows?'), we cosmopolitan literates arrive at *one* complete

---

[44] Spenser 1970 (= 1579): 450, 'The Shepheardes calender, August', 131–6.
[45] In the songs themselves—necessarily: that is the point of bucoholism—we trip over and stumble upon a discursive world of human/animal sociality and (quasi-?) relations: *canibus...nostris* (v. 67, 'our (my?) dogs') *vs. aeriae...palumbes* (v. 69, 'pigeons high in the sky'); *tu sectaris apros* (v. 75, 'you chase boar') *vs. cum faciam uitula* (v. 77, 'when I sacrifice a heifer'); cf. vv. 83, 85, 86, 91, 93–103 *passim*.
[46] Callim. *Aet*. fr. 1.23–4, Verg. *Ecl*. 6.5.

answer to *Eclogue* 3's question.[47] This particular animal fattening nicely for sacrifice, and eventually a feast in store for somebody, *belongs to Theocritus*, word for word. Does the Latin poem belong, then, to Theocritus?[48] Or has it been transferred, faithfully translated, handed down and handed over, to Virgil's custody and care? This is, it dawns, exactly the preoccupation of the commentators, whose thoughts are so dominated by the fidelity, the subservience, of this *Eclogue* to its Greek avatar. What could it mean to find that the poem still belongs to its previous owner? To the author, that is to say, who had *his* herdsman pose precisely this question for himself? To answer the question is always already to ask it once more, transposed along the line of tradition. And we should turn this round, too: whose poem shall this tralatician text prove to be? Who are destined to take up the theme and repeat the age-old question? *cuium... carmen?* This intricates the broader question 'Whom's poetry?' And that may put to us the question: in what sense do we think that poetry 'belongs' to someone; that literature is a dispute and criticism an arbitration; that the arts are the sort of thing that can be 'owned'; that 'appropriation' is a *regrettably* inescapable model for cultural exchange.[49] From the year dot, whether Damoetas/Menalcas', Theocritus/Virgil's, Segal's/Powell's, your-my *amour propre*? From before

---

[47] Segal 1967: 281, 'Vergil could not have begun the *Third Eclogue* on a more conventionally pastoral note.'

[48] Theocritus' most immediate 'answer' appears at 5.1, || αἶγες ἐμαί. *Eclogue* 3's multi-evocation of *Idylls* usurps and undoes the schemata of *Id.* 1, even as the poem pastes together *Id.* 4 and 5, destabilizing all three (four, ... more) structures of power and valuation as it does so, and providing us with too many 'answers'—and this is exactly the riddle of intertextuality, where the practice of reading begins its productivity, and of sociality, where it'll never be known how Battus (*Id.* 4) would have got on with Lakon (*Id.* 5) or Thyrsis (*Id.* 1), nor Goatherd (*Id.* 1) with Korydon (*Id.* 4) or Komatas (*Id.* 5), nor Menalcas and Damoetas with any of their *m*ummies and *d*addies, nor what 'our' poets would have made of them, with us. And these questions engross the politics as well as the poetics of pastoral, since Virgil turned *Id.* 1.1–11 into the entrée to both the exchange between pensioned Tityrus and expropriated Meliboeus, and to the book of triumviral *Eclogues* (cf. Farrell 1992).

[49] Let's drink to that: but if the poem that brought us to the dilemma of our art icons, a heifer's milk for her twins, or beech-cups never yet slurped by human lips, was itself a 'healthy or perhaps hefty drink for the meadows' of the pastoral literary space (*sat prata biberunt* ||, v. 111), the riddle remains in our reading, or re-reading, whether we have taken our fill, are ready to imbibe, or know what it might be, in our world, to store up the pristine texts we prize, or to absorb life itself through the nourishment that courses through them.

before, even, since Battus' question in Theocritus 'may allude to the stolen cattle' in the Hesiodic tale of 'Battus' Watch', when Hermes caught Battus informing on him, to him, for rustling *Apollo's* cows?[50] 'Whom's cows?'

> The whole race is a poet that *writes down*
> The eccentric propositions of its fate.[51]

—I'll tell you later—
 —I'll tell *on* you later—
—by and by—

[50] Keith 1992: 95–114, esp. 114. Cf. Gutzwiller 1991: 35–44, 'The Animal Thief and Intellectual Activity', esp. 40 on *Ecl.* 3.16–20.
[51] Stevens 1965: 76, 'Men Made out of Words'.

8

Virgil's Fourth *Eclogue*: Easterners and Westerners

R. G. M. Nisbet

It has often been pointed out that there are two main schools of thought about the Fourth *Eclogue*.[1] Some, such as Norden,[2] have looked for analogies in the religions of the East, notably in Jewish hopes for a Messiah or $Χριστός$. Others have seen the poem in essentially Western terms, as a reasonably normal representative of a tradition that goes back to Hesiod and Theocritus; on this side Jachmann's article[3] has been particularly influential. As an easy method of reference Norden's party are here called 'Easterners' and Jachmann's 'Westerners'. It will be remembered that in the strategic debates of the First World War the Easterners preferred large-scale diversions through unfamiliar terrain to concentrated attacks on heavily manned positions for limited gains. They underestimated

---

This paper appears here as it was published in 1978 and reprinted in R. G. M. Nisbet 1995: 47–75, with the addition of translations of the quotes from Greek and Latin. These are by the author, except for those from the Sibylline Oracles, which are taken from Collins 1983, and from the Bible, which are taken in the main from the Revised Standard Version.

A shorter version of this paper was given as a special lecture in the University of London on 21 October 1977. I owe much to the colleagues and graduate students who took part in a class on the subject in Oxford the previous term: Colin Clarkson, Kathleen Coleman, Anna Crabbe, Malcolm Davies, Don Fowler, Jasper Griffin, Nigel Kay, Perilla Kinchin, Peta Moon (now Mrs Fowler), Donald Ringe.

[1] The bibliography is vast; for general surveys of the poem cf. Büchner 1955–8: 1195 ff., Hommel 1950, G. Williams 1974.
[2] Norden 1924.   [3] Jachmann 1952*a*.

the difficulties of the logistics and the vulnerability of exterior lines, but their imagination was rewarded in unintended ways, and though they failed to reach the Golden Horn they played their part in the liberation of Jerusalem. It will be convenient to examine the poem section by section, and, as only some aspects can be covered, to assess the strength in particular of the Easterners' case.

> Sicelides Musae, paulo maiora canamus.
> non omnes arbusta iuvant humilesque myricae.
> si canimus silvas, silvae sint consule dignae. (1–3)

Sicilian Muses, let us sing of things a little greater. Not everybody is pleased by trees and lowly tamarisks. If we sing of woods, let the woods be worthy of a consul.

These three lines form a proem in the Western tradition.[4] A pastoral note is struck in the first two words by the allusion to a refrain of 'Moschus' (3.8 Σικελικαί ... Μοῖσαι), but though Virgil promises grander themes, the urbanity of *paulo* (pointedly incongruous with the more poetical *canamus*) suggests the manner of Cicero rather than of John the Divine. Even if the lowly tamarisks are rejected, the very literary play on *humilitas* encourages no inflated expectations. By admitting that he sings of woods Virgil shows that he is still writing within the bucolic genre, and though they are woods with a difference, they owe their special character not to Eastern mysticism but to the solemnities of Roman public life.

> ultima Cumaei venit iam carminis aetas;
> magnus ab integro saeclorum nascitur ordo.
> iam redit et virgo, redeunt Saturnia regna;
> iam nova progenies caelo demittitur alto.
> tu modo nascenti puero, quo ferrea primum
> desinet ac toto surget gens aurea mundo,
> casta fave Lucina, tuus iam regnat Apollo. (4–10)

The last age of the Sibylline song has now come; the great sequence of the centuries is born afresh. Now both the Virgin returns and returns the reign of Saturn; now a new stock is sent down from high heaven. If you but favour the baby being born, with whom the iron generation will first come to an

---

[4] *Rhet. Her.* 1.7 *attentos habebimus si pollicebimur nos de rebus magnis novis inusitatis verba facturos.*

end and through the whole world a golden generation will arise, chaste Lucina, your Apollo is already reigning.

After the restrained bucolic invocation, the emphatic *ultima* suddenly transports us to the world of eschatology. The *Cumaeum carmen* has nothing to do with Hesiod's descent from the Asiatic Cyme (Probus): 'to say that the last of that poet's ages has come is extremely stale news'.[5] The expression must refer to the Sibylline oracles (Servius), which in this context cannot mean the western collection destroyed on the Capitol in 83 BC, and later imperfectly replaced from a variety of sources;[6] these seem to have dealt with prodigies and sacrifices, and access to them was controlled by the quindecimviri. 'Cumaean' must be used for 'Sibylline' in an extended sense, and refer to one of the unofficial sorts of oracle so prevalent in the period; but while ordinary Greek Sibyls might offer time-schemes and prophecies of doom, they could not so easily accommodate a child whose appearance would regenerate the world (see below on line 8). The case is different with the Eastern Sibylline oracles[7] produced by the Hellenized Jews of Egypt, and Lactantius was surely right to see a similarity to Virgil (*Inst.* 7.24.12), though it must still be determined whether the eclogue draws directly on such a Jewish oracle or on a pagan Eastern production of the same general type (Norden's theory). Before we consider correspondences in detail, it is important to record a general resemblance of literary form: both the eclogue and the oracles offer an unusual blend of the Hesiodic, the eschatological, and the political.[8] The anti-Roman stance of much Jewish apocalyptic is not a decisive argument against a connection (in spite of Norden 1924: 53); Virgil

---

[5] Rose 1942: 177.   [6] Rzach 1923: 2105 ff., Diels 1890.

[7] Texts by Rzach 1891, Geffcken 1902, Kurfess 1951. See further Rzach 1923: 2117 ff., Nikiprowetzky 1970, Fraser 1972: 1.708 ff., 2.989 ff., Collins 1974a, summarized in Collins 1974b. For their influence on Virgil, cf. F. Marx 1898: 121 ff., Jeanmaire 1939. [Addendum from R. G. M. Nisbet 1995: 432: For the Sibylline Oracles see also Schürer 1986: 618–54, Collins 1983 and 1987, Parke 1988, esp. 145–51, and Potter 1990: 95–140.]

[8] There are also some stylistic resemblances (Austin 1927, Du Quesnay 1976: 77 ff.), but they are mainly either Hesiodic or typical of oracles in general; Virgil's end-stopped and sometimes rhyming lines (5 ff., 50 ff.) suggest the hypnotic rhythms of an incantation, but they have less in common with the Sibyl than with the Parcae of Catullus 64. On the other hand it seems significant that the groups of seven lines (4 ff., 11 ff., 46 ff., 53 ff.) can be paralleled at *Orac. Sib.* 3.227 ff.

could have reversed any such tendency in his model, just as he does with the pessimism of Catullus 64. But could Virgil have known the Eastern Sibylline oracles? The surviving collection presents difficult problems of chronology:[9] pagan, Jewish, and Christian elements seem to have been jumbled by the wind, plagiarism is a normal principle of composition, and *vaticinia post eventum* obscure the historical sequence. The bulk of the third book, which is the oldest and for our purposes the most important, has recently been assigned by Nikiprowetzky 1970 to 42 BC, but it is implausible to give a unified origin to so amorphous a conglomeration, and there is much more to be said for the orthodox view that places the early strata in the middle of the second century BC.[10] The book seems to have mainly an Egyptian provenance (so far as any indications are given), and the reign of Cleopatra must have encouraged the Roman interest in such oracles.[11] Alternatively it has been supposed that the poet learned about the Jews from Pollio,[12] who met Herod when consul in 40 (and later gave hospitality to his sons);[13] amid the hectic intrigues of the year, when a Parthian protégé ruled in Jerusalem and Herod received his kingdom in Rome, eastern prophecies would have attracted particular attention. But while Pollio's versatile tastes might have suggested the direction of the eclogue, Virgil cannot have seen much of him during the troubles of his consulship; and though Herod's visit was a spectacular occasion, it probably came too late to influence the poem significantly except by giving an extra topicality to Jewish matters. Virgil must have expected from his readers a familiarity with Sibylline oracles of the relevant type, and they are more likely

---

[9] Geffcken 1902, Fraser 1972: 1.708 ff., 2.989 ff., Collins 1974a: 21 ff.
[10] Cf. especially 3.608 ff. ὁπόταν Αἰγύπτου βασιλεὺς νέος ἕβδομος ἄρχῃ τῆς ἰδίης γαίης ἀριθμούμενος ἐξ Ἑλλήνων ἀρχῆς ἧς ἄρξουσι Μακηδόνες ἄσπετοι ἄνδρες. Cleopatra VII (not an ancient title) could not possibly be described in this way; probably the oracle refers to Ptolemy Philometor, the seventh Macedonian ruler of Egypt, and a pro-Jew (cf. Collins 1974a: 29 ff.).
[11] Cf. Tarn 1932: 135 ff., Collins 1974a: 61 ff. Horace's sixteenth epode may show some influences (Ableitinger-Grünberger 1971: 73–4); compare also line 10 with *Orac. Sib.* 8.41 (a Christian denunciation of Rome) καὶ τὰ θέμειλα λύκοι καὶ ἀλώπεκες οἰκήσουσιν.
[12] F. Marx 1898: 124 ff., Feldman 1953.
[13] Joseph. *AJ* 14.388, 15.343. The relationship with Herod suits Asinius Pollio's cosmopolitan interests (cf. his later patronage of Timagenes).

to have associated them with Cleopatra and Egypt than with Herod and Judaea.

To turn now to the details, the Easterners may help with the chronological problems of lines 4 and 5. Servius comments that 'last' means 'tenth', and the extant Sibylline oracles often mention ten ages;[14] but as more than one system was possible, it is pointless to pursue what the poet has left unspecified. It is more important to decide whether the *ultima aetas* is the predecessor of the Golden Age (6) or the Golden Age itself.[15] The former view can hardly be right: *iam* here would have a different reference from *iam* in lines 6 and 7, and the *ultima aetas* would either last a very short time or take a very long time to be recognized. This conclusion seems to be supported by the stereotyped form of eschatological proclamation: 'the time has come'.[16] The perfect *venit* is not seriously contradicted by the present tenses below: the last age has arrived, and so various things are happening or about to happen.

Line 5 offers a different time-scheme. In the first place a *saeculum*[17] is a Western concept, not a period of the world (like *aetas*) but the maximum age of a man; the doctrine was topical, as one Vulcacius had announced the tenth or last *saeculum* in 44 BC,[18] and by another calculation the new age began in 39,[19] only a month or two after the purported time of writing (see below). Secondly, the system here is not simply linear (as in the previous line), but involves a cyclic element: *ab integro nascitur*[20] alludes to the παλιγγενεσία (rebirth)[21] of the Stoics and others. On the other hand *magnus saeclorum ordo* cannot directly represent the Stoic *magnus annus*[22] (where *magnus*

---

[14] Jeanmaire 1939: 100 ff.
[15] Gatz 1967: 93 ff. At *Orac. Sib.* 4.47 the tenth age is a time when felicity is achieved.
[16] Gal. 4: 4 ὅτε δὲ ἦλθεν τὸ πλήρωμα τοῦ χρόνου, Mk. 1: 15 πεπλήρωται ὁ καιρός, Jn. 4: 23 ἔρχεται ὥρα καὶ νῦν ἐστιν. As Norden points out, ideas found in both Paul and Mark are deeply rooted (1924: 33).
[17] Nilsson 1920: 1709–10, Weinstock 1971: 191 ff.
[18] Serv. Auct. *Ecl.* 9.46; cf. Censorinus 17.6 *nonum et decimum superesse, quibus transactis finem fore nominis Etrusci.*
[19] Sudhaus 1901: 38 ff.
[20] Cf. Sen. *Q Nat.* 3.30.8 *omne ex integro animal generabitur dabiturque terris homo inscius scelerum et melioribus auspiciis natus.*
[21] See G. Kittel (ed.) 1933: 685 ff.
[22] Van der Waerden 1952, Pease 1955–8 *ad* Cic. *Nat. D.* 2.51.

marks a contrast with the solar year); nor is the apparent identity of the *ultima aetas* with the new age compatible with the Stoic view that the old cycle ends in κατακλυσμός (inundation) and ἐκπύρωσις (conflagration); nor indeed is Virgil thinking of a cycle in the full sense, as there is no suggestion that the new Golden Age will be displaced in turn. It is sometimes supposed that the poet has inconsistently juxtaposed a linear Hesiodic system with a cyclic Stoic one; yet lines 4 and 5 belong closely together (as do 6 and 7), and though Virgil's syncretism sometimes produces inconsistencies, they should not be as blatant as is suggested here. It may therefore be relevant that in Jewish and Christian eschatology the Messianic age is sometimes represented as the end of the old series (corresponding to the seventh day in *Genesis*), sometimes as an additional 'day' (compared by Christians to the Sunday of the resurrection);[23] sometimes the two systems are harmonized (the same period is regarded as both an end and a beginning,[24] or the terrestrial 'millennium' is followed by an eternal heavenly kingdom), sometimes they are uneasily juxtaposed.[25] But when the new creation is complete there is no second deterioration, exactly the situation that seems to be implied in the eclogue. As Virgil's confusing time-scheme bears some resemblance to the Jewish system, and as he has just proclaimed his dependence on the Sibyl, it seems possible that a Jewish oracle is one of the sources of his chronology.

The sixth line is claimed by the Westerners, but it owes more to the Eastern tradition than is sometimes realized. The Virgo is obviously the Δίκη (Justice) of Aratus, who left the earth apparently for good (*redit* is paradoxical), and was translated to the sky as Parthenos[26] (the Latin name similarly suggests an astronomical reference). But even where Virgil depends ultimately on Greek didactic, his words can often be harmonized with the Sibylline poems, which themselves were written

---

[23] Schürer 1907: 636 ff., Daniélou 1948.

[24] 2 Baruch 74.2 'From that time is the consummation of that which is corruptible and the beginning of that which is not corruptible', [Barnabas], *Epist.* 6.13 δευτέραν πλάσιν ἐπ᾽ ἐσχάτων ἐποίησεν. λέγει δὲ κύριος· ἰδού, ποιῶ τὰ ἔσχατα ὡς τὰ πρῶτα (Lake 1912–13: 1.362).

[25] [Barnabas] 15.5–9; the inconsistency is pointed out by H. Windisch in his commentary (1920: 384).

[26] Arat. *Phaen.* 133 ff., Verg. *G.* 2.473–4, Ov. *Met.* 1.149–50, Symm. *Or.* 3.9 *dicerem caelo redisse Iustitiam.*

in the Hesiodic manner: thus it is highly relevant that an oracle from the time of Cleopatra describes the return of Justice from the stars and the consequent cessation of bloodshed and strife.[27] There is indeed something oracular about the allusive reference to the Virgin, and her juxtaposition with the young child; and though nobody now accepts the naïve formulation of Philargyrius *id est Iustitia vel Maria* ('that is to say, Justice or Mary'), the word might derive some of its resonance from Jewish prophecies that mention a κόρη or girl (see below). The case is much clearer with *redeunt Saturnia regna*: though Hesiod assigned the Golden Age to the time of Saturn (*Op*. 111), the notion of its return is unparalleled in the Western tradition before Virgil.[28] It is therefore extremely significant that a passage in the third book of Sibylline oracles describes a future age of abundance and peace in terms traditionally applied to the past (3.744–5 and 749–51):

> γῆ γὰρ παγγενέτειρα βροτοῖς δώσει τὸν ἄριστον
> καρπὸν ἀπειρέσιον σίτου οἴνου καὶ ἐλαίου…
> πηγάς τε ῥήξει γλυκερὰς λευκοῖο γάλακτος·
> πλήρεις δ' αὖτε πόλεις ἀγαθῶν καὶ πίονες ἀγροί
> ἔσσοντ'· οὐδὲ μάχαιρα κατὰ χθονὸς οὐδὲ κυδοιμός.[29]

For the all-bearing earth will give the most excellent unlimited fruit to mortals, of grain, wine, and oil… And it will break forth sweet fountains of white milk. And the cities will be full of good things and the fields will be rich. There will be no sword on earth or din of battle.

Here the pessimism of Hesiod is alleviated by an apocalyptic vision of Paradise Regained, exactly the development that we find in the eclogue.

Line 7 is also claimed by the Westerners. Yet the *nova progenies*[30] that descends from heaven is not quite a race of men in the Hesiodic mould; it is clearly contrasted with the *gens aurea* that arises over the

---

[27] 3.373–4 εὐνομίη γὰρ πᾶσα ἀπ' οὐρανοῦ ἀστερόεντος ἥξει ἐπ' ἀνθρώπους ἠδ' εὐδικίη, μετὰ δ' αὐτῆς ἡ πάντων προφέρουσα βροτοῖς ὁμόνοια σαόφρων, Collins 1974a: 57 ff. The theme of ὁμόνοια suited the Western situation in 40 BC when *concordia* was the watchword (*ILS* 3784, Weinstock 1971: 262–3).

[28] Gatz 1967: 25, V. Schmidt 1977: 56 ff. The use of the theme in imperial panegyric is modelled on Virgil (Gatz 1967: 138–9).

[29] The line is reminiscent of Aratus (*Phaen*. 109 κυδοιμοῦ, 131 μάχαιραν).

[30] *nova* balances *ab integro* above; the child corresponds to the age. Norden 1924: 47 calls attention to the importance of newness in the world of the New Testament.

whole world (9 *surget*). *progenies* ('stock') is admittedly more general than *puero* below, in that it contains the suggestion of future descendants, but Virgil's attention is concentrated on the supernatural origin of the child himself. In the same way *caelo demittitur* implies not a general descent but a special mission, as when Juno in the *Aeneid* sends Iris from Olympus.[31] The belief that the soul is from heaven is attested in Greek philosophy from the fifth century, and is applied by Cicero especially to rulers;[32] so Virgil's reference, if it had appeared in isolation, could be explained entirely on Western lines. But in view of the other borrowings in this part of the poem, it becomes relevant to record a Sibylline parallel here also: when an early section of the extant oracles describes a 'king from the sun',[33] it is probably referring not to the East but to the sky, a conclusion that is supported by a similar passage (though it also has been disputed) in the Egyptian 'Oracle of the Potter'.[34] It is true that according to orthodox Jewish monotheism the Messiah seems to have pre-existed only in a very notional sense,[35] but the doctrine might have been extended under alien influences. With the later enhancement of his status the Christian view was formulated of a divine descent from heaven;[36] yet even this can be paralleled to some extent in the

---

[31] Verg. *Aen.* 4.694 *Irim demisit Olympo*, CH, *Kore Kosmou* fr. 24.4 καταπέμπονται δὲ ἐκεῖθεν εἰς τὸ βασιλεύειν... αἱ ψυχαί. Some compare Lucr. 2.1153–4, but that is irrelevant (Norden 1924: 48).

[32] Cic. *Rep.* 6.13 *hinc profecti huc revertuntur*, Hor. *Carm.* 1.2.45 *serus in caelum redeas*, Festugière 1944–54: 3.27 ff., Nock 1972: 935 ff.

[33] 3.652 καὶ τότ' ἀπ' ἠελίοιο θεὸς πέμψει βασιλῆα (cited tentatively by Norden 1924: 147). Jachmann 1952*a*: 43–4 thinks that this refers to a king from the East like Cyrus in Isaiah (41: 2 ἀφ' ἡλίου ἀνατολῶν); cf. also the kings in the Oracle of Baalbek (§180, ed. Alexander 1967). Norden 1924: 55 also cites 3.286 καὶ τότε δὴ θεὸς οὐρανόθεν πέμψει βασιλῆα, but there the correct reading seems to be οὐράνιος.

[34] Collins 1974*a*: 40 ff., citing *P.Oxy.* 22.2332.63 ff. καὶ τότε ἡ Αἴγυπτος αὐξηθήσεται ἐπὰν ὁ τὰ πεντήκοντα πέντε ἔτη ἀπὸ Ἡλίου παραγενόμενος ἀγαθῶν δοτὴρ καθεστάμενος ᾖ ὑπὸ θεᾶς μεγίστης (interpreted otherwise by Jachmann 1952*a*: 42), *OGIS* 90 υἱοῦ τοῦ Ἡλίου (the Rosetta Stone on Ptolemy V).

[35] Strack and Billerbeck 1924: 333 ff., Vermes 1973: 138–9. Some have seen a reference to a pre-existent Messiah in Enoch 70.1 (Mowinckel 1956: 370 ff.); but the relevant section (the 'Book of Parables') has not appeared at Qumran, and is dated by the latest editor to the Christian era (Milik and Black 1976: 91 ff.).

[36] 1 Cor. 15: 47 ὁ δεύτερος ἄνθρωπος ἐξ οὐρανοῦ, Jn. 3: 13 ὁ ἐκ τοῦ οὐρανοῦ καταβάς, *Orac. Sib.* 8.458 οὐρανόθεν δὲ μολὼν βροτέην ἐνεδύσατο μορφήν (could the first half of the line have come from a pre-Virgilian oracle?).

Hermetic Corpus, where Isis and Osiris are lent to earth for a while[37] (it is hard to believe that this is simply a retort to Christianity). The question that now presents itself is this: could Virgil's Sibylline source have marked an intermediate stage between the 'king from the sun' and the fully developed Pauline theory? If the notion appears fanciful let us formulate it another way: if we assume for the moment what has still to be established, that these lines are modelled on a Messianic oracle, would it not be strange if the child's descent from the sky had nothing to do with similar doctrines about the Messiah?

This brings us to the *nascens puer*,[38] who must surely have been mentioned in the 'Cumaean song': what is his relationship to the infant of the Gospels?[39] The ages of faith believed in a prophecy,[40] the age of scepticism would prefer a coincidence; neither explanation is satisfactory. Semi-divine children are familiar from traditional Greek religion, and human 'saviours' were common in Hellenistic kingdoms, but here we have a baby who will not just rule a nation or benefit mankind but in some sense regenerate the world. The idea of an infant god was widespread in the Near East, and as we seem to be moving in an Egyptian context the cult of Isis and the baby Horus (the Greek Harpocrates) may ultimately be relevant, but Horus was not a saviour in the real sense. Bultmann,[41] who made this point against Norden, looked farther east, but we are less concerned with the remote origins of such beliefs than with Virgil's immediate source. As so many features of the eclogue (some still to be mentioned) are compatible with a Jewish prototype, it is natural to associate the child with Messianic doctrines (it must be emphasized here as elsewhere that the arguments are not so much deductive as mutually supporting). The nativity stories of Matthew and Luke (not in Paul or Mark) are usually regarded as a comparatively

---

[37] *Kore Kosmou* fr. 23.62 ff. (cited by Nock 1972: 937–8); note especially 64 ὁ μόναρχος θεός... τὸν μέγιστόν σου πρὸς ὀλίγον ἐχαρίσατο πατέρα Ὄσιριν καὶ τὴν μεγίστην θεὰν Ἶσιν, ἵνα τῷ πάντων δεομένῳ κόσμῳ βοηθοὶ γένωνται, 69 ταῦτα πάντα ποιήσαντες, ὦ τέκνον, Ὄσιρίς τε κἀγώ, τὸν κόσμον πληρέστατον ἰδόντες ἀπῃτούμεθα λοιπὸν ὑπὸ τῶν τὸν οὐρανὸν κατοικούντων.

[38] *nascenti* refers to the critical moment of birth, not the months of pregnancy (thus Corssen 1925: 42); when an epithalamium mentions Lucina, it is not thinking of antenatal care (see also below in the text).

[39] Norden 1924: 76 ff., Erdmann 1932.

[40] Cf. Courcelle 1957.

[41] Bultmann 1924: 321, contradicting Norden 1924: 73–4, 113.

late accretion to the tradition: how then are we to explain the infant of the eclogue a generation before the birth of Christ? Perhaps the most promising prototype is the Emmanuel of Isaiah 7: 14 ἰδοὺ ἡ παρθένος ἐν γαστρὶ ἕξει καὶ τέξεται υἱόν, καὶ καλέσεις τὸ ὄνομα αὐτοῦ Ἐμμανουήλ ('behold, a virgin shall conceive and bear a son, and shall call his name Emmanuel'; in this context the Old Testament must naturally be quoted from the Septuagint). Though not in origin a Messiah, Emmanuel influenced later Messianic speculations, and Isaiah's verse is cited in Matthew's infancy narrative (1: 25) as a prophecy of the birth of Jesus.

It is necessary at this point to consider how the baby's influence will operate. The echo of 5 *saeclorum nascitur ordo* underlines the poem's organizing principle: the life of the world moves in harmony with the life of the child. *quo* implies not a deliberate achievement but an automatic consequence ('with whom'). The baby inaugurates the age not by anything he does but because he is there: it is misleading for Carcopino to compare the cock-crow that marks the rising sun,[42] for if there is no baby the day will not dawn. This strange notion well suits the Western situation in 40 BC, when the child of a dynastic marriage might bring peace by his mere existence (see below), but its origins are religious, no doubt being ultimately derived from the sympathetic magic by which seasons were revolved and vegetation renewed. Norden cited the Alexandrian festival of Helios when the initiates proclaimed ἡ παρθένος τέτοκεν, αὔξει φῶς ('the virgin has given birth, it is growing light'),[43] and though his account contains much that is uncertain, this sentence at least shows the concept that underlies Virgil's *quo*. It will be objected that so passive a role does not suit the triumphant Messiah of contemporary Jewish eschatology; on the other hand the original Emmanuel of Isaiah 'becomes a sign simply by being born',[44] and this view of him may have survived later developments. In much Christian as well as pre-Christian theology the effect of the Messiah seems to be automatic (i.e. not directly related to his teaching and example), and even

---

[42] Carcopino 1943: 29.
[43] Norden 1924: 24 ff., Usener 1911: 27 ff., R. Kittel 1924: 21 ff. The festival of Helios attested for 25 December is probably to be conflated with that of Aeon attested for 6 January (the later Epiphany); see further Tarn 1932: 144–5, who is very sceptical about Norden's interpretation.
[44] Mowinckel 1956: 116.

today when a Greek congregation hails the risen Christ, it may greet the good news not just as a promise of future immortality but as an immediate and actual regeneration of the world.

Lucina in line 10 reminds us of the eclogue's affinities with Western epithalamium,[45] perhaps also of Eilytheia's part in secular rites;[46] yet her role here is completely subordinate to her brother's. *tuus iam regnat Apollo* is not simply a parenthetic encouragement (as seems always to be assumed), but the apodosis of the sentence and climax of the section: 'provided that Lucina helps the birth' (i.e. *modo* points forward, not backwards), 'Apollo is as good as reigning' (on this interpretation *iam* refers to the new age as in lines 4, 6, and 7). This confirms that Apollo's reign is not, as is often supposed, the penultimate age or even a transitional period, but begins with the baby's birth; it is not distinct from *Saturnia regna*, but expresses the same idea in modern, non-Hesiodic terms. Virgil was perhaps aware of a neo-Pythagorean view, apparently of Eastern origin, that assigned the last age to Apollo,[47] but it may be more relevant that the Sibyl assigned it to the sun: Servius explains that this means Apollo, which he would not have had to do if he had simply fabricated his information out of Virgil's text.[48] It would certainly be anachronistic to explain the allusion on Western lines as a tribute to Octavian; it might be better to look to Antony, whose connection with such beliefs can be shown later by Alexander Helios,[49] his son by Cleopatra. Of course, Virgil's Apollo is harmonized with traditional Roman religion in a way that would have been impossible for Sol at this date, and he has associations of civilization and peace that suit the Western political situation.

> teque adeo decus hoc aevi, te consule, inibit,
> Pollio, et incipient magni procedere menses.
> te duce, si qua manent sceleris vestigia nostri,

---

[45] Stat. *Silv.* 1.2.269 ff., Slater 1912: 114 ff.

[46] Hor. *Carm. saec.* 14, *ILS* 5050.117, Zosimus, *Hist. Nov.* 2.6.9 (Diels 1890: 134).

[47] Serv. Auct. *ad loc. nonnulli etiam ut magi aiunt Apollinis fore regnum* (his gloss that this may refer to a final conflagration is irrelevant to the poem), Carcopino 1943: 52 ff., Rose 1942: 174 ff.

[48] *dixit etiam quis quo saeculo imperaret et solem ultimum, id est decimum, voluit; novimus autem eundem esse Apollinem.* Augustan poets did not directly identify Apollo with the sun, but Virgil could be influenced here by Sibylline conventions; cf. the extant oracle attributed to 17 BC (Diels 1890, lines 16–17) Φοῖβος Ἀπόλλων ὅστε καὶ ἠέλιος κικλήσκεται.

[49] Tarn 1932: 144 ff.

inrita perpetua solvent formidine terras.
ille deum vitam accipiet, divisque videbit
permixtos heroas et ipse videbitur illis,
pacatumque reget patriis virtutibus orbem. (11–17)

With *you*, to be sure, with *you* as consul, this glory everlasting will be inaugurated, Pollio, and the potent months will begin to advance. With *you* as guide, if any traces remain of our wickedness, by coming to nothing they will free the world from continuous dread. *He* will receive the life of the gods, and with gods will see heroes mingled and himself be seen by them, and will rule a world pacified by his father's prowess.

This section must be explained primarily on Western lines, but not so exclusively as is often supposed. *decus hoc aevi* cannot refer to the baby (though the personified use of *decus* is common in Roman panegyric):[50] this would not suit *inibit*,[51] or lead well to the temporal *incipient procedere menses*, or produce a correspondence between the age (11–12) and the child (15–17) to balance the similar correspondence in the preceding section (4–5 and 8–10). On the other hand Norden was too mystical when he suggested that the new century is the glory of all time (1924: 41): eternity is too vast to be embellished by one of its own subdivisions. Yet perhaps he was right that *aevi* is 'eternity' as opposed to *saeculi* or even *aetatis*; 'this glory everlasting' presumably means *aeternum Apollinis regnum* (another reason for thinking that *tuus iam regnat Apollo* is the climax of the preceding sentence). Virgil has given us an Eastern analogue of such slogans as *gloria saeculi*;[52] his expression may even be modelled on something in the Sibylline oracles on the lines of εὐφροσύνην αἰῶνος,[53] 'eternal joy'. In the same way *magni . . . menses*

---

[50] Ov. *Her.* 15.94 *o decus atque aevi gloria magna tui*, ThLL 5.1.243.6 ff.

[51] Cf. Serv. *ad loc. inchoabit, exordium accipiet, scilicet saeculum*, ThLL 7.1295.49 ff. (on *ex ineunte aetate* and similar expressions). It is argued on the other side that 15 *ille* needs a recent point of reference; but for the stereotyped *ille* (here contrasted with *te*) see below in the text.

[52] The legend *gloria novi saeculi* is found on coins of Gratian (Mattingly *et al.* 1923–67: 9.54); significantly he was addressed by Symmachus (*Or.* 3) in terms borrowed from the eclogue (see below, nn. 100, 111). The genitive *aevi* indicates concomitance, not identity; Virgil's commentators are wrong to compare Plautine expressions like *monstrum mulieris*.

[53] 3.786 (= 3.771 αἰώνιον εὐφροσύνην); the phrase looks like a Hebraism (Ecclesiasticus 2.9 εὐφροσύνην αἰῶνος, 17.12 διαθήκην αἰῶνος). The first Sibylline passage was understood by Norden to refer to the divine child (Norden 1924: 147), inconsistently

has a more portentous note than is sometimes realized (the adjective is found in the eclogue also at lines 5, 22, 36, 48, 49). *menses* cannot refer to subdivisions of the Stoic great year (the metaphor is pointless unless it is applied to a cycle), or directly to the pregnancy of the baby's mother (as at line 61); rather it describes a corresponding cosmic parturition, and when combined with the contrasting *aevi* suggests that the splendour of eternity will soon be only a few months distant.

The emphatic *te... consule* makes a thought-provoking contrast with *decus hoc aevi* by connecting the political with the cosmic timescale. Norden (1924: 42–3) thought that the poem was written for Pollio's assumption of office at the beginning of 40, and hence was an early specimen of a type of panegyric later familiar in both prose and verse.[54] But Pollio could not have been associated with peace at the beginning of the year, when the Perusine War was approaching its tragic conclusion, or during the summer, when his friend Antony was expected to invade Italy, or indeed at any time till the Treaty of Brundisium in the autumn, the supreme achievement of his distinguished career.[55] If the poet's language suggests an inauguration it is not the consul's but the baby's and the age's, and an extension of the sort of thing said in Eastern inscriptions about rulers' birthdays.[56]

Lines 13–14 belong to the Westerners. *duce* is a political term, glossed by Servius as *auctore*;[57] this dates the poem not just to 40 but to the context of the Treaty. *sceleris* here means the crime of civil war, though a Sibylline prototype could have combined Eastern notions about deliverance from sin with Hesiodic language about the wickedness of the Iron Age. *perpetua formidine* would suit both a religious litany and the historical reality, when the chain of calamity must have seemed never-ending and inescapable. *si qua manent vestigia* is

---

with himself (57) and quite wrongly (Deubner 1925: 164, Jachmann 1952a: 45–6). For the use of *aevi* cf. also Sil. *Pun.* 3.480 *aevi glacie* ('eternal ice').

[54] For the characteristics of such poems see Du Quesnay 1976: 43 ff.

[55] Tarn 1932: 151 ff., Du Quesnay 1976: 48. The latter still sees a celebration of Pollio's entry into office, but in spite of his prolonged absence from Rome he was *consul ordinarius* from the beginning of the year.

[56] OGIS 458.40–1 (on Augustus) ἦρξεν δὲ τῷ κόσμῳ τῶν δι' αὐτὸν εὐαγγελιῶν ἡ γενέθλιος ἡμέρα τοῦ θεοῦ.

[57] *dux* and *auctor* are sometimes combined in Cicero (*ThLL* 5.1.2317.58 ff.).

appropriate to prophetic utterances about expiation (for instance Sibylline oracles of the Western type); the phrase suggests in three different ways that the trouble is now virtually over (Virgil says *manent*, not *manebunt*), and would have been nonsensical at any time before the Treaty was signed. One of the main provisions was the dynastic marriage of Antony and Octavia, from which a child might be conceived with luck before the end of the year.[58] When a poem addressed to Pollio within two months of his Treaty talked of a baby who would bring peace and rule the world, it would have been impossible for a contemporary not to think of the purpose of the recent wedding;[59] by the end of the year Octavian's earlier marriage to Scribonia was unimportant,[60] and Pollio must have deplored that alliance. Of course Virgil speaks inexplicitly, as a sensible oracle should, and the implications of the poem were forgotten when the baby turned out a girl,[61] and especially when Octavian and Antony quarrelled.

Lines 15 ff. again seem to belong to the Westerners, but here there are greater ambiguities. As parallels to *ille deum vitam accipiet* commentators cite expressions for 'living like gods',[62] but *accipiet* implies the grant of a more clearly defined status, and in that case Virgil means (or at least suggests) something more than earthly felicity (this argument should be closely scrutinized, as much depends on it). The next clause in isolation might refer to the θεοξενία,[63] by which the gods entertained favoured mortals in the Golden Age and later Greek cult, but an anticlimax is avoided if it again refers to the future immortality of the child (the mention of heroes may hint obliquely

---

[58] It is clear from Virgil's language in 11–12 (where *inibit* precedes *menses*) that the new age is connected with Pollio by the conception rather than the birth of the child.

[59] The wedding of Catullus 64 (to which the eclogue is to some extent a rejoinder) ends with sinister prophecies of the birth of Achilles.

[60] It is not even plausible to see an ambiguous allusion to both marriages (thus Witte 1922/3: 43–4, G. Williams 1974: 45).

[61] The elder Antonia was born by the autumn of 39 (Plut. *Ant.* 33.3). This goes some way towards refuting the story that at the time of her marriage Octavia was pregnant by her dead husband Marcellus (Dio 48.31.4); cf. Hammond 1937: 1860.

[62] Hes. *Op.* 112 ὥστε θεοὶ δ' ἔζωον ἀκηδέα θυμὸν ἔχοντες, Ter. *Haut.* 693 *deorum vitam apti sumus.*

[63] Hes. fr. 1.6 M.-W. ξυναὶ γὰρ τότε δαῖτες ἔσαν, ξυνοὶ δὲ θόωκοι ἀθανάτοις τε θεοῖσι καταθνητοῖς τ' ἀνθρώποις, (cf. Gatz 1967: 36–7); for later cult cf. Nock 1972: 586–7. Virgil cannot be thinking simply of renewed visits by the gods to earth (Catull. 64.384 ff., 407–8), for then they would see everybody they met.

that he will enjoy a similar position). Such immortality can be explained entirely in terms of early Greek mythology and Hellenistic ruler-cult, so it will probably be thought over-speculative to look beyond Virgil's normal sources. Yet once it is accepted that the poet is drawing on Eastern eschatology, the same sort of question arises as with the descent from the sky (7): might he have transmuted to Western terms something about the ultimate ascension of the Messiah?[64] There seems to be no clear authority for such a view in orthodox Judaism, but the Christian doctrine must link up somehow with similar beliefs in other religions. Could Jews of the Diaspora have ventured, even before the birth of Christ, to give the Messiah a celestial destiny? Before dismissing such a notion out of hand, we must consider the implications of line 17.

Here we are met by further difficulties of interpretation, or rather calculated ambiguities; these may be accepted in oracles (though not indiscriminately in other sorts of poetry) even when one meaning seems more obvious than the other.[65] Thus *patriis virtutibus* from a linguistic point of view goes most easily with *pacatum* (which is improved by a supplement)[66] rather than with *reget* (which is not); yet in a panegyric it is natural to say that somebody will repeat the deeds of his father,[67] and particularly in a poem that has affinities with epithalamium.[68] In the same way *patriis* can be interpreted as equivalent to *patrum*, 'ancestors', but more particularly as *patris* ('Antony' to contemporaries). *pacatum* suits the Roman context, where *pax* was associated with *victoria*, but peace-making in a more beneficent sense was ascribed to Hellenistic rulers; the same variation of emphasis is found in Messianic writing.[69] Perhaps Antony will pacify the world in the old-fashioned Roman sense, but the baby will rule it as a peace-maker ($εἰρηνοποιός$).

---

[64] Cf. Jn. 6: 62 ἐὰν οὖν θεωρῆτε τὸν υἱὸν τοῦ ἀνθρώπου ἀναβαίνοντα ὅπου ἦν τὸ πρότερον.

[65] The natural interpretation was the wrong one at Enn. Ann. 179 *aio te, Aeacida, Romanos vincere posse.*

[66] Cf. Ov. Her. 9.13 *respice vindicibus pacatum viribus orbem* (of Hercules).

[67] Theoc. 17.13 ἐκ πατέρων οἷος μὲν ἔην τελέσαι μέγα ἔργον, Stat. Silv. 4.7.43 *crescat in mores patrios.*

[68] Cf. Catull. 64.348 and 357 (the future *virtutes* of Achilles).

[69] Contrast Orac. Sib. 3.373–4 (n. 27) with 3.653 ὃς πᾶσαν γαῖαν παύσει πολέμοιο κακοῖο. See further Windisch 1925: 240 (linking pagan and Christian concepts), Mowinckel 1956: 176–7.

Another obscurity seems particularly significant. In a Roman context one naturally assumes that the child's future domain is an earthly one; but as the first clause in the series points to a future immortality (see above on *accipiet*), and as it can easily carry the second clause with it, the obvious interpretation of the third clause involves an anticlimax. The awkwardness would be explained, though not indeed avoided, if we could suppose that Virgil is reverting to his Sibylline oracle, and that it referred at this point to an eternal kingdom. Norden well compared Luke 1: 32–3 (Gabriel to Mary) οὗτος ἔσται μέγας καὶ υἱὸς Ὑψίστου κληθήσεται, καὶ δώσει αὐτῷ Κύριος ὁ Θεὸς τὸν θρόνον Δαυὶδ τοῦ πατρὸς αὐτοῦ, καὶ βασιλεύσει ἐπὶ τὸν οἶκον Ἰακὼβ εἰς τοὺς αἰῶνας καὶ τῆς βασιλείας οὐκ ἔσται τέλος ('he will be great, and will be called the Son of the Most High; and the Lord God will give to him the throne of his father David; and he will reign over the house of Jacob forever; and of his kingdom there will be no end').[70] The significance of the parallel lies in more than the hieratic series of future tenses; here we have a conflation of the temporal and eternal kingdoms such as seems to be presupposed by Virgil's line. This conflation was natural among Jews who hoped for a Davidic Messiah, which is how Jesus is regarded in the infancy narrative of Luke and even more conspicuously in that of Matthew; as these two gospels are independent of one another, this feature must go back to the common source of the extant accounts. Indeed, Professor Raymond E. Brown in his illuminating book on the nativity considers that 'the idea of an annunciation of the birth of the Davidic Messiah…may have already existed in pre-Christian Judaism.'[71]

Annunciations in the developed sense were an Eastern phenomenon. Norden divined that Gabriel's prophecy was derived from the acclamation of Egyptian god-kings, but he did not discuss more immediate models in the Septuagint: see Gen. 16: 11–12 καὶ τέξῃ υἱόν, καὶ καλέσεις τὸ ὄνομα αὐτοῦ Ἰσμαήλ … οὗτος ἔσται ἄγροικος ἄνθρωπος… ('and you shall bear a son; you shall call his name

---

[70] Norden 1924: 125–6, following Boll 1914: 12–13. They also cited Hephaestion 65.17 Engelbrecht (= 1 p. 28 Pingree) ἐκ θεῶν σπαρήσεται καὶ ἔσται μέγας καὶ μετὰ θεῶν θρησκευθήσεται καὶ ἔσται κοσμοκράτωρ καὶ πάντα αὐτῷ ὑπακούσεται (though nothing in Virgil corresponds to the naïve καί found here and in Luke).
[71] R. E. Brown 1977: 310–11.

Ishmael...he shall be a wild ass of a man'), 17: 19 τέξεταί σοι υἱόν, καὶ καλέσεις τὸ ὄνομα αὐτοῦ ʼΙσαάκ ('she shall bear you a son, and you shall call his name Isaac'), Judg. 13: 5 (Samson), 1 Chron. 22: 9–10 (Solomon) ἰδοὺ υἱὸς τίκτεταί σοι. οὗτος ἔσται ἀνὴρ ἀναπαύσεως... οὗτος οἰκοδομήσει οἶκον τῷ ὀνόματί μου ('behold, a son shall be born to you; he shall be a man of peace...he shall build a house for my name'), Isa. 7: 14 (so Mt. 1: 21–3, Lk. 1: 13–17). οὗτος in such passages corresponds to *ille* in the eclogue; one may compare the 'Er-Stil' that Norden analyzed elsewhere in the praises of gods.[72] The annunciations in the early Greek poets are rudimentary by comparison;[73] it is therefore all the more striking when the Theocritean Tiresias prophesies about Heracles[74] (24.73 ff.) in terms that recall the pattern[75] of the Old Testament and of Luke. He says to Alcmene θάρσει ('be of good cheer' 73; she is alarmed by the episode of the snakes), which might be an adaptation of the reassurance normal at epiphanies (Lk. 1: 30 μὴ φοβοῦ, Μαριάμ, 'do not be afraid, Mary'); he calls her ἀριστοτόκεια γύναι ('mother of noble children' 73), following the form of Jewish annunciations in addressing the fortunate parent by a relevant periphrasis (Lk. 1: 28 χαῖρε κεχαριτωμένη, 'hail, o favoured one'); he proceeds σέβας δ' ἔσῃ Ἀργείαισι ('you shall be honoured among the Argive women' 78; a shame-culture's equivalent of Lk. 1: 42 εὐλογημένη σὺ ἐν γυναιξίν, 'blessed are you among women'); he prophesies τοῖος ἀνὴρ ὅδε μέλλει ἐς οὐρανὸν ἄστρα φέροντα ἀμβαίνειν τεὸς υἱός ('your son, so great a man, shall rise to the star-laden heaven' 84; an ascent that corresponds to Virgil and Luke more than to anything in the Septuagint); he leads up to the climax γαμβρὸς δ' ἀθανάτων κεκλήσεται ('he shall be called son-in-law of the immortals' 84), where the very pagan

---

[72] Norden 1913: 163 ff.
[73] Hom. *Od.* 11.248–9 χαῖρε, γύναι, φιλότητι· περιπλομένου δ' ἐνιαυτοῦ τέξεις ἀγλαὰ τέκνα, Orac. ap. Hdt. 5.92 β .2, Pind. P. 9.59 ff. τόθι παῖδα τέξεται...θήσονταί τέ νιν ἀθάνατον.
[74] Without noticing the Theocritean annunciation Friedrich Pfister cited other parallels between Heracles and Christ, which led him to posit influence on the prototype of the Gospels by a Stoic-Cynic biography of the Greek hero (1937: 42 ff.). The issues seem much more complex than he suggests; one must not think of a lost source that will explain all, but of a society where many people variously combined in their patterns of thought the most diverse cultural traditions.
[75] R. E. Brown 1977: 155 ff. gives a valuable analysis of Jewish annunciations, but he does not include pagan material.

γαμβρός (rather than υἱός) recalls the last line of the eclogue, but κεκλήσεται (though it can be paralleled at Hom. Od. 7.313 ἐμὸς γαμβρὸς καλέεσθαι) in the context of an annunciation seems remarkably close to the Jewish formula (Isa. 7: 14, Lk. 1: 32 υἱὸς Ὑψίστου κληθήσεται, etc.). The Theocritean passage suggests that though the Greek and Graeco-Jewish cultures of Alexandria were curiously separate, the Septuagint might have had some influence on Hellenistic poetry,[76] whether directly or indirectly. Borrowings in the other direction were obviously easier, especially two centuries later, and one asks whether Virgil's Sibylline model could have been coloured in turn by Hellenistic panegyrics on divine Ptolemaic infants.

> at tibi prima, puer,[77] nullo munuscula cultu
> errantis hederas passim cum baccare tellus
> mixtaque ridenti colocasia fundet acantho.
> ipsae lacte domum referent distenta capellae
> ubera, nec magnos metuent armenta leones.
> ipsa tibi blandos fundent cunabula flores.
> occidet et serpens, et fallax herba veneni
> occidet; Assyrium vulgo nascetur amomum.   (18–25)

But for you, baby boy, as your first presents the earth without cultivation will pour out ivy wandering with baccar all over the place and Indian lotus mingled with smiling acanthus. Of their own accord the she-goats will bring home udders swollen with milk, nor will the herds of cattle be afraid of great lions. Of its accord the cradle will pour out for you winsome flowers. The serpent will die, and the plant that conceals its poison will die, and Syrian amomum will be born at large.

The fragrant and unusual *munuscula* of this section mark the special position of the baby, just like the frankincense and myrrh of the Magi (Mt. 2: 11), but no close relationship can be posited, as the evangelist's story is obviously Eastern. Virgil's flowers, on the other hand, belong to the Western tradition, where they are a property of pastoral from Theocritus to Milton, and a conventional decoration

---

[76] For other alleged influences of the Septuagint on Callimachus and Theocritus see the discussion by Fraser 1972: 2.1000 ff.

[77] There is no particular significance in the parallel at Lk. 1: 76 καὶ σὺ δέ, παιδίον, προφήτης Ὑψίστου κληθήσῃ (Erdmann 1932: 32); an alteration of third-person statement and second-person address is natural in genethliacon, and indeed in other types of panegyric.

of houses at the birth of a child; in particular the infant Bacchus was surrounded by ivy,[78] Iamus and Hermes covered in blossoms, while Delos flowered in gold for Apollo. The oriental colocasia and baccar are derived from no Sibylline prototype, but are mentioned from the Roman standpoint as exotic plants, possibly with Dionysiac or even Antonian associations;[79] similarly *amomum* below (25) had been linked with the Golden Age in an earlier eclogue (3.89), and the supposed derivation of its name ('blameless') suggests a contrast with deceitful snakes and plants. The baccar grows with as little cultivation as the ivy, and the colocasia and amomum are unfamiliarly profuse (*fundet, vulgo*); such spontaneous abundance was a feature of the Golden Age from the time of Hesiod, though as such it naturally merges in a Sibylline context.[80] The situation is less conventional in line 23 where the cradle produces flowers of its own accord,[81] but commentators fail to note that even this miracle is recorded of the birth of Dionysus.[82] The cradle is not just the place of birth (as Servius and others have suggested), but has ritual parallels in the Dionysiac λίκνον; in the same way the Christian manger (a food-trough rather than *praesaepe*) not only developed a sacred significance[83] but may have had antecedents in cult.[84] The common source can ultimately be found in the near-Eastern worship of divine infants.

The animals of the section suit the pastoral setting no less than the flowers. The homing goats are derived from Theocritus,[85] though the

[78] Eur. *Phoen.* 651 ff., Philostr. *Imag.* 1.14.3, Nonnus, *Dion.* 9.12 (cf. also Dionys. Per. 941 τῷ καὶ γεινομένῳ κηώδεα φύετο πάντα). For Iamus cf. Pind. *O.* 6.55, for Hermes cf. Philostr. *Imag.* 1.26.2, for Apollo cf. *H. Ap.* 135 ff., Callim. *Hymn* 4.260 ff.

[79] Baccar must have been associated with Bacchus, colocasia came from Egypt (cf. Serv. *ad loc.*, Thiselton-Dyer 1918: 299 ff.), ivy was Dionysiac.

[80] Hes. *Op.* 117–18, Gatz 1967: 229, *Orac. Sib.* 1.297–8.

[81] *ipsa* must mean *sua sponte* to balance 21 *ipsae*; this is misunderstood by Jachmann 1952*a*: 58–9.

[82] Nonnus, *Dion.* 7.344–5 καὶ αὐτοφύτοισι πετήλοις ὄρχατος ἀμπελόεις Σεμέλης περιδέδρομεν εὐνήν (cf. 10.171 ff.).

[83] Usener 1911: 286 ff., Berliner 1955.

[84] The φάτνη at Lk. 2:7 is clearly regarded as important (R. E. Brown 1977: 418 ff.), but its motivation is not very clear; it ought to be a substitute for a cradle, not for 'room in the inn'. At *Protevangelium Jacobi* 22.2 the trough turns up for a different purpose, to hide Jesus from Herod. Did the prop exist before the play?

[85] Theoc. 11.12 (when the love-lorn Cyclops neglects his work) πολλάκι ταὶ ὄιες ποτὶ τωὔλιον αὐταὶ ἀπῆνθον (αὐταί = *ipsae*).

context there is quite different; the parallel in Horace's sixteenth epode may be ignored, as that poem's Theocritean element is mediated through Virgil.[86] It is significant that the goats bring their milk not simply to the baby (there is no *tibi*); there is an alternation not only of flowers and animals, but of the local and the universal, the cradle and the world.[87] This variation does not detract from the importance of the child, but on the contrary underlines his superhuman status. In the same way in bucolic poetry all nature mourns for Daphnis; though it is true that the Messiah's influence is often portrayed as universal (cf. 9 *toto... mundo*), Virgil's formulation here surely owes more to Theocritus than the Sibyl.

An Eastern interpretation is more naturally encouraged by the following reference to the cattle and the lions (22). Virgil is not thinking of a total absence of wild animals (as is often supposed) but of their pacific behaviour;[88] this is the more vivid explanation (especially in view of *magnos*),[89] is supported by Horace's imitation (below, n. 92), and coheres with the general view of the Golden Age as a time of vegetarianism.[90] Yet peace among animals is not directly ascribed to the Golden Age before our poem,[91] though it is mentioned in similar contexts very soon after;[92] the tame beasts of Empedocles (fr. 130 D.-K.) are not quite the same (their relation to man is emphasized rather than to each other), nor are proverbial adynata of the type πρίν κεν λύκος οἶν ὑμεναιοῖ ('till a wolf weds a ewe').[93] Under

---

[86] Snell 1938.

[87] Kloucek obscured this simultaneous action when he transposed 23 to follow 20 (which is made unattractive in any case by the repetition of *fundere*). The disjointedness of Virgil's arrangement suggests a feature of the bucolic style.

[88] It is sometimes argued that 24 *occidet et serpens* implies that the lion will also perish (Sudhaus 1901: 47). In fact *et* may join *serpens* and *herba* (in spite of the repetition of the verb); for a somewhat similar schema cf. 6 *iam redit et Virgo, redeunt Saturnia regna* (for parallels see Wagner's note).

[89] Wagenvoort 1956: 8.

[90] Barwick 1944: 36–7.

[91] Gatz 1967: 165 ff.

[92] Cf. Verg. *G.* 1.130, Hor. *Epod.* 16.33 *credula nec ravos metuent armenta leones*, *Carm.* 1.17.8–9, 3.8.13.

[93] Ar. *Pax* 1076, Kenner 1970: 63–4. There is a much closer parallel to Virgil at Theoc. 24.86–7 (on the deification of Heracles) ἔσται δὴ τοῦτ' ἆμαρ ὁπηνίκα νεβρὸν ἐν εὐνᾷ καρχαρόδων σίνεσθαι ἰδὼν λύκος οὐκ ἐθελήσει (cited by Lagrange 1931: 613–14); but that passage seems to be an interpolation (see the commentaries of Gow 1952*b* and Dover 1971).

these circumstances it becomes relevant to compare the passage from Isaiah where the calf and the young lion lie down together and the child plays on the hole of the asp (11: 6–9). The resemblance of the eclogue is increased by the reference to snakes; though the poet, unlike the prophet, makes them disappear altogether, he may have been attracted by the dire oracular *occidet*, especially when it is combined with the paradoxical *serpens* ('the creeping one will fall'). Yet it is not easy to suppose that Virgil had direct knowledge of the Hebrew scriptures or even of the Septuagint. Those who posit such curious learning still have to explain how the area of discourse could have been intelligible to the eclogue's readers.

The case is very different with the close paraphrase of Isaiah in an early section of the Sibylline Oracles (3.788–95):

> ἠδὲ λύκοι τε καὶ ἄρνες ἐν οὔρεσιν ἄμμιγ' ἔδονται
> χόρτον, παρδάλιές τ' ἐρίφοις ἅμα βοσκήσονται·
> ἄρκτοι σὺν μόσχοις νομάδες αὐλισθήσονται·
> σαρκοβόρος τε λέων φάγεται ἄχυρον παρὰ φάτνῃ
> ὡς βοῦς· καὶ παῖδες μάλα νήπιοι ἐν δεσμοῖσιν
> ἄξουσιν· πηρὸν γὰρ ἐπὶ χθονὶ θῆρα ποιήσει.
> σὺν βρέφεσίν[94] τε δράκοντες ἅμ' ἀσπίσι κοιμήσονται
> κοὐκ ἀδικήσουσιν· χεὶρ γὰρ θεοῦ ἔσσετ' ἐπ' αὐτούς.

Wolves and lambs will eat grass together in the mountains. Leopards will feed together with kids. Roving bears will spend the night with calves. The flesh-eating lion will eat husks at the manger like an ox, and mere infant children will lead them with ropes. For he will make the beasts on earth harmless. Serpents and asps will sleep with babies and will not harm them, for the hand of God will be upon them.

It is particularly important that both the Sibyl and the eclogue set the scene in the future: 'peace among animals' might in isolation be regarded as a coincidence (for though unparalleled before Virgil, the theme fits Western notions easily enough), but the coincidence becomes very considerable when one takes into account the prophetic nature of both passages and Virgil's acknowledged debt to the Sibyl. It is particularly significant that Isaiah's account of the animal-peace comes only four chapters later than his mention of the baby

---

[94] Isa. 11: 8 mentions a παιδίον νήπιον in the singular, which some have connected with an infant Messiah, but the extant oracle rightly regards the reference as general.

Emmanuel (see above); whatever the doubts of modern scholars, the Jewish composers of the Sibylline oracles are not likely to have dissociated these two chapters. Of course if Virgil were relying only on our form of the Sibylline oracle, Emmanuel (who is not there mentioned) would become irrelevant; but the text was exceptionally fluid, and it is clear that the poet was using an oracle that is now lost. The miraculous child and the animal-peace are in both Isaiah and Virgil, but only the animal-peace in the Sibyl; it would avoid an awkward coincidence if we could suppose that Virgil's version of the Sibyl made some allusion to the child.

In this connection some attention should be given to the lines of the Sibyl that immediately precede the passage on the animals (3.785–7):

> εὐφράνθητι, κόρη, καὶ ἀγάλλεο· σοὶ γὰρ ἔδωκεν
> εὐφροσύνην αἰῶνος ὃς οὐρανὸν ἔκτισε καὶ γῆν.
> ἐν σοὶ δ' οἰκήσει· σοὶ δ' ἔσσεται ἀθάνατον φῶς.

Rejoice, maiden, and be glad, for to you the one who created heaven and earth has given joy everlasting. He will dwell in you. You will have immortal light.

At the most obvious level the κόρη is the 'Daughter of Zion', i.e. Jerusalem itself; the passage is modelled on Zach. 2: 10 τέρπου καὶ εὐφραίνου, θύγατερ Σίων, διότι ἰδοὺ ἐγὼ ἔρχομαι καὶ κατασκηνώσω ἐν μέσῳ σου, λέγει κύριος ('sing and rejoice, o daughter of Zion; for lo, I come and will dwell in the midst of you, says the Lord'; cf. also Zach. 9: 9, Zeph. 3: 14, Jer. 31(38): 4 ἔτι οἰκοδομήσω σε καὶ οἰκοδομηθήσῃ, παρθένος Ἰσραήλ). Yet in the Sibyl's Isaian context the words might have referred ambiguously, or later been taken to refer, to the virgin mother of the new Emmanuel (cf. Isa. 7: 14, cited above). οἰκεῖν not only suits God's habitation of Zion (like κατασκηνώσω cited above), but was later used by Christians of the 'dwelling' of the Pneuma within an individual (1 Cor. 3: 16, Rom. 8: 9); the Sibyl's remark about spiritual habitation might be the sort of thing that led to the evangelists' more physical account of the Messiah's conception. It is important to note that without using the Sibylline passage some theologians have suggested that the Virgin in Luke's nativity actualizes things said in the Old Testament about the

Daughter of Zion.[95] Such a theory may seem fanciful at first sight, but it makes sense of 2: 35 καὶ σοῦ δὲ αὐτῆς τὴν ψυχὴν διελεύσεται ῥομφαία, ὅπως ἂν ἀποκαλυφθῶσιν ἐκ πολλῶν καρδιῶν διαλογισμοί ('and a sword will pierce through your own soul also, that thoughts out of many hearts may be revealed';[96] the two clauses must be taken together if the characteristically Semitic balance of the passage is to be maintained, yet 'many hearts' is difficult to understand if a single individual is being talked about). It is not of course being suggested here that Luke or his source is drawing on the extant version of the Sibyl, but that a late refabrication of the Sibyl's lines, where the birth of the Messianic child was made explicit, might have exemplified some of the ideas that lie behind the evangelist's account.

> at simul heroum laudes et facta parentis
> iam legere et quae sit poteris cognoscere virtus,
> molli paulatim flavescet campus arista,
> incultisque rubens pendebit sentibus uva,
> et durae quercus sudabunt roscida mella.
> pauca tamen suberunt priscae vestigia fraudis,
> quae temptare Thetim ratibus, quae cingere muris
> oppida, quae iubeant telluri infindere sulcos.
> alter erit tum Tiphys et altera quae vehat Argo
> delectos heroas; erunt etiam altera bella,
> atque iterum ad Troiam magnus mittetur Achilles. (26–36)

But as soon as you can now read of heroes' praises and your father's deeds and learn what manhood means, the open plain will gradually turn brown with soft bristles, and a reddening cluster will hang from untended thickets, and hard oaks will exude honey-dew. Yet a few traces of the old wickedness will lurk to bid men try out the sea with ships, encircle towns with walls, and cleave furrows on the earth. There will then be another Tiphys and another Argo to carry chosen heroes; there will be also another series of wars and a second time there will be despatched to Troy a great Achilles.

---

[95] See Hebert 1950: 403 ff., Laurentin 1957: 64 ff., 159 ff., and on the other side R. E. Brown 1977: 320 ff.

[96] See especially Benoit 1963: 251 ff. Some have seen here a borrowing from *Orac. Sib.* 3.316 ῥομφαίη γὰρ σεῖο διέρχηται διὰ μέσσον (Erdmann 1932: 13), but the resemblance shows no more than a common attitude to the Septuagint (Ezek. 14: 17, combined in Luke's case with Ps. 21: 21, 36: 15).

The Easterners fail in their attempt to claim this section. *at simul* (ἀλλ ὁπόταν) suits the manner of prophecies in general and is not simply Sibylline: oracles regularly follow the pattern 'when A then B'. The childhood of the θεῖος ἀνήρ is often said to foreshadow his future qualities,[97] but when the boy of the eclogue gets his moral education from books, that sets him firmly in the world of reality.[98] The Greek *heroum laudes* leads to the Roman *facta parentis*,[99] which must allude to the *res gestae* of a historical person rather than to the πράξεις of a god; in the same way *virtus* points unequivocally to the ideals of Virgil's own society. The spontaneous abundance of the Golden Age (28–30) belongs to the Western tradition,[100] and though the transference of the description to the future is most easily paralleled in the Sibyl (see above), Virgil's rhythm and colouring are more reminiscent of Catullus. If the soft yellowing bristles of the corn correspond to the first down of adolescence, the symbolism is derived from Greek erotic poetry rather than Jewish apocalyptic, and when nature matures with the development of the boy, though the notion is mystical it is certainly not Messianic. Norden compares the rites of the Egyptian Aeon (1924: 42 ff.), but the agricultural setting might suggest a less abstract year-spirit; even if the infant 'saviour' is derived from a Sibylline oracle, his gradual growth seems to come from other models. But though Jachmann was presumably right to see here a Virgilian elaboration (1952*a*: 58 ff.), there is no serious inconsistency with the appearance of the Golden Age in 18 ff.: the smiling flowers and security from snakes are appropriate for a child, the young man enjoys a

[97] Lk. 2: 52 καὶ Ἰησοῦς προέκοπτεν ἐν τῇ σοφίᾳ καὶ ἡλικίᾳ καὶ χάριτι παρὰ θεῷ καὶ ἀνθρώποις, Bieler 1935–6: 1.34 ff.

[98] Plut. *Cat. Mai.* 20.5 καὶ τὰς ἱστορίας δὲ συγγράψαι φησὶν αὐτὸς ἰδίᾳ χειρὶ καὶ μεγάλοις γράμμασιν ὅπως οἴκοθεν ὑπάρχοι τῷ παιδὶ πρὸς ἐμπειρίαν τῶν παλαιῶν καὶ πατρίων ὠφελεῖσθαι. Norden is quite unconvincing when he cites parallels for 'das lesende Götterkind' (1924: 134 ff.).

[99] Those who deny the parentage of any individual statesman would find advantages in the variant *parentum*, but the singular is supported by the *testimonia* of Nonius (521 L), Servius, and Eusebius (πατρός τε μεγίστου). Carcopino 1943: 27 n. considers that *parentis* might be a Christian interpolation, but the reading of Nonius tells against him; if anything, *parentum* might have been interpolated when the original reference was lost.

[100] The open *campus* does not usually produce grain; cf. the elaboration by Symm. *Or.* 3.9 *nunc mihi in patentibus campis sponte seges matura floresceret.*

gradual extension of nature's bounty, but complete deliverance from work comes only to the fully adult.

The references to navigation and agriculture in the next sentence suit Western accounts of the Iron Age, while the Argo recalls the fall from innocence in Catullus 64. The reasons for this interlude have been much debated. Some have thought that Virgil is reversing the Hesiodic sequence to produce a new race of heroes, some that he is repeating it on the lines of a Stoic cycle;[101] neither theory can be made to fit, as the Golden Age starts coming at the birth of the child and is completed at his maturity. Others have compared Jewish eschatology, where the Messiah must destroy the wicked before the age of peace can begin; but Virgil seems to have moved out of this range of ideas, and there is no close analogy in the Sibylline passage where foreign kings lead a counter-revolution.[102] In fact the interlude of war balances the turbulence of youth, and makes a bridge between the innocence of childhood and the felicity of middle age. The retrogression may seem out of line with what has gone before, but Virgil is too good a Roman to accept the eschatological myth without qualification: manly achievements were naturally predicted in the epithalamium and genethliacon, and true *virtus* seemed impossible in a paradise where there was nothing to do. The second Troy is clearly not Rome (which is thus represented in the Sibylline Oracles), but presumably Parthia: in the context of 40, when Syria and Cilicia had so recently been overrun, a reference to contemporary Western aspirations is hard to avoid. The new Achilles who is to be despatched[103] to the wars cannot be Antony; though he claimed descent from the original Achilles, he must not wait so long for his triumphs. Surely he is the child himself,[104] who should be allowed to repeat the *facta parentis* (26) with *facta* of his own (54): here as elsewhere Virgil is contradicting Catullus, who had seen Achilles as a man of blood.[105]

---

[101] For the former view cf. Rose 1942: 184; for the latter cf. Serv. *Ecl.* 4.34 *videtur tamen locus hic dictus per apocatastasin.*

[102] *Orac. Sib.* 3.663–4, cited by Norden 1924: 147 and Erdmann 1932: 85, but rejected by Jachmann 1952a: 40 ff.

[103] *mittere* is a Roman technicality for despatching a general to the wars (*ThLL* 8.1183.55 ff.).

[104] Tarn 1932: 155. [105] 64.348 ff., Bramble 1970: 25–6.

hinc, ubi iam firmata virum te fecerit aetas,
cedet et ipse mari vector, nec nautica pinus
mutabit merces; omnis feret omnia tellus.
non rastros patietur humus, non vinea falcem;
robustus quoque iam tauris iuga solvet arator,
nec varios discet mentiri lana colores,
ipse sed in pratis aries iam suave rubenti
murice, iam croceo mutabit vellera luto;
sponte sua sandyx pascentis vestiet agnos.   (37–45)

Next when your age has now grown firm and made you a man, even the very trader will retire from the sea, nor will the ship of pine-wood exchange merchandise; every land will produce everything. The soil will not be subjected to mattocks nor the vine to the pruning-hook; the sturdy ploughman too will now loose the yoke from the oxen, nor will wool learn to counterfeit variegated colours, but the ram of himself in the meadows will change his fleece now with sweetly reddening purple, now with saffron-coloured yellow; of its own accord scarlet will clothe the grazing lambs.

The description of the child's maturity also conforms to the Western tradition. The absence of navigation follows Hesiod and Aratus,[106] not Eastern apocalyptic: the sea that was no more in *Revelation* represents the primeval anarchy of the world, and has nothing to do with Graeco-Roman ideas on the corrupting influence of commerce.[107] The disappearance of work and the automation of the Golden Age are also conventional (n. 80), and though the transference of the theme to the future suits the Sibyl,[108] the actual phraseology recalls Lucretius and especially Catullus (64.38 ff.). On the other hand the sweetly blushing ram is a novel embellishment of the topic: Virgil has characteristically transmuted a piece of Etruscan antiquarianism recently translated by Tarquitius.[109] His sentimental and humorous[110]

---

[106] Hes. *Op.* 236–7, Arat. *Phaen.* 110–11, Gatz 1967: 229. Virgil's *et ipse* suggests the sea's irresistible magnetism for the merchant.
[107] Rev. 21: 1 καὶ ἡ θάλασσα οὐκ ἔστιν ἔτι, Caird 1966: 262.
[108] 7.146–7 (a late section) οὐκέτι τις κόψει βαθὺν αὔλακα γύρῳ ἀρότρῳ, οὐ βόες ἰθυντῆρα κάτω βάψουσι σίδηρον (Kurfess 1951 gives Jewish parallels).
[109] Macrob. *Sat.* 3.7.2 *purpureo aureove colore ovis ariesque si aspergetur, principi ordinis et generis summa cum felicitate largitatem auget*, Serv. Auct. *ad loc.*, Wagenvoort 1962: 139 ff.; for Tarquitius see Heurgon 1953: 402 ff.
[110] Hor. *Sat.* 1.10.44 *molle atque facetum*.

fantasy, which does not deserve the scorn of the critics, makes an agreeable contrast with the monstrosities of Daniel and Revelation.

> 'talia saecla' suis dixerunt 'currite' fusis
> concordes stabili fatorum numine Parcae.
> adgredere o magnos (aderit iam tempus) honores,
> cara deum suboles, magnum Iovis incrementum!
> aspice convexo nutantem pondere mundum,
> terrasque tractusque maris caelumque profundum;
> aspice, venturo laetentur ut omnia saeclo! (46–52)

'Speed such ages' said the Fates to their spindles, concordant by the constant will of destiny. Assume, I pray, great dignities (the time will soon be here), dear offspring of the gods, great increase of Jupiter. Look at the cosmos swaying with its vaulted weight, the lands and the stretches of the sea and the deep sky—look how everything rejoices in the coming age.

From one point of view this passage belongs to the Western tradition, as it is a rejoinder to the sinister epithalamium of the Parcae at the wedding of Peleus and Thetis (n. 105). The first line obviously echoes the Catullan refrain *currite ducentes subtegmina, currite fusi* (64.327); Virgil like his model is addressing the spindles, not (as is often thought) the centuries.[111] The section is framed by references to *saecula* (46 and 52), which do not appear in Catullus, but though this suits Virgil's preoccupation with time-schemes, the idea is now expressed in Roman terms. The same is true of *stabili...numine*: the movement predicted by the Parcae (*currite*) is fixed immovably by divine decree, just as in Horace's *Carmen Saeculare* (25 ff.).

The following lines are more portentous,[112] and go far beyond the sentimental hopes of Graeco-Roman epithalamium. At first sight *adgredere...honores* seems to suggest the assumption of a public career, and to refer therefore to the boy's maturity; the reader is allowed this escape-route if he wishes to take it.[113] But *aderit iam*

---

[111] *talia*, which associates the Parcae with the preceding prophecies, would be unacceptably vague for a vocative. For the internal accusative *saecula* cf. again the imitation of Symm. *Or.* 3.9 *iamdudum aureum saeculum currunt fusa Parcarum*.

[112] This portentousness might seem to support the view that 48–52 should be assigned to the Parcae (thus Kurfess 1938: 815–16), who otherwise have little to say. But it is strange that they should address the baby rather than the parents or the world, and as *adgredere* and *aspice* lead up to *incipe*, these imperatives should all be spoken by the poet.

[113] It makes 53 *tum* easier; yet see below, n. 125.

tempus has an eschatological ring (see above on 4), and the development of events would be disrupted if the words referred to anything but the birth. In that case *magnos* is a sacral word (like *o*) masquerading as political, and *honores* refers not to future magistracies but to more immediate homage; like the adoration of the Magi, this alone marks out the baby as superhuman. The movement of the poem as the birth approaches recalls the Hellenistic poets' practice of describing a ceremony in a running commentary, but it would be misleading here to speak simply of a literary technique. With his feeling for the spirit as well as the externals of religion Virgil has suggested not a pageant but a vigil, not a commemoration but an experience (n. 43). This feature seems neither Roman nor Jewish, but belongs to the world of mystery cults.

The sonorous acclamation of line 49 adds to the religious atmosphere, but it would be dangerous to assume that Virgil took it over from a Sibylline model: though the emphatic σπονδειάζων can easily be paralleled in the Sibyl, it is more probably suggested by Catullus 64. Norden compared *cara suboles* with God's address to Christ, σὺ εἶ ὁ υἱός μου ἀγαπητός ('thou art my beloved son', Mk. 1: 11), but the meaning there is something like 'chosen',[114] and *cara* has far more sentimental associations. Munro[115] even interpreted *magnum Iovis incrementum* as 'promise of Jupiter to be'; but though Roman emperors could later be called 'Jove', such a reference seems impossible at this date, especially after *deum*. The homely *incrementum* is used of additions to a flock or with some tenderness of human offspring,[116] yet there are also difficulties about translating 'child of Jupiter'; this is repetitive after *deum suboles*, and the portentous *magnum* implies that the augmentation will be great rather than just the baby.[117] Perhaps on the surface we are allowed to understand 'great offspring

---

[114] Norden 1924: 132. 'Son of God' was not in fact a regular appellation of the pre-Christian Messiah; cf. Strack and Billerbeck 1924 on Rom. 1: 3, Cullmann 1963: 272 ff., Vermes 1973: 197 ff.

[115] Cited by Mayor, Fowler, and Conway 1907: 111 ff. Cf. Ov. *Met.* 3.103 *vipereos dentes, populi incrementa futuri*, Apollonides, *Anth. Pal.* 9.287.6 (on Tiberius) Ζῆνα τὸν ἐσσόμενον.

[116] Serv. *ad loc. et est vulgare, quod bucolico congruit carmini*, Frank 1916: 334 ff., Norden 1924: 129 ff., Carcopino 1943: 88 ff.

[117] Büchner 1955–8: 1209, citing *Pan. Lat.* 4(10) 37.5 *Constantine Caesar, incrementum maximum boni publici*.

Virgil's Fourth Eclogue 183

of Jupiter', but once we see the force of *magnum* we are encouraged to think of the destiny of a hero: the child will be a 'great addition' to the divine family, just like Hercules or the Dioscuri.[118] Lines 50–2 transport us from the infant to the firmament. The world conventionally shook in response to Zeus,[119] and objects nodded and swayed at the epiphany of a god,[120] but cosmic manifestations at the birth of a baby go beyond the Western precedents. When Theognis[121] describes Apollo's birth, the land rejoices and the sea laughs, but when the theme is taken over by a Christian Sibylline oracle the whole universe exults (8.474–5): τικτόμενον δὲ βρέφος ποτὶ ἕπτατο γηθοσύνῃ χθών, οὐράνιος δ' ἐγέλασσε θρόνος καὶ ἀγάλλετο κόσμος ('The joyful earth fluttered to the child at its birth. The heavenly throne laughed and the world rejoiced').[122] Gladness was the predominant emotion on such occasions: the angel of the evangelist brings tidings of great joy,[123] and at the coming of the Kingdom of God John the Divine hears a voice crying εὐφραίνεσθε, οὐρανοί.[124] So in these lines at least it is plausible that Virgil had an Eastern antecedent, and possible that he had a Sibylline one; τικτόμενον βρέφος is the Greek for *nascens puer* (Norden 1924: 149), and may suggest a common source in an earlier Jewish oracle.

> o mihi tum longae maneat pars ultima vitae,
> spiritus et quantum sat erit tua dicere facta:
> non me carminibus vincet nec Thracius Orpheus
> nec Linus, huic mater quamvis atque huic pater adsit,
> Orphei Calliopea, Lino formosus Apollo.
> Pan etiam, Arcadia mecum si iudice certet,
> Pan etiam Arcadia dicat se iudice victum. (53–9)

O that the last part of a long life may then remain to me and enough breath to tell of your achievements: then in song neither Thracian Orpheus will surpass me nor Linus, though his mother is of help to one and his father to

---

[118] Liv. 1.7.10 *aucturum caelestium numerum*, Verg. Aen. 8.301 *decus addite divis* (both of Hercules), *Ciris* 398 *cara Iovis suboles, magnum Iovis incrementum* (of the Dioscuri; the singular suggests 'augmentation' rather than 'children').
[119] Hes. *Theog.* 839 ff., Catull. 64.205–6, Hor. *Carm.* 1.34.9 ff.
[120] Callim. *Hymn* 2.1 ff., Verg. Aen. 3.90–1, Pfister 1924: 319.
[121] Thgn. 9–10 ἐγέλασσε δὲ γαῖα πελώρη, γήθησεν δὲ βαθὺς πόντος ἁλὸς πολιῆς.
[122] For such portents, cf. ps-Callisthenes (on the birth of Alexander) ὥστε τὸν πάντα κόσμον συγκινηθῆναι, *Protevangelium Jacobi* 18.2 (an unnatural stillness at the birth of Jesus), Norden 1924: 58 n.
[123] Lk. 2: 11, Norden 1924: 57–8.   [124] Rev. 12: 12, echoing Isa. 44: 23.

the other, Calliopea to Orpheus, fair Apollo to Linus. Even Pan if he were to compete with me with Arcadia as judge, even Pan with Arcadia as judge would say that he was defeated.

'May I live to describe the day' was a conventional thought in panegyric[125] that particularly suited eulogies of the young,[126] but it can hardly be a coincidence that similar hopes are found in eschatological writings and particularly in the Sibylline oracles.[127] On the other hand lines 55–9 with their singing match and Arcadian umpires revert to the pastoral tradition, and it is pointless to seek a mystical significance in bards of the countryside like Orpheus and Linus. The repetition of these names in different cases suggests the bucolic idiom, as does the Greek accidence of *Orphei* and the feminine caesura in 57; in the same way the verbal juggling of 58–9 belongs to the style that Theocritus had established with the opening lines of his first idyll. The reference to Pan is an echo of Moschus[128] that balances the invocation of the first line. The dread voice[129] of Eastern apocalyptic has now given place to more familiar melodies.

> incipe, parve puer, risu cognoscere matrem
> (matri longa decem tulerunt fastidia menses).
> incipe, parve puer: qui non risere parentes,
> nec deus hunc mensa, dea nec dignata cubili est.   (60–3)

Begin, little baby, to recognise your mother with a laugh (ten months have brought long discomfort to your mother). Begin, little baby: those who have not laughed to their parents—him neither a god thought worthy of his table nor a goddess of her bed.

With the birth of the child, the eclogue once again becomes enigmatic. The humanity of the scene shows a truly Italian sentiment (cf. Catullus

---

[125] Cf. *Ecl.* 8.7–8 *en erit umquam ille dies mihi cum liceat tua dicere facta?* As *tum* in our passage suits this pattern, it should not be changed to *tam*; though the new age begins immediately, Virgil looks forward to its full development.

[126] See Hor. *Epist.* 1.4.8 ff., Pers. 2.37 ff. for nurses' prayers for their charges.

[127] *Orac. Sib.* 3.371–2 ὦ μακαριστός, ἐκεῖνον ὅς ἐς χρόνον ἔσσεται ἀνήρ... (just before the passage on εὐνομίη cited above, n. 27), 4.192, *Psalm. Sal.* (first century BC) μακάριοι οἱ γινόμενοι ἐν ταῖς ἡμέραις ἐκείναις, Lk. 2: 30 (the 'Nunc Dimittis') ὅτι εἶδον οἱ ὀφθαλμοί μου τὸ σωτήριόν σου, Erdmann 1932: 45.

[128] 3.55–6 Πανὶ φέρω τὸ μέλισμα; τάχ᾽ ἂν καὶ κεῖνος ἐρεῖσαι τὸ στόμα δειμαίνοι μὴ δεύτερα σεῖο φέρηται.

[129] Milton, *Lycidas* 132; he understood the mixing of the genres (Johnson did not).

61.212–13), and suggests that a real baby is meant rather than some vague abstraction; the mother is presumably Octavia, whose patronage of letters may be significant.[130] No mystical reason[131] need be sought for the ten months of pregnancy, for the inclusive method is often used in such contexts. On the other hand ordinary children do not smile till they are forty days old;[132] it is only a Wunderkind like Dionysus[133] or Zoroaster[134] who does this on the day of his birth. The Westerners may claim that the exact date is unspecified, but there is less point in stressing the months of pregnancy if there is a significant gap between the birth and the laugh. The right answer may once again be that the ambiguity is deliberate: if we choose to be hard-headed Westerners we need see no more than an encouragement to hurry up and show signs of personality, but for the reader who has understood the message of the poem there is a hint that the infant is out of the ordinary. Such a transcendental note is quite compatible with the domesticity of the scene; if Isis and Harpocrates touched the hearts of men, it was because they combined the human with the divine.

The poem ends with another enigma, though not where commentators have found it: it is clear from the structure and sense of the passage that the baby is doing the laughing and not the parents (that is to say, the *cui* of Virgil's manuscripts is impossible against the *qui* implied by Quintilian 9.3.8).[135] The last line is more difficult. Norden pointed to Eastern legends where the hero receives a divine bride,[136] and nearer home to the Dionysiac mysteries, where the god

[130] Cichorius 1922: 277 ff.
[131] Carcopino 1943: 94–5, 225 ff., contradicted by Norden 1924: 61 n., Fabia 1931: 33 ff., ThLL 8.749.54 ff.
[132] Arist. *Hist. An.* 587b5 ff., Antigonus, *Hist. Mir.* (Keller, *Rer. Nat. Script.* 42) τῇ δὲ τεσσαρακοστῇ προσλαμβάνειν τὸ γελαστικὸν καὶ ἄρχεσθαι ἐπιγινώσκειν μητέρα, Censorinus, *DN* 11.7, Lydus, *Mens.* 4.21 (p. 85 W.).
[133] Nonnus, *Dion.* 9.35–6 καὶ πόλον ἐσκοπίαζεν ἀήθεα, θαμβαλέος δὲ πατρῴην ἐγέλασσεν ἴτυν δεδοκημένος ἄστρων.
[134] Plin. *HN* 7.72, Norden 1924: 65 ff.; for more remote analogies cf. Stuart 1921: 216 ff.
[135] Norden 1924: 62 n. It is not so certain that *parentes* must be changed to *parenti*; the more general formulation has some attractions. *ridere* with the accusative may describe amusement rather than derision (cf. Ov. *Ars am.* 1.87 *hunc Venus... ridet*), and the crowing of babies betrays a robuster emotion than benevolence; thus the infant Dionysus laughed at the stars (above, n. 133).
[136] Norden 1924: 68 ff.; he regarded the symbolical marriage of Christ at Rev. 19: 7 as an attenuated version of this myth.

was acclaimed as a bridegroom;[137] but though this range of ideas may ultimately lie behind Virgil, we need not assume that he is imitating a Sibylline or other mystical prototype. It is simpler to suppose that he is recalling the story of Heracles, who feasted with Zeus and took Hebe to wife;[138] yet even to this it might be replied that the poet's general formulation (with its implication that every good baby ought to smile) does not suggest so special a privilege. Warde Fowler[139] got round the difficulty by referring to the Roman custom by which at the birth of upper-class children a table was placed for Hercules in the atrium and a bed for Juno; Virgil would then be suggesting a nurses' saw to the effect that the unsmiling baby comes to no good. On the other hand, it seems likely that a bed was placed for Juno only at the birth of a girl,[140] which would make the last words of the poem surprisingly irrelevant; and *dignata cubili est* surely points to something more than an antiquarian symbol. Perhaps one could propose a compromise, or rather recognise another oracular ambiguity; at a superficial level Virgil may be alluding to a nursery saying (this would explain the generalisation of *qui non*), but by his form of words he has ensured that the reader will think primarily of superhuman destiny.

Virgil claims at the beginning of the eclogue to be drawing on the Sibyl, and he ought to be believed. So many features suit the Eastern oracles that cumulatively they seem decisive, the proclamation of the eschatological period, the ambiguous chronological system, the descent of Justice from the stars, the return of the Golden Age, the prayer to share in the coming felicity, the pervasive blend of the Hesiodic and the prophetic. As the animal-peace in particular points to a Jewish oracle, so too should the infant saviour, especially as both pictures are found in the same area of Isaiah. The association of the Messiah with Emmanuel might have proved attractive to the Hellenized Jews of Egypt, who could have been influenced by Greek

---

[137] Firm. Mat. *Err. Prof. Rel.* 19 νύμφιε χαῖρε.
[138] Hom. *Od.* 11.602–3, Pind. *N.* 1.71–2, Theoc. 24.84 (see above in the text).
[139] Mayor, Fowler, and Conway 1907: 75 ff., citing Schol. Bern. *ad loc. Iunoni Lucinae lectus, Herculi mensa.*
[140] Cf. Hesychius στέφανον ἐκφέρειν· ἔθος ἦν, ὁπότε παιδίον ἄρρεν γένοιτο παρὰ Ἀττικοῖς, στέφανον ἐλαίας τιθέναι πρὸ τῶν θυρῶν· ἐπὶ δὲ τῶν θηλειῶν, ἔρια διὰ τὴν ταλασίαν (I owe this reference to Mr S. G. Pembroke).

legends as well as by indigenous cults. It may be significant that though the infancy narratives of the Gospels are basically Jewish, some features suggest a Hellenistic origin,[141] the virgin birth[142] (apparently encouraged by the Septuagint's translation of Isaiah 7: 14), the mystical Pneuma (paralleled in Philo),[143] the curiously literal notion (however muted) of divine parentage, one might add more subjectively the naïve realism of the Greek Luke's pastoral scene, so imaginatively contrasted (just as in Virgil) with the cosmic revolution it portends. Hellenized Jews of the less sophisticated sort are still rather shadowy people: one would be glad to know more about how they formulated the eschatological message in the pre-Christian period. The extant Sibylline oracles provide one dismal answer, but if Virgil's source had caught more of the Greek spirit, it might have given the abstract and colourless myth a more human aspect, such as later appeared also in parts of Luke's nativity story.

In the end the learning and the vision of the Easterners give no more than a background to the interpretation of the eclogue.[144] Virgil has no interest in Jewish eschatology for its own sake, but is ingeniously adapting it to Western modes of thought (a process that has continued over the centuries to our own day); if we read between the lines the true saviour is not an alien Messiah but a Roman boy, who will owe his existence to an imaginative political achievement and bring the world a peace based on the realities of Western imperialism. If the poem expresses itself in allegories, that suits the general pattern of the book as well as the ambiguous manner of prophetic writing; in the *Aeneid* Virgil was to use other mythological forms to convey a modern message. It could fairly be urged against Norden that instead of interpreting the poet's symbols in a Western political context, he was lured into the mists of oriental religion (though without saying enough about the Sibyl, who alone can guide us through the murk); but even if he failed to give a satisfactory account of the poem, his book is salutary in other directions. In the

---

[141] Dibelius 1932 (= Dibelius 1953–6: 1.1–78).
[142] Dibelius 1932: 42 ff., Bultmann 1963: 291–2 (= 316 in third German edition).
[143] Norden 1924: 78–9, Dibelius 1932: 31–2.
[144] For criticisms of Norden's approach see Deubner 1925: 160 ff. (in his review of W. Weber, *Der Prophet und sein Gott*), Jachmann 1952a: 13 ff. Yet there is also much to criticize in the Westerners' underestimation of this supremely beautiful poem.

first place as a Jew he was able to see Christianity historically, that is to say as a Jewish heresy centring on a Messiah (as its name shows); seeing that the inter-Testamental period is of such critical importance, the uncertain evidence of the eclogue may in fact deserve more attention than he gave it. Secondly, he refused to detach the Greek Bible from the main body of classical literature, but applied his unique ear for form to both impartially (as in the *Kunstprosa* of his youth, where St Paul rubs shoulders with Antiochus of Commagene). These questions of form are so crucial in New Testament studies, and the analyses of the theologians have such far-reaching implications, that more classical scholars ought to follow the Easterners' example. War is too serious a business to be left entirely to the generals.

9

The Sixth *Eclogue*: Virgil's Poetic Genealogy

David O. Ross, Jr.

By the time Virgil published his *Eclogues*—in 35 BC, as now seems likely[1]—the course that Latin poetry was to follow for the next century had been firmly set. When Catullus died in 54 BC there were still a number of possibilities open: the first generation of new poets had broadened poetic horizons by their discoveries and experiments—in technique, in verse forms, and in subjects. It is hard to imagine what Latin poetry, even in the next generation, would have been like without their experiments and innovations; yet the very diversity of the new poetry makes it equally hard to predict a future course. But after 35 BC there remained only one way a poet could write, only one direction in which he could set out. Instead of a number of possibilities open to the poet, there was only one narrow road: the future of poetry suddenly became clear and definite, so much so that it soon was to cease to exist as a future at all.

Latin poetry matured almost overnight, and its brief maturity produced great achievement from men of genius and splendid poetry from good poets. The pages to follow will deal with two basic aspects of the achievement of the Augustan poets, how the sudden definition of poetry came about, and how it led easily and naturally to the expression of the deepest concerns of the time. The peace that came

---

This paper was first published in Ross 1975: 18–38 and appears here virtually unchanged except for the addition of translations of Greek and Latin quotations by the author. The author would like to dedicate this republication to the memory of his teacher, Wendell V. Clausen.

[1] See Bowersock 1971: 73–80 and Clausen 1972: 201–5.

after September of 31 BC to a vast empire had been bought at tremendous cost, of which the last and largest payment had just been made; over the next few years it became more and more likely that stability and order had returned to stay, that the recent domination of fear and chaos was past for good. There have been few such times in Western history, and even fewer in which poets have been able to voice with complete conviction the profound relief and pride of achievement felt by the people. That Augustan poets were able to do so when the time came was the unlikely result of the discovery of Callimachus' narrow road some years before.

It may seem a paradox that the greatness of Augustan poetry was a direct result of a narrowing of poetic horizons, and even more a paradox that the poets who spoke for the national experience in the decade or so following the battle of Actium were able to do so only because in the preceding decade poetry had become private, personal, and esoteric. The previous chapter [= Ross 1975: 1–17, 'Introduction: From Catullus to Gallus'] was a summary of what Catullus had accomplished, the discovery of the poet's place in poetry—the ability to write as an individual in both direct and (what was more important) abstract forms of verse, and the realization of a poetic history that included a role for the poet of the present. This realization, however, remained without clear definition or formulation until Virgil and Gallus in the next generation. From Catullus we look forward, and from the *Eclogues* back, to the process that set the course, and consequently we can see its evolution only dimly; but following the publication of Gallus' *Amores* and the completion of the *Eclogues*, there was only one position a serious poet could assume: how this single tradition was specified and what it meant for the poets who followed is the subject of this chapter.

It should be obvious that the Sixth Eclogue is largely concerned with poetry,[2] but it is far from obvious just what sort of poetry Virgil intends, and even less clear what he is saying about it. The twelve-line introduction takes the form of a *recusatio* (the refusal to write epic,

---

[2] For scholarly discussions and opinions concerning the questions raised here, see the bibliographical notes to the following: Büchner 1955–8: 1219–24; Stewart 1959; Wimmel 1960: 132–47; Elder 1961.

reges et proelia, 3; *tristia bella*, 7) and includes three lines (3–5) translated directly from Callimachus' prologue to the *Aetia*—this, in fact, the first formal, fully-developed *recusatio* in Latin poetry. As a Callimachean statement it includes words denoting elegance and refinement (*deductum... carmen*, 5; *tenui... harundine*, 8) and neoteric lightness opposed to gravity (*ludere* vs *cum canerem*, 1 and 3). At the same time the poetry is to be pastoral (*Syracosio... versu*, 1; *silvas*, 2; *agrestem Musam*, 8; *myricae* and *nemus*, 10–11), obvious enough, perhaps, in a book of pastoral poetry, but emphasized by Virgil in the one important departure he has made from the Callimachean original: instead of Apollo's address to the poet concerning the fat sacrificial victim (as Callimachus had put it, ἀοιδέ, τὸ μὲν θύος ὅττι πάχιστον | θρέψαι, 'poet, raise the sacrificial victim as fat as possible', fr. 1.23–4 Pf.), Virgil's Apollo tells the shepherd to fatten his flock (*pastorem, Tityre, pinguis | pascere oportet ovis*, 'Tityrus, the shepherd should pasture fat sheep', 4–5).[3]

The setting of what follows (Silenus' capture) is indeed pastoral, but the subject is not: Silenus is a seer, and reveals his secrets only after ritual binding.[4] The song itself, though containing enough pastoral suggestions and motifs to have led some critics to stress this aspect of it,[5] seems to have eluded all scholars in their attempts to discover its unity: cosmogony, psychotic love, and metamorphoses are hardly the most convenient and conventional subjects for pastoral. Yet here too poetry itself is obviously prominent:[6] it is stressed in the introductory scene (*carminis*, 18; *carmina... carmina*, 25; *canebat*, 31); the whole song is at its conclusion associated with Apollo (*quae Phoebo... meditante... ille canit*, 82–4); and central and prominent in the song is the ritual initiation of the poet Gallus:

> tum canit errantem Permessi ad flumina Gallum
> Aonas in montis ut duxerit una sororum,
> utque viro Phoebi chorus adsurrexerit omnis;

---

[3] R. Pfeiffer 1928: 322.

[4] See Klingner's clear recapitulation (1967: 106).

[5] Elder, for instance, 'the poem may contain a brief... for his own kind of Latin pastoral' (1961: 121); cf. his discussion of the pastoral motifs (116–20).

[6] Büchner stresses poetry as the central theme of the *Eclogue* ('Das Gedicht zeigt die Macht, Fülle, Verzauberung des Gesanges', Büchner 1955–8: 1223); cf. Becker 1955: 317–18.

>   ut Linus haec illi divino carmine pastor
>   floribus atque apio crinis ornatus amaro
>   dixerit: 'hos tibi dant calamos, en accipe, Musae,
>   Ascraeo quos ante seni, quibus ille solebat
>   cantando rigidas deducere montibus ornos.
>   his tibi Grynei nemoris dicatur origo,
>   ne quis sit lucus quo se plus iactet Apollo.'   (64–73)

Then he sings of how one of the Muses led Gallus, wandering at the waters of the Permessus, onto the Aonian mountains, and how the whole chorus of Phoebus rose to greet the man; how Linus, shepherd of divine song, crowned with bitter parsley, said to him: 'The Muses give you these pipes—here, take them—which before they gave to the old man of Ascra, with which *that one*, with his singing, used to make the stiff oaks walk down the mountains. On these pipes let the story of the origin of the Grynean grove be told by you, that there be no grove in which Apollo takes more pride'.

Much of the extensive literature on the Sixth Eclogue that deals with the unity of the themes of Silenus' song fails to find a satisfactory explanation for the intrusion of these lines, and conversely scholars primarily concerned with Gallus seldom deal in any detail with the context surrounding what is, with the Tenth Eclogue, our most important, and elusive, source for the poetry of Virgil's friend and contemporary.[7]

Few, I think, would not grant that there must be some reason behind the diversity of theme and subject in Silenus' song, and if we may also be allowed the assumption that poetry of some sort is a primary concern in this Eclogue, then we may with equal validity expect a unity in Virgil's conception of poetry: it may be possible to find some thread to follow from the pastoral and the neoteric to poetry as revelation, to cosmogony and science, to the strange and unnatural. We may begin conveniently at the center, with the details of Gallus' initiation.

---

[7] The striking exception is F. Skutsch 1901 and 1906. It may be fairly said that Skutsch is the only scholar to have dealt properly with both Gallus and the other themes of Silenus' song, and to have realized fully the importance of *Ecl.* 6 and 10 as a source for Gallus' poetry: his extreme and unwarranted inferences and conclusions, however, effectively scared subsequent scholars away from profitable inquiry along similar lines.

Gallus, wandering by the river Permessus, was led by one of the Muses to the Aonian mountains, where the whole chorus of the Muses (*Phoebi... chorus omnis*, 66) rose in greeting and Linus, with a speech, presented him with the pipes of Hesiod, on which he was to sing of the Grynean Grove. Why should Linus be given a role of such importance? Who is he, and what does he have to do with Apollo and the Muses, with the pipes of Hesiod, and particularly with Gallus? Modern commentators are of little or no help with such questions: 'There seems no evidence that Linus was supposed ever to have been a shepherd, but it was natural for a pastoral poet to conceive of him as such.'[8]

It was not natural at all. Linus, at different places and at different times, had assumed several forms: as poet and musician (commonly the son of Apollo and sometimes of a Muse) he had come to be associated with the dirge, credited with the invention of certain instruments and even of the hexameter, and often appears as a semi-divine singer much like Musaeus or Orpheus. Linus' role as mythical singer could be taken for granted by Virgil, as in the Fourth Eclogue:

> non me carminibus vincet nec Thracius Orpheus,
> nec Linus, huic mater quamvis atque huic pater adsit,
> Orphei Calliopea, Lino formosus Apollo.   (55–7)

Neither Thracian Orpheus nor Linus will conquer me in song, though his mother lend support to the one, and his father to the other—to Orpheus Calliope, to Linus handsome Apollo.

But only here in the Sixth Eclogue does Linus appear as a shepherd: if we can see why and how Virgil has created this new role for Linus, presumably we will be closer to understanding why he acts as spokesman for the Muses at Gallus' initiation.

---

[8] Conington and Nettleship 1898 *ad loc*. On the Linus figure in Greek religion and myth, see the article by Abert and Kroll 1926. Stewart notes Linus' associations with the lament and suggests that 'it would be not unreasonable to assume that Linus is meant to represent the earlier and simpler form of elegy, that which was later combined with a Hesiodic tradition to produce, in Hellenistic times, the kind of poem which Gallus is urged to write' (1959: 193). But the parsley crown need not be a symbol of mourning, and there is no particular reason to see in Virgil's Linus the inventor of the dirge which then becomes real elegy.

In Theocritus (24.105–6) Linus had made a brief appearance as teacher 'of letters' to the young Heracles:

γράμματα μὲν τὸν παῖδα γέρων Λίνος ἐξεδίδαξεν,
υἱὸς Ἀπόλλωνος μελεδωνεὺς ἄγρυπνος ἥρως.

Old Linus taught the boy his letters, (Linus) the son of Apollo, the hero of the midnight oil, (Heracles') guardian.

This too is an odd role for Linus:[9] he has, in fact, become an Alexandrian singer, literate and learned. The epithet ἄγρυπνος indicates the labored polish demanded of the new poets of Alexandria, a title of distinction.[10] μελεδωνεύς, 'guardian', remains unexplained in this context: perhaps it contains a pun on μέλος, referring to the usual tradition where Linus is indeed a musician; if so, it would be a characteristic Alexandrian touch.

More to the point, though, is the Linus Virgil found in the first book of Callimachus' *Aetia* (fr. 26–8 Pf.).[11] The mythographer Conon, in his *Diageseis* (published between 36 BC and AD 17), gives us a full account which must depend on Callimachus: Linus, son of Apollo and the Argive princess Psamathe, daughter of Crotopus, was raised by a shepherd and torn apart by the shepherd's dogs one day; a plague sent by Apollo led to the propitiation of Psamathe and Linus by the festival Arneis (the lamb festival), to the naming of the month Arneus ('because Linus had been reared amongst lambs'), and to the dirge.[12] Here was an easy aetiological explanation not only for the dirge, but also for the custom of killing stray dogs on the day of the festival: the names Arneis and Arneus were more troublesome, but finally yielded when Linus, the bastard exposed as an infant, was found to have been brought up by a convenient shepherd.

It is a pity we have so little of Callimachus' version of this story. One couplet, though, is eloquent:

[9] See the comment of Gow 1952b *ad loc.* Theocritus is here unusual in that Linus teaches γράμματα to Heracles (also reported by 'Suidas', s.v. Λίνος); Eumolpus becomes the music master.
[10] Cf. below, n. 34.
[11] See the convenient summary of the story given by Trypanis 1975: 24–6 and von Wilamowitz-Moellendorff 1925: 230–4.
[12] See Pfeiffer's note to *Aetia* fr. 26.1, citing Conon fr. 19 (Jacoby *FGH* 1.195–6), μῆνά τε ὠνόμασαν Ἀρνεῖον, ὅτι ἀρνάσι Λίνος συνανετράφη· καὶ θυσίαν ἄγουσι καὶ ἑορτὴν Ἀρνίδα ('and they named the month "Arneion", since Linus was raised with lambs (*arnasi*); and they celebrate a sacrifice and a festival called "the Arnis"').

ἄρνες τοι, φίλε κοῦρε, συνήλικες, ἄρνες ἑταῖροι
ἔσκον, ἐνιαυθμοὶ δ' αὔλια καὶ βοτάναι.   (fr. 27 Pf.)

Lambs were your fellows, dear boy, your companions, and your abodes were their folds and pastures.

On this couplet Pfeiffer observes, 'in anaphora post diaeresin bucolicam "pastorale" quiddam inest cf. Theoc. 1.64 et passim': it may be that Callimachus has used this device purposely to mark the bucolic nature of the passage.[13] We may suppose that Callimachus developed the pastoral character of Linus at some length and, with characteristic wit, gave the young Linus a new literary occupation, that of shepherd.

Virgil's Linus, though, is neither the mythical *Ursänger*, nor the somewhat mock-heroic poet-scholar-teacher suggested by Theocritus, nor the pastoral figure we can imagine in Callimachus, but rather all three at once, something new and undoubtedly more significant than the prototypes: *divino carmine pastor*. Whether Virgil himself was responsible for this transformation, or to what extent, is a question to be asked shortly.

Such is the Linus, then, who acts as spokesman for Apollo and the Muses in handing on Hesiod's pipes to Gallus:

> hos tibi dant calamos, en accipe, Musae
> Ascraeo quos ante seni, quibus ille solebat
> cantando rigidas deducere montibus ornos.

The Muses give you these pipes—here, take them—which before they gave to the old man of Ascra, with which *that one*, with his singing, used to make the stiff oaks walk down the mountains.

---

[13] Pfeiffer's Index Rerum Notabilium (R. Pfeiffer 1949–53: 2.127, s.v. anaphora 'bucolica') lists *Epigram* 22.3 as the only other occurrence of this anaphora in Callimachus, in which 'pastorale quiddam' should also be noted:

> Ἀστακίδην τὸν Κρῆτα τὸν αἰπόλον ἥρπασε Νύμφη
> ἐξ ὄρεος, καὶ νῦν ἱερὸς Ἀστακίδης.
> οὐκέτι Δικταίῃσιν ὑπὸ δρυσίν, οὐκέτι Δάφνιν
> ποιμένες, Ἀστακίδην δ' αἰὲν ἀεισόμεθα.

(A nymph stole the goatherd Astacides the Cretan from the mountain, and now Astacides is divine. No longer will we shepherds under the oaks of Dicte sing of Daphnis, no, but always now of Astacides.)

Once again, in these lines, there is something new, as Heyne noted in a comment repeated by most subsequent editors: 'Novum vero hoc, quod nunc Hesiodo tribuitur, id quod de Orpheo sollenne est, silvas eius cantum esse sequutas.' The attribution to Hesiod of the Orphic ability to charm forests would indeed be unusual, especially as Virgil in an earlier Eclogue had specifically given Orpheus what was rightfully his (*Orpheaque in medio posuit silvasque sequentis*, 'and in the center he set Orpheus and the trees following him', 3.46). But there is no need to disfigure Hesiod in such a way. The two relative clauses (*quos... quibus...*) can be taken separately, and *ille*, in the second, can be understood in its common Latin function as indicating a change of subject: '...which before they gave to Hesiod, on which that (other well-known singer, Orpheus) used to play to charm the ash trees down from the mountains.'

The ambiguity was undoubtedly intentional, for Hesiod does, by implication, receive a share in Orpheus' powers and is brought into the same line of poetic descent, but Virgil had a further purpose. The second relative clause is, in effect, a riddle, a poetic elegance used to avoid the obvious.[14] A similar 'riddle' occurs in *Ecl.* 3.40–2, when Menalcas puts up his wager, the cups, *caelatum divini opus Alcimedontis* ('the relief work of the divine Alcimedon'):

> in medio duo signa, Conon, et—quis fuit alter,
> descripsit radio totum qui gentibus orbem,
> tempora quae messor, quae curvus arator haberet?

...in the center two figures, Conon and—but who was the other, who with his compass marked off the whole globe for its peoples, and marked what seasons the reaper should observe, what the bent plowman?

The answer, Aratus, needed no gloss for Virgil's readers.[15] The chief function of Menalcas' forgetfulness here seems almost to be a

---

[14] The proper riddles of *Ecl.* 3.104–7 remain unsolved. Silenus' first words in *Ecl.* 6 are worth noting in this connection: *quo vincula nectitis?'* inquit. | *'solvite me, pueri...'*('Why do you bind me?' says he. 'Free me, children', 23–4); *solvere* can be used in Latin of 'solving' a riddle (Petron. 58.8, *qui de nobis longe venio, late venio? solve me* ('Who am I who come far, right out from us, and wide, too? Answer me.')— though *solve* here of course involves a further pun).

[15] There is no real reason why Eudoxos of Cnidos, the astronomer whose writings Aratus versified, should be assumed here rather than, or to the exclusion of, Aratus himself, who has ample reason to appear.

preparation for the riddle at *Ecl.* 6.70–1; the Alexandrian scientist and scientist-poet are in fact balanced by Orpheus himself, whom Alcimedon has set in the cup Damoetas offers as his stake:

> Orpheaque in medio posuit silvasque sequentis.   (3.46)

... and in the center he set Orpheus and the trees following him.

It is no mere coincidence (as I hope to make clear) that in the Third Eclogue Conon and Aratus appear with Orpheus, who is identified by the magic power of his song over nature. There should be no difficulty in granting Orpheus his own proper magic in a similar (riddling) context in the Sixth Eclogue and allowing him to appear with Hesiod.

We have met Orpheus already in following various other questions involving these lines, not perhaps by accident: Orpheus and Linus appear together at *Ecl.* 4.55–7, and Orpheus with Conon and Aratus at 3.40–6; at *Ecl.* 8.55–6 Orpheus occurs again as a singer, *in silvis*, and with Arion (*certent et cycnis ululae, sit Tityrus Orpheus, | Orpheus in silvis, inter delphinas Arion*, 'let screech owls vie with swans, let Tityrus be Orpheus, Orpheus in the woods, and be Arion among his dolphins'). But it is in the Sixth Eclogue that the most important appearance occurs. When Silenus begins his song,

> tum vero in numerum Faunosque ferasque videres
> ludere, tum rigidas motare cacumina quercus;
> nec tantum Phoebo gaudet Parnasia rupes,
> nec tantum Rhodope miratur et Ismarus Orphea.   (6.27–30)

Then indeed you would see Fauns and wild beasts sport in time with his music, and the stiff oaks nod their heads to the rhythm. Not so much does the peak of Parnassus rejoice in Phoebus, nor do Rhodope and Ismarus wonder so at Orpheus.

The proemium to Silenus' song ends with Orpheus, and in the preceding parallel line stands Apollo. Silenus' song thus is clearly associated in this introduction with both Apollo and Orpheus, an association expanded by Virgil in the language of lines 27–8. First, *Faunosque ferasque*. The use of *-que -que* connecting two items is archaic-epic (that is, solemn, ritualistic, and ancient), and is naturally infrequent in the *Eclogues*.[16] The appearance of the Fauni cannot be set down simply to their being pastoral creatures, as they occur nowhere else in the *Eclogues*; rude deities of ancient Latium, who spoke in Saturnians,[17] they were banished by Ennius, along with the older poets: *versibus quos olim Fauni vatesque canebant* ('in verses which once the Fauns and seers used to sing').[18] Secondly, *ludere*, repeated from the first line of the Eclogue, carries not only its pastoral associations there, but a certain neoteric connotation as well:[19] the magic of Silenus' song brings about a union of the old and the new, the old Fauns return to participate in the new poetry. Thirdly, *rigidas* (*quercus*) anticipates *rigidas* (*ornos*) of line 71. Here again is the magic power of Orphic song, associated with Silenus and Apollo, just as later (70–1) it is extended to Hesiod and so to Gallus. A poetic unity is beginning to appear, with Orpheus providing a focus.

In this setting, then, Silenus begins his song. The cosmogony with which it opens has too often been associated by modern scholars simply with Lucretius. The language, at least in some details, is indeed Lucretian, but it would have been difficult and odd for Virgil or any poet of his time to write on such a theme without a certain Lucretian flavor.[20] We should not be misled by this general poetic flavor to see in the passage a compliment to Lucretius and no more, or to consider him the sole 'source' for the lines. Not only are the lines not entirely Epicurean, but the language itself immediately points to other sources.[21] In the first book of Apollonius'

---

[16] On *-que -que* connecting two items see Leumann, Hofmann and Szantyr 1965: 515, with refs. (esp. for the poets, Norden 1957: 228 and Christensen 1908). Elsewhere in the *Eclogues -que -que* appears only at 8.22 (again in a line suggestive of the magic of poetry over nature, *Maenalus argutumque nemus pinusque loquentis* | *semper habet...*) and in 10.23 and 65–6.

[17] Varro, *Ling.* 7.36 (*Fauni* < *fari*), commenting on Ennius' line.

[18] Enn. *Ann.* 214: see O. Skutsch 1968: 31–4 and 119–29.

[19] Cf. *ludere* in Catullus, and on the 'Ludus Poeticus' in general, Wagenvoort 1956: 30–42.

[20] See Jachmann 1923: 290: 'Das [dass Vergil sich in der Diktion an Lukrez angeschlossen hat] ist aber so gut wie selbstverständlich, für diese Dinge war damals Lukrez in Rom eben das grosse Muster. Der Inhalt entspricht dem durchaus nicht.'

[21] Stewart 1959 has a fine summary of the work done to establish the eclectic nature of these lines: for Empedoclean elements see nn. 25–30 (pp. 200–1), with related text (184–5); for correspondences with Apollonius, p. 186 and n. 35, pointing

Argonautica, Orpheus sings for the heroes a song which begins with a very similar cosmogony (496–502); Silenus' Creation is in fact framed by lines closely corresponding to the first and last lines of Orpheus':

> ἤειδεν δ' ὡς γαῖα καὶ οὐρανὸς ἠδὲ θάλασσα (496) =
> namque canebat uti magnum per inane coacta
> semina terrarumque animaeque marisque fuissent (31–2)[22]

he sang how the earth and heavens and sea = for he sang how the atoms of earth and air and sea had been driven together through the great void

> οὔρεά θ' ὡς ἀνέτειλε, καὶ ὡς ποταμοὶ κελάδοντες
> αὐτῆσιν νύμφῃσι καὶ ἑρπετὰ πάντ' ἐγένοντο (501–2) =
> incipiant silvae cum primum surgere, cumque
> rara per ignaros errent animalia montis (39–40)

how the woods arose, how the resounding rivers with their nymphs, and all the creatures came into being = when the woods first began to arise, and when creatures, then few, wandered through the strange mountains

Within this Orphic framework a rich suggestion of various philosophical doctrines points to Virgil's purpose: a poetry of 'science', rather than of a particular school or sect, is suggested. The power of the mythical Orpheus—his ability to charm all nature—takes on a real poetic form in these lines, and the reference to Apollonius' Orpheus suggests the continuation and transformation of this poetic magic from the distant past to Alexandria; once again, old and new are united.

We may return now to lines 70–1 (... *quibus ille solebat / cantando rigidas deducere montibus ornos*), which I feel certain are to be understood as a direct reference to Orpheus, not as an Orphic

---

out as well 'Stoic and Neo-Pythagorean' elements; Stewart 1959: 201 n. 36 also notes that 'Orpheus' song in Apollonius appears to imitate what must have been a prominent passage in Parmenides: ... πῶς γαῖα καὶ ἥλιος ἠδὲ σελήνη, etc.' But that *Ecl.* 6.31–40 is eclectic and goes beyond Lucretius and Epicurean doctrine is by no means generally accepted: see, most recently and with extensive bibliography, Spoerri 1970: 144–63.

[22] Virgil has added a fourth element in the following line (*et liquidi simul ignis*), as if emphasizing the addition. That the language of these lines is not simply Lucretian has been clearly indicated by Virgil by the Grecism *-que -que -que* (*et*). Only once elsewhere in the *Eclogues* does *-que* occur three times in one line: *terrasque tractusque maris caelumque profundum* (4.51).

characteristic attributed to Hesiod (though this, of course, is implied as well).[23] One word, by its position at the center of the line, demands attention: *deducere*. We have noted that the neoteric *ludere* of the first line is repeated as Silenus begins to sing, suggesting the neoteric quality of Silenus' song, and by extension in the context, attributing this quality to Apollo and Orpheus as well. *Deducere*, similarly, must suggest *deductum* in line 5. This is no chance recall, nor one to be explained by the mystical workings of the poetic subconscious. In the three lines of the opening *recusatio* translated directly from Callimachus, *deductum carmen* reproduces τὴν Μοῦσαν λεπταλέην, and has been thoroughly studied in the context of neoteric terminology.[24] We have, in fact, become so accustomed to the term that we need to be reminded of its boldness in Latin: unlike *tenuis*, or even *gracilis*, it is anything but an obvious translation for the idea of λεπτός.[25] It is impossible to imagine that Virgil was unaware of the prominence he gave *deducere* in its context at line 71: the result again is that Orpheus and the new poetry are associated.

These observations on Linus and Orpheus have, perhaps, done little more than lead up to (and I hope elaborate and support) J. P. Elder's illuminating discussion of the Sixth Eclogue.[26] Elder finds that Virgil's intention was 'to associate himself with the company of

[23] Propertius (2.13.3–8, discussed below) has reassembled Hesiod, Orpheus, and Linus, surely with *Ecl*. 6.67–71 in mind. Propertius' clear suggestion of Orpheus (*aut possim Ismaria ducere valle feras*, in which *Ismaria valle* corresponds to *miratur et Ismarus Orphea*, *Ecl.* 6.30) is the best commentary on the identification of *ille in Ecl.* 6.70–1, though the authority of E. Reitzenstein in his influential article (1931: 49–51) has perhaps caused hesitation in many minds: he refers Prop. 2.13.5–6 to Hesiod (as well as *Ecl*. 6.70–1).

[24] First and most thoroughly by E. Reitzenstein 1931: 25–40; cf. Wimmel 1960, Stichwortindex s.v. λεπτός, and *passim*.

[25] *Deducere* in the sense of 'spinning a fine thread': here, at least, the poet of the *Culex* knew what he was doing when he wrote, after Virgil, *lusimus, Octavi, gracili modulante Thalia, | atque ut araneoli tenuem formavimus orsum. | lusimus...* ('We played, Octavius, with slender Thalia leading our song, and like spiders we shaped a fine web. We played...', 1–3). Note *gracili* and *tenuem* (= λεπτός), that the idea of *deducere* is conveyed by the spider and the web, and that *Thalia* and *lusimus* are repeated from the opening lines of *Ecl*. 6. In this connection, the terms used by the poets of the spider's spinning are not generally noted: cf. Catull. 68.49 (*nec tenuem texens sublimis aranea telam*), Ov. Am. 1.14.7 (*vel pede quod gracili deducit aranea filum*).

[26] See also O. Skutsch 1956: 193–201.

other inspired poets in the great tradition—with Apollo, Linus, Orpheus, Hesiod, Silenus, and Gallus', though only indirectly, because 'His is usually a connotative world, in which things are not "spelled out"; that is the business of prose.'[27] He then marks 'the chief points of interconnection' between these inspired singers, in more detail than can be repeated here,[28] and shows 'how subtly Virgil has used these associations, one by one, to build up throughout the poem his House of Inspiration, and delicately to include himself within the edifice.'

I would substitute for Elder's 'House of Inspiration' the term 'poetic genealogy' (the descent of the pipes that Gallus finally receives might almost be diagrammed in a stemma). The founder of the line is, of course, Apollo, and with Apollo stand the Muses (*Phoebi... chorus omnis*).[29] In the next generation appear Linus and Orpheus, the mythical, semi-divine singers (together in *Ecl.* 4.55–7, where Apollo is Linus' father and Calliope Orpheus' mother, permitting us to speak properly of a generation). Then Hesiod, the inheritor of Orpheus' pipes (as we have read the lines), which represent what may be considered 'scientific poetry'—poetry as the power over, and understanding of, nature. All these figures have participated directly

[27] Elder 1961: 114.
[28] I have touched upon most of Elder's points above, but should add here a few more of his observations (1961: 115–16). 'Virgil's song of Silenus' was originally Apollo's song. '... the phrase *Linus divino carmine pastor* (line 67) brings divinity and the bucolic together (cf. *E.* 10.17 where Gallus is hailed as *divine poeta*)'—and where, I might add, divinity and the bucolic are again associated: *stant et oves circum* (*nostri nec paenitet illas,* | *nec te paeniteat pecoris, divine poeta*) ('the sheep, too, stand around (they are not ashamed of us, and may you, divine poet, feel no shame for the flock)'). Line 8 (*agrestem tenui meditabor harundine Musam*) is recalled at the end of the poem, *omnia, quae Phoebo quondam meditante beatus* | *audit Eurotas* (82–3): 'The succession, via Silenus, is from Apollo to Virgil, and both "meditate" it; *now* at least it is a pastoral song (*agrestem Musam*) and in the Alexandrian style (*tenui harundine*).' Elder finds in uses of *canere* (*cantare*) throughout the Eclogue 'the obvious verb employed as a kind of formalizing link between Silenus, Hesiod, and Virgil, with Apollo in the background' (at 71 *cantando* I would see Orpheus instead of Hesiod).
[29] It is strange that we do not have a good study devoted to Apollo in Latin poetry. (Gagé 1955 has little to say of the Callimachean Apollo who merged so opportunely with the Actian Apollo.) The Callimachean Apollo (of the *Aetia* prologue and *Hymn* 2, esp. lines 105–12; cf. on the 'Museum' at Alexandria, its religious character, and the poets as ἱερεῖς, R. Pfeiffer 1968: 96–9) comes to Rome first with the *recusatio* in *Ecl.* 6: there is no such Apollo in Catullus—Virgil was definitely aware of the literary origin of his innovation.

in Gallus' initiation, but we may add a further poetic generation present in the scene by implication and specified elsewhere in the *Eclogues*, the Alexandrians: Callimachus (*Ecl.* 6.3–5), Aratus[30] (with Conon, and associated with Orpheus, in *Ecl* 3.40–6), Theocritus of course, Apollonius (here through his Orpheus, just as Virgil through his Silenus), then (as discussed below) Euphorion and Parthenius. Finally, as the last representative, Gallus receives from Linus the pipes on which Orpheus and Hesiod had played. Silenus, who tells of the scene as one of his *carmina*, seems both to represent and to be an integral part of this poetic genealogy.[31] We may perhaps begin to understand now why Virgil presents Silenus in a pastoral setting, but as a seer who must be ritually bound, a figure foreign to pastoral: in Silenus the pastoral and the 'scientific' are united, just as they are in the Orphic-Hesiodic pipes which Gallus receives through the *pastor* Linus.

We must, for a moment, expand somewhat and attempt to clarify this idea of scientific poetry, though our discussion must necessarily be very incomplete. Some apology must be made for the term 'scientific' itself, both because it reproduces nothing in Latin and because it is far from apt to our ears (though unfortunately the best single term I found): in what follows, then, it must be understood to have a special sense and significance, which did exist for Virgil. For us, science and poetry are incompatible, and the appeal of Aratus' *Phaenomena* to the Hellenistic and Roman worlds remains something of a mystery.[32] Virgil's own debt to Aratus was acknowledged in a characteristic way. When in the first book of the *Georgics* Virgil comes to the weather signs given by the moon, he translates the corresponding passage of Aratus unusually closely. In this passage Aratus had set an acrostic in a period of five lines, beginning with the line (783) ΛΕΠΤΗ μὲν καθαρή τε περὶ τρίτον ἦμαρ ἐοῦσα ('being

[30] Though Aratus, of course, never lived and worked at Alexandria, he may be considered an Alexandrian poetically.

[31] O. Skutsch 1956: 193–4 acutely observes, 'Die leicht begreifliche Umgestaltung Silens von Verkünder der Weisheit zum Vertreter der wahren Poesie ist Alexandrinisch', a remark noted by Elder.

[32] The *Phaenomena* was graced with at least 27 commentaries, and was translated at Rome by Varro Atacinus, Cicero, Germanicus, and Avienus. Cicero, for instance, praises Aratus for his *ornatissimis atque optimis versibus,* though conceding that the poet was *ignarum astrologiae* (*De Or.* 1.69).

SLENDER and fresh on the third day'), and continuing so that the first letters of each line in the period spell ΛΕΠΤΗ. Virgil, also within five lines (G. 1.429–33), has signed his passage in a somewhat different way: 429 MAximus, 431 VEntus, 433 PUra; that is, in reverse order, PUblius VErgilius MAro.³³ By this device Virgil may be pointing particularly to the key word (almost a stylistic *terminus technicus* for the new poets) λεπτή. Aratus' acrostic was recognized by Callimachus; a reference to it may conclude his epigram (27 Pf.) on the *Phaenomena* (beginning Ἡσιόδου τό τ' ἄεισμα καὶ ὁ τρόπος, 'Hesiod's the content and the style'): χαίρετε λεπταί | ῥήσιες, Ἀρήτου σύμβολον ἀγρυπνίης ('hail "slender" diction, the token of the midnight oil of Aratus').³⁴ 'Hesiod's is the content and the manner': how Hesiod came to replace Homer as the poetic exemplar for the Alexandrians need not be recited here, but for Virgil the 'manner', or style, of scientific poetry had already been defined, and acclaimed, by Callimachus, and Aratus' direct succession in the line of Hesiod clearly established.

Virgil's singular contribution, however, seems to be Orpheus, and Orpheus stands for something far greater than 'manner'. Orpheus has the power to charm nature, and, as it develops, the knowledge and understanding of it. The poetry Orpheus represents can thus properly be called scientific. Virgil has described such poetry most fully and evocatively in the famous passage at the end of the second book of the *Georgics* (475–94), introducing the lines with a suggestion of himself as priest of the Muses³⁵ (*me vero primum dulces ante omnia Musae,* | *quarum sacra fero ingenti percussus amore,* | *accipiant...,* 'then first may the Muses, dear to me beyond all else, receive me,

---

³³ See Jacques 1960, with a good review of the significance of λεπτός following Aratus; and E. L. Brown 1963: 96–105. Though I cannot follow Brown in all his observations, I find it difficult not to believe in his discovery of Virgil's 'acrostic' signature. Note, also, in Aratus, καθαρή (783) = *pura* in Virgil (433): it became another key term in Callimachus (*Hymn* 2.111) and was taken over by the Latin poets (e.g., to be discussed below, Prop. 2.13.12).

³⁴ σύμβολον, an emendation by Ruhnken accepted by Pfeiffer, may thus be confirmed and explained ('λεπταί' is the σφραγίς = σύμβολον of Aratus). Note also ἀγρυπνίης, and cf. above on Linus (Theoc. 24.106) as ἄγρυπνος ἥρως, Alexandrian singer (cf. Cinna's epigram (*FPL*, p. 89 Morel) with the words *Arateis multum invigilata lucernis carmina*).

³⁵ Cf. above n. 29.

whose sacred tokens I carry, struck with deep love for them'), but with the request that they *receive* him and *teach* him 'science' (... *caelique vias et sidera monstrent,* | *defectus solis varios lunaeque labores...,* 'may they show me the paths of the heavens and the stars, the varied eclipses of the sun and the labors of the moon'). The power of such knowledge extends over the underworld itself (*felix qui potuit rerum cognoscere causas,* | *atque metus omnis et inexorabile fatum* | *subiecit pedibus strepitumque Acherontis avari,* 'happy he who could learn nature's workings and who cast beneath his feet every fear, inexorable destiny, and the roar of greedy Acheron', 490–2). Here too it is still generally assumed that in the entire passage Virgil had Lucretius in mind, and that Lucretius is referred to directly in lines 490–2,[36] but here again the associations extend farther and Virgil's reference should not be limited to a particular individual or philosophical sect. It is Orpheus who, in the corresponding section of Book Four, can exert power, through his poetry, over the underworld,[37] and it would seem to be the whole tradition of 'Orphic' poetry (as we have attempted to outline it) that is suggested here. Moreover, lines 477–8 are an allusion to Aratus;[38] Stewart has discussed this passage in emphasizing most usefully the eclectic nature of Virgil's conception of scientific poetry in *Ecl.* 6.31–40.[39]

[36] That the *felix qui potuit...* is a *macarismos* is a fact too often overlooked or ignored: the convention is necessarily a generality—Lucretius may be *suggested* by the lines, but he cannot be referred to *directly*. That Virgil is not referring specifically to Lucretius here is made clear by the parallel *fortunatus et ille*: whom does Virgil have in mind there?

[37] Orpheus, with his divine power, can achieve what mortality cannot (... *manisque adiit regemque tremendum* | *nesciaque humanis precibus mansuescere corda.* | *at cantu...,* 'he approached the Shades and the fearsome King and those hearts that know no pity at the prayers of men', G. 4.469–71); it is particularly Virgilian, however, that it is his 'humanity' that causes the final loss of Eurydice.

[38] See the discussion by Paratore 1939: 180 n. 6; Paratore sees the lines immediately following, however, as simply Lucretian. We should note that Aratus is adapted again by Virgil in the first couplet of the singing contest in *Ecl.* 3.60–1, after the wager of the cups with representations of Conon, Aratus, and Orpheus: *ab Iove principium musae: Iovis omnia plena* = ἐκ Διὸς ἀρχώμεσθα ... μεσταὶ δὲ Διὸς πᾶσαι μὲν ἀγυιαί κ.τ.λ., *Phaen.* 1–4.

[39] Stewart 1959: 185 concludes on *Ecl.* 6.31–40: 'By taking traits from different, partly opposed, doctrines Virgil has made a new formulation which represents "scientific" poetry in general, not one school or one work.' He supports his conclusion with a discussion of G. 2.475–92, pointing to elements of Lucretius, Empedocles, and Aratus.

The most striking aspect of *G.* 2.475–94 is the opposition of the scientific and the pastoral. (Here again I must ask for the reader's temporary indulgence, this time for taking liberties with the term 'pastoral'.) Lines 475–82 (scientific poetry) are followed by the pastoral alternative (483–9); the balance is repeated immediately by the opposition in lines 490–4 (*felix qui potuit rerum cognoscere causas... fortunatus et ille deos qui novit agrestis | Panaque Silvanumque senem Nymphasque sorores*, 'happy he who could learn nature's workings... and blessed too he who knows the gods of the countryside, Pan, old Sylvanus, and the sister nymphs'). The whole passage seems to be a comment on (and a revision of) the poetic genealogy represented in Gallus' initiation in the Sixth Eclogue. One difficulty one would have in drawing a proper stemma of the genealogy would be that Linus and Orpheus cannot be related linearly, one descended from the other—both are, as it were, 'brothers' by separate parents.[40] Such an oversimplification undoubtedly never occurred to Virgil, but it suggests nonetheless what does seem to have been Virgil's purpose, that Linus and Orpheus each represent, on the same level, different aspects of poetry.[41] Virgil's poetic genealogy is an attempt to relate, and unify, a poetic diversity: Gallus' inheritance becomes that of a single tradition.

Gallus was wandering by the Permessus (*errantem Permessi ad flumina Gallum*); one of the Muses led him to the Aonian mountains where Linus gave him the pipes with instructions that with them he sing the *aetion* (*origo*) of Apollo's Grynean Grove. Here is a further unifying point in the tradition, and one of great importance. We are reliably informed by Servius (on line 72), 'hoc autem Euphorionis continent carmina quae Gallus transtulit in sermonem Latinum', and Gallus' interest in Euphorion is confirmed by Virgil himself when in the Tenth Eclogue Gallus says, *ibo et Chalcidico quae sunt mihi condita versu | carmina pastoris Siculi meditabor avena* ('I will go,

---

[40] Cf. again *Ecl.* 4.55–7; that Orpheus and Linus are brothers is reported (for what it is worth) by Apollodorus 1.3.2. Those who have noted that Linus was Orpheus' teacher (Page 1965 in his comment on *Ecl.* 6.67; Elder 1961: 115) seem to be repeating not Virgil but a worthless remark in 'Suidas' (s.v. Ὀρφεύς), καί φασι μαθητὴν γενέσθαι αὐτὸν Λίνου: cf. also Apollodorus 2.4.9.

[41] But not that noted by Servius on *Ecl.* 4.58: '*PAN ETIAM* redit ad rustica numina: nam satis excesserat dicendo Linum poetam, Orphea theologum'.

and the songs which I based on Chalcidian verse I will (now) play on the reed of the Sicilian shepherd', 50–1). We can also be certain about the reason for Gallus' interest in Euphorion and in the Grynean Grove: Stephanus of Byzantium gives us the information that the ethnic form Γρύνειος—the form used by Virgil here, *Grynei nemoris*—occurred in Parthenius' poem *Delos* (λέγεται καὶ Γρύνειος Ἀπόλλων ὡς Παρθένιος Δήλῳ, 'the "Grynean Apollo" is to be found in Parthenius' poem "Delos"').[42] Virgil has extended his poetic genealogy to include Euphorion and Gallus' friend and poetic mentor Parthenius, for there can be little doubt now that it was Parthenius who was largely responsible not only for the general direction of Gallus' poetic career, but for the specific subject of the Grynean Grove. The impression is conveyed that Parthenius, as much as Linus, stands as the Muses' surrogate in presenting Gallus with the pipes.

We now come to a crucial point in our discussion, one which concerns the actual poetic production of Gallus, the author of four books of elegies (only so much can be said with any certainty). Are we to understand from the scene of his initiation that he is leaving elegy and is henceforth to write a new and different sort of poetry such as is suggested by the Grynean Grove—Alexandrian aetiology, in whatever form? This is what scholars have generally concluded from the passage, and the only question remaining, it seems, is whether Virgil is urging this as a change for his friend or is reporting a new course already taken. Almost all the details of Gallus' poetic career are open to debate, but all are crucial for an understanding of the development of Augustan poetry. We must therefore discuss certain details of Gallus' initiation again, to see what assumptions we may or may not make and to place the scene in the context of Virgil's poetic genealogy as we have developed it thus far.

First, the river Permessus. The identification of it as 'the stream of elegy', and hence the conclusion that Gallus leaves elegy for another sort of poetry (represented by the Aonian mountains, or Helicon), are based entirely on a couplet of Propertius:

---

[42] For this point, and for Parthenius' relationship to Gallus, see the decisive remarks by Clausen 1964: 191–3: Clausen's demonstration (pp. 188–91) of the importance of Parthenius for Cinna's *Zmyrna* and Catullus (esp. c. 95) should be kept in mind.

> nondum etiam Ascraeos norunt mea carmina fontis,
> sed modo Permessi flumine lavit Amor.   (2.10.25–6)

Not yet does my poetry know the springs of Ascra, but now only in the river Permessus has Love bathed my verse.

Here, at the very end of a *recusatio* (*aetas prima canat Veneres, extrema tumultus*: | *bella canam, quando scripta puella mea est*, 'let youth sing of Love, and old age of battle: I will sing of war when I have written of my love', 7–8), Propertius can only mean, we are told, that he cannot yet write epic (*Ascraeos fontis*) because his whole poetic experience has been of elegy (*Permessi flumine*): Virgil's Gallus, then, must likewise be leaving elegy for a higher sort of poetry. Leaving aside the question of what Propertius *does* mean, I do not think we are justified in drawing this conclusion, simple and obvious though it may appear. In the first place, in the opening line of the poem Propertius had referred to Helicon, a mountain which can only be Hesiod's: *sed tempus lustrare aliis Helicona choreis* ('but it is time to celebrate Helicon in different verse'). Propertius does not say that now is the time to *approach* Helicon (i.e. to write epic at Hesiod's fountains), or to *climb* Helicon, or to be *transported* there, or anything of the sort, but rather simply that it is the time 'to celebrate' (*lustrare*) Helicon (where presumably he has been for some time) with *other* (i.e. epic) choruses: the distinction does not lie in a choice of poetic localities, but rather in the sort of verse to be composed. The simple identification of epic with Hesiod's fountains becomes even more difficult, or impossible, when a few poems later Propertius places his love elegy with no uncertainty in Hesiod's grove:

> hic [Amor] me tam gracilis vetuit contemnere Musas,
> iussit et Ascraeum sic habitare nemus   (2.13.3–4)

Love forbade me to scorn such slender poetry and ordered me thus to frequent the Ascrean grove,

a passage to which we will return shortly. If there can be no question of an opposition between the *Ascraeos fontis* (2.10.25) and the *Ascraeum nemus* (2.13.4), and if both clearly refer to Hesiodic verse, then either Propertius is to be found guilty of hopeless inconsistency in saying first that his songs have not yet become acquainted with the Hesiodic fountains, then that Love has ordered him to frequent the Hesiodic grove; or something is wrong with our reading of 2.10.25–6 when we make so clear an opposition between the (elegiac) stream of Permessus and the (epic) Hesiodic fountains. Perhaps, though, all we can say for the moment is that we should not conclude from Propertius 2.10.25–6 that Virgil's Gallus has been called to abandon elegy.

Furthermore, the Permessus is in origin neither an elegiac stream nor distinct geographically or poetically from Helicon. Hesiod begins the *Theogony* with the Heliconian Muses (by whom he will be initiated as a poet); then,

> καί τε λοεσσάμεναι τέρενα χρόα Περμησσοῖο
> ἢ Ἵππου κρήνης ἢ Ὀλμειοῦ ζαθέοιο
> ἀκροτάτῳ Ἑλικῶνι χοροὺς ἐνεποιήσαντο.   (5–7)[43]

...when (the Muses) had washed their delicate bodies in the Permessus or the Horse's Spring or in the divine Olmeius, they made their dances on Helicon's height.

There is no distinction here between the Permessus and Helicon itself, and Virgil, for whom this scene of Hesiod's initiation was of such importance, could hardly have attempted to draw one in the face of Hesiod's text. The identity of the Permessus and Helicon can be followed still further: we know from Servius Auctus (on *Ecl.* 10.12, *Aonie Aganippe*) and the scholiast on Juvenal (7.6) that Callimachus had mentioned Aganippe as the '*fons Permessi fluminis*', and we now know for certain where this mention occurred: as had been suspected, it is to be placed in the introduction to the *Aetia*, in the context of Callimachus' own dream, in which he was transported to Helicon.[44] Finally and significantly, in the only other occurrence of

---

[43] See West 1966: 153–4: wherever Hesiod's Permessus actually was, there is no doubt about its being in the immediate vicinity of Helicon.

[44] Pfeiffer (on *Aetia* fr. 696), following a conjecture first made by Hecker, had suggested, 'fort. in Aetiorum "somnio"'; see also his comments on the Schol. Flor. to fr. 2. Confirmation is given by *P. Oxy.* 2262 fr. 2 (published by R. Pfeiffer 1949–53: 2.101–3, with commentary). For Callimachus' dream, see *Anth. Pal.* 7.42. It is important, in this context, to note the association of *Aonie Aganippe* with Gallus again in *Ecl.* 10.12—a further indication not to oppose, but to unite, the *Permessi flumina* and *Aonas montes* in *Ecl.* 6.

the Permessus in Greek poetry, Nicander too connects it with Ἀσκραῖος Ἡσίοδος (*Ther.* 11–12).

From a review of these contexts it seems impossible that Virgil (or perhaps Gallus previously) could have meant the Permessus to represent 'subjective love elegy' opposed to Helicon and Hesiodic-Callimachean aetiological poetry. Such an interpretation cannot stand: the Permessus and Helicon are topographically and poetically identical wherever they occur together in Greek poetry, and those occurrences are all in poets and scenes intimately connected with Virgil's poetic genealogy and Gallus' initiation. Instead of assuming that Gallus has been called from elegy to a loftier poetic genre, we must infer (a) that the geographical details (both the Permessus and Helicon) are presented by Virgil to refer in no uncertain terms to the scene of the initiations of both Hesiod and Callimachus, and therefore (b) that Gallus, wandering by the Permessus, had already written Hesiodic-Callimachean poetry which he is being rewarded and recognized for, not initiated to.

The inference that Gallus had already written Hesiodic-Callimachean poetry (in some form), and that this was recognized by Virgil in the Sixth Eclogue, can be given additional support by a different approach. A question was suggested earlier about Virgil's precedent for the figure of Linus, whose new role was created by Virgil so quietly that modern scholars have understandably overlooked its significance. Yet it seems doubtful that even the complete context (now lost) of Linus' appearance in Callimachus would have made more significant, or explicable, to contemporary Roman readers of the *Eclogues* the importance Linus suddenly assumed, for the Callimachean Linus, though a shepherd, seems only to have been an incidental figure created with literary wit for a single aetiological episode, having nothing of the ritual solemnity he emerges with in the *Eclogues*; likewise the Theocritean Linus, though a precedent of sorts, would hardly have illuminated the Virgilian context. We must assume, I think, that we have lost an important stage in Linus' transformation, that this development occurred elsewhere with fuller detail in a source which Virgil could draw on and suggest.

It seems more than likely that that source was Gallus. Scholars have suggested that some of the details of *Ecl.* 6.64–73 owe something to Gallus, that he himself had perhaps written of his own initiation by the Muses.[45] We may return now to a passage referred to previously, a pronouncement by Propertius on his own poetry:

> hic [Amor] me tam gracilis vetuit contemnere Musas,
>   iussit et Ascraeum sic habitare nemus,
> non ut Pieriae quercus mea verba sequantur,
>   aut possim Ismaria ducere valle feras,
> sed magis ut nostro stupefiat Cynthia versu:
>   tunc ego sim Inachio notior arte Lino.   (2.13.3–8)

Love forbade me to scorn such slender poetry and ordered me thus to frequent the Ascrean grove, not so that the Pierian oaks might march to my words or that I lead (in dance) the wild beasts in the Ismarian glade, but rather that Cynthia might wonder in awe at my verse: then would I be more famous in my craft than Inachian Linus.

The whole poem contains unmistakable Callimachean terms:[46] the *gracilis Musas* represent Callimachus' 'slender Muse' of the *Aetia* prologue (τὴν Μοῦσαν λεπταλέην, fr. 1.24 Pf.); shortly after this passage Propertius mentions a *docta puella*, who will approve his poetry *auribus puris* (11–12)—καθαρός is another key term for Callimachus[47]—and then scorns the *populi confusa fabula* (13–14).[48] At the same time the *personae dramatis* of Propertius' lines all seem to enter directly from Gallus' initiation in the Sixth Eclogue: the Muses, Hesiod (the *Ascraeum nemus*), Orpheus with his power to charm the oaks and wild beasts,[49] and finally Linus, distinguished in his 'art'. It may be asked, though, why Propertius should import his poetic characters wholesale from Virgil and specifically from the *Eclogues*,

---

[45] R. Reitzenstein 1896: 194–5; F. Skutsch 1901: 34 ('Nicht eigene Erfindung ist es, was Vergil hier giebt; vielmehr wiederholt er nur, was Gallus selbst in einem eigenen Gedicht von sich erzählt hatte, einem Gedicht, das eben die Schilderung seiner Dichterweihe als Prooemium und danach die Geschichte vom gryneischen Hain enthielt'); Wimmel 1960: 235 ('Vielleicht stammt die Szene in ihrer elegischen Ausformung aus Gallus selbst').

[46] On the following terms and others, see Wilkinson 1966: 141–4, who argues convincingly for the unity of this poem largely from the Callimachean elements in it.

[47] καθαρή τε καί … ὀλίγη λιβάς, *Hymn* 2.111–12; cf. above, n. 33 for the term in Aratus (with λεπτός), translated as *purus* by Virgil.

[48] σικχαίνω πάντα τὰ δημόσια, Callim. *Epigr.* 28.4 (Pf.) = e.g., *odi profanum vulgus et arceo*, Hor. *Carm.* 3.1.1.

[49] Cf. *feras, quercus,* and *Ismarus* all with Orpheus at *Ecl.* 6.27–30. E. Reitzenstein 1931, though, refers the lines to Hesiod (see above, n.23).

a tradition in which he has no need to stress his literary individuality (*non ut...sed magis ut nostro stupefiat Cynthia versu: tunc ego sim...notior arte Lino* is after all a challenge to a precedent in his own genre). If Gallus, however, had first brought these poetic exemplars together somewhere in his elegies, there is then every reason for Propertius' doing so here in this context.

That both Propertius and Virgil derive their passages from a common source, and that this source is Gallus, can be demonstrated positively, I believe. It would be gratuitous to point to details which occur in Propertius but not in Virgil (such as the specific epithet *Pieriae* (*quercus*) or the mention of the *ars* specifically of Linus), were it not that one such detail provides an essential clue that amounts almost to proof: *Inachio...Lino.*[50] Virgil, as we have seen, gives no information anywhere about Linus' provenance, and indeed provides so little information of any sort that we might well feel uncertain about the claim made previously that Callimachus' Linus, 'reared amongst lambs', provided the reason for Linus' role as *pastor* in Virgil. But the story related by Callimachus and the mythographer Conon differs in several essential features from other, both earlier and later, accounts of the attributes and activities of Linus, one of which is the setting in *Argos*, where Linus is the son of the *Argive* princess Psamathe. Had Propertius taken Linus (with the others) directly from the cast of participants in Gallus' initiation in the Sixth Eclogue, it would appear extremely unlikely that he would himself have then made a connection, independently, with Callimachus' Argive Linus and come up with the proper epithet *Inachio*—there is no evident reason that would have prompted him to have taken such an uncharacteristic step. If, however, it was Gallus who had introduced the *pastor* Linus to Latin poetry (and it has been argued above that the Virgilian Linus would hardly have been understandable even to a literary contemporary without a previous exemplar), then Gallus' Linus must have been a form of the Callimachean Linus, complete with his Callimachean provenance, and perhaps even with the epithet *Inachius*.

---

[50] Commentators have missed the point of *Inachio* entirely (just as they have overlooked the general significance of Linus); *Inachio* is interpreted to mean, simply, 'Greek' (e.g. Camps 1967 *ad loc.* 'i.e. Greek, Inachus being a legendary of Argos').

We have seen that Virgil, with his initiation scene, sets Gallus directly in the tradition of Hesiod and Callimachus. We can assume, in all probability, that Gallus had taken over the *pastor* Linus from Callimachus and made him a figure of some importance: when in the Sixth Eclogue Linus acts as the Muses' representative in handing on the pipes to Gallus, he may well be re-enacting a role he had performed earlier in Gallus' own poetry, and when he instructs Gallus to sing of the Grynean Grove, he is in fact relating what had already been performed. Finally, as we can infer from a comparison with Propertius 2.13.3–8, it is more than likely that the entire initiation scene and the actors in it come more or less directly from Gallus.[51]

What we said about a unified poetic tradition inherited by Gallus will now have to be modified in one important respect: it is not Virgil who was responsible for this conception (at least not entirely), but rather Gallus himself. In his poetic genealogy Virgil may have rearranged and organized various pieces, and may have expanded, connected, and suggested other relationships, but I do not think he can be credited with the original conception of a poetic unity. Callimachus, after all, had clearly established a single tradition for what can be termed scientific poetry; it may have been Gallus who saw Orpheus as the archetypal cosmic poet,[52] the founder of the line of Hesiod and Aratus. Linus' function is parallel, the semi-divine exemplar of the pastoral.[53] Whoever devised the position of one of these two legendary singers most likely also established the other in his corresponding role.

Whoever first enunciated what particular detail is of little importance (since we can never be certain of all the facts) beside what was actually achieved. The idea that all poetry arises from a single impulse (Apollo, the Muses) and, whatever form it may take, never departs from a single demonstrable tradition, and that the true

---

[51] To speak of an 'initiation' scene in Virgil is now no more than a convenience: Gallus may have related a proper initiation, but, as we have argued, for Virgil the scene is one of recognition and reward, not an initiation to a new poetic course.

[52] This assumption rests on my arguments for the common exemplar (Gallus) for *Ecl.* 6.64–73 and Prop. 2.13.3–8 (proved, I think, at least for the figure of Linus): the chances are, then, that Orpheus played a role of some importance in Gallus.

[53] The pastoral element in Gallus, as has often been suggested, must have been considerable.

poet of the present (the received, initiated poet, that is) inherits this unified tradition, was perhaps never before clearly realized and expressed, even by Callimachus. It has become a commonplace to say that what primarily motivated classical (and especially Roman) poetry was the expression of individuality within a confining genre. The discovery of a single unified tradition comprehending a variety of forms and genres means that genre need no longer count for much. As long as the poetic impulse is pure and the tradition undefiled—that is, as long as the poet can claim to have been initiated to the canons of Callimachean art—then, no matter what formal genre a poet assumes, there can be a universality of time and space, of reality and unreality. There is no better demonstration of this new freedom than the *Eclogues* of Virgil, in part pure Theocritean pastoral, in part disturbingly divorced from the pastoral world, set now in a timeless past, now in a present all too real, in a landscape which shifts in a similar fashion. We may assume, though, that Virgil in the *Eclogues* was not the first to have experienced the new freedom with such confidence. Everything suggests that Gallus had seen the real unity behind apparently diverse traditions, and had gone far in formulating it. We can expect his elegies to have reflected this discovery.

Carmina quae vultis cognoscite, says Silenus to his captors (line 25), and the following songs are indeed a perfect demonstration of the possibilities of the new poetry. We have mentioned precedents and associations, both literary and scientific, for the eclectic cosmogony with which Silenus begins.[54] The themes which follow defy neat classification—purposely. There are indications of epyllia. The brief mention of the Proetides (line 48) within the story of Pasiphae resembles the panel within a panel of, for instance, Catullus' epyllion;[55] the repeated *a, virgo infelix*... (lines 47 and 52) comes from Calvus' epyllion *Io* (*a, virgo infelix, herbis pasceris amaris*, 'ah, unhappy girl, you will feed on bitter grass', *FPL* p. 85 Morel); and there is a direct speech by the heroine (55–60). Other notable features of

---

[54] The cosmogony should include lines 41–2 (after which—*his adiungit*—a new *carmen* begins: cf. Orpheus' song in Apollonius, which continues in the same way with Cronos and Zeus (*Arg.* 1.503–11)). In support of this (not generally accepted) division, see Jachmann 1923: 288–94.

[55] Noted by F. Skutsch 1901: 42.

neoteric poetry are not difficult to find. F. Skutsch has called attention to the way certain themes are presented: Silenus tells *at what fountain* Hylas was lost (*quo fonte relictum*, 43), and is concerned with the specific details of Philomela's flight and plumage (*quo cursu... quibus... alis*, 80–1), both of which suggest aetiological poetry.[56] It is often observed that in lines 74–7 Virgil has conflated the two separate stories concerning a Scylla (one the monster daughter of Phorcys, the other the daughter of Nisus who became the *ciris*), but the allusion to a different tradition in the relating of another is a recognized feature of learned poetry, which Virgil makes clear with the Alexandrian *quam fama secuta est*.[57] At the same time, there is no need to point out the pastoral motifs of, for instance, the stories mentioned in lines 45–63,[58] or to do more than mention that a good case can be made for regarding Love as the prime concern of Silenus' songs:[59] the neoteric interest in the darker aspects of erotic experience is certainly evident, and many of the stories concern metamorphoses.

This summary does little justice to the richness of detail in Silenus' song, but the lines have been discussed at length by many scholars in various attempts to find a controlling unity. There seems to be a purposeful variety in the poetic forms and poetic stories Virgil suggests, so that no category, no matter how broad, can include them all comfortably.[60] Yet obviously Virgil must have had some purpose in putting them all into Silenus' song, and enough similarities and points of contact obviously exist between the separate songs to convey the impression of a whole. Gallus' initiation, I have argued, provides the clue, and Gallus' poetry supplied what is now missing to us, the discovery that behind poetic diversity, behind the variety of purpose, form, theme, or genre, lies a unity of poetic tradition, a direct line of descent from divinity to contemporary poet, represented by the pipes

---

[56] F. Skutsch 1901: 32–3.

[57] See Norden 1957: 123–4 (on line 14, *ut fama est*).

[58] Cf. again Elder's comments on the pastoral elements throughout the poem (1961: 116–20), though many of the motifs he lists I cannot accept as 'pastoral'.

[59] Klingner 1967: 109–10.

[60] To find the unity of Silenus' songs in the force and development of Love, for instance, or in metamorphoses, is to have distorted, or to leave unexplained, the opening cosmogony and Gallus' initiation.

of the poet, *hos tibi dant calamos, en accipe, Musae*...Whatever is played on these pipes will necessarily be real poetry, for style and expression are determined by the instrument. The Sixth Eclogue is itself the demonstration of the unity of poetry, and the Eclogue Book is the example of what can be achieved by the discovery that real poetry is circumscribed and defined not by genre or form, but only according to a poetic genealogy.

10

An Interpretation of the Tenth *Eclogue*

Gian Biagio Conte

It has often been said that of all the great *carmina* in Latin literature, Virgil's tenth *Eclogue* has been most resistant to critical authority. Because of its density and composite form, it has rebuffed all of the theories, which, by being too comprehensive, have explained the textual contrasts at only a superficial level. Its complexity of expression, so erratic and elliptical, impedes access to its fullest sense. Despite its effect of wholeness, it appears suddenly to shatter into separate, incongruous segments. And yet readers who have tried to chip away at the text, meticulously examining its separate elements, have found themselves confronting its compact, continuous architectonic unity and above all its dynamic poetic discourse.

At the beginning of this century, interpretation of the tenth *Eclogue* was from the outset necessarily tainted by 'original sin', which it seems never to have quite lived down. Skutsch was the first critic (but not the last) who, instead of seeing Virgil, went searching for Gallus.[1] One can understand why. The illusion that it was possible to recover complete passages of the lost poetry of Gallus (almost as if Gallus's own voice could be heard speaking) rather than

---

This paper was originally published in Italian in Conte 1980: 11–43. The revised English version presented here first appeared in Conte 1986: 100–29.

[1] F. Skutsch 1901. In answering his opponents in the later volume *Gallus und Vergil* (F. Skutsch 1906), Skutsch developed the basic line of argument put forward in this study; its corollary was that Cornelius Gallus should be identified with the author of the pseudo-Virgilian epyllion *Ciris*, which Virgil bore in mind in all his works.

oblique, uncertain echoes convinced Skutsch that Virgil was using an Alexandrian form of homage to honor his friend. Thus Skutsch believed that Virgil had conceived his sixth and tenth *Eclogues* as 'catalogues' of works by Gallus that have not come down to us. Skutsch's enthusiastic interpretation was made all the more dangerous by the power of his scholarship and his exceptional philological talent. Leo[2] objected at once, and Paul Jahn,[3] like many others, reacted decisively and immediately. The 'Kataloggedicht' theory is by now only a faded memory; it is recalled as a wrongheaded enterprise in a heroic age of classical philology in Germany.

All the same, it cannot be claimed that a great deal of progress has been made. Even Friedrich Klingner, the shrewdest interpreter to have emerged recently in German criticism, could not go past a certain point.[4] Yet he had all that was needed. He knew that the task was not easy,[5] and he possessed practically all the exegetical material accumulated by the great philologists who had almost concurrently discussed and quarreled over this eclogue: Skutsch, Leo, and Jahn, as already noted, Jacoby marginally, and then Snell;[6] nor should one forget those whose work has, in my view, offered most to a well-founded interpretation—Witte, Pfeiffer, and Pohlenz.[7] Klingner had the special advantage of a method that had a close affinity with the text. Again and again he shows his ability to trace faithfully the sequence of ideas, or 'Gedankengang'—how ideas emerge, disappear, and return in various patterns—and their concatenations in significant units (the 'Gefüge', joints—how their interaction results in the organic synthesis of the text).

Something of that early period and great debate of interpretation was left—and is still left—as an invisible underpinning for later scholars. Too many proposals for specific and general exegesis had been put forward for the interpretations to disappear even when they had been undermined or refuted. Even direct refutations sometimes

---

[2] Leo 1902: 14 ff. (= 1960: 2.29 ff.).   [3] Jahn 1902.
[4] Klingner 1967.
[5] 'The tenth eclogue is the most peculiar—so peculiar that most of its interpreters have racked their brains over it in vain' (Klinger 1967: 166).
[6] Jacoby 1905; Snell 1945 (= 1946: 233–258; translated into English in Snell 1953: 281–309).
[7] Witte 1922; E. Pfeiffer 1933; Pohlenz 1930 (= 1965: 2.97 ff.).

adopted the same logical scheme as their targets.[8] Above all, a kind of hesitancy has persisted, an inclination to distrust the intelligibility of the text, almost as if the eclogue, besides being complex, 'wanted', by its very nature, to be insidious. This inclination perhaps accounts for the feeling that we must read between the lines, above and beneath the words used. Thus even the most innocent signs have sometimes been scrutinized to yield an unlikely sense.[9] Meanings are extracted that are actually secondary or unactivated, and attributes to those meanings acquire chance symbolic values; then they are linked according to ungrounded equivalences and oppositions.

This point is worth clarifying. I quite agree that a poem does not yield its full meaning simply by being heard. Its fullness of sense can be revealed only by a systematic 'translation' from one plane of language (the text's) to another (the critic's). Its meaning is none other than this possibility of coherent recreation, which gives the critic the right to apply a hermeneutic grid to the text—an organic system of questioning. The critic is right to devise a cultural superstructure capable of revealing the 'ideology' (in the broad sense) implemented in the form and context of the poetry. But before doing so—or simultaneously—the critic must become an ingenious maker of the text (pulling it apart and remaking it), so as to capture its sense, its internal 'logic'. Critics must rely on the language and the means it uses.

In other words, we need a method that is internally coherent and also devises a critical discourse that is consistent with the text, not an undisciplined surrender to arbitrary inferences sanctioned by supposed ambiguity. A 'method' is simply a way of attaining an aim, but

---

[8] Thus Leo 1902, who defeated Skutsch and the Kataloggedicht theory, had failed to recognize the wholly literary, fictional status of Arcadia (the symbol of a poetic world, an existential myth) and so believed that Gallus, involved in war-time maneuvers, had really stayed for a time in that mountainous part of the Peloponnesus; his mistake was repeated, much later, by Rose 1942: 104 ff. But biographism, which had a naturalistic and late historicist matrix, was the vice of a whole generation, and even Leo shared its limitations (which are apparent in the theoretical work of Wilhelm Dilthey, though in his extreme old age Dilthey's initial certainties gave way to a cautious recantation). I do not wish to deny completely the legitimacy of studies based on biographical or historical data, but in general one must be extremely wary, as the damage done often exceeds the benefits obtained.

[9] This is one of my objections to the argument of Michael Putnam, a critic of talent, in Putnam 1970.

An Interpretation of the Tenth Eclogue

this way need not be straightforward. The tenth *Eclogue* is a prime example of how going through the text may mean following a path as crooked as that of Theseus. For the reader, 'unwinding' discourse, losing his way, going back, and reversing the simple logic of the straight line means following the thread that offers the only way of escaping from the maze. One must pass through the various textual levels, from the plane of the story that is narrated to that of representation by direct speech. One must recognize behind Virgil's voice the bucolic persona of Virgil the shepherd, meeting Gallus as an object of the narration and watching him make himself the subject of a soliloquy that alternates between complaints and memories, regrets and visions, the past and the future, and continually turns from one such dimension to another, as if changing spaces and landscapes were being superimposed. In this way the perception of the reader is disturbed and upset but poetically sharpened. The changing aspects of the passages make the way into the labyrinth apparently directionless, but in the end the reason for its tortuousness becomes clear. This eclogue, in fact, proves to be a finished structure of carefully elaborated tensions—an exterior, dramatic representation of an interior, imagined meaning. It is achieved as a compromise between an 'idea' into which the sense of the whole poem may be condensed at an abstract level (almost into a single point) and an ongoing, linear development which that sense takes on in its linguistic-literary expression. This dialectic gives rise to the total sense (or 'poetic unity') of the eclogue, without thereby forcing its unity.

Criticism of the *Eclogues* has always begun by surveying (in some cases, with lists and tables) Virgil's considerable debt to Theocritus. There is by this time little to add, even for the tenth *Eclogue*, to the scrupulous listing of parallels by Jahn, Hosius, and now Posch.[10] It is

---

[10] Posch 1969: 15 ff. If one wished to be pedantic, one could perhaps see *Eclogue* 10.42–3 (*hic gelidi fontes, hic...hic...hic*, 'here cool springs...here') as echoes of Theocritus, *Idyll* 8.45–7, because of their sustained movement with the quadruple anaphora of ἔνθα ('here'). Virgil's lines also echo, in regard to their content, *Idyll* 8.33 and 8.37. These lines mark the beginning of the celebrated elegiac couplets in the competition between Daphnis and Menalcas. (Even if the authenticity of the eighth *Idyll* is notoriously doubtful, it is sufficient for our purposes that it was included in the Theocritean corpus and as such could be considered valid by Virgil.)

more important to draw clear distinctions within this accumulation of Theocritean material, since not all of it, plainly, is equally relevant to an exegesis of Virgil. There are deliberate echoes, and there are mere fragments in a bucolic manner; there are also different modes and degrees in creating intentional echoes, and they cover a range of functions.

When Gallus, against the setting of the mountains of Arcadia, is lovesick and pines away, this is an evident epiphany of the agonies of Daphnis, the bucolic hero. But Virgil did not wish merely to take up the theme of the suffering and death of Daphnis (perhaps even fusing various occasions on which the Theocritean shepherds had performed). His main purpose was to produce a close calque of that first, exquisite *Idyll* by Theocritus that is named after Thyrsis, who celebrates Daphnis, and of course he intended the competent reader to recognize this fact.

The initial signal makes this relationship recognizable:

> quae nemora aut qui vos saltus habuere, puellae
> Naides, indigno cum Gallus amore peribat?   (*Ecl.* 10.9–10)

What groves, what glades were your abode, virgin Naiads, when Gallus was dying with a love unrequited?

Theocritus *Idyll* 1.66: πᾶ πόκ' ἄρ' ἦσθ', ὅκα Δάφνις ἐτάκετο, πᾶ πόκα, Νύμφαι; ('Wherever, wherever were you, Nymphs, when Daphnis was dying?'). So the song on the dying of Daphnis-Gallus begins. This striking echo, long ago identified by critics of Virgil, is of exceptional significance. It immediately reveals the specific mode in which the Virgilian 'Nachdichten' is used here with respect to Theocritus. Virgil not only changed the style but also reworked structures and situations to transform his 'character' Gallus.

When he adapts Theocritus's verses on Daphnis to his poet-friend Gallus, in a certain sense he dresses his Gallus in Daphnis's clothes (we will gradually discover the precise implications of this operation). Gallus, too, like Daphnis, receives sympathy from the whole of nature, and he too is visited by the men and gods of the bucolic world, all eager to console him. It might be objected that Theocritus's *Thyrsis* was the obvious term of comparison for an eclogue presenting lovesickness and for a poet who wished (*Eclogue* 10.6) <u>sollicitos</u>

Galli dicere amores ('to speak of the *distressful loves* of Gallus'). But to achieve this comparison, could not Virgil have made a looser, less detailed reference, less tied down by the trammels of writing poetry after a model? Yes, if he had not wished to stake a claim on the *dramatic development* underlying Theocritus's idyll and if he had not needed to take over the meaning conveyed by Daphnis's proud words to Aphrodite: Δάφνις κἠν Ἀίδα κακὸν ἔσσεται ἄλγος Ἔρωτι ('Even in the underworld, Daphnis will resist love harshly'). By going to such lengths to push home the identification of Gallus with Daphnis's suffering, Virgil invites Gallus to repeat Daphnis's resistance to love and his antagonism to Eros. And in making this invitation, Virgil was also offering to help his friend.

In the version of the myth given in *Thyrsis*, Daphnis has irritated Aphrodite by flaunting his hard-heartedness and so offending her. She takes her revenge by having Eros arouse a violent passion in him. The shepherd-singer dies of this passion rather than be forgiven by submitting to the goddess. Several visitors come in turn to grieve over their Daphnis and do all they can to make him give up his headstrong decision. Hermes, a pastoral god here, asks, 'Why do you torment yourself? Whom are you in love with?' Priapus, too, inquires, 'Why do you pine away? That girl runs from spring to spring, and from wood to wood, searching for you. You are incapable of loving, poor fool.' The last to come, lashing him with her sarcasm, is his enemy Aphrodite: 'You claimed you could make Eros yield. But isn't it you who have had to yield to terrible Eros?' Against vindictive Aphrodite, against the 'detestable, fierce goddess', Daphnis, who had said nothing earlier, now finds the strength for a proud reply: he will not surrender, nor ever yield to love. Paradoxically, Daphnis seems to give up the joys of love just when he is dying of it; and this happens when that desire could easily be satisfied: Priapus tells him that the girl he loves actually longs to be united with him. Daphnis's apparently senseless refusal and his preference for suffering reject eros as a yoke that would deprive him of his innate freedom; as a shepherd and hunter he is his own master. His resistance is due not to a fear of the pleasures of love but to the fear of finding himself the prey and slave of love.

Gallus, however, is not just an elegiac poet but also an elegiac character, if we admit that this literary genre brings life and poetry closest together. Just what Daphnis considers loathsome slavery is for Gallus the meaning of life itself—the *servitium amoris* ('slavery to love'). This purpose continues—quite illogically—to absorb and fill life even when the object of desire appears unattainable. Thus Apollo's warning in *Eclogue* 10.22–3: *Galle, quid insanis?... tua cura Lycoris | perque nives alium perque horrida castra secuta est* ('"Gallus", he said, "what madness is this? Your sweetheart Lycoris has been following another through snow and rugged camp"'), may be read as the reverse of Priapus's question. The contrast between the exhortations (the first asking Daphnis to accept love and recover his pastoral serenity and the second asking Gallus to accept clearheadedly the *discidium* ('separation') that has already occurred) exactly corresponds to the opposition between the two literary genres. Here the bucolic code and the elegiac code oppose each other.

Thus there is a structural contrast between Daphnis and Gallus. Clearly, no opposition could be implemented if it were not based on a number of shared features that justified an acknowledged relationship of homology (conjunction). Everything depends on the importance of these visually shared features. Thus we return to the problem of Virgil's 'Daphnidization' of Gallus. This identification is overwhelmingly powerful compared with all the other parallels, however useful these may be in other respects: I have in mind the comparisons with *Eclogues* 2 and 8A (and their respective Theocritean models).[11] The fact is that in this case Virgil has not just brought into play his masterly talent for fusion, crossing this with that. We find here not just stylistic echoes but an identification of character and dramatic function (Gallus becomes Daphnis); more exactly, the stylistic echoes are relevant, but they have been put in as a means and are subordinated to the literary aim of identification. For this reason it is exegetically valuable to recognize the presence of Theocritus's *Thyrsis* as dominant. It is not simply a source of learned comparison but a structurally dynamic feature that affects all the other features in Virgil's eclogue.

---

[11] See E. Pfeiffer 1933: 47 ff. and 55 and his well-judged remarks on the song of Corydon and on the *ultima verba* of Damon; but these observations have a value that is generic rather than specific: they confirm the fully bucolic character of some of the structures underlying the tenth *Eclogue*.

The 'Daphnidization' of Gallus is Virgil's gift to his friend, a gift of redemption. The poet welcomes his friend, who is suffering (the first few lines show Gallus in just this elegiac attitude and pose). Virgil accepts him with affection, which is just what Gallus expects.[12] Gallus's monologue (*Eclogue* 10.31–69) gives his reply to the invitation to join the bucolic. Gallus agrees to wear the mask of the shepherd Daphnis; he, like Daphnis, lies pining away from love, and he too is visited by the inhabitants of the wood and the various divinities who gather around him and wish—each in a different way—to be close to him and to rescue him from the suffering that is destroying him. Again like Daphnis, Gallus at first says nothing and then responds to the various appeals made to him. His answer soon becomes a heartfelt monologue. What is more, Gallus immediately displays full awareness of his metamorphosis from elegiac poet to Daphnis the shepherd, and he shows his acceptance by viewing himself as already the object of a pastoral poem. Thus when Pan tries to cut short his suffering ('the god of love is as insatiable as meadows are for water, or bees for flowers, or kids for grass: there can never be enough tears to satisfy his cruelty'), Gallus answers that the fact that he is dying—the feature which makes him like Daphnis— will, however (*Eclogue* 10.31, *tamen*), qualify him for celebration in a song by the Arcadians, now that he himself wishes to become an Arcadian just as Virgil is an Arcadian, for this poem of his fulfills his purpose of *sollicitos Galli dicere amores*. In other words, Gallus understands what Virgil is doing from *within* the poem, and Gallus

---

[12] This is what is meant by the rhetorical question in the proem (*Eclogue* 10.3), *neget quis carmina Gallo?* ('Who would deny Gallus a song?'). Virgil's readiness almost anticipates his friend's need for help; it is a sign of eager affection, of an attempt to come to his aid at once with a *confectum carmine munus* ('gift composed of verse'). It is far from being, as Pohlenz thought, a formula (full of humor) concealing the 'playful challenge' directed by Gallus to Virgil, to make him write a poem (but not a boring one!) for Lycoris—that is, an erotic-elegiac poem. Sidetracked by the 'mixture' of elegiac and bucolic themes and insensitive to their contextual dialectics and to the inner conflict that, as we shall see, underlies them, Pohlenz could not fail to conclude: 'The general tendency of the poem [the tenth *Eclogue*] led Virgil to beat Gallus at his own game, to show him mockingly (!), on the basis of his [Gallus's] own poems, that he had very little right to look haughtily— from above—on bucolic poetry on the grounds that it was incapable of bringing success in love' (1965: 2.110).

endorses it. This understanding underlies the poem's essentially metaliterary character.

This eclogue, therefore, is not about the biographical experience of Gallus; this possibility can, in fact, be excluded, because his sufferings are molded so as to convey an experience that takes shape as elegiac poetry. Virgil's considerate interest in Gallus is directed less to his friend as such than to his friend as elegiac poet, whose sufferings *are* his poems, so that saving him would mean saving him from his elegies. Gallus himself (the Gallus who is by now part of Virgil's text) grasps this point and realizes that in this case poetry knowingly involves reflections on poetry. The meaning mediated by the poetic word is directed to a reality (a conflict) intrinsic to literary forms. But I will return to this subject later.

Now that Gallus has accepted Virgil's gift and has seen himself as a shepherd, he discovers the virtues of the bucolic world (*Eclogue* 10.33–43). Tormented as it is by elegiac passion, his spirit is refreshed by the vision of a pastoral existence in the country, where even the furor of love is not a condemnation to perpetual pining but finds its own place among the simple things of that world without disturbing their quiet drift and supreme ease. Gallus, however, is never more than a guest in that world. He is welcomed with loving care but remains different—an outsider. His elegiac sensibility is such that the pleasant bucolic dream is only a wish for what might have been, a regret for a life that cannot be his. His appeal to Lycoris (*Eclogue* 10.42–3) to come share this paradise with him can be read as a further proof that he is living in a dream world where wishes are powerless and cannot come true.[13]

The dream is bound to remain unreal, but the image of joy it contains has caught Gallus's eye and has brought a sharper awareness of the dark side of elegiac passion. The fulfillment of the dream is hindered by the reality that breaks in to thwart the wish (*Eclogue*

---

[13] In the phrase *quicumque furor* ('whatever madness'), in *Eclogue* 10.38, the noun remains elegiac without being able to melt into the new bucolic atmosphere: later, *furor* is again one of the culminating words expressing Gallus's unconditional surrender to passion and his renunciation of all resistance to it (*Eclogue* 10.69): *tamquam haec sit nostri medicina furoris* ('As if this be medicine for my madness'). In Ovid's 'Triumph of Love', *Amores* 1.2.25 ff.—a mocking parody of a solemn Roman triumph (constructed by antiphrastic allusion to Virgil, *Aeneid* 1.291–6),—one of the elegiac personifications in Eros's train is, significantly, called Furor: see Labate 1971.

10.44): *nunc* ('now'). But the reality of the elegiac life lacerates the dream and inevitably casts a shadow over elegiac poetry, whose distinctive status—its encoding within literature—involves a chosen way of life. If the life of the elegiac poet is a hard one, why should the blame not be laid on the literary ideology—an artistic but also an existential code—that, as a model, actually imposes laws of behavior on its adepts? To represent the harsh reality that endangers the attractive vision to which Gallus was already yielding, Virgil simply puts into Gallus's mouth the lines that Gallus had once used to lament his misfortune.[14] They are worth examining to see how this negative reality emerges in all its destructive power to dissolve the dream:

> nunc insanus amor duri me Martis in armis
> tela inter media atque adversos detinet hostis:
> tu procul a patria, nec sit mihi credere tantum!
> Alpinas, a! dura nives et frigora Rheni
> me sine sola vides. a! te ne frigora laedant!
> a! tibi ne teneras glacies secet aspera plantas! (44–9)

But now a mad passion for the harsh god of war keeps me in arms, in the midst of weapons and the opposing enemy; while you, cruel, far from your native land—I would not believe such a report—look on Alpine snow and the ice-bound Rhine, alone and without me. Ah, may the frosts not harm you! Ah, may the jagged ice not cut your tender feet!

Instead of rural delight and unruffled union between Gallus and Lycoris, there is an irremediable separation of the two lovers, who are subject to the inflexible laws of war that not only keep them apart but are such that the wishes of the one are different from, or opposite to, those of the other. Thus Gallus must once again experience the conflict due to being an elegiac poet; his is a love that never reaches

---

[14] In commenting on *Eclogue* 10.46, Servius writes: *hi autem omnes versus Galli sunt de ipsius translati carminibus* ('These are the verses of Gallus translated from the poems of the author himself'). Propertius's elegy 1.8 confirms this point, and the obvious resemblances between this elegy and *Eclogue* 10.46–9 leave no doubt that Propertius wrote it on the model of the elegy by Gallus that Virgil is reproducing to some extent here. See Alfonsi 1949. In any case, Servius's remark applies to a larger passage—probably to virtually all of what in Virgil has become a monologue spoken by Gallus: see F. Skutsch 1901: 18 ff.; Jacoby 1905: 74 ff.; and, most specifically, my discussion below comparing the monologue with Tibullus 1.10, and the pages that follow it.

the point of achieving calm satisfaction (but would he really want calm satisfaction?) and is primarily suffering, while gratification inevitably is relegated to dreams or to a mythical golden age located in the distant past. This same elegiac reality Tibullus would express:

> quis fuit, horrendos primus qui protulit enses?
> quam ferus et vere ferreus ille fuit! (1.10.1–2)

Who first discovered the horrible sword? How harsh he was and truly of iron.

For Tibullus, or for Gallus, war divides lovers; Tibullus goes on, a few lines later:

> divitis hoc vitium est auri, nec bella fuerunt,
> faginus astabat cum scyphus ante dapes.
> non arces, non vallus erat, somnumque petebat
> securus varias dux gregis inter oves.
> tunc mihi vita foret vulgi nec tristia nossem
> arma nec audissem corde micante tubam.
> *nunc* ad bella trahor, et iam quis forsitan hostis
> haesura in nostro tela gerit latere. (1.10.7–14)

This is the curse of precious gold; nor were there wars when the cup of beech stood before the banquet. There were no citadels, no palisades, and the lord of the flock, free of care, would nap among the vari-colored sheep. Had I lived then, I would not have known the grief-inflicting wars of the common soldier nor have heard, with thrilling heart, the trumpet of war. *Now* I am drawn to war and now, perhaps, some enemy bears a weapon that will pierce my ribs.

Nunc combines temporal function with an adversative force and makes it plain that the adversative cause is none other than the present reality; indeed, it signals the return to the present. The function of *nunc* with adversative value (like the Greek νῦν δέ) may be seen, for example, in Sallust (*Jugurtha* 14.24) and with equally dramatic effect in *Aeneid* 10.628–30. But this instance from Tibullus most clearly illustrates its special thematic use. In the elegiac poets it is often used in antithesis to *utinam*, contrasting dreams with reality.

After the dream interval, the present is restored and with it the suffering, the *insanus amor*. Only now the *insania* ('madness') is no longer a matter of clinging stubbornly to a love that yields nothing but unhappiness. Apollo had ruthlessly warned Gallus (*Eclogue* 10.22–3): *Galle, quid insanis? tua cura Lycoris | perque nives alium perque horrida castra secuta est* ('Gallus, why are you mad? Your concern, Lycoris, has followed another through the snows and through the grim camps'). Now (*nunc*) that Gallus has experienced the sweetness of bucolic life, the *insania* is *amor duri Martis* ('love of harsh war').[15] Yes, he almost protests, in answering Apollo, this is true madness, the madness that keeps him tied to the world of war, which is intrinsically hostile to love (Propertius's verdict in 3.5.1 is *pacis Amor deus est, pacem veneramur amantes*, 'Love is the god of peace, we lovers venerate peace'). The contradiction within elegiac poetry (which expresses a love made of contrasting features) is felt so vividly here and comes so near to total breakdown that it produces a sign of repulsion and rejection (*Eclogue* 10.50): *ibo et* ('I shall go and').

Let us pause for a moment to reconsider the ways in which this bitter, brutal reality reemerges and, once it has won command, smothers Gallus's daydreaming. Just when the stream of thought seems to be about to distance the reader from the initial picture of grief, the reader is brought back sharply to it. The unexpected sequence of the propositions paradoxically unleashes the driving force needed to make the dramatic action surge forward again. It is not just a question of finding the initial position unchanged: the reappearance of the initial suffering itself contains an active element that, for a moment at least, will prevent the tormented mind of

---

[15] I see no serious reason for not interpreting in the following way, by linking *duri... Martis* with *insanus amor*, according to a syntactic construction that, besides being straightforward, keeps the logical subject of the sentence—the *amans* whose *insania* is asserted—connected with *me*, which (as required by the sense) bitterly subjectivizes the line, since it holds the personal pronoun in the vise of the *duri... Martis* nexus. Those who interpret the phrase by linking the genitive with *armis* are obviously thinking of its correspondence with *Eclogue* 10.22, *Galle, quid insanis?* But this approach (as noted by E. Pfeiffer 1933: 53 and n. 55) weakens the contrast between *Eclogue* 10.44–5 and the preceding lines; in addition, the lines in question seem disconnected or at least read oddly: 'If I were a shepherd I would pass my life happily and quietly with Phyllis or Lycoris, but my great passion [for Lycoris] keeps me among the weapons of Mars' (Tibullus 1.10). In any case, one should not overlook the real circumstance that Gallus was a politician and soldier; this established the specific situation (doubtless reflected in his poetry, as the lines just quoted testify) of an existential conflict that was intensely felt throughout elegiac literature. The words *insanus amor duri... Martis* ('mad love of harsh war') seem to carry the innuendo of a contrasting ambition in Gallus to be *miles tenerae Veneris* ('a soldier of tender Venus') instead—an ambition made unattainable by the harshness of life and destiny.

Gallus from falling back into elegiac pining and yearning. He does so only later (*Eclogue* 10.60), once he has seen all the opportunities for salvation offered to him by his friend's gift fail. Thereafter Gallus has no choice but to yield himself to himself—to the life of an elegiac poet. At this moment, however, his dominant impulse is an almost joyful one—to reject his own situation by taking the way out that has been given him by Virgil, who has let him take on the mythical role of Daphnis the shepherd (*Eclogue* 10.50-1):

> ibo et, Chalcidico quae sunt mihi condita versu
> carmina, pastoris Siculi modulabor avena.

I will go, and the songs I composed in Chalcidian verse I will play on a Sicilian shepherd's pipe.

Just as the return from bucolic daydreaming to the true reality of being an unhappy lover meant evoking through his own elegiac lines the painful 'realism' of his 'autobiographical' poems (*nunc*), so now his escape from the painfulness of this form of life analogously, and inevitably, appears as a refusal of the lines that represent that life— in other words, a relinquishing of elegiac poetry. It could not be otherwise, since the basic convention of such poetry is truth to life; more exactly, it makes such truth its preliminary 'pretense'—the distinctive criterion of its literary code.[16]

[16] Such an approach accounts for the apparent paradox that the elegiac poets— most strikingly Propertius—are admired as poets of ardent, personally experienced passion, as prime examples of *Erlebnisdichtung*, whereas philologists could not avoid demonstrating their use of convention and 'literariness'. This contradiction then spread from the personality of individual elegiac poets to literary genre. The Latin love elegy was called subjective in contrast with the supposed objectivity of the Greek elegy, but when it was meticulously scrutinized by philologists, all that remained was an apparatus of themes and motifs already found in Greek love poetry. Several shrewd remarks on the 'sincerity' of the Roman love elegy—interpreted not as authentically reporting autobiographical 'true-to-life' experiences but as a general stylistic manner, that is, the constitutive form and expressive function of elegiac language—are contained in Allen 1962 (the critical scope of the discussion should, however, have been widened to comprise the status of every literary text, and the function and procedures typical of the literary process). In the last analysis even that shrewd scholar David O. Ross in Ross 1975, seems to fall back, even if involuntarily and despite all his precautions, into biographism, perhaps not as regards Cornelius Gallus the soldier and politician, but at least as regards Gallus *the poet* (see n. 8). Ross had already written the valuable *Style and Tradition in Catullus* (Ross 1969), in which basic lines of interpretative theory were taken up as presuppositions; they were developed in the later volume in important discussions. Unless I am mistaken, his

In referring to a relinquishing of elegiac poetry, I meant a sacrifice only of its orientation—of the way in which that experience had been organized in forms belonging to literature and to life. What had really failed was only the context, the form of the experience, the mold given to feelings by external reality. Even harsh Lycoris turned sweet again when placed in the pastoral shade of bucolic life. But this first attempt, as we have seen, ended in failure. Gallus must now try another form of defense against the poison of love. Love remains, but the context in which it is to be fulfilled must change. Gallus will now try to experience nature in the wild state, living in uninhabited forests and hunting on the mountains. In terms of poetics, the same thing could be expressed by saying that what had been elegy must now become pastoral poetry.

It is important to note the way in which Virgil expresses himself. Gallus will not throw away his poetry; he will simply add the melody of the Sicilian shepherd to the *carmina* he has already written in Chalcidian meter. The sense of every libretto inclines to that of the music that is to accompany it, and every piece adapts itself to the register that the interpreter favors. Put in the clearest possible terms, Gallus is saying, 'I will change my way of life so as not to suffer any more, and change my way of writing poetry too. I will adapt that poetry of erotic passion, written in the elegiac mode, to the flute of a Sicilian shepherd. The bucolic hexameter will replace the elegiac couplet. The change in poetic code will be enough to confer freedom on themes otherwise marked by their subjection to the harsh yoke of Eros. The power of the register will be fully displayed in the "rewriting" of what has already been sung—and already lived—and such rewriting can, in itself, become a new way of life.'[17] The locus of Eros

suggestion in Ross 1975: 87 n. 2 is that to some extent Gallus experiences a real crisis of literary vocation and decides to abandon, of the two types of poetry he has written, the mythological type and to dedicate himself exclusively to the subjective elegy (97 n. 4). In my view, however, the literary biography of Gallus is not the right place to look for the crisis. The literary biography is simply the structural setting within which the poetic conflict that Virgil establishes between the genres—bucolic and elegiac—achieves dialectical expression and dynamic representation.

[17] The abrupt movement of these lines, which is heightened by the colloquial expressiveness of the *ibo et... modulabor* nexus, effectively and immediately conveys Gallus's decision to react decisively against the torment of a situation that has become intolerable. It also echoes the discontinuous, elliptical sequence of thought that, perhaps even earlier than Propertius (conceivably in Gallus), had been given to the

and of the suffering elegiac poet was the town; the new locus must be far from Eros and unknown to him, in the forests, near the dens of wild animals: *certum est in silvis, inter spelaea ferarum* ('It is my firm purpose (to dwell) amid the wild beasts' dens'; *Eclogue* 10.52). The way to avoid yielding to the affliction of love will be to run freely to the mountains, hunting. Venus will no longer be the one and only goddess; the chief goddess will be Diana. He now prefers—we might say—the open spaces of the forest to the closed door of the girl he loves. When Ovid, after teaching how to practice deceptions in love, began to take pleasure in prescribing remedies for it, he inevitably recommended the following cure:

> vel tu venandi studium cole: saepe recessit
> turpiter a Phoebi victa sorore Venus.
> nunc leporem pronum catulo sectare sagaci,
> nunc tua frondosis retia tende iugis,

impetuous 'Gefühlsentwicklung' (development of sentiment) of elegiac expression (see Bréguet 1948). Propertius uses very similar expressive movement marked by an initial impulse that is no less brusque in 2.10, when he tests his decision to become an epic poet and to pay tribute at last to the great period of the Roman Empire and the triumphs of its ruler. Here too the metabasis to another poetic genre takes shape as if it were an outburst of this new bard's enthusiasm in leaving behind the old love themes (which, in any case, he does not repudiate but seems to localize in his youth). He too imagines himself living in the new world he has chosen and already sees himself as a poet of wars and riots; it is another poetic world, another *cithara* ('lyre'): *nunc aliam citharam me mea Musa docet* ('Now my Muse teaches me another lyre'; Propertius 2.10.10). Thus it seems that Propertius not only drew from the tenth *Eclogue* the surface features that distinguish the soliloquy of Gallus the shepherd in Virgil but also decided to take over the metaliterary sense of the eclogue (only implicit in Virgil), making it into a personal poetic manifesto. The signals of this operation are clear (and a few of them were picked up by Rothstein, an expert detector of *loci similes*): first, from Propertius 2.10: *sed tempus*...(1); *iam libet*...(2); *iam libet*...(3); *nunc volo*...(9); *nunc*...(10); *iam*...(11); *iam*...(13). In Virgil, *Eclogue* 10, we gave the sequence: *ibo et*...(50); *certum est*...(52); *iam mihi...videor...| ire*...(58–9); *libet*...(59). For the second parallel sequence, we have in Propertius 2.10.1 *lustrare* and in Eclogue 10.55 *lustrabo* and then Propertius 2.10.10: *nunc aliam citharam me mea Musa docet* ('now my Muse teaches me another instrument') and Virgil, *Eclogue* 10.50–1: *Chalcido quae sunt mihi mihi condita versu | carmina, pastoris Siculi modulabor avena* ('I shall play on the reed of a Sicilian shepherd the songs that I composed in Chalcidian verse'). Finally, we have the parallel use of the future tense in the two sequences. Another important point must be made: the literary function that Propertius presents is like that of a *recusatio* although of a special kind. In the end he postpones to an indeterminate future his inauguration of a new kind of poetry, although at first this appeared to be a choice that he had already made: he lets his enthusiasms evaporate, like Virgil's Gallus.

> aut pavidos terre varia formidine cervos,
> aut cadat adversa cuspide fossus aper.
> (*Remedia Amoris* 199–204)

Or cultivate the pleasures of the chase; often has Venus, vanquished by Phoebus's sister, beaten a loose retreat. Now pursue with cunning hound the forward-straining hare, now stretch your nets on leafy ridges; or else with varied panic alarm the timid deer, or meet the boar and fell him with your spear thrust.

There is no doubt that Gallus here has fully decided to implement his choice and to live a new life. His resolution to leave Venus for chaste Diana is born of despair. By contrast, Propertius in 2.19 envisages a similar refusal of town life and chooses the cult of Diana the huntress, not to escape from love and from proximity to his lady, but for just the opposite reason: his choice is due to a stubborn determination to stay near her and never leave her without his kind attentions. Cynthia has moved from the town to the country, to stay in a villa. Propertius might be expected to lament her absence and feel anguish at her coldness in wishing to live far from him; but paradoxically he pretends to be glad, since he is an expert at making a virtue of necessity. There at least—so the poet consoles himself—Cynthia will be chaste. Where Diana reigns, there will be none of the mishaps of the elegiac life, no flattery by young men eager to court her, no noisy serenades under her windows, no risk of her making new men friends in town—in other words, no temptations. But even as he jokes paradoxically, Propertius does not forget that it is his duty to perform the *servitium amoris*. It is not enough to accept the capricious egoism of the girl he loves, even if he turns it into a game: the elegiac lover, even when his lady leaves him in a painful solitude, must follow her wherever she goes. An elegiac topos based on mythical exempla required him not to shun unusual hardships and distressing ordeals but rather to stay near his loved one and thus show her his unfailing constancy. As Propertius states,[18]

> Milanion nullos fugiendo, Tulle, labores
> saevitiam durae contudit Iasidos.

---

[18] The setting is the same as that chosen by Gallus: *Eclogue* 10.57 (*Partheniis... in antris*) = Propertius 1.1.11 (*Parthenios... saltus*) and *Eclogue* 10.58 (*per rupes*) = Propertius 1.1.14 (*Arcadiis rupibus*). See also Ross 1975: 61–5 and 90–1.

> nam modo Partheniis amens errabat in antris
> ibat et hirsutas ille videre feras;
> ille etiam Hylaei percussus vulnere rami
> saucius Arcadiis rupibus ingemuit.
> ergo velocem potuit domuisse puellam:
> tantum in amore preces et benefacta valent.   (1.1.9–16)

Yet Milanion shrank not, Tullus, from any labors, however hard, and so subdued the cruel heart of the unrelenting daughter of Iasus. For now he wandered love-distraught in the glens of Mt. Parthenion and went to face the shaggy creatures of the wild. Moreover, stunned by the wound from the club of Hylaeus, he groaned in pain in the rocks of Arcadia. So at last was he able to conquer the swift-footed maid; such is the reward that prayers and loyal service have for love.

Perseverance in love knows no limits. When Cynthia chooses the wild solitude of the countryside, Propertius the townsman has no alternative but to take up country life and dedicate himself to rural activities. To stay near her and please her, he too will live among solitary groves (*solae... silvae*) and meandering streams fallen from mossy ridges (*vaga muscosis flumina fusa iuga*; 2.19.29–30); he will leave his usual goddess, Venus, and will become a devotee of Diana:

> ipse ego venabor: iam nunc me sacra Dianae
> suscipere et Veneris ponere vota iuvat.[19]
> incipiam captare feras et reddere pinu
> cornua et audaces ipse monere canes.   (2.19.17–20)

---

[19] Like Barber and Camps, I read *Veneris* (this is a conjecture found in the *deteriores*, whereas the tradition gives *Veneri*, as do nearly all the editors); the proposal 'Veneris' was first made by Housman 1888: 6 (= 1972: 33). The correction seems to be indispensable, since it is required by the sense of the sentence (and by the whole elegy). Now that Propertius is to rejoin Cynthia in the chaste countryside, he himself will take up the chaste pastimes of Diana the huntress: 'By now I wish only to adopt the rites of Diana and give up the cult of Venus.' *Vota Veneris* is a metonymic variant of the previous *sacra Dianae*, and *ponere* (*simplex pro composito* (= *deponere*)) contrasts semantically with *suscipere*. The repeated attempts by Enk to justify the reading 'I will follow the cult of Diana and dedicate the trophies of hunting to Venus' are unconvincing; such gifts would be not only senseless but also in deplorable taste for a lover. The sense of the phrase lies in the contrast it establishes; one must expect a thought like that which appears in the passage (quoted above) from Ovid, *Remedia amoris* 199–200, *saepe recessit | turpiter a Phoebi victa sorore Venus*, or its equivalent (quoted below in the text) from Tibullus 4.3.19–20, *nunc sine me sit nulla Venus, sed lege Dianae | caste puer* ('Now let there be no love without me, but under the rule of Diana, chaste boy'). Of course, Propertius smilingly corrects his intentions to betray his

An Interpretation of the Tenth Eclogue

I myself will hunt; right now my joy is to perform the sacrifices of Diana and to put the vows of Venus aside. I will begin to snare wild beasts, to nail trophies of horns to the pine tree, and with my own voice to urge on the bold hounds.

This is the utmost form of *obsequium* to which Propertius yields, obedient (as Milanion had been before him) to a rule of the elegiac relationship. Ovid was to make it one of his precepts.[20]

What is more, when Tibullus speaks through his invention, Sulpicia, whose lover, Cerinthus, is fond of hunting, he does not fail to attribute the same intention to her:

> sed tamen, ut tecum liceat, Cerinthe, vagari,
>   ipsa ego per montes retia torta feram,
> ipsa ego velocis quaeram vestigia cervi,
>   et demam celeri ferrea vincla cani.
> tunc mihi, tunc placeant silvae, si, lux mea, tecum
>   arguar ante ipsas concubuisse plagas.
>   . . .
> nunc sine me sit nulla Venus, sed lege Dianae,
>   caste puer, casta retia tange manu.   (4.3.11–16 + 19–20)

goddess. He knows quite well that in this case leaving Venus for chaste Diana is the very best way of honoring the goddess of love. Venus herself, in fact, has chosen the country now that Cynthia has gone to live there, so it is not the devotee who has changed faith but the goddess who has changed her place of abode. Tibullus tells us so more openly:

> rura meam, Cornute, tenent villaeque puellam:
>   ferreus est, heu, heu, quisquis in urbe manet.
> ipsa Venus latos iam nunc migravit in agros,
>   verbaque aratoris rustica discit Amor.   (2.3.1–4)

(The countryside and my estates, Cornutus, hold my love; O he is made of iron, who remains in the city. Yes, now Venus herself has moved to the open land, and Cupid is learning the plowman's country dialect.) Tibullus, of course, intends to take up work that will be new to him—plowing.

[20] *Ars amatoria* 2.117–96. It appears to be still more significant that, earlier, Tibullus in 1.4—when Priapus composes an *ars amatoria* on seducing boys—does not fail to recommend the form of *obsequium* (*obsequio plurima vincit Amor,* 'by obedience love conquers most'; 1.4.40) that leads the lover to follow the boy he loves when the latter goes out hunting:

> nec te paeniteat duros subiisse labores
>   aut opera insuetas atteruisse manus.
> nec, velit insidiis altas si claudere valles,
>   dum placeas, umeri retia ferre negent.   (1.4.47–50)

(Do not be reluctant to endure hard labor or to callus hands unused to work; nor, if he wish to set his snares in steep glens, should your shoulders balk at carrying the nets—as long as you please him.)

Yet still, Cerinthus, that I may roam with you, I will carry the woven nets across the mountains myself, follow the tracks of the running deer myself, and undo the iron collar of the straining hound. Then, then, the forest would please me, when it can be shown that I have lain beside you, my love, right before the trap.... But now let there be no love without me; but, under the rule of Diana, chaste boy, hold the nets with a chaste hand.

Taken as a whole, Roman love elegy includes in its major theme of *servitium amoris* (equivalent to love) the lover who, through *obsequium* ('obedience') is prepared even to become a devotee of Diana.[21] The recurrence of this motif throughout the history of Latin elegy allows us to reconstruct a lineage whose founding father one may reasonably suppose to have been Gallus. One may surmise that Gallus told Lycoris, now living far from home, that, as her devoted lover, he was ready to rejoin her in any place, however wild and inhospitable, and that—if by this means he could stay beside her—he would even live in the woods and hunt wild beasts. We may observe, too, the convergence between the words of Gallus as hunter in Virgil (*Eclogue* 10.58–9): *iam mihi... videor... libet* and the movement quoted from Propertius (2.19.17–18): *iam nunc me... iuvat.* If *Eclogue* 10.52–60 (*certum est in silvis... interea... venabor... iam mihi per rupes videor lucosque*, 'I'm determined to wander in the woods... meanwhile I'll hunt... even now I seem to be wandering over rocks and through groves') are a rewriting of what Gallus had put into Chalcidic verse, Gallus must have written words like those for Lycoris in his elegies; if so, it may be inferred that Gallus really is the initiator of the line that we have just reconstructed.

Let us now examine this topos from another angle. A specific and certainly not coincidental resemblance had attracted the attention of Franz Skutsch, but it had bewildered rather than enlightened him. To understand it, he would have needed a grasp of the dialectic between the elegiac tradition, which this resemblance presupposed, and the meaning of the tenth *Eclogue*, the metaliterary meaning that underlies a conflict between genres. These lines of Gallus's soliloquy

---

[21] This behavior by the elegiac lover is brought back to the same mythical roots by Ovid. In the *Metamorphoses* 10.518–36 Venus herself, for once, is the victim—even if accidentally—of the arrows of Love, after taking on all the attributes of Diana to go hunting with her love, Adonis.

(especially *Eclogue* 10.55–60) are modeled on the delirium of lovesick Phaedra, who is longing to rejoin her stepson Hippolytus—a devotee of the chaste arts of Diana:

> πέμπετέ μ' εἰς ὄρος. εἶμι πρὸς ὕλαν
> καὶ παρὰ πεύκας, ἵνα θηροφόνοι
> στείβουσι κύνες
> βαλιαῖς ἐλάφοις ἐγκριμπτόμεναι.
> πρὸς θεῶν· ἔραμαι κυσὶ θωΰξαι
> καὶ παρὰ χαίταν ξανθὰν ῥῖψαι
> Θεσσαλὸν ὅρπακ', ἐπίλογχον ἔχουσ'
> ἐν χειρὶ βέλος.   (Euripides, *Hippolytus* 215–21)

Lead me to the mountain; I am going to the pine forest, where the deadly hounds stalk and pursue the spotted deer. O please, I have a passion to set on the dogs and to throw a Thessalian spear from beside this golden hair, aiming it with my own hand.

But something important is out of place in this close parallelism. Phaedra imagines she is on the mountains because of her uncontrollable wish to be with her beloved Hippolytus, whereas Gallus seems to yearn for those mountains for the opposite reason—to escape the torment and obsession of love. This contradiction could give rise to serious difficulties. Both Gallus and Phaedra belong to the literary lineage we have just traced through the elegiac tradition, but the elegiac poets who follow their precursor Gallus seem to repeat the ritual of *obsequium* to love first seen in Phaedra, not its opposite, found in Gallus, who aims to find freedom and a cure for love. This parallel appears to vitiate the reconstruction that led us to recognize Gallus as the originator, in Latin, of the *ipse ego venabor* motif. Instead of being (as he actually is) the earliest link through which the ἐρωτικὸν πάθημα of Phaedra became part of the 'language' of the Latin elegy, he would now have to be assigned an eccentric position with respect to the development of this theme.[22] There can be no

---

[22] Here one need only recall the active, even if not always direct, relationship linking many of the motifs of Greek tragedy with Latin love poetry. The ἐρωτικὰ παθήματα ('erotic anguishes'), which take on the dignity of tragic performance in Euripides, never ceased to exert a fascination over the elegiac poets (in some cases via Alexandrian mythological fiction, which was particularly fond of giving free play to the thoughts of its heroes and heroines in soliloquies). The story of Phaedra and the two tragic versions by Euripides seem to have been a favorite starting point

escape from this impasse until the Kataloggedicht hypothesis, in all its possible disguises, has been definitely demolished. We reject the idea that the tenth *Eclogue* harbors an inert collection of fragments from the work of Gallus, unaffected by the creation of a new relationship between them or by rearrangement within a dynamic contextual framework.

As noted above, Virgil offers Gallus, who is pining away, the gift of his poetry to bring about his friend's recovery. Virgil would be a bad doctor, however, if he simply offered Gallus, as a cure, the source of his illness—the writing of elegiac poetry. Gallus himself, convinced that the remedy will work, reveals the secret: his elegiac poetry, the root of his trouble, should be rewritten and turned into its opposite so that the cause of the harm can be rendered innocuous by its antidote. Thus his poetry, as it appears after his firm decision to take to the forest (*ibo et... modulabor... certum est*), is transformed. It is no longer an expression of elegiac motifs but the rewriting of those motifs as liberated in the bucolic register.[23] Thus a contrast is set up between the tenth *Eclogue* (whose *Virgilian* Gallus has now given poetry the stamp of freedom), and the Phaedra of Euripides plus the elegiac tradition that springs from it (through the *elegiac* Gallus).

Consequently there is no contradiction between Gallus who goes to the mountains to escape love and Phaedra who longs to be there to find it. There is a *contrast*—a contrast deliberately aiming at the redemption and recovery of Gallus by literary means. Just as the elegy can reverse its character, becoming bucolic, so too the Phaedra theme (the lover who searches to find love in the woods) can change into that of the lover who tries to escape from love in those same woods. Virgil's intervention is an affectionate rewriting of what his

---

for the concentration, expansion, and development of some of the major themes in Latin love poetry: (1) *eros-nosos*: sickness of love, a destructive force capable of enslaving lovers and exhausting them, (2) *eros anikêtos*: unconquerable love, which ruthlessly overpowers anyone who tries to oppose its divine power and only restores those who bend their necks to its yoke (see e.g. Euripides, *Hippolytus* 5–6, 443–6; Tibullus 1.8.7–8 and K. F. Smith 1913 *ad loc.*; Ovid, *Amores* 1.2.7–18), and (3) *eros didaskalos*: love, the teacher, which instills strength into lovers and teaches them how to go through any test (see Euripides, *Hippolytos Kalyptomenos*, *TGF* fr. 430; Tibullus 1.1.19–20 and K. F. Smith 1913 *ad loc.*; Ovid, *Heroides* 4.10; *Amores* 1.6.7; 3.1.49).

[23] On the concept of 'register', see Conte 1986: 88–95.

friend had already written, almost as if guiding his uncertain hand, in an attempt to free him. The man who had likened himself to Phaedra in his 'madness' (*insanire*) now declares—in words resembling the ones he had spoken then—that he wishes instead to follow the model of Daphnis.

Daphnis resisted Aphrodite, even though it cost him his life: Virgil offers Gallus this example. The fact that Gallus accepts the gift of his bucolic friend and becomes Daphnis allows him to reverse his previous behavior. He had once learned from the exemplum of Phaedra and imitated her submission to the *insania* of love: now he can try antagonism rather than servitude to Eros. Thus Virgil's help—his gift—can take effect only insofar as Gallus does *not* repeat his own experience as an elegiac poet. Refuge within the bucolic can set him free only to the extent that the bucolic register has linked it indissolubly with the suffering due to lovesickness.

It is now time that we step back to consider a feature set aside earlier so that our full attention could focus on the main level, that of the reversal of the elegiac register into a bucolic one within Gallus's soliloquy. On closer inspection, Gallus's act of refusal comprises two distinct movements, each of which involves the rewriting of an elegiac poem already written by him. The motif of the lover who finds relief for his suffering in wild, uninhabited places and cuts the name of his lady on the tender bark of trees seems itself to reveal a recognizably elegiac nature, which is warranted by its significant place among the gifts left to all the Latin elegiac poets by their master, Callimachus.[24] It is now clearer and more plausible that the freeing of Gallus begins with the resumption—now in a bucolic register—of the motif of 'suffering in the woods and cutting love into trees' (*incidere amores arboribus*). After this first stage of passive participation in the wild bucolic landscape, Gallus, with the *ipse ego venabor* motif, proceeds—in a crescendo—to the second stage, that of an active participation in that world. This participation brings a greater degree of freedom.

But the thoughtful affection of a friend can go only so far, and here the illness is stronger than the cure. Earlier, the harsh reality of a life

---

[24] Callimachus *fr.* 73 Pf. = Propertius 1.18; see also Ovid, *Heroides* 5.21 ff.; for further parallels and discussion, see Jacoby 1905: 58–9.

tied to military commitments (*Eclogue* 10.44–9, 'nunc') made the longing for a calm bucolic love recede into unreality. But now that Gallus has accepted the remedy of his friend, from despair, and has followed Daphnis's example in resisting Eros, he realizes that a capacity to resist does not guarantee the end of suffering. For Gallus, freedom from Eros means freedom from pain; the first effect of the remedy should have been to free his heart from pain. Conversely, when Daphnis resisted Eros, his ability to stand firm demanded a virile willingness to suffer: pain was the necessary complement to an integrity he defended until he died. So when Gallus realizes his suffering will continue in any case, he inevitably succumbs, yielding to his old self:

> ... tamquam haec sit nostri medicina furoris,
> aut deus ille malis hominum mitescere discat.
> iam neque Amadryades rursus nec carmina nobis
> ipsa placent; ipsae rursus concedite silvae.   (*Eclogue* 10.60–4)

As if this could heal my frenzy or as if that god would learn to grow gentle toward human sorrows. Now neither Hamadryads nor even songs have charms for me; ye very woods, once more withdraw.[25]

This outcome was only to be expected. It is true that if the hardest *labores* are accepted in an elegiac spirit, they may win the favor of the loved girl, but it is also true that they are powerless to change the cruel nature of the god of love. As often in Latin love poetry, the invincibility of Eros is made plain in a whole series of hyperboles (*Eclogue* 10.64–8),[26] and it is now given its most perfectly elegiac formulation: *omnia vincit Amor, et nos cedamus Amori* ('Love conquers all—we, too, must yield to love'; *Eclogue* 10.69).[27]

---

[25] The use of the imperative of *concedere* is a standard formula in comedies; it shows when a character must leave the stage. It is almost as if Gallus, at this point in the action, finds he must dismiss the bucolic setting that has been set up for him as an ephemeral mise-en-scène.

[26] *Sithŏnius* for 'Thracian' is a rare toponym whose appearance here seems to call for the hypothesis of its use by Gallus, who may well have been responsible for its introduction into the lexis of Latin poetry (if so, Virgil's use of it is an allusion!); in the precious Alexandrian poet Euphorion, much admired by Gallus, its only occurrence (Euphorion fr. 63.2 van Groningen) has the same prosodic form, with -ŏ-.

[27] This line displays several features suggesting that its author was Gallus. In any case, in the last line Virgil could most effectively have given Gallus his own words to speak—words that mark an elegiac climax. More specific considerations, too, arouse

An Interpretation of the Tenth Eclogue

Gallus's decision to give up definitely terminates contact between the elegiac and bucolic forms. Any possibility of resolving the elegiac conflict in bucolic terms is now excluded. Gallus goes his own way again; Virgil, now left alone, returns to his muses.[28] But his gift has not disappeared. As a remedy it may have failed, but the poem written for Gallus remains. Could it not be said, too, that, even if Virgil's Gallus has not fulfilled his thoughtful friend's plans for him, the very fact stands as a proof to Lycoris of the irresistible strength of Gallus's love for her? This, I believe, is the gift Virgil wished to offer, a gift dedicated to Lycoris as well as to Gallus: *quae legat ipsa Lycoris* ('something that Lycoris herself may read'). The elegiac convention made each poem a proof of love, an act of homage capable of winning over a lady, a piece of courting.[29] This was just what Gallus needed to flatter Lycoris. He must, in fact, have been the first to perform this lover's act of homage to his lady (an act that came to be

---

the suspicion that Gallus was responsible for line 69, at least (even if it was probably reworked by Virgil). First, *omnia vincit amor* ('love conquers all'), as shown by Grondona 1977: 26–7, resembles a hemistich from an elegiac pentameter, and its metrical and semantic structure was often imitated within the diadochê of the Roman elegiac poets (see the various comments on this line). Second, there is the predilection shown by Tibullus (and, through his influence, by later elegiac poets) for ending elegies with the anaphora, with polyptoton, of a single word that moves from the first hemistich to the second in the last line (Grondona 1977: 28), as here: *amor... amori*. Might this stylistic device go back to Gallus? Third, Ovid allusively reworks the second half of the line in a proemial (and programmatic) elegy near the beginning of the first book of *Amores*, in 2.9–10: *cedimus an subitum luctando accendimus ignem? | cedamus: leve fit, quod bene fertur, onus* ('Shall I yield or by resisting ignite the latent flame? Let me yield. Light grows the burden that is well borne'). This too seems to derive from an authoritative model by Gallus.

[28] Virgil now reconsiders his work with a reflective attitude; serene and detached, the poet sits weaving the symbol of poetry itself: *gracili fiscellam texit hibisco* ('he weaves a basket from pliant reeds'; *Eclogue* 10.71); on this symbol, see Pöschl 1964. He has finished his last eclogue and with it his *libellus*, so the shepherd-poet is ready to leave his flock. He has carried out the poetic program he had set himself in the proem to his sixth *Eclogue*: the declaration of a poetics valid for the whole of his bucolic poetry. His task was *deductum dicere carmen* ('to recite fine-spun verse') and also *pingues pascere oves* ('to pasture *well-fed sheep*'). His flock is now well fed, and the poet can say farewell to it: *ite domum saturae, venit Hesperus, ite capellae* ('Get yourselves home, my *full-fed* goats—the Evening Star comes—get home'; *Eclogue* 10.77).

[29] See the valuable study of Stroh 1971. It investigates the function of the elegy in winning the love of a woman by courting her (for our purposes, see especially 204 and 228, but in this connection see also Antonio La Penna's review of Stroh (1975: 139)).

expected of an elegiac poet), as a recently discovered papyrus has confirmed.[30] This find has, incidentally, finally dispelled a nightmare that obsesses (or ought to obsess) any philologist who tries to reconstruct a poet's work conjecturally, on the basis of a few scattered bits of evidence.

Before the find occurred, all inferences about Gallus, including mine, were condemned to circularity. We might in fact say that, to be understood, the tenth *Eclogue* requires us to posit the existence of an earlier, extraneous text with which Virgil's eclogue was to be contrasted. But information about this earlier text had necessarily to be drawn from Virgil's text, which became the end point of all inferential reasoning and also a source of proof. As one might imagine, proof in this matter is not so simple; in rebuilding the Gallan model, one must actually have recourse to texts by Propertius and Tibullus, as we have done here. Now, however, the chance discovery of poetry by Gallus on papyrus places us in a strong position. Even if what has been recovered is all too small (about ten lines, some of them incomplete), these fragments allow us to draw at least three basic conclusions. First, they confirm that Gallus wrote in elegiac couplets on a subjective theme; second, one of the phrases to have survived happens to be addressed directly to Lycoris—*tristia nequitia...Lycori tua* ('grievous...by your wantonness, Lycoris')—where all four words taken singly and together show Gallus in the lamenting attitude attributed to him in the tenth *Eclogue*; and, third, it is striking (and for our purposes this is the most significant discovery) that Lycoris appears as the *domina* and addressee of the poem, so that Virgil's *quae legat ipsa Lycoris* should be compared with Gallus' own *carmina | quae possem domina dicere digna mea* ('verses that I might speak worthy of my mistress').

Bucolic poetry just this once, in the tenth *Eclogue,* approaches the condition of 'werbende Dichtung'—the poetry of courting. Its presupposition is that, when Lycoris reads the eclogue, she will be flattered to see that the yoke of love she has placed on Gallus's shoulders has stayed firmly in place; the attempt to shake it off has only made him feel its weight bearing down more ineluctably. This does not mean that the bucolic relinquishes its literary distinctiveness

---

[30] Anderson, Parsons, and Nisbet 1979.

and undergoes a kind of fusion with the elegy. Just the opposite is true: the sense of the tenth *Eclogue* is actually founded on a display of the difference between these two genres. The specific individuality of each of the two opposed elements can be fully grasped only when a clearly defined area is occupied by each in turn. The possibility of hearing the same *carmina* sung on the elegiac and bucolic registers brings home the 'formative' function each possesses.

The eclogue's metaliterary depth (the fact that what it says is directed to its own specific literary quality, its precise encoding within literary conventions) allows it to achieve an *exploration of the boundaries* of a poetic genre—an inquiry into features located very close to those of another genre but which, for that very reason, are distinctive and peculiar to it. The different genres that compose a literary culture are mutually definable by virtue of the systematic relationships differentiating them. The aim of Virgil's exploration here is not to link and blur two poetics but to gain a deeper insight into that which divides them. The outcome transcends a greater formal awareness, since it involves more than poetics. The opposition, within a single context, between elegiac and bucolic poetry necessarily involves a parallel opposition between the life and setting of the town and that of the country. In the tenth *Eclogue,* light is shed on this second-level opposition by the nature of the term of comparison—the elegy—where acceptance of the town and refusal of the country had a thematic status and were constitutive features of the literary code. As we can now understand, the analogous parallel opposition between Venus and Diana is not only brought into play here as a mythical scheme or anthropological archetype; it also mediates symbolically—in terms of practical activity and the choice of a way of life—between the elegiac/bucolic opposition and the referents of each, town and country, respectively. When statements about 'poetics' are read globally, without detaching them from statements about life, they take on a deeper meaning that has nothing to do with their metaliterary nature.

If we refuse to separate the text from its intentions (which means not ingenuously guessing at the author's intentions but uncovering the living relationship that linked the text with the world and with its immediate public), the writing of this poetry can be seen as a vital use of language in a form brimming with sense. The eclogue's starting point is an exploration of the boundaries of a genre, and the outcome is to have suggested the need for an existential choice that is not universal or easy and may even be impossible to make. One need hardly recall here the apparently great importance of the theme of τίς ἄριστος βίος ('What is the best way of life?'), especially in Augustan culture (evidence of this importance is the debate on this topic in both philosophy and poetry). Statements about genre and the forms of poetic expression aim not only to plot the contours of the artistic process (the range that defines them in the expectations of the public and in the collective literary consciousness) but also to explore and delimit a way of living. Virgil appeals to us to take his writing of poetry seriously, as a real form of life. Here, in short, poetry may be said to project the model of order, of structure, that is fundamental to life. Literary genre, with the reciprocal constraints and definitions of function that it implies, is an analogue, on the level of rhetorical form, of a larger ordering process that it projects upon life and the world. Poetic writing, as a heightened realization of language in practice, works toward an intense identification and interpretation of word and thought, of the signifier and the signified. It works as reflection not *above* but *within* the text: it stands entirely within that lived relation of humans with the world that is ideology.[31]

The problem comes into focus, I believe, if it is expressed in terms of a sociology of literary forms. In the tenth *Eclogue*, the confrontation between two adjacent genres makes their relationship come to life, rescuing both from the conventionally static nature of literary institutions. By being made vivid and vital in this way, the conflict between forms is able to mediate (not only *per imaginem*) a conflict

---

[31] Erich Köhler uses the stimulating expression 'grounding in life' ('Sitz im Leben') to indicate the relationship which, in his view, each literary genre has with an aspect or given stage of a community's development; it aims to signal the specific function that genre exercises in assimilating and interpreting social reality (Köhler 1977). But the idea itself (of theological origin) is more impressive than its critical application to literary texts. The danger lies in automatizing the relationship between the series of social events (which is historical) and the series of truly literary events (which is historical too, but has its own rhythms and development, which are often out of step with respect to the concurrent social rhythms). This point may be obvious enough (even to Köhler, I believe, and to Niklas Luhmann, whose sociological theory of systems is a basic presupposition of Köhler's thesis), but when using this approach it is much easier to formulate fascinating pseudoscientific hypotheses than to gain objective knowledge of literary phenomena.

present in life. This mediation, however, appears in the eclogue less as a *gnoseological* mirroring of sociological reality than as a dialectical, dynamic representation of social *behavior*—most specifically, as the behavior of the poet as a participant in, and critic of, this contradictory social situation. Even if Virgil presents himself as standing outside the drama, he is involved in it and is a necessary element in it. He takes part in it and experiences it—even if in a different way from Gallus, and even if he is capable of a certain degree of detachment. Without him, the dialectic essential to the poem could never have come into being.

On the one hand, there is Virgil, enclosed and sheltered in his universe; on the other, Gallus, the elegiac poet, who remains such even when welcomed into bucolic poetry. He is a guest there, invited with affectionate consideration but still a guest, a favorite friend, still an officer and statesman. Even if he is a poet, he does not belong to Virgil's literary universe, so closed in on itself and so averse to any real referent that it deliberately mixes and mingles Sicily and Arcady, farmers and shepherds, sheep and vineyards, Sicilian nymphs, and rural and Olympic gods.[32] In fact, this basic heterogeneity of the elegiac and the bucolic sustains the eclogue. On the one hand there is history (the town) and on the other its negation (the country). Bucolic poetry creates a world without history or, to be more precise, a world sheltered from the fascination and terror exercised by history. For the moment, this suffices for Virgil; Virgil makes it suffice for

---

[32] The representation of the agropastoral world here is assigned to abstractly symbolic language and takes shape in a topography made up of signs that are heterogeneous but have a mythical effect overall. As it appears in Latin elegies, the town has a much higher degree of credibility; it is drawn concretely and consists of objects and environments that are mentioned or described as if viewed from a much shorter distance. The comparison (here an opposition) should thus be drawn between a 'country form' and a 'town form', where the second is the real model on which the derivative, fictitious image of the first is built by antithesis. So the two forms are not strictly comparable. The Town as Power described by Tityrus in *Eclogues* 1.19–25 is impressively large (*stultus ego... sic parvis componere magna solebam*, 'foolish, I used to compare great things with small in this way'). It is the habitat of the real gods, beside which the pastoral deities appear as lowly and basically powerless. The country is excluded from power and lives in a glow that deprives it of its reality, aestheticizes it. By being made the result of a rhetorico-linguistic transformation that reverses the reality of town life by antithesis, it easily passes into literariness.

him even if he finds it cramping. History steals into that world but only to be detached from the logic of daily events; it soon falls back into the grip of a time that is unchanging.[33] It is an Epicurean world, one not governed by mankind. Grief is there; it can be overcome not by thickskinned endurance or unflinching resistance but by acceptance, with a sense of limitations that springs from an awareness of human weakness rather than from human strength. It is a world of tolerance, of obedient consolation. But already the brief references to contemporary events betray the intrusion of reality.

[33] The 'unmoving' time of the country form is qualitative and radically different from the ongoing, quantitative time of elegiac life defined by the rhythms of the town. One may recall the polemic by the Epicureans—by a certain Epicureanism, in particular—against 'infinite' or quantitative time (which leads to anguish: some of the *divites* of Lucretius and Horace's *strenua... inertia* ['laborious laziness'; *Epistles* 1.11.28] spring to mind) and in favor of the 'catastematic' pleasure peculiar to qualitative time, located here at dusk, the calmest, most melancholy time of day, when passion has gently drifted away.

11

Eclogues *in extremis*: On the Staying Power of Pastoral

Seamus Heaney

As a mode of writing, the pastoral requires at least a minimal awareness of tradition on the part of both the poet and the audience. It usually involves a self-consciously literary performance, so it becomes vulnerable to accusations of artificiality, as in Dr Johnson's famous stricture on Milton's 'Lycidas', a poem which was 'not to be considered as the effusion of real passion; for passion runs not after obscure allusions'. 'Where there is leisure for fiction', Johnson famously declared, 'there is little grief.'[1] And it has to be admitted that pastoral does run the danger of ending up as fine writing, of being an upholstered convention rather than a first-time discovery. What I am interested in, therefore, is how successfully the mode has continued to account for itself. For example, one recent critic has written that in order to take pastoral seriously, 'we must be able to say... that its reductions produce accounts of life and art in which one can take a serious interest and from which one can derive a serious pleasure'.[2] I want to end up considering whether pastoral does indeed survive this particular challenge, but I thought it would be interesting to begin with a poem by Michael Longley. Entitled 'The beech tree', it alludes to the first poem in Virgil's *Eclogues* and the last one in his

---

This paper was first presented as a discourse to those present at an ordinary general meeting of the Royal Irish Academy on 6 June 2002. It was published as Heaney 2003 and is reprinted here virtually unchanged.

[1] Abrams (ed.) 1993: 1.2406.   [2] Alpers 1996: 161.

Georgics and thereby manages to suggest how pervious consciousness remains to the inherited past even as it dwells in the copiousness and immediacy of the present:

> Leaning back like a lover against this beech tree's
> Two-hundred-year-old pewter trunk, I look up
> Through skylights into the leafy cumulus, and join
> Everybody who has teetered where these huge roots
> Spread far and wide their motionless mossy dance,
> As though I'd begun my eclogues with a beech
> As Virgil does, the brown envelopes unfolding
> Like fans their transparent downy leaves, tassels
> And prickly cups, mast, a fall of vermilion
> And copper and gold, then room in the branches
> For the full moon and her dusty lakes, winter
> And the poet who recollects his younger self
> And improvises a last line for the georgics
> About snoozing under this beech tree's canopy.[3]

Michael Longley has one important thing in common with the shepherds and goatherds of classical eclogue: like them, he is a love poet, devoted to expressing himself in images drawn from the world of nature. But Longley isn't just playing at being a character *in* an eclogue: he is presenting himself as the latest practitioner of the genre, in dialogue with its past masters—'Everybody who has teetered where these huge roots | Spread far and wide...'. There is indeed intertextuality here, but there is little post-modern belatedness. The irony involved is affectionate, a matter of tone; there is a trust in historical continuity and the viability of classical techniques. Longley's verse line moves with the hush and sureness of Virgil's own hexameters, and his poem, moreover, consists of a single sentence which manifests all the syntactical reach, ramification and suspension of a classic Latin period.

The fact that Michael Longley studied the classics at Trinity is, of course, important: his learning sets the beech tree image in a long perspective. But equally important is his refusal to abandon the personal note associated with what he has often called 'the great indoors'. For decades, it was the great outdoors of life in Northern

---

[3] Longley 2000: 62 (reproduced with the kind permission of the author).

Ireland that clamoured for attention, asking that its unremitting violence be treated in terms dictated by the old sectarian and ideological divisions, but Longley on the whole resisted these expectations and put his faith in images of the peaceable kingdom of the flora and fauna. So when he sets his beech tree deliberately in line with the ones in poems by the young Virgil, he is also putting his faith in the staying power of pastoral as a mode.

What keeps a literary kind viable is its ability to measure up to the challenges offered by new historical circumstances, and pastoral has been confronted with this challenge from very early on. Virgil himself, for example, in his first eclogue, is actually testing the genre he inherited from Theocritus and proving that it is fit for life in his own deadly Roman times. By the third line Meliboeus is lamenting the troubles that farmers must face in contemporary Italy. Eviction, expropriation, refugee status overnight. It is all as arbitrary as it is irresistible: the anonymous power of Rome and the brutal might of the legions are shown to have the force of fate. One man is struck by misfortune, the next, for no reason, is immune. Tityrus plays his flute at ease under the beech tree, but Meliboeus speaks for the victims of the system:

> nos patriae finis et dulcia linquimus arva.
> nos patriam fugimus; tu, Tityre, lentus in umbra
> formosam resonare doces Amaryllida silvas.[4]

It is a plaintive anthem. Inside two lines, the word *patria* is heard twice, while the verb *linquimus* is reinforced by the verb *fugimus* and the repetitions of *nos* (the victims) and *tu* (the lucky Tityrus addressed in the first line of the eclogue) keep adding to the pathos: *Tityre, tu patulae recubans sub tegmine fagi*...

Tityrus, there you are, stretched out in the shade of the broad beech, practising on your reed, getting it right for the green-sleeved muse of the woods. But we are bound away from our homeland and the fields we love, away from the home ground. And there you are, Tityrus, giving music lessons to trees, telling them all about the lovely Amaryllis.[5]

---

[4] Ferry 1999: 2.   [5] Author's translation.

This is already very literary, very conscious of earlier work done by Theocritus in Greek. The muses of Sicily who inspired the earlier poet's idylls are always at the back of the Latin poet's mind. Virgil, to put it another way, is himself very much the learned poets' poet; he may have come from a country background but he has an eye on an audience very different from the shepherds and goatherds he would have known in his boyhood, on the farm from which his father was eventually expelled. The expulsion happened in the course of the big land confiscations that were organised in order to resettle Julius Caesar's legionaries after the civil war with Pompey, and it's usually assumed that the eviction theme of the first eclogue derives from Virgil's family's experience. Which is to say that in spite of the literary nature of the performance, the covenant with life and the times is nevertheless being maintained. If, for example, the editors of the 1974 *Penguin Book of English Pastoral Verse* had printed a translation of this poem in their anthology, they could hardly have got away with announcing in their introduction that 'the pastoral vision is, at base, a false vision, positing a simplistic, unhistorical relationship between the ruling, landowning class—the poet's patrons and often the poet himself—and the workers of the land; as such its function is to mystify and to obscure the harshness of actual social and economic organization'.[6]

This statement is in itself a bit simplistic and unhistorical, not least because the relationship between the landowning classes and the workers of the land figures immediately and conspicuously in the first eclogue in Virgil's book. Tityrus's account of how he managed to keep possession of his smallholding gives a clear idea of the relations that pertained in the latter half of the first century BC between the powerful ones at the Roman centre and the poor ones in the Italian regions. In fact, a good bit of the poem consists of Tityrus's recollection of the harsh conditions he endured as a tenant farmer and of a visit to Rome where he made a successful plea to an unnamed but charismatic young man, as a result of which he ended up being granted the freehold on his land. Naturally, therefore, the aging Tityrus utters a paean to this young god, as he calls him, and this might well be regarded as a mystification and even as a piece of

[6] Barrell and Bull (eds.) 1974: 4.

propaganda on Virgil's part, insofar as it seems to be the poet's way of paying tribute to the emperor Octavian and thanking him for having restored his father's estates. But propaganda or not, the poem still keeps harsh reality in mind, and Meliboeus's rehearsal of the facts of his situation and the situation of others like him acts as a rebuke to Tityrus's hymn of praise and even to some extent as a rebuttal of it. 'But the rest of us must go from here', says Meliboeus, in Cecil Day Lewis's translation,

> and be dispersed—
> To Scythia, bone-dry Africa, the chalky spate of Oxus,
> Even to Britain—that place cut off at the world's end.
> Ah, when shall I see my native land again? After long years,
> Or never?—see the turf-dressed roof of my simple cottage,
> And wondering gaze at the ears of corn that were all my kingdom?
> To think of some godless soldier owning my well-farmed fallow,
> A foreigner reaping these crops! To such a pass has civil
> War reduced us.[7]

What these poems prove is that literariness as such is not an abdication from the truth. The literary is one of the methods human beings have devised for getting at reality: if it is concerned with its own appearance, that is only because it wants to show up or to get behind other appearances. Its diversions are not to be taken as deceptions but as roads less travelled by where the country we thought we knew is seen again in a new and revealing light. A simpler light, maybe, but still a true one.

Virgil, it seems to me, passes the test—the honesty test, let's call it—that the theatre director Peter Brook proposes for others working in the creative field. A remark in a newspaper interview may be off the cuff but seems to me right on target. 'Once you enter into this field [called art]', Brook says, 'like in any field, you have a responsibility... Your responsibility is, within your own limitations, to be as honest as you can. Being honest means, on the one hand, opening your eyes totally to the world as it is and, on the other, not trying to give a lying view of the world to other people... The responsibility of anyone in the arts is to look... for the other side of every coin. The moment you see a black side, your obligation is to look for a

---

[7] Day Lewis 1983: 5–6.

luminous side.'[8] Brook doesn't mean by this that you are to cultivate a Panglossian optimism. He wants writers to do what the Greeks and Shakespeare and Beckett did, to confront 'the pitiless nature of human experience in a way that makes you at the end very positive, full of courage, in a sense stronger than when you came in'.[9] Obviously, I wouldn't claim that pastoral is always or often going to fulfill this expectation, but I still believe that at its high points it does indeed 'leave you stronger than when you came in'.

Paul Alpers's book *What is pastoral?* is ready to concede that pastoral has its limitations but that it also has its ways of making up for and occasionally exceeding them. Taking its bearings from Schiller's essay 'On naive and sentimental poetry', and approaching the topic with the aid of more recent critics such as Kenneth Burke and William Empson, Alpers provides one of the fullest investigations of the mode, and one which alerts us to the fact that within the mode there are different genres, such as eclogue and pastoral lyric, pastoral elegy and pastoral comedy. More to the point, however, is Alpers's honest admission which I quoted at the beginning, his readiness to concede that 'to take this literary kind seriously, we must be able to say... that its reductions produce accounts of life and art in which one can take a serious interest and from which one can derive serious pleasure'.[10]

It is possible, of course, to enjoy the literary-historical hall of mirrors in which traditional motif and classical allusion repeat and reflect one another for their own sweet sake, but sooner or later we will come up against the Johnsonian objection referred to earlier. Essentially, this boils down to asking what, after all, is the human value of the perfectly made-up thing? And the answer must be that it depends on the seriousness of what is at stake beyond the attainment of artistic finish, and on the depth of the poet's engagement with considerations other than the technical and the aesthetic. In Virgil's ninth eclogue, for example, you can sense that there is much at stake for Virgil. Again, the setting involves the kind of land grabbing that his father had suffered, and the deeper theme is essentially asking thequestion 'How with this rage shall beauty hold a plea?' This is the question that Shakespeare would ask fifteen hundred years later

---

[8] O'Toole 2001. [9] Ibid. [10] Alpers 1996: 161.

(in Sonnet 65), and it's the one which always presents itself when art feels called upon to stay power. In Virgil's poem the representative artist is a master singer, a goatherd called Menalcas, a figure who doesn't actually appear on the scene, although clearly his songs are cherished by Lycidas and Moeris. Again, the situation is as in the first eclogue, where an older man has had his land confiscated and now seems to be working as a labourer for the one who has taken over.

Moeris is on his way to the market in town, charged with the task of selling for the new owner kids that until lately had probably been his own. There is a strong sense of devastated order. Both Moeris and Lycidas have been shocked out of a trust in an older world whose securities were until recently taken for granted, a world where omens were heeded and spells prevailed, where the biggest contest was the song contest and where song was credited with the power to ward off danger. The fiction of the poem has them travelling the road, but from Virgil's time to our own, the image of displaced persons on a highway, on the move with their old possessions, is as realistic as it is literary and is capable of compelling a serious interest as well as giving serious pleasure:

> *Lycidas*: Where are you headed, Moeris? Into town?
>
> *Moeris*: The things we have lived to see... The last thing
> You could have imagined happening has happened.
> An outsider lands and says he has the rights
> To our bit of ground. 'Out, old hands,' he says,
> 'This place is mine.' And these kid-goats in the creel—
> Bad cess to him—these kids are his. All's changed.
>
> *Lycidas*: The story I heard was about Menalcas,
> How your song-man's singing saved the place.
> From where the hills start doubling back and the ridge
> Continues gently sloping to the water,
> Right down to those old scraggy-headed beech trees.
>
> *Moeris*: That's what you would have heard. But songs and tunes
> Can no more hold out against brute force than doves
> When eagles swoop. The truth is, Lycidas,
> If I hadn't heard the crow caw on my left
> In our hollow oak, I'd have kept on arguing
> And that would have been the end of the road, for me
> That's talking to you, and for Menalcas even.

> *Lycidas*: Shocking times. Our very music, our one consolation,
> Confiscated, all but. And Menalcas himself
> Nearly one of the missing.[11]

The tree that Tityrus was stretched beneath in the first eclogue (and that is remembered in the Longley poem) was *patula fagus*, a broad-spreading beech, one with a strong suggestion of the Keatsian 'beechen green and shadows numberless', a tree that was rooted deep in the land of heart's desire, but what we hear about now are *veteres, iam fracta cacumina, fagos*—old ones, with their tops broken, scraggy-headed old beech trees rooted in a desolate and no longer nourishing landscape of fact. All that the landscape of the past can provide are warnings from crows and memories of better times. Indeed, this ninth eclogue could well carry as its epigraph a line from Brian Friel's play, *Translations*, where a character who is being forced into the desolation of historical reality declares that 'it can sometimes happen that a civilization becomes imprisoned in a linguistic contour that no longer matches the landscape of fact'.[12] Virgil would surely have felt the force of this, caught as he was between his devotion to a venerable poetic language contoured by Sicily and Theocritus and his awareness of a contemporary landscape full of displaced persons and properties that had changed hands at sword point, knowing that the firmness of the hexameter was no illusion but knowing equally that it was no effective help, no stabiliser of a destabilised country. And yet pastoral cannot actually function as a mode without writer and audience being completely alert to the ill fit that prevails between the beautifully tinted literary map and the uglier shape that reality has taken in the world. Indeed, it is because of this shared understanding of the kind of representation that is going on that a pastoral poet does not need constantly to prove that his reality principle is in working order. He and his audience know that eclogues which make no explicit reference to reality as it is actually experienced are every bit as clued in to it as ones that do.

Virgil's *Eclogues*, you could say, are a kind of Crystal Palace, beautifully structured and strong because of inner relationships and symmetries; the author in late Republican Rome, like the engineer in Victorian England, was fully aware that artificial conditions were

---

[11] Heaney 2001: 31–2.   [12] Friel 1981: 43.

being created, but he was also proud of his extraordinary ability to contrive the transparent tegument. In each case the art asks us to see through it, to view it from all sides, to enter in and to stand back, to regard it as both a revelation and an intervention, a *locus amoenus* where you can choose to remember or forget the legions or the locomotives, depending upon how much reality you are ready to accommodate or are accustomed to bear.

The integrity, consonance and radiance that I've claimed for Virgil's *Eclogues* can also be claimed for another sequence written almost two thousand years later by the poet whom I regard as the greatest one alive among us today. Czeslaw Milosz's lyric sequence entitled 'The world' is a poem in sections written in Warsaw during the Nazi occupation.[13] Although not spoken by a shepherd, 'The world' is definitely a version of pastoral, since it is in a strict sense idyllic. Schiller's essay on naive and sentimental poetry, to which I referred earlier, is worth returning to here, first of all for his reflections on the idyll:

All peoples who possess a history have a paradise, a state of innocence, a golden age; indeed, every man has his paradise, his golden age, which he recalls, according as he has more or less of the poetic in his nature, with more or less inspiration. Experience itself therefore supplies enough for the depiction of which the pastoral idyll treats. For this reason it remains always a beautiful, an elevating fiction, and the poetic power in representing it has truly worked on behalf of the ideal.[14]

The *locus amoenus* in Milosz's poem is a secure home in a settled countryside, a place which obviously contains memories of the poet's own childhood. Milosz had grown up as a landowner's son, on a small estate in the woodlands of Lithuania, in conditions where the physical and metaphysical worlds must have seemed equally safe and settled, and it was to this innocent place that he returned in memory at one of the most atrocious moments of World War II. What is important, however, is not so much the consoling innocence of the memories themselves as the artistic intransigence with which the innocence is presented. There is something bulletproof about

[13] Milosz 1988: 36–55.
[14] Alpers 1996: 33, quoting Schiller from H. B. Nisbet (ed.)1985.

Milosz's crystal palace. 'The world' is significantly subtitled 'A naive poem', and we must surely understand this subtitle to be something more than an announcement that the poem is written in the language of a child's primer; it also has to be an ironical nod in the direction of Schiller, who characterised the naive poet as one 'who only follows nature and feeling' and 'can only have a single relationship with his subject'. Once, however, the poet begins to reflect, once that single relationship with the world that is so powerfully evident in Homer is lost, once consciousness of the division between self and not self develops, complication begins to set in. Schiller gives the name 'sentimental' to poetry arising from this experience of primal separation from nature and actuality, and this means that he would have placed Virgil's *Eclogues* and Milosz's 'The world' in the 'sentimental' rather than the 'naive' category. For Schiller, 'sentimental' was a specialised aesthetic term, without the pejorative connotations which the word now carries. The 'sentimental' is where the poet finds himself after consciousness of self has occurred. Unlike the naive poet in his state of undifferentiated harmony with nature, this new poet

reflects upon the impression objects make upon him, and only in that reflection is the emotion grounded which he himself experiences and which he excites in us...[15]

In Milosz's 'The world', the emotion is certainly grounded in reflection, in ironical, even tragic reflection on the impression objects make upon him, and so the poem falls into the German theorist's 'sentimental' category, although it has to be said that Milosz's first Polish audience may well have thought of it as 'sentimental' in the more common sense of the term. 'The world' is reported to have puzzled the listeners when it was first read at one of Warsaw's clandestine literary gatherings. Robert Hass, who co-translated the poem with Robert Pinsky, comments:

It is not surprising that it did [puzzle the first audience]. Of all the responses to the European horror of the years 1935–45—Eliot's 'Little Gidding', Akhmatova's *Requiem*, Vallejo's 'Spain, let this cup pass', Celan's 'Todesfuge', Pound's *Pisan Cantos*—it is the most radically strange. In the middle of

---

[15] Alpers 1996: 29.

Eclogues in extremis 255

the horror when the whole world seemed to be playing out the most terrible of the songs of experience, Milosz, beginning with a glimpsed image of a schoolgirl's hat on a wooded path in the early spring, wrote what has been called 'the most serene poem in the Polish language'.[16]

The opening section, as translated by Hass and Pinsky, goes like this:

> Down where the green valley opens wider,
> Along the path with grass blurring its border,
> Through an oak grove just broken into flower,
> Children come walking home from school together.
>
> In a pencil case with a lid that slides open,
> Bits of bread roll around with stumps of crayon,
> And the penny hidden away by all children
> For spring and the first cuckoo in the garden.
>
> The girl's beret and her brother's school-cap
> Bob, as they walk, above the fringe of bushes.
> A jay screams, hopping in a tree-top;
> Over the trees, clouds drift in long ridges.
>
> Now, past the curve, you can see the red roof:
> Father leans on his hoe in the front garden,
> Then bends down to touch a half-opened leaf;
> From his tilled patch he can see the whole region.[17]

Before going any further with this discussion, it will be instructive to hear what the author had to say about his poem four decades after he wrote it. He described it as 'a rather ironic operation', 'an act of magic to depict the exact opposite' of the way the world was at the time of the poem's composition. He was striving, he said, for a pure calligraphic line because 'given the way the world was, if you actually wanted to say something about it, you'd have had to scream, to speak'.[18] And Milosz's explanation of his procedures and aims would surely have gained a sympathetic understanding from Virgil, and for that matter, from Longley. What he is talking about is what I have been calling 'the literary', meaning the deliberate choice of a genre and a perfect nonchalance in execution of its demands, although Milosz's case is a very clear reminder that in order for the literary to be of human value it must be at the service of human need.

[16] Hass 1981: 42.   [17] Milosz 1981: 41.
[18] Czarnecka and Fiut 1987: 127.

If the requirements of genre gain sway over or become substitutes for the poet's own personal injuries or energies, then what we have is a mock-up rather than an act of magic. What we want, after all, is poetry as Wallace Stevens conceived of it, the result of imagination pressing back against the pressure of reality.

I gave this talk a slightly melodramatic title—'Eclogues *in extremis*'—because I want to end with a case where the eclogue comes into play as a tragic resource, a case where the genre produced the kind of work that Alpers requires, namely an account of life in which we can take a serious interest. The poems in question were again produced in the atrocious conditions created by the Nazis in Eastern Europe, but before I turn to them, I'd like to look at some pre-war eclogues which foreshadowed the terrible operations that Hitler would set in motion a few years later. In December 1933 Louis MacNeice completed the first of three eclogues which would eventually appear in his Faber volume in 1935, and indeed that same work, 'An eclogue for Christmas', would stand as the opening poem of the collection.[19]

No Tityrus or Meliboeus here, no kids in baskets or reed pipes, and yet as in Virgil's first and ninth eclogues, the road to town is still the meeting place and the ones who meet and talk are every bit as shadowed by disastrous times as Virgil's goatherds ever were; neither of MacNeice's protagonists is heading into exile but each is alienated and angst-ridden, and the subject of their conversation is the threatened state of the country. Economic depression, collapsing confidence in traditional faiths and institutions, revolution on the horizon at home, war on the horizon abroad—the familiar 1930s backdrop is ever so slightly de-familiarised by the decidedly classical word 'eclogue' in the title and by the conventional utterance, the unapologetically literary arc described by the seven simple words that open the poem: 'I meet you in an evil time.'[20]

This brief sentence, somewhat stiff and reminiscent indeed of a piece of translated Latin, serves notice that the pastoral convention is alive and well. And for all the ritzy up-to-dateness of the poem as a whole, for all its modern dress and de-classicising of its shepherd characters to a pair of speakers called A and B, 'An eclogue for

[19] MacNeice 1966: 33–6.   [20] Ibid. 33.

Christmas' ploughs up the old Virgilian ground and plays some highly sophisticated variations on themes that had become traditional in later pastoral. A and B, for example, represent among other things the town-dweller and the country-dweller, and their conversation is to some extent a subversion of the time-honoured convention that truth and morals are enshrined in country ways whereas the giddier vanities and the stronger corruptions are rooted in towns and courts. A is the townsman, conscious of his deracination, slightly proud of it but also slightly panicked. Hence he is ready to seek guidance from B, the country-dweller, the one supposed to be in touch with immemorial wisdom, the one whose 'morose routine', as A calls it, allows time for contemplation, in a place where there is traditionally room for reflection. 'Therefore,' says A,

> [W]hen we bring out the old tinsel and frills
> To announce that Christ is born among the barbarous hills
> I turn to you whom a morose routine
> Saves from the mad vertigo of being what has been.
> B. Analogue of me, you are wrong to turn to me,
> My country will not yield you any sanctuary,
> There is no pinpoint in any of the ordnance maps
> To save you when your town and town-bred thoughts collapse,
> It is better to die *in situ* as I shall,
> One place is bad as another. Go back where your instincts call
> And listen to the crying of the town-cats and the taxis again
> Or wind your gramophone and eavesdrop on great men.[21]

The eclogue structure calls forth from MacNeice a poetry that can sound at once off the cuff and oracular; its express subjects are public ones, the state of the nation and all the rest of those 1930s concerns, but the strength of the work is that it confirms Joseph Brodsky's exhilarating contention that if art teaches us anything, it is that the human condition is private. And that deep reach into the private strata is felt in many oddly nightmarish images that surface all through these poems, nowhere more powerfully than in the well-known, doom-laden lines spoken by B a little later in the poem:

[21] Ibid.

B. In the country they are still hunting, in the heavy shires
   Greyness is on the fields and sunset like a line of pyres
   Of barbarous heroes smoulders through the ancient air
   Hazed with the factory dust and, orange opposite, the moon's glare,
   Goggling yokel stubborn through the iron trees,
   Jeers at the end of us, our bland ancestral ease;
   We shall go down like palaeolithic man
   Before some new Ice Age or Genghis Khan.[22]

The full flowering of all this, the rhetorical and spiritual climax of the eclogue phase in MacNeice's development, would arrive two years later, when Auden and he were in Iceland, in retreat in the religious rather than the military sense; or else you could say they were in the wings, readying themselves for the moral and artistic spotlight that would shine down on them once they returned to a European stage where the Spanish Civil War was in full swing and the signs of Hitler's terrible intentions could no longer be ignored. Thinly disguised as Ryan and Craven, the visitors to Iceland are interrogated and instructed in the course of the poem by an oracle called The Voice of Europe and by the ghost of the saga hero Grettir. What awaits them at home may be the ranked armies of the Fascists, what Ryan/MacNeice calls 'the wall | Of shouting flesh',[23] but Grettir at the end can only recommend one course of action. In these concluding lines of 'Eclogue from Iceland', G and C are the initials, respectively, of Grettir and Craven/Auden:

G. Minute your gesture but it must be made—
   Your hazard, your act of defiance and hymn of hate,
   Hatred of hatred, assertion of human values,
   Which is now your only duty.
C. Is it our only duty?
G.   Yes, my friends.
   What did you say? The night falls now and I
   Must beat the dales to chase my remembered acts.
   Yes, my friends, it is your only duty.
   And, it may be added, it is your only chance.[24]

---

[22] MacNeice 1966: 34.　　[23] Ibid. 47.　　[24] Ibid.

This marks MacNeice's exit from the pastoral mode and as an exit line, it is considerably more vigorous than the last line of Virgil's tenth eclogue (which it may or may not be remembering): *Ite domum saturae, venit Hesperus, ite capellae.*[25] 'Go on home now with your bellies full, my goats, the evening star is rising, go on, go on.'[26] Virgil's conclusion inclines you to agree with another judgment of Schiller's to be found in the essay I quoted from earlier. 'We can love [pastoral idylls]', Schiller writes, 'and seek them out only when we stand in need of peace.' Then he adds 'Only for the sick in spirit can they provide healing, but no nourishment for the healthy; they cannot vivify, only assuage.'[27] But when Grettir says 'The night falls now and I | Must beat the dales to chase my remembered acts', and when he goes on to urge the poets to do their duty in the extreme conditions, you are inclined to disagree with Schiller's claim that pastoral 'cannot vivify', and with his claim that they do not suit us 'when our forces are striving for motion and activity'. Late in the history of the genre, MacNeice comes along and proves the case to be otherwise, proves in fact that the eclogue is more than capable of providing 'nourishment for the healthy'.

Not every poet is called upon to fulfil these large demands. But when the call comes, there is evidence that the pastoral mode is by no means an exhausted resource, and that it can vivify the spirit as well as touch the heart. Going back to the terrible conditions which prevailed in Europe during World War II, I want to conclude with a brief reference to the tragic eclogues written by the Hungarian poet Miklos Radnoti. Composed in labour camps and in the course of a forced march during which Radnoti met his death, these poems were found in a notebook in his overcoat pocket, after the war, when his body was exhumed from a mass grave.

In Radnoti's 'Eighth Eclogue', the situation envisaged in Virgil's first, where the outcast on the road encounters a more secure singer, is drastically revised.[28] The crystal dome has been smashed, the landscape is the actual landscape of war, and the poet—the one in

---

[25] Ferry 1999: 84. [26] Author's translation.
[27] Alpers 1996: 33–4. [28] Radnoti 2000: 61–2.

the poem and the one who is writing the poem—is being herded from the camp towards death either by starvation or mass execution, but even in these extreme conditions the genre comes to his aid. Radnoti meets not a Tityrus under a broad beech but the biblical prophet Nahum, the one who had prophesied the fall of Assyria; and his news for Nahum is more terrible than news of an eviction:

> On every hand, young children are dashed in pieces against
> the walls, the church tower is a torch, the house an oven,
> the householder roasting inside, and factories go up in smoke.
> The street runs with burning people, then it faints, thrumming,
> the bomb's great bed heaves, the heavy mortise bursts
> asunder, and like cowpats in the pasture, the dead lie scattered
> and shrivel pell-mell about the squares of the town.[29]

For all the terrible realism of this, we can still invoke Peter Brook's phrase and say that we go out stronger than we came in, not least because of the final turn which the dialogue takes. When the poet complains that 'this time still grinds me down like a stone in a swift-surging stream', the prophet answers:

> Thou only thinkest so. I know thy latest poems. Poison
> keepeth us alive. A prophet's rage is kin to a poet's:
> meat for the people, and drink![30]

But we might go further and say that because this particular poet's rage is expressed in the eclogue form, that form (and the pastoral mode in general) can also provide 'meat for the people, and drink'— can provide, in fact, vivification, nourishment for the healthy, an account of life in which we can take a serious interest.

[29] Radnoti 2000: 61.   [30] Ibid. 62.

Bibliography

Abbe, E. (1965). *The Plants of Virgil's Georgics*. Ithaca: Cornell University Press.
Abert, H. and Kroll, W. (1926). 'Linos 1'. *Pauly-Wissowa* 13: 715–17.
Ableitinger-Grünberger, D. (1971). *Der junge Horaz und die Politik: Studien zur 7. und 16. Epode*. Heidelberg: Winter.
Abrams, M. H. (ed.) (1993). *The Norton Anthology of English Literature*, 2 vols., 6th edn. New York: Norton.
Alexander, P. J. (1967). *The Oracle of Baalbek: The Tiburtine Sibyl in Greek Dress*. Washington: Dumbarton Oaks Center for Byzantine Studies.
Alfonsi, L. (1949). 'Nota properziana'. *RBPh* 27: 5–27.
Allen, A. W. (1962). 'Sunt qui Propertium malint'. In J. P. Sullivan (ed.), *Critical Essays on Roman Literature: Elegy and Lyric*. London: Routledge & Kegan Paul, 107–48.
Alpers, P. (1979). *The Singer of the Eclogues: A Study of Virgilian Pastoral*. Berkeley: University of California Press.
—— (1990). 'Theocritean Bucolic and Virgilian Pastoral'. *Arethusa* 23: 19–47.
—— (1996). *What Is Pastoral?* Chicago: University of Chicago Press.
Anderson, R. D., Parsons, P. J., and Nisbet, R. G. M. (1979). 'Elegiacs by Gallus from Qasr Ibrîm'. *JRS* 69: 125–55.
Anderson, W. S. (1982). 'The Orpheus of Virgil and Ovid: *flebile nescio quid*'. In J. Warden (ed.), *Orpheus: The Metamorphoses of a Myth*. Toronto: University of Toronto Press, 25–50.
Arnaldi, F. (1943). *Studi Vergiliani*. Naples: Loffredo.
Austin, R. G. (1927). 'Virgil and the Sibyl'. *CQ* 21: 100–5.
Axelson, B. (1945). *Unpoetische Wörter: Ein Beitrag zur Kenntnis der lateinischen Dichersprache*. Lund: Ohlssons Boktryckeri.
Barra, G. (1952). 'Le Bucoliche e la formazione spirituale e poetica di Virgilio'. *RAAN* 27: 7–31.
Barrell, J. and Bull, J. (eds.) (1974). *The Penguin Book of English Pastoral Verse*. London: Penguin.
Barrett, A. A. (1970). 'The Authorship of the Culex: An Evaluation of the Evidence'. *Latomus* 29: 348–62.
Barwick, K. (1944). 'Zur Interpretation und Chronologie der 4. Ecloge des Vergil und der 16. und 7. Epode des Horaz'. *Philologus* 96: 28–67.

Batstone, W. W. (1997). 'Virgilian Didaxis: Value and Meaning in the *Georgics*'. In Martindale (ed.), 125–44.
Baumbach, M. (2001). 'Dichterwettstreit als Liebeswerbung in Vergils 5. Ekloge'. *Philologus* 145: 108–20.
Bayet, J. (1930). 'L'évolution de l'art de Virgile des origines aux Géorgiques'. *Revue des cours et conférences* 31: 231–41, 372–84, 547–59, 606–20.
Beaujeu, J. (1982). 'L'enfant sans nom de la *IVe Bucolique*'. *REL* 60: 186–215.
Becker, C. (1955). 'Virgils Eklogenbuch'. *Hermes* 83: 314–49.
Benko, S. (1980). 'Virgil's Fourth Eclogue in Christian Interpretation'. *ANRW* 2.31.1: 646–705.
Benoit, P. (1963). ' "Et toi-même, un glaive te transpercera l'âme!" (Luc 2,35)'. *Catholic Biblical Quarterly* 25: 251–61.
Berg, W. (1974). *Early Virgil*. London: Athlone Press.
Berliner, R. (1955). *Die Weihnachtskrippe*. Munich: Prestel.
Bethe, E. (1892). 'Vergilstudien II: Zur ersten, neunten und achten Ecloge'. *RhM* 47: 577–96.
Bieber, M. (1961). *The Sculpture of the Hellenistic Age*. New York: Columbia University Press.
Bieler, L. (1935–6), ΘΕΙΟΣ ANHP: *Das Bild des 'göttlichen Menschen' in Spätantike und Frühchristentum*, 2 vols. Vienna: Höfels.
Binder, G. (1983). 'Lied der Parzen zur Geburt Octavians: Vergils vierte Ekloge'. *Gymnasium* 90: 102–22.
Bloom, H. (1973). *The Anxiety of Influence: A Theory of Poetry*. New York: Oxford University Press.
—— (1975). *A Map of Misreading*. New York: Oxford University Press.
—— (1976). *Poetry and Repression: Revisionism from Blake to Stevens*. New Haven: Yale University Press.
—— (1982). *Agon: Towards a Theory of Revisionism*. New York: Oxford University Press.
Boll, F. (1914). *Aus der Offenbarung Johannis: Hellenistische Studien zum Weltbild der Apokalypse*. Leipzig: Teubner.
Borgeaud, P. (1988). *The Cult of Pan in Ancient Greece*. Transl. by K. Atlass and J. Redfield. Chicago: University of Chicago Press.
Böschenstein-Schäfer, R. (1967). *Idylle*. Stuttgart: Metzler.
Bowersock, G. W. (1971). 'A Date in the *Eighth Eclogue*'. *HSPh* 75: 73–80.
—— (1978). 'The Addressee of Virgil's Eighth Eclogue: A Response'. *HSPh* 82: 201–2.
Boyle, A. J. (1975). 'A Reading of Virgil's Eclogues'. *Ramus* 4: 187–203.
—— (1976). *The Eclogues of Virgil*. Melbourne: The Hawthorne Press.
—— (1986). *The Chaonian Dove: Studies in the Eclogues, Georgics and Aeneid of Virgil*. Leiden: Brill.

Bradbury, M. (1978). *Eating People is Wrong*. London: Secker & Warburg.
Bramble, J. C. (1970). 'Structure and Ambiguity in Catullus LXIV'. *PCPhS* 16: 22–41.
Breed, B. W. (2006a). *Pastoral Inscriptions: Reading and Writing Virgil's Eclogues*. London: Duckworth.
—— (2006b). 'Time and Textuality in the Book of the *Eclogues*'. In Fantuzzi and Papanghelis (eds.), 333–67.
Bréguet, E. (1948). 'Les *Élégies* de Gallus d'après la Xe *Bucolique* de Virgile'. *REL* 26: 204–14.
Brelich, A. (1969). *Paides e Parthenoi*. Rome: Edizioni dell'Ateneo.
Briggs, W. W., Jr. (1981). 'A Bibliography of Virgil's "Eclogues" (1927–1977)'. *ANRW* 2.31.2: 1267–1357.
Brown, E. L. (1963). *Numeri Vergiliani: Studies in 'Eclogues' and 'Georgics'*. Brussels: Latomus.
—— (1978). 'Damoetas' Riddle: Euclid's *Theorem* 1.32'. *Vergilius* 24: 25–31.
—— (1981). 'The Lycidas of Theocritus' *Idyll* 7'. *HSPh* 85: 59–100.
Brown, R. E. (1977). *The Birth of the Messiah: A Commentary on the Infancy Narratives in Matthew and Luke*. Garden City, New York: Doubleday.
Brugioni, B. (1940). 'Antiarcadia Virgiliana'. *MC* 10: 102–11.
Brummer, J. (1912). *Vitae Vergilianae*. Leipzig: Teubner.
Büchner, K. (1955–8). 'P. Vergilius Maro'. *Pauly-Wissowa* 8: 1021–1486 (= Büchner 1957).
—— (1957). *P. Vergilius Maro: Der Dichter der Römer*. Stuttgart: Druckenmüller.
Bultmann, R. (1924). Rev. of Norden 1924. *Theologische Literaturzeitung* 49: 319–23.
—— (1963). *The History of the Synoptic Tradition*. New York: Harper & Row.
Caird, G. B. (1966). *A Commentary on the Revelation of St. John the Divine*. New York: Harper & Row.
Cairns, F. (1972). *Generic Composition in Greek and Roman Poetry*. Edinburgh: Edinburgh University Press.
—— (1999). 'Virgil *Eclogue* 1.1–2: A Literary Programme?'. *HSPh* 99: 189–93.
Calame, C. (1977). *Les choeurs de jeunes filles en Grèce archaïque*, 2 vols. Rome: Edizioni dell'Ateneo & Bizzarri.
Campbell, J. S. (1982/3). 'Damoetas's Riddle: A Literary Solution'. *CJ* 78: 122–6.
Camps, W. A. (1967). *Propertius: Elegies, Book II*. Cambridge: Cambridge University Press.

Cancik, H. (1986). ' "Delicias domini": Ein kulturgeschichtlicher Versuch zu Vergil, Ekloge 2'. In U. J. Stache, W. Maaz, and F. Wagner (eds.), *Kontinuität und Wandel: Lateinische Poesie von Naevius bis Baudelaire. Franco Munari zum 65. Geburtstag.* Hildesheim: Weidmann, 15–34.

Carcopino, J. (1943). *Virgile et le mystère de la IVe Églogue.* Paris: L'Artisan du Livre.

Cartault, A. (1897). *Étude sur les Bucoliques de Virgile.* Paris: Colin.

Cassio, A. C. (1973). 'L'*incipit* della *Chioma* callimachea in Virgilio'. *RFIC* 101: 329–32.

Christensen, H. (1908). 'Que - que bei den römischen Hexametrikern (bis etwa 500 n. Chr.)'. *ALL* 15: 165–211.

Cichorius, C. (1922). *Römische Studien: Historisches, Epigraphisches und Literaturgeschichtliches aus vier Jahrhunderten Roms.* Leipzig: Teubner.

Clausen, W. V. (1964). 'Callimachus and Latin Poetry'. *GRBS* 5: 181–96.

—— (1972). 'On the Date of the *First Eclogue*'. *HSPh* 76: 201–5.

—— (1987). *Virgil's Aeneid and the Tradition of Hellenistic Poetry.* Berkeley: University of California Press.

—— (1994). *A Commentary on Virgil, Eclogues.* Oxford: Clarendon Press.

Clay, J. S. (1974). 'Damoetas' Riddle and the Structure of Vergil's Third Eclogue'. *Philologus* 118: 59–64.

Coleiro, E. (1979). *An Introduction to Vergil's Bucolics with a Critical Edition of the Text.* Amsterdam: Grüner.

Coleman, R. (1977). *Vergil: Eclogues.* Cambridge: Cambridge University Press.

Collins, J. J. (1974*a*). *The Sibylline Oracles of Egyptian Judaism.* Missoula, Mont.: Society of Biblical Literature for the Pseudepigrapha Group.

—— (1974*b*). 'The Provenance of the Third Sibylline Oracle'. *Bulletin of the Institute of Jewish Studies* 2: 1–18.

—— (1983). 'Sibylline Oracles (Second Century B.C.—Seventh Century A.D.)'. In J. H. Charlesworth (ed.), *The Old Testament Pseudepigrapha*, Vol. 1. London: Darton, Longman & Todd, 317–471.

—— (1987). 'The Development of the Sibylline Tradition'. *ANRW* 2.20.1: 421–59.

Commager, S. (ed.) (1966). *Virgil: A Collection of Critical Essays.* Englewood Cliffs, New Jersey: Prentice-Hall.

Comparetti, D. (1997). *Vergil in the Middle Ages.* Transl. by E. F. M. Benecke. Princeton: Princeton University Press.

Conington, J. and Nettleship, H. (1881). *P. Vergili Maronis Opera*, Vol. 1, 4th edn. London: Whittaker.

—— and Nettleship, H. (1898). *P. Vergili Maronis Opera*, Vol. 1, 5th edn. London: Bell.

Connolly, J. (2001). 'Picture Arcadia: The Politics of Representation in Vergil's *Eclogues*'. *Vergilius* 47: 89–116.
Conte, G. B. (1980). *Il genere e i suoi confini: Cinque studi sulla poesia di Virgilio*. Turin: Stampatori.
—— (1986). *The Rhetoric of Imitation: Genre and Poetic Memory in Virgil and Other Latin Poets*. Transl. by C. Segal. Ithaca: Cornell University Press.
Corssen, P. (1925). 'Die vierte Ekloge Virgils'. *Philologus* 81: 26–71.
Corti, M. (1969). *Metodi e Fantasmi*. Milan: Feltrinelli.
Courcelle, P. (1957). 'Les exégèses chrétiennes de la quatrième églogue'. *REA* 59: 294–319.
Courtney, E. (1990). 'Vergil's Sixth *Eclogue*'. *QUCC* 34: 99–112.
Cremona, V. (1977). 'Distrazioni critiche e unità poetica della prima bucolica'. In (no ed.), *Atti del Convegno Virgiliano sul Bimillenario delle Georgiche*. Naples: Istituto Universitario Orientale, 287–308.
Cullmann, O. (1963). *The Christology of the New Testament*, 2nd edn. Transl. by S. C. Guthrie and C. A. M. Hall. Philadelphia: Westminster Press.
Currie, H. M. (1976). 'The Third *Eclogue* and the Roman Comic Spirit'. *Mnemosyne* 29: 411–20.
Czarnecka, E. and Fiut, A. (1987). *Conversations with Czeslaw Milosz*. Transl. by R. Lourie. San Diego: Harcourt Brace Jovanovich.
Daniélou, J. (1948). 'La typologie milléllariste de la semaine dans le christianisme primitif'. *VChr* 2: 1–16.
Davis, G. (2004). 'Consolation in the Bucolic Mode: The Epicurean Cadence of Vergil's First Eclogue'. In D. Armstrong *et al.* (eds.), *Vergil, Philodemus, and the Augustans*. Austin: University of Texas Press, 63–74.
Day Lewis, C. (1983). *Virgil: The Eclogues and Georgics*. Oxford: Oxford University Press.
De Saint-Denis, E. (1942). *Virgile: Bucoliques*. Paris: Les Belles Lettres.
Deremetz, A. (1987). 'Le *carmen deductum* ou le fil du poème: À propos de Virgile, *Buc.*, VI'. *Latomus* 46: 762–77.
Deubner, L. (1925). Rev. of W. Weber, *Der Prophet und sein Gott*. *Gnomon* 1: 160–9.
Dibelius, M. (1932). 'Jungfrauensohn und Krippenkind: Untersuchungen zur Geburtsgeschichte Jesu im Lukas-Evangelium'. *SHAW* 22.4 (= Dibelius 1953–6: 1.1–78).
—— (1953–6). *Botschaft und Geschichte: Gesammelte Aufsätze*, 2 vols. Ed. by G. Bornkamm. Tübingen: Mohr.
Diehl, E. (1911), *Die Vitae Vergilianae und ihre antiken Quellen*. Bonn: Marcus und Weber.
Diels, H. (1890). *Sibyllinische Blätter*. Berlin: Reimer.

Bibliography

Dix, T. K. (1995). 'Vergil in the Grynean Grove: Two Riddles in the Third *Eclogue*'. *CPh* 90: 256–62.

Dover, K. J. (1971). *Theocritus: Select Poems*. London: Macmillan.

Dryden, J. (1961). *The Works of Virgil*. Oxford: Oxford University Press.

—— (1970). 'A Discourse Concerning the Original and Progress of Satire'. In J. Kinsley and G. A. E. Parfitt, *John Dryden: Selected Criticism*. Oxford: Clarendon Press, 208–78.

Duckworth, G. E. (1969). *Vergil and Classical Hexameter Poetry: A Study in Metrical Variety*. Ann Arbor: University of Michigan Press.

Du Quesnay, I. M. Le M. (1976). 'Vergil's Fourth *Eclogue*'. *Papers of the Liverpool Latin Seminar* 1: 25–100 (= Hardie (ed.) 1999: 1.283–350).

—— (1976/7). 'Virgil's Fifth *Eclogue*: The Song of Mopsus and the New Daphnis'. *PVS* 16: 18–41 (= Hardie (ed.) 1999: 1.351–84).

—— (1979). 'From Polyphemus to Corydon: Virgil, *Eclogue* 2 and the *Idylls* of Theocritus'. In D. West and T. Woodman (eds.), *Creative Imitation and Latin Literature*. Cambridge: Cambridge University Press, 35–69.

—— (1981). 'Vergil's First *Eclogue*'. *Papers of the Liverpool Latin Seminar* 3: 29–182.

Egan, R. B. (1996). 'Corydon's Winning Words in *Eclogue* 7'. *Phoenix* 50: 233–9.

Elder, J. P. (1961). '*Non iniussa cano:* Virgil's Sixth Eclogue'. *HSPh* 65: 109–25 (= Hardie (ed.) 1999: 1.388–403).

Erdmann, G. (1932). *Die Vorgeschichten des Lukas- und Matthäus-Evangeliums und Vergils vierte Ekloge*. Göttingen: Vandenhoeck & Ruprecht.

Faber, R. (1995). 'Vergil Eclogue 3.37, Theocritus 1, and Hellenistic Ekphrasis'. *AJPh* 116: 411–7.

Fabia, P. (1931). '*Decem menses* (Virgile, Églogue IV, 61)'. *REA* 33: 33–40.

Fairclough, H. R. (1999). *Virgil 1: Eclogues, Georgics, Aeneid I–VI*, rev. by G. P. Goold. Cambridge, Mass.: Harvard University Press.

Fantazzi, C. (1966). 'Virgilian Pastoral and Roman Love Poetry'. *AJPh* 87: 171–91.

—— and Querbach, C. W. (1985). 'Sound and Substance: A Reading of Virgil's Seventh Eclogue'. *Phoenix* 39: 355–67.

Fantuzzi, M. and Papanghelis, T. D. (eds.) (2006). *Brill's Companion to Greek and Latin Pastoral*. Leiden: Brill.

Faraone, C. A. (1989). 'Clay Hardens and Wax Melts: Magical Role-reversal in Vergil's Eighth *Eclogue*'. *CPh* 84: 294–300.

Farrell, J. (1991*a*). 'Asinius Pollio in Vergil Eclogue 8'. *CPh* 86: 204–11.

—— (1991*b*). *Vergil's Georgics and the Traditions of Ancient Epic: The Art of Allusion in Literary History*. New York: Oxford University Press.

—— (1992). 'Literary Allusion and Cultural Poetics in Vergil's Third *Eclogue*'. *Vergilius* 38: 64–71.
Feldman, L. H. (1953). 'Asinius Pollio and His Jewish Interests'. *TAPhA* 84: 73–80.
Ferry, D. (1999). *The Eclogues of Virgil: A Translation*. New York: Farrar, Straus, and Giroux.
Festugière, A.-J. (1944–54). *La Révélation d'Hermès Trismégiste*, 4 vols. Paris: Lecoffre.
Flintoff, T. E. S. (1975/6). 'Characterisation in Virgil's Eclogues'. *PVS* 15: 16–26.
Fraenkel, E. (1957). *Horace*. Oxford: Clarendon Press.
Frank, T. (1916). 'Magnum Jovis Incrementum, *Ciris* 398, and Verg. *Ec.* iv. 49'. *CPh* 11: 334–6.
Fraser, P. M. (1972). *Ptolemaic Alexandria*, 3 vols. Oxford: Clarendon Press.
Friel, B. (1981). *Translations*. London: Faber & Faber.
Frischer, B. D. (1975). *At tu aureus esto: Eine Interpretation von Vergils 7. Ekloge*. Bonn: Habelt.
Fuchs, F. (1930/1). 'Vergiliana'. *Hochland* 28.2: 75–80.
Gagé, J. (1955). *Apollon Romain: Essai sur le culte d'Apollon et le développement du 'ritus Graecus' à Rome des origines à Auguste*. Paris: Boccard.
Gagliardi, P. (2003). *Gravis cantantibus umbra: Studi su Virgilio e Cornelio Gallo*. Bologna: Pàtron.
Galinsky, G. K. (1965). 'Vergil's Second *Eclogue*: Its Theme and Relation to the *Eclogue* Book'. *C&M* 26: 161–91 (= Hardie (ed.) 1999: 1.203–30).
Gallavotti, C. (1966). 'Le coppe istoriate di Teocrito e di Virgilio'. *PP* 111: 421–36.
Gatz, B. (1967). *Weltalter, goldene Zeit und sinnverwandte Vorstellungen*. Hildesheim: Olms.
Geffcken, J. (1902). *Komposition und Entstehungszeit der Oracula Sibyllina*. Leipzig: Hinrichs.
Gerber, D. E. (1969). 'Semonides of Amorgos, Fr. 1.4'. *TAPhA* 100: 177–80.
Gercke, A. (1921). 'Auch ich war in Arkadien geboren'. *NJb* 47: 313–17.
Giangrande, G. (1967). ' "Arte Allusiva" and Alexandrian Poetry'. *CQ* 17: 85–97.
Gigante, M. (ed.) (1981). *Lecturae Vergilianae I: Le Bucoliche*. Napoli: Giannini.
Gimm, R. (1910). 'De Vergilii stilo bucolico quaestiones selectae'. Diss. Leipzig.
Gow, A. S. F. (1952*a*). *Bucolici Graeci*. Oxford: Oxford University Press.
—— (1952*b*). *Theocritus*, 2 vols, 2nd edn. Cambridge: Cambridge University Press.

Bibliography

Green, R. P. H. (1996). 'Octavian and Vergil's Eclogues'. *Euphrosyne* 24: 225–36.

Griffiths, F. T. (1979). 'Poetry as Pharmakon in Theocritus' Idyll 2'. In G. W. Bowersock, W. Burkert, and M. C. J. Putnam (eds.), *Arktouros: Hellenic Studies Presented to Bernard M. W. Knox on the Occasion of his 65th Birthday*. Berlin: De Gruyter, 81–8.

Grondona, M. (1977). 'Gli epigrammi di Tibullo e il congedo delle elegie (su Properzio e Virgilio)'. *Latomus* 36: 3–29.

Grumach, E. (1949). *Goethe und die Antike: Eine Sammlung*, 2 vols. Berlin: De Gruyter.

Gutzwiller, K. J. (1991). *Theocritus' Pastoral Analogies: The Formation of a Genre*. Madison: University of Wisconsin Press.

Hagen, H. (1867). *Scholia Bernensia ad Vergili Bucolica atque Georgica* (= *Jahrbücher für Classische Philologie Suppl.* 4.5). Leipzig: Teubner.

Hahn, E. A. (1944). 'The Characters in the *Eclogues*'. *TAPhA* 75: 196–241.

Halperin, D. M. (1983). *Before Pastoral: Theocritus and the Ancient Tradition of Bucolic Poetry*. New Haven: Yale University Press.

Hammond, M. (1937). 'Octavius 96) Octavia minor'. *Pauly-Wissowa* 17: 1859–68.

Hardie, P. R. (1998). *Virgil*. Oxford: Oxford University Press.

—— (ed.) (1999). *Virgil: Critical Assessments of Classsical Authors*, 4 vols. London: Routledge.

Harrison, S. J. (1990). 'Some Views of the *Aeneid* in the Twentieth Century'. In Harrison (ed.), 1–20.

—— (ed.) (1990). *Oxford Readings in Vergil's* Aeneid. Oxford: Oxford University Press.

Hass, R. (1981). ' "The World": A Note on the Translation'. *Ironweed* 9 (2).

Hatzikosta, S. (1987). 'Non-Existent Rivers and Geographical "Adynata" '. *MPhL* 8: 121–33.

Heaney, S. (2001). *Electric Light*. London: Faber.

—— (2003). 'Eclogues *in extremis*: On the Staying Power of Pastoral'. *Proceedings of the Royal Irish Academy* 103C: 1–12.

Hebert, A. G. (1950). 'The Virgin Mary as the Daughter of Zion'. *Theology* 53: 403–10.

Heinze, R. (1903). *Virgils epische Technik*, Leipzig: Teubner.

Henderson, J. (1998*a*). 'Virgil, *Eclogue* 9: Valleydiction'. *PVS* 23: 149–76.

—— (1998*b*). 'Virgil's Third *Eclogue*: How Do You Keep an Idiot in Suspense?'. *CQ* 48: 213–28 (= Henderson 1999: 146–69).

—— (1999). *Writing Down Rome: Satire, Comedy, and Other Offences in Latin Poetry*. Oxford: Clarendon Press.

Herrmann, L. (1930). *Les Masques et les visages dans les Bucoliques de Virgile*. Brussels: Éditions de la Revue de l'Université de Bruxelles.

Heurgon, J. (1953). 'Tarquitius Priscus et l'organisation de l'ordre des haruspices sous l'empereur Claude'. *Latomus* 12: 402–17.

Heuzé, P. (1970). 'Formosus Alexis, formosam Amaryllida'. *Caesarodunum* 5: 147–9.

Himmelmann-Wildschütz, N. (1973). 'Ein antikes Vorbild für Guercinos "Et in Arcadia ego"?'. *Pantheon* 31: 229–36.

Holtorf, H. (1953). 'Das neue Bild Vergils: Ein Forschungsbericht'. *AU* 1.5: 46–65.

Holzberg, N. (2006). *Vergil: Der Dichter und sein Werk*. Munich: Beck.

Hommel, H. (1950) 'Vergil's "messianisches" Gedicht'. *Theologia Viatorum* 2: 182–212 (= Oppermann (ed.) 1963: 368–425).

Hopkinson, N. (1982). 'Juxtaposed Prosodic Variants in Greek and Latin Poetry'. *Glotta* 60: 162–177.

Horsfall, N. (ed.) (1995). *A Companion to the Study of Virgil*. Leiden: Brill.

Hosius, C. (1930). 'Zu Vergils zweitausendstem Geburtstag'. In id., *Zwei Rektoratsreden*. Würzburg: Stürtz, 29–50.

Housman, A. E. (1888). 'Emendationes Propertianae'. *JPh* 16: 1–35 (= Housman 1972: 29–54).

—— (1972). *The Classical Papers of A. E. Housman*, 3 vols. Ed. by J. Diggle and F. R. D. Goodyear. Cambridge: Cambridge University Press.

Hubaux, J. (1927). *Le réalisme dans les bucoliques de Virgile*. Liège: Vaillant-Carmanne.

—— (1929). 'Et in Arcadia ego (Virgile, *Buc.*, X, 31)'. *Le Musée Belge* 33: 57–65.

Hubbard, T. K. (1993). 'Poetic Succession and the Genesis of Alexandrian Bucolic'. *SyllClass* 4: 27–42.

—— (1995). 'Allusive Artistry and Vergil's Revisionary Program: Eclogues 1–3'. *MD* 34: 37–67.

—— (1995/6). 'Intertextual Hermeneutics in Vergil's Fourth and Fifth Eclogues'. *CJ* 91: 11–23.

—— (1998). *The Pipes of Pan: Intertextuality and Literary Filiation in the Pastoral Tradition from Theocritus to Milton*. Ann Arbor: University of Michigan Press.

Jachmann, G. (1922). 'Die dichterische Technik in Vergils Bukolika'. *NJb* 49: 101–20.

—— (1923). 'Vergils sechste Ekloge'. *Hermes* 58: 288–304.

—— (1952*a*). 'Die Vierte Ekloge Vergils'. *ASNP* 21: 13–62.

—— (1952*b*). 'L'Arcadia come paesaggio bucolico'. *Maia* 5: 161–74.

Jacoby, F. (1905). 'Zur Entstehung der römischen Elegie'. *RhM* 60: 38–105.

Jacques, J.-M. (1960). 'Sur un acrostiche d'Aratos (*Phén.*, 783–787)'. *REA* 62: 48–61.
Jahn, P. (1902). 'Aus Vergils Frühzeit'. *Hermes* 37: 161–72.
Jakobson, R. (1981). 'Linguistics and Poetics'. In S. Rudy (ed.), *Roman Jakobson, Selected Writings III: Poetry of Grammar and Grammar of Poetry*. The Hague: Mouton, 18–51.
Jeanmaire, H. (1939). *La Sibylle et le retour de l'âge d'or*. Paris: Leroux.
Jenkyns, R. (1989). 'Virgil and Arcadia'. *JRS* 79: 26–39.
—— (1992). 'Pastoral'. In id. (ed.), *The Legacy of Rome: A New Appraisal*. Oxford: Oxford University Press, 151–75.
—— (1998). *Virgil's Experience: Nature and History, Times, Names, and Places*. Oxford: Clarendon Press.
Karanika, A. (2006). 'Agonistic Poetics in Virgil's Third Eclogue'. In Skoie and Velázquez (eds.), 107–14.
Katz, J. T. and Volk, K. (2006). 'Erotic Hardening and Softening in Vergil's Eighth *Eclogue*'. *CQ* 56: 169–74.
Keith, A. M. (1992). *The Play of Fictions: Studies in Ovid's* Metamorphoses *Book 2*. Ann Arbor: University of Michigan Press.
Kennedy, D. F. (1983). 'Shades of Meaning: Virgil, *Eclogue* 10.75–7'. *LCM* 8: 124.
—— (1987). '*Arcades ambo*: Virgil, Gallus and Arcadia'. *Hermathena* 143: 47–59.
Kenner, H. (1970). *Das Phänomen der verkehrten Welt in der griechisch-römischen Antike*. Klagenfurt: Geschichtsverein für Kärnten.
Kenney, E. J. (1983). 'Virgil and the Elegiac Sensibility'. *ICS* 8: 44–59 (= Hardie (ed.) 1999: 1.68–83).
Kerkhecker, A. (2000). 'Pan, Deus Arcadiae'. *CR* 50: 414–15.
Kittel, G. (ed.) (1933). *Theologisches Wörterbuch zum Neuen Testament*, Vol. 1. Stuttgart: Kohlhammer.
Kittel, R. (1924). *Die hellenistische Mysterienreligion und das Alte Testament*. Stuttgart: Kohlhammer.
Klingner, F. (1927a). 'Rom als Idee'. *Die Antike* 3: 17–34 (= id. (1961), *Römische Geisteswelt*, 4th edn. Munich: Ellermann, 631–52).
—— (1927b). 'Virgils erste Ekloge'. *Hermes* 62: 129–53 (= Klingner 1956a: 294–308).
—— (1927c). Rev. of G. Rohde, *De Vergili eclogarum forma et indole*. *Gnomon* 3: 576–83.
—— (1930). 'Die Einheit des virgilischen Lebenswerkes'. *MDAI(R)* 45: 43–58 (= Klingner 1956a: 256–74. English version in Hardie (ed.) 1999: 1.3–17).

—— (1931a). 'Über das Lob des Landlebens in Virgils Georgica'. *Hermes* 66: 159–89 (English version in Hardie (ed.) 1999: 2.184–210).
—— (1931b). 'Virgil als Bewahrer and Erneuerer'. *Das humanistische Gymnasium* 42: 123–36.
—— (1942). 'Virgil'. In H. Berve (ed.), *Das neue Bild der Antike*, Vol. 2. Leipzig: Koehler & Amelang, 219–245 (= Klingner 1956a: 221–55).
—— (1943): 'Virgil und die geschichtliche Welt'. In id., *Römische Geisteswelt*, 1st edn. Leipzig: Dieterich, 91–112 (= Klingner 1956a: 275–93).
—— (1947) *Dichter und Dichtkunst im alten Rom* (= *Leipziger Universitätsreden* 15). Leipzig: Barth (= Klingner 1956a: 142–76).
—— (1956a). *Römische Geisteswelt*. 3rd edn. Munich: Ellerman.
—— (1956b). 'Virgil'. In (no ed.), *L'influence grecque sur la poésie latine de Catulle à Ovide* (= *Entretiens Hardt* 2). Vandœuvres-Geneva: Fondation Hardt, 131–55.
—— (1967). *Virgil: Bucolica, Georgica, Aeneis*. Zurich: Artemis.
Köhler, E. (1966). 'Wandlungen Arkadiens: Die Marcela-Episode des *Don Quijote* (I, 11–14)'. In id., *Esprit und arkadische Freiheit: Aufsätze aus der Welt der Romania*. Bonn: Athenäum, 302–27.
—— (1977). 'Gattungssystem und Gesellschaftssystem'. *Romanistische Zeitschrift für Literaturgeschichte* 1: 7–22.
Köhnken, A. (1984). ' "Sola...tua carmina" (Vergil, Ecl. 8,9 f.)'. *WJA* 10: 77–90.
Kollmann, E. D. (1973a). 'A Study of the Vocabulary of Vergil's Eclogues'. *RELO* 3: 1–24.
—— (1973b). 'Die Stimme Vergils in seinen Eklogen'. *StudClas* 15: 69–85.
—— (1974). 'The World of the Eclogues'. *RELO* 4: 1–24.
—— (1975). 'A Study of Proper Names in Vergil's Eclogues'. *CW* 69: 97–112.
Korenjak, M. (2003). 'Tityri sub persona: Der antike Biographismus und die bukolische Tradition'. *A&A* 49: 58–79.
Korfmacher, W. C. (1960). 'Classical Type Characterization: The Pastoral Phase'. In L. B. Lawler, D. M. Robathan, and W. C. Korfmacher (eds.), *Studies in Honor of Ullman, Presented to him on the Occasion of his Seventy-fifth Birthday*. St. Louis: The Classical Bulletin, 60–8.
Krauss, W. (1938). 'Über die Stellung der Bukolik in der ästhetischen Theorie des Humanismus'. *Archiv für das Studium der neueren Sprachen* 174: 180–98.
Kroll, W. (1924). *Studien zum Verständnis der römischen Literatur*. Stuttgart: Metzler.
Kuhn, D., Hofmann, A., and Kunz, A. (1966). *Auch ich in Arcadien: Kunstreisen nach Italien 1600–1900*. Marbach: Schiller-Nationalmuseum.

Kumaniecki, C. F. (1926). 'Quo ordine Vergilii eclogae conscriptae sint'. *Eos* 29: 68–79.

Kurfess, A. (1938). 'Hat Linkomies' Auffassung der vierten Ekloge wirklich dem Rätselraten ein Ende bereitet?'. *Philologische Wochenschrift* 58: 812–16.

—— (1951). *Sibyllinische Weissagungen*. Munich: Heimeran.

Labate, M. (1971). 'Il trionfo d'amore in Ovidio e un passo dell' "Eneide"'. *Maia* 23: 347–8.

Lagrange, M.-J. (1931). 'À propos du messianisme de la IVe églogue de Virgile'. *Revue Biblique* 40: 613–14.

Lake, K. (1912–13). *The Apostolic Fathers*, 2 vols. Cambridge, Mass.: Harvard University Press.

Lallemant-Maron, J. (1972). 'Architecture et philosophie dans l'œuvre virgilienne'. *Euphrosyne* 5: 447–55.

La Penna, A. (1963). 'La seconda ecloga e la poesia bucolica di Virgilio'. *Maia* 15: 484–92.

—— (1975). Rev. of Stroh 1971. *Gnomon* 47: 134–42.

—— (1981). 'Lettura della terza bucolica'. In Gigante (ed.), 129–69.

—— (2005). *L'impossibile giustificazione della storia: Un'interpretazione di Virgilio*. Bari: Laterza.

Lattimore, S. (1973). 'Battus in Theocritus' Fourth *Idyll*'. *GRBS* 14: 319–24.

Laurentin, R. (1957). *Structure et théologie de Luc I–II*. Paris: Gabalda.

Leach, E. W. (1974). *Vergil's Eclogues: Landscapes of Experience*. Ithaca: Cornell University Press.

Lecrompe, R. (1970). *Virgile, Bucoliques: Index verborum, relevés statistiques*. Hildesheim: Olms.

Lee, G. (1977). 'A Reading of Virgil's Fifth Eclogue'. *PCPhS* 203: 62–70.

—— (1984). *Virgil: The Eclogues*. New York: Penguin.

Lee, M. O. (1989). *Death and Rebirth in Virgil's Arcadia*. Albany: State University of New York Press.

Lefèvre, E. (2000). 'Catulls Parzenlied und Vergils vierte Ekloge'. *Philologus* 144: 62–80.

Lembach, K. (1970). *Die Pflanzen bei Theokrit*. Heidelberg: Winter.

Leo, F. (1902). 'Vergil und die Ciris'. *Hermes* 37: 14–55.

—— (1903). 'Vergils erste und neunte Ecloge'. *Hermes* 38: 1–18.

—— (1960). *Ausgewählte kleine Schriften*, 2 vols. Ed. by E. Fraenkel. Rome: Edizioni di Storia e Letteratura.

Lerner, L. (1984). 'The *Eclogues* and the Pastoral Tradition'. In C. Martindale (ed.), *Virgil and his Influence: Bimillennial Essays*. Bristol: Bristol Classical Press, 193–213.

Leumann, M., Hofmann, J. B., and Szantyr, A. (1965). *Lateinische Syntax und Stilistik*. Munich: Beck.
Levi, P. (1967/8). 'Arcadia'. *PVS* 7: 1–11.
Lieberg, G. (1982). *Poeta Creator: Studien zu einer Figur der antiken Dichtung*. Amsterdam: Gieben.
—— (1985). *Zu Idee und Figur des dichterischen Schöpfertums*. Bochum: Lieberg.
Lipka, M. (2001). *Language in Vergil's Eclogues*. Berlin: De Gruyter.
Lipking, L. (1981). *The Life of the Poet: Beginning and Ending Poetic Careers*. Chicago: Chicago University Press.
Lodge, D. (1984). *Small World*. Harmondsworth: Penguin.
Lohmeyer, D. (1975). *Faust und die Welt*. Munich: Beck.
Longley, M. (2000). *The Weather in Japan*. London: Cape.
Luther, A. (2002). *Historische Studien zu den Bucolica Vergils* (= *Österreichische Akademie der Wissenschaften, Phil.-hist. Kl., Sitzungsberichte* 698). Vienna: Verlag der Österreichischen Akademie der Wissenschaften.
MacNeice, L. (1966). *The Collected Poems*. Ed. by E. R. Dodds. London: Faber & Faber.
Mahaffy, J. P. (1878). *Rambles and Studies in Greece*, 2nd edn. London: Macmillan.
Mähl, H.-J. (1965). *Die Idee des goldenen Zeitalters im Werk des Novalis: Studien zur Wesensbestimmung der frühromantischen Utopie und ihren ideengeschichtlichen Voraussetzungen*. Heidelberg: Winter.
Mambelli, G. (1940). *Gli studi virgiliani nel secolo XX*, 2 vols. Florence: Sansoni.
Mankin, D. (1988). 'The Addressee of Virgil's Eighth Eclogue: A Reconsideration'. *Hermes* 116: 63–76.
Marchetta, A. (1994). 'L' incipit bucolico di Virgilio: ecl. 2,1'. In id., *Due studi sulle Bucoliche di Virgilio*. Rome: Gruppo Edit. Internazionale, 7–88.
Marmorale, E. V. (1960). *Pertinenze e impertinenze*. Napoli: Armanni.
Martindale, C. (1997a). 'Green Politics: The *Eclogues*'. In Martindale (ed.), 107–24.
—— (1997b). 'Introduction: "The Classic of All Europe"'. In Martindale (ed.), 1–18.
—— (ed.) (1997). *The Cambridge Companion to Virgil*. Cambridge: Cambridge University Press.
Marx, F. (1898). 'Virgils vierte Ekloge'. *NJb* 1: 105–28.
Marx, L. (1964). *The Machine in the Garden: Technology and the Pastoral Ideal in America*. New York: Oxford University Press.

Mattingly H. *et al.* (1923–67). *Roman Imperial Coinage*, 9 vols. London: Spink.

Maury, P. (1944). 'Le secret de Virgile et l'architecture des Bucoliques'. *Lettres d'Humanité* 3: 71–147.

Mayer, R. (1983a). 'Missing Persons in the *Eclogues*'. *BICS* 30: 17–30.

—— (1983b). 'The Civil Status of Corydon'. *CQ* 33: 298–300.

Mayor, J. B., Fowler, W. W., and Conway, R. S. (1907). *Virgil's Messianic Eclogue: Its Meaning, Occasion, and Sources*. London: Murray.

Milik, J. T. and Black, M. (1976). *The Books of Enoch: Aramaic Fragments of Qumrân Cave 4*. Oxford: Clarendon Press.

Milosz, C. (1981). 'The World'. Transl. by R. Hass and R. Pinsky. *Ironweed* 9 (2).

—— (1988). *The Collected Poems, 1931–1987*. New York: Ecco Press.

Momigliano, A. (1948). *Studi di Poesia*, 2nd edn. Bari.

Monteleone, C. (1994). *Palaemon. L'ecloga III di Virgilio:* lusus *intertestuale ed esegesi*. Naples: Loffredo.

Moore-Blunt, J. (1977). 'Eclogue 2: Virgil's Utilisation of Theocritean Motifs'. *Eranos* 75: 23–42.

Mowinckel, S. (1956). *He that Cometh*. Oxford: Blackwell.

Muecke, F. (1975). 'Virgil and the Genre of Pastoral'. *AUMLA* 44: 169–80.

Mynors, R. A. B. (1969). *P. Vergili Maronis opera*. Oxford: Clarendon Press.

Najock, D. (2004). *Statistischer Schlüssel zum Vokabular in Vergils Eklogen*. Hildesheim: Olms.

Nauta, R. R. (2006). 'Panegyric in Virgil's *Bucolics*'. In Fantuzzi and Papanghelis (eds.), 301–32.

Nikiprowetzky, V. (1970). *La troisième Sibylle*. Paris: Mouton.

Nilsson, M. (1920). 'Saeculares ludi, Säkularfeier, Säkulum'. *Pauly-Wissowa* 2. Reihe, lA.2: 1696–1720.

Nisbet, H. B. (ed.) (1985). *German Aesthetic and Literary Criticism: Winckelmann, Lessing, Hamann, Herder, Schiller, Goethe*. Cambridge: Cambridge University Press.

Nisbet, R. G. M. and Hubbard, M. (1970). *A Commentary on Horace:* Odes, Book I. Oxford: Clarendon Press.

—— (1978). 'Virgil's Fourth Eclogue: Easterners and Westerners'. *BICS* 25: 59–78 (= R. G. M. Nisbet 1995: 47–65 = Hardie (ed.) 1999: 1.256–82).

—— (1991). 'The Style of Virgil's *Eclogues*'. *PVS* 20: 1–14 (= R. G. M. Nisbet 1995: 325–37).

—— (1995). *Collected Papers on Latin Literature*. Ed. by S. J. Harrison. Oxford: Clarendon Press.

Nock, A. D. (1972). *Essays on Religion and the Ancient World*, 2 vols. Ed. by Z. Stewart. Oxford: Clarendon Press.

Norden, E. (1913). *Agnostos Theos: Untersuchungen zur Formengeschichte religiöser Rede.* Leipzig: Teubner.

—— (1924). *Die Geburt des Kindes: Geschichte einer religiösen Idee.* Leipzig: Teubner.

—— (1957). *P. Vergilius Maro: Aeneis Buch VI*, 4th edn. Stuttgart: Teubner.

O'Hara, J. J. (1996). *True Names: Vergil and the Alexandrian Tradition of Etymological Wordplay.* Ann Arbor: University of Michigan Press.

O'Toole, F. (2001). 'Between Horror and Transcendence'. *Irish Times* 1 October 2001: 15.

Oppermann, H. (ed.) (1963). *Wege zu Vergil: Drei Jahrzehnte Begegnungen in Dichtung und Wissenschaft.* Darmstadt: Wissenschaftliche Buchgesellschaft.

Otis, B. (1964). *Virgil: A Study in Civilized Poetry.* Oxford: Clarendon Press.

Otto, W. F. (1931). 'Vergil: Festrede zur Feier der zweitausendsten Wiederkehr seines Geburtstags' (= *Schriften der Strassburger Wissenschaftlichen Gesellschaft an der Universität Frankfurt* 13). Berlin: De Gruyter (= Oppermann (ed.) 1963: 69–92).

Page, T. E. (1965). *P. Vergili Maronis Bucolica et Georgica.* London: Macmillan.

Panofsky, E. (1936). 'Et in Arcadia ego: On the Conception of Transience in Poussin and Watteau'. In R. Klibansky and H. J. Paton (eds.), *Philosophy and History: Essays Presented to Ernst Cassirer.* Oxford: Oxford University Press, 223–54.

—— (1955). '*Et in Arcadia ego*: Poussin and the Elegiac Tradition'. In id., *Meaning in the Visual Arts: Papers in and on Art History.* Garden City, New York: Doubleday Anchor Books, 295–320.

Papanghelis, T. D. (1997). 'Winning on Points: About the Singing-Match in Virgil's Seventh Eclogue'. In C. Deroux (ed.), *Studies in Latin Literature and Roman History* 7. Brussels: Latomus, 144–57.

—— (1999). 'Eros Pastoral and Profane: On Love in Virgil's *Eclogues*'. In S. M. Braund and R. Mayer (eds.), *Amor: Roma. Love and Latin Literature.* Cambridge: Cambridge Philological Society, 44–59.

Paratore, E. (1939). 'Spunti Lucreziani nelle "Georgiche"'. *A&R* 7: 177–202.

Parke, H. W. (1988). *Sibyls and Sibylline Prophecy in Classical Antiquity.* London: Routledge.

Parry, H. (1988). 'Magic and the Songstress: Theocritus Idyll 2'. *ICS* 13: 43–55.

Paschalis, M. (ed.) (2007). *Pastoral Palimpsests: Essays in the Reception of Theocritus and Virgil.* Heraklion: Crete University Press.

Pasquali, G. (1951). 'Arte allusiva'. In id., *Stravaganze quarte e supreme.* Venice: Pozza, 11–20 (= Pasquali 1968: 273–82).

Pasquali, G. (1968). *Pagine stravaganti*. Florence: Sansoni.
Patterson, A. (1987). *Pastoral and Ideology: Virgil to Valéry*. Berkeley: University of California Press.
Pease, A. S. (1955–8). *M. Tulli Ciceronis De natura deorum*, 2 vols. Cambridge, Mass.: Harvard University Press.
Perkell, C. G. (1978). 'A Reading of Virgil's Fourth Georgic'. *Phoenix* 32: 211–21.
—— (1981). 'On the Corycian Gardener of Vergil's Fourth *Georgic*'. *TAPhA* 111: 167–77.
—— (1989). *The Poet's Truth: A Study of the Poet in Virgil's Georgics*. Berkeley: University of California Press.
—— (1990a). 'On *Eclogue* 1.79–83'. *TAPhA* 120: 171–81.
—— (1990b). 'Vergilian Scholarship in the Nineties: Eclogues'. *Vergilius* 36: 43–55.
—— (1996). 'The "Dying Gallus" and the Design of *Eclogue* 10'. *CPh* 91: 128–40.
—— (2001). 'Vergil Reading His Twentieth-Century Readers: A Study of *Eclogue* 9'. *Vergilius* 47: 64–88.
Petriconi, H. (1930). 'Über die Idee des goldenen Zeitalters als Ursprung der Schäferdichtungen Sannazaros und Tassos'. *Die neueren Sprachen* 38: 265–83.
—— (1948). 'Das neue Arkadien'. *A&A* 3: 187–200.
—— (1959). 'Die verlorenen Paradiese'. *Romanistisches Jahrbuch* 10: 167–99.
Pfeiffer, E. (1933). *Virgils Bukolika: Untersuchungen zum Formproblem*. Stuttgart: Kohlhammer.
Pfeiffer, R. (1928). 'Ein Neues Altersgedicht des Kallimachos'. *Hermes* 63: 302–41.
—— (1949–53). *Callimachus*, 2 vols. Oxford: Clarendon Press.
—— (1968). *History of Classical Scholarship from the Beginnings to the End of the Hellenistic Age*. Oxford: Clarendon Press.
Pfister, F. (1924) 'Epiphanie'. *Pauly-Wissowa Suppl.* 4: 277–323.
—— (1937). 'Herakles und Christus'. *ARW* 34: 42–60.
Pietzcker, C. (1965). 'Die Landschaft in Vergils Bukolika'. Diss. Freiburg.
Poggioli, R. (1975). *The Oaten Flute: Essays on Pastoral Poetry and the Pastoral Ideal*. Cambridge, Mass.: Harvard University Press.
Pohlenz, M. (1930). 'Das Schlussgedicht der Bucolica'. In (no ed.), *Studi Virgiliani*. Mantua: 205–25.
—— (1965). *Kleine Schriften*, 2 vols. Ed. by H. Dörrie. Hildesheim: Olms.
Posch, S. (1969). *Beobachtungen zur Theokritnachwirkung bei Vergil*. Innsbruck: Wagner.
Pöschl, V. (1964). *Die Hirtendichtung Virgils*. Heidelberg: Winter.

Potter, D. S. (1990). *Prophecy and History in the Crisis of the Roman Empire: A Historical Commentary on the Thirteenth Sibylline Oracle*. Oxford: Clarendon Press.

Powell, B. B. (1976). 'Poeta Ludens: Thrust and Counter-Thrust in *Eclogue* 3'. *ICS* 1: 113–21.

Poynton, J. B. (1936). *Versions*. Oxford: Blackwell.

Putnam, M. C. J. (1965). *The Poetry of the Aeneid: Four Studies in Imaginative Unity and Design*. Cambridge, Mass.: Harvard University Press.

—— (1970). *Virgil's Pastoral Art: Studies in the* Eclogues. Princeton: Princeton University Press.

—— (1979). *Virgil's Poem of the Earth: Studies in the* Georgics. Princeton: Princeton University Press.

Radnoti, M. (2000). *Camp Notebook*. Transl. by F. R. Jones. Todmorden: Arc.

Raper, R. W. (1908). 'Gods in the *Eclogues* and the Arcadian Club'. *CR* 22: 40–3.

Rapin, R. (1659). *Renati Rapini Eclogae cum dissertatione de carmine pastorali*. Paris: Barbou.

Reitzenstein, E. (1931). 'Zur Stiltheorie des Kallimachos'. In (no ed.), *Festschrift Richard Reitzenstein*. Leipzig: Teubner, 23–69.

Reitzenstein, R. (1893). *Epigramm und Skolion: Ein Beitrag zur Geschichte der alexandrinischen Dichtung*. Giessen: Ricker.

—— (1896). 'Properz-Studien'. *Hermes* 31: 185–220.

Richter, A. (1970). *Virgile: La huitième bucolique*. Paris: Les Belles Lettres.

Robinson, D. M. and Fluck, E. J. (1937). *A Study of the Greek Love-Names*. Baltimore: Johns Hopkins University Press.

Rohde, G. (1963). *Studien und Interpretationen zur antiken Literatur, Religion und Geschichte*. Berlin: De Gruyter.

Rose, H. J. (1942). *The Eclogues of Vergil*. Berkeley: University of California Press.

Rosenmeyer, T. G. (1969). *The Green Cabinet: Theocritus and the European Pastoral Lyric*. Berkeley: University of California Press.

Ross, D. O., Jr. (1969). *Style and Tradition in Catullus*. Cambridge, Mass.: Harvard University Press.

—— (1975). *Backgrounds to Augustan Poetry: Gallus, Elegy and Rome*. Cambridge: Cambridge University Press.

Rudd, N. (1976). *Lines of Enquiry*. Cambridge: Cambridge University Press.

Rüdiger, H. (1959). 'Schiller und das Pastorale'. *Euphorion* 53: 229–51.

Rumpel, I. (1961). *Lexicon Theocriteum*. Hildesheim: Olms.

Rumpf, L. (1996). *Extremus labor: Vergils 10. Ekloge und die Poetik der Bucolica*. Göttingen: Vandenhoeck & Ruprecht.

Rumpf, L. (1999). 'Bukolische Nomina bei Vergil und Theokrit: Zur poetischen Technik des Eklogenbuchs'. *RhM* 142: 157–75.

Rundin, J. (2003). 'The Epicurean Morality of Vergil's *Bucolics*'. *CW* 92: 159–76.

Rupprecht, K. (2004). 'Warten auf Menalcas: Der Weg des Vergessens in Vergils neunter Ekloge'. *A&A* 50: 36–61.

Rutherford, R. B. (1989). 'Virgil's Poetic Ambitions in Eclogue 6'. *G&R* 36: 42–50.

Rzach, A. (1891). *Chresmoi sibylliakoi / Oracula sibyllina*. Vienna: Tempsky.

—— (1923).'Sibyllinische Orakel'. *Pauly-Wissowa* 2. Reihe, 2.2: 2103–83.

Sainati, A. (1919). *La lirica latina del Rinascimento I*. Pisa: Spoerri.

Sallmann, K. (1995). 'Poesie und Magie: Vergils 8. Ekloge'. *ŽAnt* 45: 287–301.

—— (1998). 'Wer singt Damons Lied?: Noch einmal zu Vergils 8. Ekloge'. In A. E. Radke (ed.), *Candide iudex: Beiträge zur augusteischen Dichtung. Festschrift für Walter Wimmel zum 75. Geburtstag*. Stuttgart: Steiner, 275–81.

Sannazaro, J. (1504). *Arcadia*. Naples: Mayr.

—— (1961). *Opere Volgari*. Ed. by A. Mauro. Bari: Laterza.

Santucci, E. (1930). 'Il dolore nella poesia virgiliana'. *Annuario del R. Liceo scientifico Fulcieri Paolucci di Calboli (Forlì)*, anni scolastici 1928/29, 1929/30: 42–50.

Sargeaunt, J. (1920). *The Trees, Shrubs, and Plants of Virgil*. Oxford: Blackwell.

Saxl, F. (1927). *Antike Götter in der Spätrenaissance: Ein Freskenzyklus und ein Discorso des Jacopo Zucchi*. Leipzig: Teubner.

Scaliger, I. C. (1561). *Poetices libri septem*. Lyon: Vincentius.

—— (1994). *Poetices libri septem: Sieben Bücher über die Dichtkunst*, Vol. 1. Ed. by L. Deitz. Stuttgart: Frommann-Holzboog.

Schadewaldt, W. (1931). 'Sinn und Werden der vergilischen Dichtung'. *Das Erbe der Alten* 20: 69–95 (= Schadewaldt 1970: 701–722 = Oppermann (ed.) 1963: 43–68).

—— (1970). *Hellas und Hesperien: Gesammelte Schriften zur Antike und zur neueren Literatur*, 2 vols., 2nd edn. Zurich: Artemis.

Schäfer, A. (2001). *Vergils Eklogen 3 und 7 in der Tradition der lateinischen Streitdichtung: Eine Darstellung anhand ausgewählter Texte der Antike und des Mittelalters*. Frankfurt: Lang.

Schiller, F. (1989). 'Über naive und sentimentalische Dichtung'. In id., *Sämtliche Werke*, Vol. 5, 8th edn. Munich: Hanser, 694–780.

Schmidt, E. A. (1972). *Poetische Reflexion: Vergils Bukolik*. Munich: Fink.

—— (1974). *Zur Chronologie der Eklogen Vergils*. Heidelberg: Winter(= E. A. Schmidt 1987: 197–237).

—— (1975). 'Arkadien: Abendland und Antike'. *A&A* 21: 36–57 (= E. A. Schmidt 1987: 239–64).
—— (1987). *Bukolische Leidenschaft oder Über antike Hirtenpoesie*. Frankfurt: Lang.
—— (1998). 'Freedom and Ownership: A Contribution to the Discussion of Vergil's First *Eclogue*'. *Papers of the Leeds International Latin Seminar* 10: 185–201.
Schmidt, V. (1977). 'Redeunt Saturnia Regna: Studien zu Vergils vierter Ecloga'. Diss. Groningen.
Schoepsdau, K. (1974). 'Motive der Liebesdichtung in Vergils dritter Ecloge'. *Hermes* 102: 268–300.
Schott, R. (1930). 'Vergil und Homer'. *Allgemeine Rundschau* 27: 842–4.
Schultz, C. E. (2003). '*Latet anguis in herba*: A Reading of Vergil's Third *Eclogue*'. *AJPh* 124: 199–224.
Schunck, P. (1970). 'Sannazaros Arcadia'. *Romanistisches Jahrbuch* 21: 93–106.
Schürer, E. (1907). *Geschichte des jüdischen Volkes im Zeitalter Jesu Christi*, Vol. 2, 4th edn. Leipzig: Hinrichs.
—— (1986). *The History of the Jewish People in the Age of Jesus Christ*, Vol. 3, 2nd edn. Ed. by G. Vermes, F. Millar, and M. Goodman. Edinburgh: Clark.
Segal, C. P. (1965). '*Tamen cantabitis, Arcades:* Exile and Arcadia in *Eclogues* One and Nine'. *Arion* 4: 237–66 (= Segal 1981: 271–300 = Hardie (ed.) 1999: 1.172–202).
—— (1967). 'Vergil's *caelatum opus*: An Interpretation of the Third *Eclogue*'. *AJPh* 88: 279–308 (= Segal 1981: 235–64 = Hardie (ed.) 1999: 1.231–55).
—— (1981). *Poetry and Myth in Ancient Pastoral: Essays on Theocritus and Virgil*. Princeton: Princeton University Press.
—— (1985). 'Space, Time, and Imagination in Theocritus' Second Idyll'. *ClAnt* 4: 103–19.
—— (1987). 'Alphesiboeus' Song and Simaetha's Magic: Virgil's Eighth Eclogue and Theocritus' Second Idyll'. *GB* 14: 167–85.
Seng, H. (1999). *Vergils Eklogenbuch: Aufbau, Chronologie und Zahlenverhältnisse*. Hildesheim: Olms.
Sergent, B. (1986). *Homosexuality in Greek Myth*. Transl. by A. Goldhammer. Boston: Beacon Press.
Serpa, F. (1987). *Il punto su Virgilio*. Bari: Laterza.
Skoie, M. and Velázquez, S. B. (eds.) (2006). *Pastoral and the Humanities: Arcadia Re-inscribed*. Exeter: Bristol Phoenix Press.
Skutsch, F. (1901). *Aus Vergils Frühzeit*. Leipzig: Teubner.
—— (1906). *Gallus und Vergil*. Leipzig: Teubner.
Skutsch, O. (1956). 'Zu Vergils Eklogen'. *RhM* 99: 193–201.

Skutsch, O. (1968). *Studia Enniana*. London: Athlone.
Slater, D. A. (1912). 'Was the Fourth Eclogue Written to Celebrate the Marriage of Octavia to Mark Antony?: A Literary Parallel'. *CR* 26: 114–19.
Smith, K. F. (1913). *The Elegies of Albius Tibullus, the Corpus Tibullianum*. New York: American Book Company.
Smith, R. R. R. (1991). *Hellenistic Sculpture: A Handbook*. London: Thames and Hudson.
Snell, B. (1938). 'Die 16. Epode des Horaz und Vergils 4. Ekloge'. *Hermes* 73: 237–42.
—— (1945). 'Arkadien: Die Entdeckung einer geistigen Landschaft'. *A&A* 1: 26–41 (= Snell 1946: 233–258 = Snell 1955: 371–400 = Oppermann (ed.) 1963: 338–67. English version in Snell 1953: 281–309 = Commager (ed.) 1966: 14–27 = Hardie (ed.) 1999: 1.44–67).
—— (1946). *Die Entdeckung des Geistes: Studien zur Entstehung des europäischen Denkens bei den Griechen*, 1st ed. Hamburg: Claassen & Goverts.
—— (1953). *The Discovery of the Mind: The Greek Origins of European Thought*. Transl. by T. G. Rosenmeyer. Oxford: Blackwell.
—— (1955). *Die Entdeckung des Geistes: Studien zur Entstehung des europäischen Denkens bei den Griechen*, 3rd edn. Hamburg: Claassen.
Solodow, J. B. (1977). '*Poeta Impotens*: The Last Three Eclogues'. *Latomus* 36: 757–71.
—— (1986). '*Raucae, tua cura, palumbes*: Study of a Poetic Word Order'. *HSPh* 90: 129–153.
Spenser, E. (1970). *Poetical Works*. Oxford: Oxford University Press.
Spoerri, W. (1970). 'Zur Kosmogonie in Vergils 6. Ekloge'. *MH* 27: 144–63.
Springer, C. (1983/4). 'Aratus and the Cups of Menalcas: A Note on Eclogue 3.42'. *CJ* 79: 131–4.
Stégen, G. (1957). *Commentaire sur cinq Bucoliques de Virgile (3, 6, 8, 9, 10)*. Namur: Wesmael-Charlier.
Stephan, R. (1971). *Goldenes Zeitalter and Arkadien: Studien zur französischen Lyrik des ausgehenden 18. und des 19. Jahrhunderts*. Heidelberg: Winter.
Stevens, W. (1965). *Selected Poems*. London: Faber & Faber.
Stewart, Z. (1959). 'The Song of Silenus'. *HSPh* 64: 179–205.
Strack, H. L. and Billerbeck, P. (1924). *Kommentar zum Neuen Testament aus Talmud und Midrasch*, Vol. 2. Munich: Beck.
Stroh, W. (1971). *Die römische Liebeselegie als werbende Dichtung*. Amsterdam: Hakkert.
Stroppini, G. (1993). *Amour et dualité dans les* Bucoliques *de Virgile*. Paris: Klincksieck.
Stroux, J. (1932). *Vergil*. Munich: Hueber.

Bibliography

Stuart, D. R. (1921). 'On Vergil Eclogue iv.60–63'. *CPh* 16: 209–30.

Sudhaus, S. (1901). 'Jahrhundertfeier in Rom und messianische Weissagungen'. *RhM* 56: 37–54.

Sullivan, M. B. (2002). '*Et eris mihi magnus Apollo*: Divine and Earthly Competition in Virgil's Seventh *Eclogue*'. *Vergilius* 48: 40–54.

Tarn, W. W. (1932). 'Alexander Helios and the Golden Age'. *JRS* 22: 135–60.

Tarrant, R. J. (1978). 'The Addressee of Virgil's Eighth Eclogue'. *HSPh* 82: 197–9

Terzaghi, N. (1963). *Studia Graeca et Latina*. Turin: Bottega d'Erasmo.

Theodorakopoulos, E. (1997). 'Closure: The Book of Virgil'. In Martindale (ed.), 155–65.

Thibodeau, P. (2006). 'The Addressee of Vergil's Eighth Eclogue'. *CQ* 56: 618–23.

Thiselton-Dyer, W. T. (1918). 'On Some Ancient Plant-Names'. *JPh* 34: 290–312.

Thomas, R. F. (1982). 'Catullus and the Polemics of Poetic Reference (Poem 64.1–18)'. *AJPh* 103: 144–64 (= Thomas 1999: 12–32).

—— (1986). 'Virgil's *Georgics* and the Art of Reference'. *HSPh* 90: 171–98 (= Thomas 1999: 114–41 = Hardie (ed.) 1999: 2.58–82).

—— (1990). 'Vergilian Scholarship in the Nineties: Ideology, Influence, and Future Studies in the *Georgics*'. *Vergilius* 36: 64–70.

—— (1998). 'Voice, Poetics, and Virgil's Sixth *Eclogue*'. In J. Jasanoff, H. C. Melchert, and L. Oliver (eds.), *Mír Curad: Studies in Honor of Calvert Watkins*. Innsbruck: Institut für Sprachwissenschaft der Universität Innsbruck, 669–76 (= Thomas 1999: 288–96).

—— (1999). *Reading Virgil and His Texts: Studies in Intertextuality*. Ann Arbor: University of Michigan Press.

Timpanaro, S. (1978). *Contributi di filologia e di storia della lingua Latina*. Rome: Edizioni dell'Ateneo & Bizzarri.

Töns, U. (1973). 'Vergil und die Ekloge in den romanischen Ländern'. Habilitationsschrift Münster, unpublished.

—— (1977). 'Sannazaros Arcadia: Wirkung und Wandlung der vergilischen Ekloge'. *A&A* 23: 143–61.

Tracy, S. (2003). 'Palaemon's Indecision'. In P. Thibodeau and H. Haskell (eds.), *Being There Together: Essays in Honor of Michael C. J. Putnam on the Occasion of his Seventieth Birthday*. Afton, Minn.: Afton Historical Society Press, 66–77.

Trypanis, C. A. (1975). *Callimachus*: Aetia, Iambi, *Lyric Poems*, Hecale, *Minor Epic and Elegiac Poems, and Other Fragments*. Cambridge, Mass.: Harvard University Press.

Usener, H. (1911). *Das Weihnachtsfest*, 2nd edn. Bonn: Cohen.

Vaccaro, A. J. (1966). 'Adjetivación atributiva en las Églogas'. *REC* 10: 7–23.
Van der Waerden, B. L. (1952). 'Das Grosse Jahr und die ewige Wiederkehr'. *Hermes* 80: 129–55.
Van Sickle, J. (1978). *The Design of Virgil's Bucolics*. Rome: Edizioni dell'Ateneo & Bizzarri (2nd ed. 2004).
—— (1980). 'The Book-Roll and Some Conventions of the Poetic Book'. *Arethusa* 13: 5–42.
—— (1981). '*Commentaria in Maronem commenticia*: A Case History of Bucolics Misread'. *Arethusa* 14: 17–34.
—— (1986). *Poesia e potere: Il mito Virgilio*. Bari: Laterza.
—— (1987). ' "Shepherd Slave": Civil Status and Bucolic Conceit in Virgil, Eclogue 2'. *QUCC* 56: 127–9.
—— (1992). *A Reading of Virgil's Messianic Eclogue*. New York: Garland.
—— (2004). 'Virgil *Bucolics* 1.1–2 and Interpretive Tradition: A Latin (Roman) Program for a Greek Genre'. *CPh* 99: 336–53.
Veit, W. (1961). 'Studien zur Geschichte des Topos der Goldenen Zeit von der Antike bis zum 18. Jahrhundert'. Diss. Cologne.
Vermes, G. (1973). *Jesus the Jew: A Historian's Reading of the Gospels*. New York: Macmillan.
Vidal-Naquet, P. (1986). *The Black Hunter: Forms of Thought and Forms of Society in the Greek World*. Transl. by A. Szegedy-Maszak. Baltimore: Johns Hopkins University Press.
Volk, K. (2002). *Die Poetics of Latin Didactic: Lucretius, Vergil, Ovid, Manilius*. Oxford: Oxford University Press.
Von Albrecht, M. (2006). *Vergil: Bucolica, Georgica, Aeneis. Eine Einführung*. Heidelberg: Winter.
Von Finckenstein, F. L. K. (1806). *Arethusa oder die bukolischen Dichter des Alterthums*, Vol. 1. Berlin: Unger.
Von Wilamowitz-Moellendorff, U. (1906). *Die Textgeschichte der griechischen Bukoliker*. Berlin: Weidmann.
—— (1925). 'Die griechische Heldensage. II.' *Preussische Akademie der Wissenschaften Berlin, Phil.-Hist. Kl., Sitzungsberichte* 1925.17: 214–42.
Vossler, K. (1906). 'Tassos Aminta und die Hirtendichtung'. *Studien zur vergleichenden Literaturgeschichte* 6: 26–40 (= Vossler 1965: 181–93).
—— (1950). *Poesie der Einsamkeit in Spanien*, 2nd edn. Munich: Beck.
—— (1965). *Die Romanische Welt: Gesammelte Aufsätze*. Munich: Piper.
Wagenvoort, H. (1956). *Studies in Roman Literature, Culture and Religion*. Leiden: Brill.
—— (1962). 'Indo-European Paradise Motifs in Virgil's 4th Eclogue.' *Mnemosyne* 15: 133–45.
Waltz, R. (1927). 'La Ire et la IXe Bucolique'. *RBPh* 6: 31–58.

Webster, T. B. L. (1964). *Hellenistic Poetry and Art.* London: Methuen.
Weinstock, S. (1971). *Divus Julius.* Oxford: Clarendon Press.
Weisbach, W. (1930). 'Et in Arcadia ego: Ein Beitrag zur Interpretation antiker Vorstellungen in der Kunst des 17. Jahrhunderts'. *Die Antike* 6: 127–45.
Wellek, R. and Warren, A. (1949). *Theory of Literature.* New York: Harcourt & Brace.
Wendel, C. (1900). 'De nominibus bucolicis', *Jahrbücher für classische Philologie Suppl.* 26: 1–90.
—— (1920). *Überlieferung und Entstehung der Theokrit-Scholien.* Berlin: Weidmann.
Wendel, H. (1933). *Arkadien im Umkreis bukolischer Dichtung in der Antike und in der französischen Literatur.* Giessen: Selbstverlag des Romanischen Seminars.
Werner-Fädler, M. (1972). *Das Arkadienbild und der Mythos der goldenen Zeit in der französischen Literatur des 17. und 18. Jahrhunderts.* Salzburg: Institut für romanische Philologie der Universität Salzburg.
West, M. L. (1966). *Hesiod: Theogony.* Oxford: Clarendon Press.
Westendorp Boerma, R. E. H. (1949). *P. Vergili Maronis libellus qui inscribitur Catalepton*, Vol. 1.Assen: De Torenlaan.
Whitaker, R. (1988). 'Did Gallus Write "Pastoral" Elegies?'. *CQ* 38: 454–8.
Wili, W. (1930). *Vergil.* Munich: Beck.
Wilkinson, L. P. (1966). 'The Continuity of Propertius ii. 13'. *CR* 16: 141–4.
Williams, F. J. (1971). 'A Theophany in Theocritus'. *CQ* 21: 137–45.
Williams, G. (1974). 'A Version of Pastoral: Virgil, *Eclogue* 4'. In A. J. Woodman and D. West (eds.), *Quality and Pleasure in Latin Poetry.* Cambridge: Cambridge University Press, 31–46.
Williams, G. D. (1994). *Banished Voices: Readings in Ovid's Exile Poetry.* Cambridge: Cambridge University Press.
Williams, R. D. (1972/3). 'Virgil Today'. *PVS* 12: 25–35.
—— (1979). *Virgil: The Eclogues and Georgics.* New York: St. Martin's Press.
Wimmel, W. (1960). *Kallimachos in Rom: Die Nachfolge seines apologetischen Dichtens in der Augusteerzeit.* Wiesbaden: Steiner.
—— (1968). *Der frühe Tibull.* Munich: Fink.
—— (1998). 'Vergils Tityrus und der perusinische Konflikt: Zum Verständnis der ersten Ekloge'. *RhM* 141: 348–61.
Windisch, H. (1920). *Der Barnabasbrief* (= *Handbuch zum Neuen Testament, Ergänzungsband: Die apostolischen Väter 3*). Tübingen: Mohr.
—— (1925). 'Friedensbringer-Gottessöhne: Eine religionsgeschichtliche Interpretation der 7. Seligpreisung'. *Zeitschrift für neutestamentliche Wissenschaft* 24: 240–60.

Winterbottom, M. (1976). 'Virgil and the Confiscations'. *G&R* 23: 55–9 (= I. McAuslan and P. Walcot (eds.) (1990). *Virgil*. Oxford: Oxford University Press, 65–8).
Witte, K. (1922). *Der Bukoliker Vergil: Die Entstehungsgeschichte einer römischen Literaturgattung*. Stuttgart: Metzler.
—— (1922/3). 'Virgils vierte Ekloge: Eine Studie zur Poetik der römisch-hellenistischen Dichtung'. *WS* 43: 35–44.
Wormell, D. E. W. (1960). 'The Riddles in Virgil's Third Eclogue'. *CQ* 10: 29–32.
Worstbrock, F. J. (1963). *Elemente einer Poetik der Aeneis: Untersuchungen zum Gattungsstil vergilianischer Epik*. Münster: Aschendorff.
Wright, J. R. G. (1983). 'Virgil's Pastoral Programme: Theocritus, Callimachus and *Eclogue* 1'. *PCPhS* 209: 107–60 (= Hardie (ed.) 1999: 1.116–71).
Yeats, W. B. (1965). *Selected Poetry*. Harmondsworth: Penguin.
Zetzel, J. E. G. (1984). 'Servius and Triumviral History in the *Eclogues*'. *CPh* 79: 139–42.
Zinn, E. (1956). 'Die Dichter des alten Rom und die Anfänge des Weltgedichts'. *A&A* 5: 7–26.
Ziolkowski, T. (1993). *Virgil and the Moderns*. Princeton: Princeton University Press.

Acknowledgements

Permission to reprint the following items is gratefully acknowledged:

E. A. Schmidt, 'Arkadien: Abendland und Antike', in *Bukolische Leidenschaft oder Über antike Hirtenpoesie* (Frankfurt: Peter Lang Verlag, 1987), 239–64.

L. Rumpf, 'Bukolische Nomina bei Vergil und Theokrit: Zur poetischen Technik des Eklogenbuchs', *Rheinisches Museum* 142 (1999), 157–75.

R. G. M. Nisbet, 'The Style of Virgil's *Eclogues*', *Proceedings of the Virgil Society* 20 (1991), 1–14.

T. K. Hubbard, 'Allusive Artistry and Vergil's Revisionary Program: Eclogues 1–3', *Materiali e discussioni per l'analisi dei testi classici* 34 (1995), 37–67.

C. G. Perkell, 'On *Eclogue* 1.79–83', *Transactions and Proceedings of the American Philological Association* 120 (1990), 171–81.

J. Henderson, 'Virgil's Third *Eclogue*: How Do You Keep an Idiot in Suspense?', *Classical Quarterly* 48 (1998), 213–28.

R. G. M. Nisbet, 'Virgil's Fourth Eclogue: Easterners and Westerners', *Bulletin of the Institute for Classical Studies* 25 (1978), 59–78.

D. O. Ross, Jr., 'The Sixth Eclogue: Virgil's Poetic Genealogy', in *Backgrounds to Augustan Poetry: Gallus, Elegy and Rome* (Cambridge: Cambridge University Press, 1975), 18–38.

G. B. Conte, 'An Interpretation of the Tenth *Eclogue*', in *The Rhetoric of Imitation: Genre and Poetic Memory in Virgil and Other Latin Poets* (Ithaca: Cornell University Press, 1986), 100–29.

S. Heaney, 'Eclogues *in extremis*: On the Staying Power of Pastoral', *Proceedings of the Royal Irish Academy* 103C (2003), 1–12.

Passages cited

Biblical

Gen. 16:11–12: 170
   17:19: 171

Judg. 13:5: 171

1 Chron. 22:9–10: 171

Ps. 21:21: 177 n. 96
   36:15: 177 n. 96

Eccl. 2:9: 166 n. 53

Isa. 7:14: 164, 171, 172, 176, 187
   11:6–9: 175
   11:8: 175 n. 94
   41:2: 162 n. 33
   44:23: 183 n. 123

Jer. 31(38):4: 176

Ezek. 14:17: 177 n. 96

Zeph. 3:14: 176

Zach. 2:10: 176
   9:9: 176

2 Baruch 74:2: 160 n. 24

Mt. 1:21–3: 171
   1:25: 164
   2:11: 172

Mk. 1:11: 182
   1:15: 159 n. 16

Lk. 1:13–17: 171
   1:28: 171
   1:30: 171
   1:32–3: 170
   1:32: 172

1:42: 171
1:76: 172 n. 77
2:11: 183 n. 123
2:30: 184 n. 127
2:35: 177
2:52: 178 n. 97

Jn. 6:62: 169 n. 64

Rom. 8:9: 176

1 Cor. 3:16: 176
   15:47: 162 n. 36

Gal. 4:4: 159 n. 16

Rev. 12:12: 183 n. 124
   19:7: 185 n. 136
   21:1: 180 n. 107

Greek

Antigonus, *Hist. Mir.*: 185 n. 132
Apollod. *Bibl.* 1.3.2: 205 n. 40
   2.4.9: 205 n. 40
   3.9.2: 103 n. 46
Apollonides, *Anth. Pal.* 9.287.6: 182 n. 115
Ap. Rhod. *Argon.* 1.496–502: 199
   1.496: 199
   1.501–2: 199
   1.503–11: 213 n. 54
Arat. *Phaen.* 1–4: 204 n. 38
   109: 161 n. 29
   110–11: 180 n. 106
   131: 161 n. 29
   133 ff.: 160 n. 26
   738: 202–3
Ar. *Pax* 1076: 174 n. 93
Arist. *Hist. An.* 587b5 ff.: 185 n. 132

[Barnabas], *Epist.* 6.13: 160 n. 24
   15.5–9: 160 n. 25

Callim. *Aet.* fr. 1.23–4: 152 n. 46, 191
  fr. 1.24: 210
  fr. 1.29–30: 91 n. 26
  fr. 26–8: 194
  fr. 26.1: 194 n. 12
  fr. 27: 195
  fr. 73: 237 n. 24
  fr. 110.1: 105
  Epigr. 22: 195 n. 13
  Frag. inc. sed. fr. 689: 96 n. 38
    27: 203
    28.4: 210 n. 48
  Hymn 2.1 ff.: 183 n. 120
    2.9–11: 52
    2.105–12: 201 n. 29
    2.108–9: 87 n. 18
    2.110–12: 87 n. 18
    2.111–12: 210 n. 47
    2.111: 203 n. 33
    4.260 ff.: 173 n. 78
Conon fr. 19: 194 n. 12
Crinagoras, *Anth. Pal.* 9.545.1: 139 n. 18

Dionys. Per. 941: 173 n. 78

Empedocles fr. 130: 174
Euphorion fr. 63.2: 238 n. 26
Eur. *Hipp.* 5–6: 236 n. 22
  215–21: 235
  443–6: 236 n. 22
  Hipp. Kalypt. fr. 430: 236 n. 22
  Phoen. 651 ff.: 173 n. 78

Hephaestion 65.17: 170 n. 70
Hdt. 5.93 β .2: 171 n. 73
Hes. *Op.* 111: 161
  112: 168 n. 62
  117–18: 173 n. 80
  236–7: 180 n. 106
  Theog. 5–7: 208
    839 ff.: 183 n. 119
  fr. 1.6: 168 n. 63
Hom. *Od.* 7.313: 172
  11.248–9: 171 n. 73
  11.602–3: 186 n. 138
Hymn. Hom. Ap. 135 ff.: 173 n. 78

Joseph. *AJ* 14.388: 158 n. 13

Kore Kosmou fr. 23.62 ff.: 163 n. 37
  fr. 24.4: 162 n. 31

Lydus, *Mens.* 4.21: 185 n. 132

Mosch. 3.8: 156
  3.55–6: 184 n. 128

Nic. *Ther.* 11–12: 209
Nonnus, *Dion.* 7.344–5: 173 n. 82
  9.12: 173 n. 78
  9.35–6: 185 n. 133

Orac. Sib. 1.297–8: 173 n. 80
  3.227 ff.: 157 n. 8
  3.286: 162 n. 33
  3.316: 177 n. 96
  3.371–2: 184 n. 127
  3.373–4: 161 n. 27, 169 n. 69
  3.608 ff.: 158 n. 10
  3.652: 162 n. 33
  3.653: 169 n. 69
  3.663–4: 179 n. 102
  3.744–5: 161
  3.749–51: 161
  3.771: 166 n. 51
  3.786: 166 n. 53
  3.788–95: 175
  3.785–7: 176
  4.47: 159 n. 15
  4.192: 184 n. 127
  7.146–7: 180 n. 108
  8.41: 158 n. 11
  8.458: 162 n. 36
  8.474–5: 183

Philostr. *Imag.* 1.14.3: 173 n. 78
  1.26.2: 173 n. 78
Pind. *Nem.* 1.71–2: 186 n. 138
  Ol. 6.55: 173 n. 78
  Pyth. 9.59 ff.: 171 n. 73
Plut. *Cat. Mai.* 20.5: 178 n. 98
PMG 852: 53 n. 6
P. Oxy. 20.2262 fr. 2: 208 n. 44
  22.2332.63 ff.: 162 n. 34
Protevangelium Jacobi 18.2: 183 n. 122
  22.2: 173 n. 84
Psalm. Sal.: 184 n. 127

Passages cited

Theoc. *Id.* 1.1 ff.: 119
1.1–11: 153 n. 48
1.1–3: 83
1.4–6: 51–2
1.25–60: 104
1.25–6: 85
1.29–30: 51
1.52: 91 n. 26
1.64: 51, 195
1.66: 220
1.103: 221
1.134: 49
2.1–2: 90
2.18–19: 90 n. 24
2.59–62: 90 n. 24
2.82: 49
3.1–5: 84
3.1: 77 n. 26
3.2: 77 n. 26
3.3–4: 84
3.6–9: 89
3.6: 77 n. 26
3.22: 77 n. 26
3.34–6: 97
3.38: 83 n. 14
4.1 ff.: 55
4.1–2: 102
4.1: 152
4.3: 102
4.13: 102
4.28–30: 96 n. 36
4.36: 77 n. 26
4.38: 77 n. 26
5.1: 153 n. 48
5.6: 77 n. 25
5.8: 96 n. 36
5.20: 77 n. 25
5.41–2: 103
5.81: 77 n. 25
5.82: 106
5.88–9: 107 n. 53
5.90–1: 107
5.104–7: 105 n. 49
6.6–22: 107
6.21–41: 101
6.34–8: 95
6.42–6: 95
7.21–3: 89–90
7.72: 77 n. 26, 84
7.73: 77 n. 25
7.78–9: 77 n. 25
7.78: 77 n. 25
7.88–9: 77 n. 25, 82 n. 11, 119
7.96–127: 92
7.131–9: 93
7.131–4: 91
7.135–42: 86–7
7.135–7: 91
7.135–6: 91 n. 27
7.138–9: 91
9.1–2: 51
10.7: 77 n. 25
10.12: 77 n. 25
11.12: 173 n. 85
11.25–7: 98
11.30: 95
11.34–40: 94
11.34: 94
11.40–1: 97
11.44–9: 95
11.56–9: 98
11.65–6: 95
11.72–81: 99
11.72: 51
12.3–6: 71 n. 11
14.1–2: 55
15.19–20: 56
17.13: 169 n. 67
24.73 ff.: 171
24.73: 171
24.78: 171
24.84: 171, 186 n. 138
24.86–7: 174 n. 93
24.105–6: 194
24.106: 203 n. 34
[Theoc.] *Id.* 8.3: 93, 101
8.11–20: 104, 105 n. 49
8.15–16: 101 n. 44
8.33: 219 n. 10
8.37: 219 n. 10
8.41–4: 54
8.45–7: 219 n. 10
8.47: 77 n. 25
8.90–1: 104
Σ *Id.* 8.53-6d Wendel: 104 n. 48
Thgn. 9–10: 183 n. 121
Zosimus, *Hist. Nov.* 2.6.9: 165 n. 46

Latin

Calp. *Ecl.* 4.64: 74
Calvus *FPL* 85: 213
Catull 5.4–6: 37 n. 67
  61.212–13: 184–5
  61.224–5: 108 n. 60
  62.45: 49 n. 1
  62.56: 49 n. 1
  64.38 ff.: 180
  64.205–6: 183 n. 119
  64.327: 181
  64.348 ff.: 179 n. 105
  64.348: 169 n. 68
  64.357: 169 n. 68
  64.384 ff.: 168 n. 63
  64.407–8: 168 n. 63
  66.1: 105
  66.47: 104, 105
  68.49: 200 n. 25
Censorinus, *DN* 11.7: 185 n. 132
  17.6: 159 n. 18
Cic. *Aratea* fr. 1: 106
  De or. 1.69: 202 n. 32
  Leg. 2.3.7: 106
  Rep. 6.13: 162 n. 32
Cinna *FPL* 89: 203 n. 34

Donat. 742 Hagen: 35 n. 59
  Vit. Verg. 43: 50

Enn. *Ann.* 179: 169 n. 65
  214: 198 n. 18

Firm. Mat. *Err. Prof. Rel.* 19: 186 n. 137

Hor. *Carm.* 1.2.45: 162 n. 32
  1.34.9 ff.: 183 n. 119
  1.17.8–9: 174 n. 92
  3.1.1: 210 n. 48
  3.8.13: 174 n. 92
  Carm. saec. 14: 165 n. 46
  25 ff.: 181
  Epist. 1.4.8 ff.: 184 n. 126
  1.11.28: 244 n. 33
  Epod. 16.33: 174 n. 92
  Sat. 1.10.44–5: 59 n. 11
  1.10.44: 180 n. 110
Hyg. *Fab.* 185: 103 n. 46

Juv. 7.120: 56–7
Σ Juv. 7.6: 208

Lactant. *Inst.* 7.24.12: 157
Liv. 1.7.10: 183 n. 118
Lucr. 2.1153–4: 162 n. 31

Macrob. *Sat.* 3.7.2: 180 n. 109

Ov. *Am.* 1.2.7–18: 236 n. 22
  1.2.9–10: 239 n. 27
  1.2.25 ff.: 224 n. 13
  1.6.7: 236 n. 22
  1.14.7: 200 n. 25
  3.1.49: 236 n. 22
  Ars am. 1.87: 185 n. 135
  2.117–96: 233 n. 20
  Her. 4.10: 236 n. 22
  5.21 ff.: 237 n. 24
  9.13: 169 n. 66
  15.94: 166 n. 50
  Met. 3.103: 182 n. 115
  10.518–36: 234 n. 21
  10.686–704: 103 n. 46
  Rem. am. 199–204: 231
  199–200: 232 n. 19
  Tr. 3.3.76: 33 n. 55

Pan. Lat. 4(10) 37.5: 182 n. 117
Pers. 1.78: 49
  2.37 ff.: 184 n. 126
Petron. 58.8: 196 n. 14
Plin. *HN* 7.72: 185 n. 134
  36.35: 96
Prop. 1.1.9–16: 231–2
  1.1.11: 231 n. 18
  1.1.14: 231 n. 18
  1.8.7–8: 60 n. 14
  1.17.21–4: 33 n. 55
  2.10.1: 207, 230 n. 17
  2.10.2: 230 n. 17
  2.10.3: 230 n. 17
  2.10.7–8: 207
  2.10.9: 230 n. 17
  2.10.10: 230 n. 17
  2.10.11: 230 n. 17
  2.10.13: 230 n. 17
  2.10.25–6: 207, 208

2.10.25: 207
2.13.3–8: 200 n. 23, 210, 212 + n. 52
2.13.3–4: 207
2.13.4: 207
2.13.5–6: 200 n. 23
2.13.11–12: 210
2.13.12: 203 n. 33
2.13.13–14: 210
2.19.17–20: 232–3
2.19.17–18: 234
2.19.29–30: 232
3.3.31: 56
3.5.1: 227

Quint. *Inst.* 6.3.20: 59
  9.3.8: 185

Rhet. Her. 1.7: 156 n. 4

Sall. *Iug.* 14.24
Sen. *Q Nat.* 3.30.8: 159 n. 20
Serv. *ad* Verg. *Aen.* 3.113: 103 n. 46
  ad Verg. *Ecl.* 1.1: 74
  3.105: 107 n. 57
  4.11: 166 n. 51
  4.20: 173 n. 79
  4.34: 179 n. 101
  4.49: 182 n. 116
  4.58: 205 n. 41
  6.72: 205
  10.46: 225 n. 14
Serv. Auct. *ad* Verg. *Ecl.* 4. 10: 165 + n. 47
  4.37: 180 n. 109
  9.46: 159 n. 18
  10.12: 208
Sil. *Pun.* 3.480: 167 n. 53
Stat. *Silv.* 1.2.269 ff.: 165 n. 45
  4.7.43: 169 n. 67
Suet. *Aug.* 70: 21 n. 13
Symm. *Or.* 3.9: 160 n. 26, 178 n. 100, 181 n. 111

Ter. *Haut.* 693: 168 n. 62
Tib. 1.1.19–20: 236 n. 22
  1.1.61 ff.: 33 n. 54
  1.1.35–48: 36
  1.3.63–4: 37
  1.4.40: 233 n. 20

1.4.47–50: 233 n. 20
1.8.7–8: 236 n. 22
1.10.1–2: 226
1.10.7–14: 226
2.3.1–4: 233 n. 19
4.3.11–16: 233
4.3.19–20: 232 n. 19, 233

Varro, *Ling.* 7.36: 198 n. 17
Verg. *Aen.* 1.291–6: 224 n. 13
  3.90–1: 183 n. 120
  4.328: 50
  4.694: 162 n. 31
  5.163: 50
  8.301: 183 n. 118
  8.660: 50
  10.628–30: 226
Ecl. 1: 82–8 *passim*, 110–24 *passim*
  1.1: 69 n. 8, 252
  1.3–5: 247
  1.4: 34, 74
  1.6: 50
  1.13: 74
  1.18: 74
  1.19–25: 243 n. 32
  1.27: 76
  1.30–2: 92
  1.30: 77 n. 26
  1.31: 77 n. 26
  1.34: 50
  1.36: 77 n. 26
  1.38: 74
  1.51–8: 92
  1.55: 50
  1.57: 56
  1.58: 52–3
  1.64–72: 249
  1.65: 94 n. 33
  1.71: 34
  1.74: 51
  1.77: 125
  1.81: 50
  2: 88–101 *passim*
  2.1: 76 n. 22
  2.3–4: 69 n. 8
  2.4–5: 125
  2.3: 83 n. 14
  2.6: 58
  2.10: 77 n. 26

Verg. (cont.)
  2.14: 77 n. 26
  2.15–6: 101, 103
  2.15: 75
  2.24: 58
  2.26: 76 n. 22
  2.31–3: 44
  2.35–9: 104, 107
  2.36–9: 101
  2.37: 76 n. 22
  2.39: 76 n. 22
  2.52: 77 n. 26
  2.65: 58
  2.69: 51
  3: 101–8 passim, 125-54 passim
  3.1–2: 56
  3.1: 50, 76 n. 22
  3.8: 56
  3.12–13: 76 n. 22
  3.17: 76 n. 22
  3.20: 74
  3.21–4: 76 n. 22
  3.23–4: 75 n. 20
  3.37: 83 n. 14
  3.40–6: 197, 202
  3.40–2: 196
  3.40: 56
  3.56: 50
  3.60–1: 204 n. 38
  3.64: 77 n. 26
  3.72: 77 n. 26
  3.78–9: 58–9
  3.81: 77 n. 26
  3.93: 55
  3.96: 74, 75
  3.102: 50
  3.104–7: 196 n. 14
  4: 155–88 passim
  4.1–3: 75 n. 19
  4.4–10: 61
  4.28: 61
  4.43: 50
  4.48–9: 62
  4.50–2: 62
  4.51: 199 n. 22
  4.55–9: 62
  4.55–7: 197, 201, 205 n. 40
  4.58–9: 43
  4.62: 50
  4.87–103: 36 n. 61
  5.4: 75 n. 21
  5.12: 74
  5.13–14: 69 n. 8
  5.13: 83 n. 14
  5.14: 54
  5.25: 50
  5.36: 50
  5.51–2: 51
  5.52: 58
  5.61: 50
  5.72: 76 n. 22
  5.73: 76 n. 22
  5.85–7: 75, 102
  5.86–7: 74
  5.86: 76 n. 22
  5.87: 76 n. 22
  6: 189–215 passim
  6.4–5: 75, 84, 239 n. 28
  6.4: 75
  6.5: 152
  6.14 ff.: 54
  6.20–1: 51
  6.31–2: 59–60
  6.35: 50
  6.43–4: 60
  6.44: 58
  6.53: 58
  6.76: 50
  7.29–30: 60
  7.32: 50
  7.37: 77 n. 26
  7.55: 76 n. 22
  7.61–8: 53
  7.65–6: 54
  7.67: 76 n. 22
  8.6–13: 9
  8.6–7: 9
  8.7–8: 184 n. 125
  8.17 ff.: 54
  8.22–4: 44
  8.22–3: 46
  8.22: 198 n. 16
  8.26: 76 n. 22
  8.29: 76 n. 22
  8.41: 48
  8.48–50: 52
  8.55–6: 197
  8.55: 75

8.58: 49
8.80: 60
8.96: 76 n. 22
8.98: 76 n. 22
8.108: 58
8.109: 55
9.1–17: 251–2
9.1: 56
9.2–4: 55
9.6: 50
9.9: 28, 69 n. 8, 83 n. 14, 252
9.19–20: 78
9.22: 77 n. 26
9.23–5: 57
9.23–4: 75
9.37–8: 55
9.39: 77 n. 26
9.46: 76 n. 22
9.50: 76 n. 22
10: 216–44 *passim*
10.1–8: 42
10.12: 58, 208 n. 44
10.17: 201 n. 28
10.20: 75
10.22: 56 n. 9

10.23: 198 n. 16
10.31ff.: 18 n. 2
10.33: 33 n. 55
10.34: 32 n. 54
10.48–51: 60
10.65–6: 198 n. 16
10.70–7: 42
10.71: 49
10.75–7: 63
G. 1.130: 174 n. 92
1.429–33: 203
2.473–4: 160 n. 26
2.475–94: 203–4, 205
2.475–92: 204 n. 39
2.475–82: 205
2.477–8: 204
2.483–9: 205
2.490–4: 205
2.490–2: 204
4.469–71: 204 n. 37
4.475–7: 120
4.511–15: 120
[Verg.] *Ciris* 398:
    183 n. 118
Culex 1–3: 200 n. 25